One Hundred Great Guns

"Das ist Gemacht
wers besser kan,
der mag ein neues
fangen Ann"

Felix Fuchs, 1633.

ONE HUNDRED

GREAT GUNS

An illustrated history of firearms

By MERRILL LINDSAY

Photographs by Bruce Pendleton
Book designed by Verne Noll
Lock illustrations by Peter Parnall

WALKER & CO., NEW YORK

First published in the United States of America
in 1967 by Walker and Company, a division of
Publications Development Corporation.

Library of Congress Catalog Card Number: LC 67-23653.

Printed and bound in Japan.

ACKNOWLEDGEMENTS

*Many hundreds of people have helped us in the production of this book. If all of the professional personnel
in the 14 different museums who have given generously of their time and knowledge were to be listed, this
would become a chapter. I do, however, want to give special thanks to a few who have gone out of their way to help:*

BRUSSELS, BELGIUM
Roger Malengret Lebrun

Edgar Ley

Jean Squilbeck, Curator
Musée Royal de la Porte de Hal

CHESHIRE, CONNECTICUT
Dr. Harman Leonard

CHICAGO, ILLINOIS
John Amber, Editor
The Gun Digest

COPENHAGEN, DENMARK
Dr. Arne Hoff, Curator
Tøjhus Museet

EDINBURGH, SCOTLAND
R. B. Stevenson
National Museum of Antiquities
of Scotland

HARTFORD, CONNECTICUT
Henry P. Maynard, Curator
Wadsworth Atheneum

R. L. Wilson, Advisor to the Atheneum

LENINGRAD, U.S.S.R.
Dr. Leonid Tarassuk
The Hermitage

LIEGE, BELGIUM
Jean Puraye, Curator
Le Musée d'Armes de Liège

Albert van Zuylen

LONDON, ENGLAND
Claude Blair, Keeper, Dept. of
Metalwork
Victoria and Albert Museum

John Hayward
Sotheby and Company

A. Norris Kennard,
Master of the Armouries
Tower of London

William Reid, Assistant Keeper,
The Armouries, Tower of London

MADRID, SPAIN
Ann K. Lindsay

MARKESAN, WISCONSIN
Samuel E. Smith

MUNICH, GERMANY
Dr. A. Frhr. von Reitzenstein
Bayerisches Armeemuseum

Dr. Edwin Schalkhausser, Curator
Bayerisches Armeemuseum

NEW HAVEN, CONNECTICUT
Robert Barry

Anthony D. Darling

Thomas E. Hall, Curator
Winchester Gun Museum

George Rowbottom

Harry Sefried

Harold Whelpley

NEW YORK, NEW YORK
Robert Abels

Frederick B. Adams, Jr.
Morgan Library

Russell B. Aitken

Randolph Bullock, Curator
Metropolitan Museum of Art

Steven V. Grancsay, Curator Emeritus
Metropolitan Museum of Art

James Humphry III, Chief Librarian
Metropolitan Museum of Art

Otto von Kienbusch

Irving Moskowitz

Helmut Nickel, Ass. Curator
Metropolitan Museum of Art

PARIS, FRANCE
Count Alain de la Falaise

Robert Jean Charles
Musée de l'Armée

Colonel Jacques Wemaere, Curator
Musée de l'Armée

PRINCETON, NEW JERSEY
Leonard Heinrich (deceased)

RAMSEY, NEW JERSEY
Warren Moore

RINGOES, NEW JERSEY
Lewis H. Gordon, Jr.

SANTA ANA, CALIFORNIA
Captain Calvin Hurd
"Le Petit Soldat"

STOCKHOLM, SWEDEN
Countess Kerstin Bernadotte

TURIN, ITALY
Gen. Agostino Gaibi

Guido Amoretti, Curator
Museo Civico "Pietro Micca"

Reg. Roberto Biasiol

Dr. Raffaele Natta-Soleri
Armeria Reale

Gen. Pietro Roggero, Curator
Museo Storico Nazionale d'Artiglieria

Agnoletto Walter
"La Bottega dell'Armarolo"

UPPER ARLINGTON, OHIO
Geoffrey Jenkinson

VIENNA, AUSTRIA
Dr. Bruno Thomas, Director
Kunsthistorisches Museum

Dr. Ortwin Gamber
Kunsthistorisches Museum

Wilhelm Schlag
Minister of Cultural Affairs

WASHINGTON, D.C.
Harold L. Peterson

WEST POINT, NEW YORK
Robert Fisch, Ass. Curator
West Point Museum

All of the color photography in this volume was done with indirect stroboscopic light from one or two sources bounced from nylon umbrellas. The objects were usually photographed against noseam paper. A special set was designed by Mr. Pendleton for the purpose of photographing guns and this literally went around the world in the process of taking over 6,000 photographs.

THE MUSEUMS WHO CO-OPERATED WITH US IN ALLOWING US TO REMOVE GUNS FROM CASES

FOR PHOTOGRAPHY ARE LISTED ALPHABETICALLY.

Armeria Reale, Turin, Italy
Bayerisches Armeemuseum, Munich, Germany
Kunsthistorisches Museum, Vienna, Austria
Musée de l'Armée, Paris, France
Musée d'Armes, Liège, Belgium
Musée Royal de la Porte de Hal, Brussels, Belgium
Museo Storico Nazionale d'Artiglieria, Turin, Italy
The Metropolitan Museum of Art, New York, New York
Tøjhus Museet, Copenhagen, Denmark
The Tower of London, London, England
Victoria and Albert Museum, London, England
Wadsworth Atheneum, Hartford, Connecticut
West Point Museum, West Point, New York
Winchester Gun Museum, New Haven, Connecticut

IN ADDITION TO THE MUSEUMS, A NUMBER OF PRIVATE COLLECTORS
GRACIOUSLY ALLOWED US TO PHOTOGRAPH IN THEIR HOMES.

Charles Addams, New York, New York
Russell B. Aitken, New York, New York
Otto von Kienbusch, New York, New York
Joe Kindig Jr., York, Pennsylvania
Harman Leonard, Cheshire, Connecticut
Irving Moskowitz, New York, New York
Geoffrey Jenkinson, Upper Arlington, Ohio
George Rowbottom, Hamden, Connecticut
Harry Sefried, New Haven, Connecticut
Fred Stevens, Stevenson, Connecticut
Albert van Zuylen, Brussels, Belgium
Agnoletto Walter, Turin, Italy
Harold Whelpley, Westville, Connecticut

The source of the individual guns illustrated is indicated in the picture captions. All of the guns illustrated from any individual museums or collection can be located by consulting the bold type listings in the General Index.

CONTENTS

One Hundred Great Guns

Refining saltpeter, *sketched by Basil Wefring for*
Georgius Agricola De Re Metallica *before 1553.*

CHAPTER I

THE INVENTION OF GUNPOWDER *Fact and Fiction*

WE KNOW THAT gunpowder was first used to make a noise rather than to propel a projectile. We also know the approximate date of its first use in warfare—around 1250. Its place of origin was the Near East. Its first use was in a battle between the Saracens and the Spanish. Its first chroniclers were Roger Bacon, who had studied the scientific texts of the Arabian scholars, and Albertus Magnus, who reported the use of cannon by the Moors. But like many other important discoveries such as the wheel, the wedge and the smelting of metal, the invention of gunpowder cannot be attributed to any one person.

With the noise and flash and smoke that resulted from the first explosion of gunpowder, there must have been such confusion and excitement that no one thought to record the time, the place or the inventor. Instead of a factual account, two contradictory myths, both hoary with age, still survive as explanations for the invention. Both are unprovable and with a little research, both should be discredited.

The first myth is that gunpowder was invented in 1354 by a diabolical monk named Berthold Schwarz. He was supposed to have lived in Freiburg, Germany. If this were true, the neighbors must have made him move after his first successful experiment. Though a statue was erected 500 years later to commemorate this supposed event, there is no record in the contemporary archives of the town to substantiate his existence. Several other south German towns claim the honor of being his birthplace, as well as one in Sweden and one in Italy.

In 1877 an eminent historian of arms and armor, Auguste Demmin, asserted without offering proof, that Schwarz's real name was Anklitzen and that he was also a cannon founder. Just by coincidence, there was a cannon founder by the name of Anklitzen who had been thrown in jail for casting some defective cannons for the Venetian Doges. This was in 1380. Even if Schwarz (his name is an English corruption of "Der Schwarze Berthold" or in Latin "Bertholdus Niger") or Anklitzen had existed, they could not possibly have been born early enough to have discovered gunpowder. Bacon's

description of gunpowder dates from 1267 and Albertus Magnus' account of the use of cannons from 1280—almost a century before the fictional friar.

The theory of the Chinese invention of gunpowder has had as long a life and about as little substance as Black Berthold. Even as late as the mid-nineteenth century, French orientalists were offering translations of early Chinese manuscripts to prove that the Chinese had known about gunpowder first. The manuscripts range from 618 B.C. to 1300 A.D. One, "The Annals of the Moguls," was "improved" in translation; weapons mentioned in it becoming cannons which helped Kublai Khan reduce the city strongholds along the Chinese coast. If Kublai Khan or the Chinese had discovered gunpowder, why did the Great Khan commission Marco Polo to build a Venetian-style, stone-throwing ballista? It is interesting to note that nowhere in the famous "Travels" does Marco Polo mention the tiniest Chinese firecracker, gun, or bomb. It's mystifying when you consider that all of Polo's waking hours, when he wasn't building this ballista, or governing the city of Yangchow, were spent in making keen observation of mechanical inventions and unusual objects, which formed the basis of his book. Marco Polo was also a soldier—he dictated his memoirs as a prisoner-of-war in a Genoese dungeon—and it is evident from 23 versions of his work that he didn't smell any gunpowder in the length and breadth of his travels in China.

The Chinese theory has a long history, as we discover in a reference and disclaimer to it in a compendium of information published early in the 17th century:

"Some have sayled a long course as farre as *China* the farthest part of fhe world to fetch the invention of guns from thence, but we know the Spanish Proverb, *Long wayes, long lies.* One writeth I know not upon whose credit, that Roger Bacon commonly called Frier Bacon knew to make an engine, which with Saltpeter and Brimstone, should prove notable for batterie, but he tendring the safety of mankind would not discover it."
So wrote the English historian William Camden in his

Berthold Schwarz. *An imaginary portrait from André Thevet's* Pourtraits et vies des hommes illustres, *Paris 1584.*

Stamping gunpowder in a hand mortar. *Jean Appier,* Pyrotechnia of Hanzelet, *Paris, 1630.*

"Remaines / concerning / Britanie: / But especially England and the Inhabitants thereof: Artillarie," in 1614. He went on:

"The best approved Authors agree that they were invented in Germanie, by Berthold Swarte a Monk skillful in Gebers Cookery or Alchimy, who tempering up the stone, which covered it when a sparke fell into it. But one saith he consulted with the divell for an offensive weapon, who gave him answer in this obscure Oracle:

Vulcanus gignat, pariat Natura, Minerva
Edoceat, nutrix ars erit atque dies.
Vis mea nihilo, tria dent mihi corporapastum:
Sunt soboles strages, vis, furor, atque fragor.

"By this instruction he made a trunck of yron with learned advice, crammed it with sulphure, bullet, and putting thereto fire, found the effects to bee destruction, violence, fury, and roaring cracke. This being begunne by him, by skill and time is now come to that perfection, not onely in great yron and brasse pieces, but also in small, that all admire it; having names given them, some from serpents, or ravenous birds, as Culverines or Colubrines, Serpentines, Basilisques, Faulcons, Sacres; others in other respects, as Canons, Demicanons, Chambers, Slinges, Arquebuze, Caliver, Handgun, Muskets, Petronils, Pistoll, Dagge &c. and Petarras of the same brood lately invented."[1]

A fair claim to the invention of gunpowder is that of Roger Bacon, who described the devilish substance in 1267 and named the ingredients and the effect, although he disguised the formula and proportions in the form of an anagram. Some said that Bacon got the idea from a Marcus Graecus, who, it now seems, didn't exist. Others attributed Bacon's discovery to Arabian sources. Fortunately, to offset this hodgepodge of myth, there are some facts. Albertus Magnus, the thirteenth-century German philosopher, describes the role of cannons in the siege of Seville in 1247, *and he wrote about it in 1280,* within the span of his personal recollection.

City records and many arms historians record a cannon built in Amberg, Germany, dated 1301.[2] Duille Grete—"Crazy Gerty"—Ghent's giant cannon, was built as an anti-siege weapon in 1313. In 1326, still before Berthold, someone drew a picture of guns, more precisely, a hand cannon and a *pot-de-fer* to illustrate Walter de Melemete's *De Officiis Regum*—a University of Oxford manuscript (library of Christ Church, Oxford, manuscript 92). An inventory of war materials at Windsor Castle made during 1330 and 1331 lists "una magna balista de cornue quae vocatur Domina Gunilda" (a big ballista with a barrel [cannon] which is named Mistress Gunilda).

Camden continues, in his *Remaines:*

"The very time of their first invention is uncertaine, but certaine it is that King *Edward* the third used them at the siege of Calice, 1347,[3] for *Gunnarii* had their pay there, as appeareth by record. About 33 yeares before they were seene in Italy, and about that time they began, as it seemeth, to be used in Spaine, but named by writers *Dolia igniuoma,* fire flashing vessels.

"Yet the French, as *Polidore Virgil*[4] noteth, skant knew the use of them untill the yeare 1425, when the English by great ordinance had made a breach in the wals of *Mans,* under the conduct of *Thomas Montacute,* last Earle of Salisburie of that surname, who was slaine at Orleans with a great shotte, and is noted to be the first English gentleman slaine thereby. Albeit now hee is thought the most unfortunate, and cursed in his mother's wombe, who dieth by great shotte."

Gibbon suggests that guns and gunpowder traveled from Europe to the Orient along the ancient caravan routes that the Polos followed—but more than a century later. In any event, they arrived in plenty of time to be loaded, cocked, and aimed to salute the arrival of Henry the Navigator's Vasco da Gama when he arrived at Goa in 1498.

If all this seems complicated, there is a simple, straightforward answer—if one is a fundamentalist:

"Uzziah . . . made in Jerusalem engines, invented by

---

[1] *These names were given to different sizes of cannon in diminishing order of caliber or bore.*

[2] *Rathgen* Das Geschütz im Mittelalter, *Berlin, 1928, says the cannon in the armory of Amberg, Bavaria, has the inscription 1303—probably a false date—he says it should be 1403. Freiherr von Reitzenstein, Curator of the Bavarian Army Museum, says in* Allgemeiner Militär-Zeitung: *"large cannon were first used by Herzog Albrecht II of Brunswick-Grubenhayen in 1365." The first picture of a German gun is in Codex 600—Munich Bibliothek, dated circa 1350. Differing opinions as to the cannon's age can be found in: P. A. Lenz,* Nouvelles Archives, Philosophiques et Litteraires, *1840, Auguste Dem-*

min Arms and Armour, *London, George Bell and Sons, 1877; and Oscar Guttman, London, 1906; Van der Haegen,* Mem. couonnes Acad. Roy. Belg. *1899; and Clephan* The Earliest Hand Fire-arms. *Walter Scott pub. 1906. Hime says Guttman and Greenhill could not find the record in Ghent and the dates may be fudged a few years out of local pride.*

[3] *Also at Cressy in 1346, according to Velani and Froissart (in the recently discovered French edition of his work).*

[4] *Polidore Virgil,* De Inventoribus Rerum. *Born Urbino c. 1470, he died 1555; lived in England 1501-1550, was Archdeacon of Wells 1508, also wrote* History of England.

Goat-powered mill *for crushing iron pyrites.*
Basil Wefring sketch. De Re Metallica, Basel, 1556.

cunning men, to be on the towers and upon the bulwarks, to shoot arrows and great stones withal.''

II Chronicles 26:15

Or, for those who prefer the classical, or enlightened, approach, Alexander the Great's invasion of India, according to his biographer, was resisted by fiery and explosive defense weapons. This is not entirely without logic, because gunpowder, that is, black powder, is made of saltpeter, sulphur and charcoal; and the only place in the ancient world where saltpeter existed in a reasonably pure and abundant state was India. If gunpowder did come from India[5] it was a much better kept secret than Greek fire—first used in the sieges of Constantinople in 716 A.D.—whose ingredients were kept a secret from the Saracen invaders for the next 400 years.[6]

Whatever the source, gunpowder was a rare and valuable commodity at a time when the entire British arsenal contained *in toto* a couple of dozen full barrels of black powder, and in the fourteenth century an English royal edict prohibited the export of gunpowder or any of its ingredients.

Black powder has not changed much since the earliest records were kept. In 1350 the formula was 41% saltpeter, 29½% charcoal and 29½% sulphur.[7] In 1781 the British Ordinance formula called for 75% saltpeter, 15% charcoal and 10% sulphur. The formula remains essentially the same today in DuPont's FG or FFFG black powder, the only difference between these modern designations being the coarseness of the grind.

Powder mixing in the old days allowed more latitude for originality—up to a point.[8] For example, larch was recommended for the charcoal if the powder was to be used in large guns or cannons, but dogwood was preferred for small bore or pistol work: large tree—large charge, small tree—small charge. Also, a Frenchman discovered that one increased the potency of gunpowder by spreading it out in the sun and pouring brandy over it.

There were drawbacks, too. One set of do-it-yourself instructions says to first grind and powder the ingredients,

Firing a Petard. *Ancient Armour from Francis Grose,* Military Antiquities, *London 1786.*

then roughly mix them together and put the mixture between millstones; a jackass could be employed to turn the mill, which further mixed and refined the powder. The author of these instructions, a humanitarian, suggests it is not necessary to stay with the jackass during the final stages!

Black powder has undergone only one major improvement during its 600 years of known existence. At first, dry grinding was enough to produce the desired effects, but the product was highly uneven; fine powders were touchy, yet coarser bits did not burn. This was overcome by "corning" the mix. In corning, the ground powder is mixed with water until it resembles dirty oatmeal. Dissolving the saltpeter blends the ingredients still further, and after drying and sieving, results in a consistently uniform grain, or corn, of homogenous composition. The development of corned gunpowder took place in England about the time of Cromwell, some time during the middle 1600's and even earlier in France.

Some two hundred years were to pass before the invention of smokeless powders; they had to wait on two mid-nineteenth century discoveries—guncotton, and Nobel's nitroglycerin. However, these were not instant discoveries. The spirit of scientific inquiry of the 18th century led Berthollet to discover that it was possible to substitute potassium chlorate for saltpeter. Berthollet and Lavoisier *(Regisseur des Poudres et Salpetres de France)* did research with fulminate of mercury before 1800—a necessary prelude to Forsythe's invention. The Englishman Howard, who nearly blew himself up with his experiments, reported on a "new fulminating mercury" to the Royal Society in 1800.

Finally, Christian Friedrich Schonbein, the nineteenth-century German chemist, reported the discovery of guncotton in 1840.[9] Guncotton is cotton that has been soaked in a mixture of nitric and sulphuric acids. The resultant cellulose nitrate is carefully and repeatedly washed to remove all traces of residual acid, which would make it unstable. It is soluble in such solvents as ether and acetone, and the resulting colloid dries to a stable, even-burning substance.

English gunsmiths developed a powder for which they claimed even greater stability at high temperatures. This is the nitroglycerin-based powder called cordite. White hunters in Africa in the 1880's and 1890's hunted ivory with huge single- and double-barreled rifles shooting large-bore cartridges loaded with cordite.

Cordite or smokeless, the resulting improvements were splendid. By eliminating the smoke- and residue-producing ingredients of black powder, two important advances had been made in the art of shooting. The telltale smoke which gave away the hunter's position and blinded artillery observers disappeared. So did the romantic nonsense of the smoke of battle, as did much of that acrid and nostalgic smell that went with an autumn day. Gone also was the "crud"[10] that had to be gouged, scraped and scratched out of the barrel, sometimes after every shot, if the bullets were tight and the hunter, consequently, wasn't using patches.

Not only did smokeless powders make shooters' lives happier, they made practical reality of many an inventive genius' dreams of dependable repeating firearms. The heavy fouling of black powders forced breech-loading and multiple-firing weapons to remain rather impractical theory, despite the inventiveness and sometimes jewel-like workmanship of the best craftsmen: after the first few shots such weapons failed to function. This explains why pirates are represented as they are in illustrations—wearing half a dozen guns tucked

[5] *Joinville describes iron rockets which he claims to have seen there. Also, see reference to a translation of* Gentoo Laws *in Francis Grose's* History of the English Army, *(1789).*

[6] *Greek fire is thought to have been a blend of naphtha, crude oil and sulphur—naphtha and bitumen, or crude oil, occurring naturally on the surface in some areas of what is today Turkey. Anna Comnena in her* Alexias *(c. 1100) provides the formula noted, in Chapter XIX. According to Gibbon the fire was used both as a defensive weapon fired from the city walls of Constantinople, and as an aggressive weapon from the bows of the Eastern Empire's fighting galleys.*

[7] *Partington,* Greek Fire and Gunpowder, *(Cambrdige: Heffer, 1960). This work contains many historic formulas.*

[8] *See* The Art of Warre, Certain Ways . . . *Peter Whitehorne, Imprinted at London by W. Williamson for John Wight, Anno 1575.*

[9] *Ascanio Sobrero of Torino discovered nitroglycerin the same year. Nobel's 122 patents for explosives were taken out between 1864 and 1888, but it was a Frenchman, Paul Vieille, who discovered modern colloidal powders in 1887.*

[10] *See* Krud, *Danish name for gunpowder (German:* Kraut—Om Bysse—Krud—Naas dit er opfunded i Europa . . . SKRIFTER, *(H. Aram, Copenhagen, 1745).*

GUNPOWDER

into their pantaloons. Each pistol represented a single shot. With all the artillery in his belt, Long John Silver didn't have as much firepower as a present-day youngster with a .22 caliber target gun.

When gunpowder was invented—or came to be used in warfare—there were already some rather fancy machines for destruction in the hands of medieval soldiers. It is worth taking a look at these before getting on to guns proper. Some of these mechanisms were more sophisticated than the early hand cannon, and their triggers and escapements were to appear later in modified form in the wheel locks of the famous Reiters (cavaliers) of Germany.

14th century French *breech-loading cannon. Separate breech secured by driving in the two wedges. Cast in Metz, cal. 100mm, length 1840mm. Stone bullet weight approx. 1 kilo. Museo Storico Nazionale d'Artiglieria, Turin.*

Great bronze mortar. *Probably cast at the siege of Jerusalem c. 1480. Cast by the order of Grand Master Pierre d'Aubusson. Inscribed F PETRUS DAVBUSSON M HOSPITALIS IHER. Wt. 3,325 kilos, shot granite balls weighing 261 kilos. Musée de l'Armée, Paris.*

An example of autofrettage. *This leather cannon was built for King Gustavus Adolphus. It is a copper tube strapped with iron, covered with leather and wound with cord. loa. 77½", bores 3". Note #270, Musée de l'Armee, Paris*

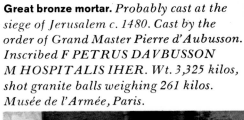

LA CATHERINE. *Cast at Innsbruck in 1404, inscribed "My name is Catherine, beware of me, I punish injustice. Georg Endorfer cast me." Wt. 4,597 kilos, cal. 390mm. loa. 3.65 meters Provenance, Rhodes. Musée de l'Armée, Paris.*

Beer-mug breech loader. *This is a model of the 14th century excavated guns which have been found in Spain.*

Huge bronze bombard. *One of two cannon cast at Constantinople around 1453. The other cannon, a mate to this, was melted by Napoleon. The bore is big enough to sit in. Museo Storico Nazionale d'Artiglieria, Turin.*

Espringale or spring engine.
*The released plank drove the
arrow. Vegetius, De Re Militari,
page 158, Paris, 1553.*

Trebuchet of small size. *The man is afraid because the stone should have been released by now. Vegetius, De Re Militari, page 24 Paris, 1553.*

MACHINES BEFORE GUNS

Trebuchet *model built by Randolph Bullock, after the plans of Ralph Payne-Gallwey. Metropolitan Museum of Art, New York.*

Ballista model. *18th-century French. The Metropolitan Museum of Art, New York, No. 54. 46.5. Bequest of Alan Rutherford Stuyvesant, 1954.*

Onager or catapult. *This model of an ancient siege machine has a simple trigger. The rope pulls the hook out of the eye holding down the beam against tension.*

Combination crossbow and wheel lock. *This is an exact miniature made by Agnoletto Walter of Turin of the weapon with the Da Vinci-designed wheel lock, external "U" main spring. The original in the Palazzo Ducale in Venice is engraved RENALDO DA VISINDI ASOLO 1562.*

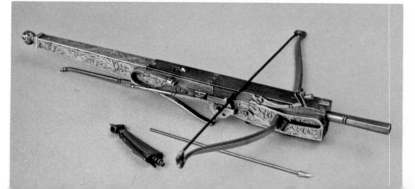

German flintlock sword pistol *with silver mounts and jade grips. c. 1670. Joe Kindig Jr. Collection, York, Pa.*

Miniature metal crossbow *marked with the cross of Savoy. 16th or 17th century, length 9½" bow 7". Armeria Reale, Turin.*

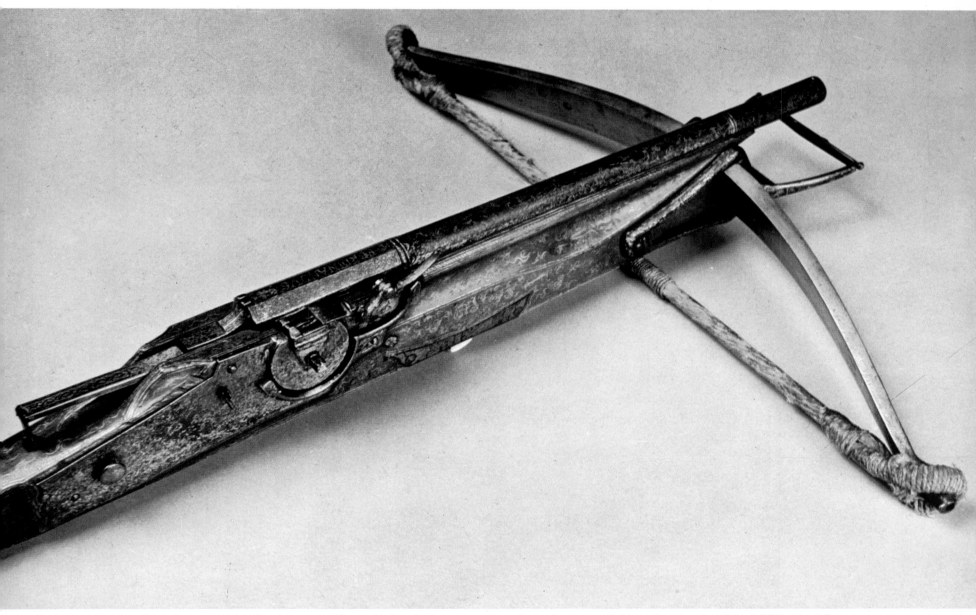

Earliest dateable wheel lock *combined with a crossbow. Painted wooden stock with the initials F.A. repeated, and the crest of Archduke Ferdinand of the Netherlands. The top of the barrel is marked FERDINANDUS. Note primitive outside spring. The* weapon dates between 1521 and 1526. loa. 28¾" bbl. 15¾" bow span 21" bore. cal. .36". Smooth bore. No. #1498 Bayerisches Armeemuseum, Munich.

Great hunting crossbow *with crannequin, rhino horn inlaid on shaft. No #VII/7 Musée de la Porte de Hal, Brussels.*

Two wheel lock pistols on a halberd *or hunting pike. Nuremberg strap engraved. bbls 8⁵⁄₁₆ long, cal. .34". Musée de la Porte de Hal, Brussels.*

Dated and signed *ivory-inlaid crossbow. German, 1628. Charles Addams Collection, New York.*

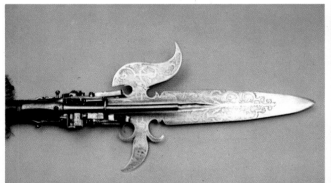

CHAPTER II

MACHINES BEFORE GUNS

ARMA VIRUMQUE CANO . . .

"At other times, but especially when my Uncle Toby was so unfortunate as to say a syllable about cannons, bombs, or petards my father would exhaust all the stores of his eloquence (which indeed were very great) in a panegyric upon the *Battering Rams* of the ancients—the *vinea* which Alexander made use of at the siege of Tyre. He would tell my uncle Toby of the *catapultae* of the Syrians, which threw such monstrous stones so many hundred feet and shook the strongest bulwarks from their very foundations . . . he would go on and describe the wonderful mechanism of the *ballista*, which Marcellinus makes so much rout about; the terrible effects of the *pyraboli*, which cast fire . . . the danger of the terebra and scorpio which cast javelins."[1]

Anything which can be thrown—a stone or a battle axe, or shot—a bolt or an arrow, or blown—a dart from a blow pipe, becomes a ballistic missile. With these the hunter has an advantage over the beasts of the field—an artificial weapon enabling him to increase the area in which he can create an offensive or defensive zone.

Shooting an arrow or hurling a javelin is a personal matter requiring strength, skill and practice in order to be done effectively. It was always a major problem to train a group of working men into skillfulness in these gymnastic arts. The Greeks had more or less success in maintaining skilled groups of fighting men, but the English fought a long losing battle trying to maintain an effective body of long-bowmen.

With the advent of the crossbow, however, the matter of personal virtuosity and strength became secondary. With a machine that could shoot a knight in armor off his horse, all that was required was effective recruitment of enough manpower when the need arose. The crossbow became such a threat to society that it warranted a papal encyclical denouncing the weapon and enjoining the use of it against fellow Christians. Its use was recommended for the extermination of Moors, Turks, Saracens and unbelievers. But in this period of history, noted for its lack of humanistic concern,

no one took the Pope's edict seriously. It soon became a commonplace for combatants to hire a regiment or two of German or Genovese crossbowmen.

The crossbow had a long and documented series of antecedents. The ancients had all manner of large machines for heaving arrows, stones, firebrands—any of a variety of missiles, including an occasional out-of-luck enemy, over castle walls and through the roofs of fortified cities. Some of these machines were king-sized versions of the crossbow of the Middle Ages. Spring tension was achieved in a number of ways. Sometimes it was done with a rope of grass fibers, skin or braided hair pulling against the set of a bow of wood or metal. Other machines achieved motive power by the uncoiling action of a heavy twisted skein of ropes, while still other siege machines worked like an unbalanced seesaw. A heavy weight on one end, suddenly released, tossed the lighter object (the projectile) up into the air from the other end of the seesaw and, hopefully, in the general direction of the enemy. The Romans developed machines capable of throwing huge stones a considerable distance. These same machines could hurl a first-rate bonfire on to the heads of any enemy who felt secure hiding behind a wall. There were alternate loads for specific circumstances: depending on the objectives and the materials on hand, hot lead, boiling water, fire-tipped arrows, incendiary spears or even horse manure are known to have been used.

For each specialized war machine of the Romans, there seems to have been a medieval counterpart. The original Latin models had been forgotten and were invented all over again near the end of the Dark Ages. The falerica of the ancients became the Teutonic springal; the ballista, the arbalist, the onager—named by the Romans for the wild ass because it bucked when the massive coil spring was released —became the Gothic mangonel; and the trap-gate of earlier times became a trebucket, hurling stones from the end of a counter-balanced tree trunk. Since these medieval weapons never attained the size of their reputed Roman counterparts,

---

[1] *Laurence Sterne,* Tristram Shandy, *Vol. III.*

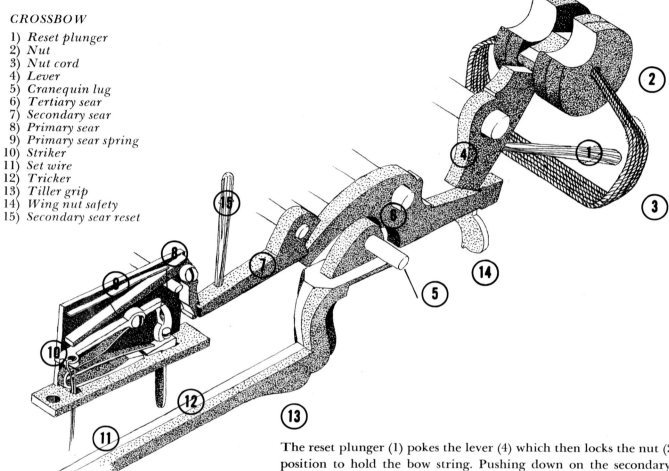

CROSSBOW

1) *Reset plunger*
2) *Nut*
3) *Nut cord*
4) *Lever*
5) *Cranequin lug*
6) *Tertiary sear*
7) *Secondary sear*
8) *Primary sear*
9) *Primary sear spring*
10) *Striker*
11) *Set wire*
12) *Tricker*
13) *Tiller grip*
14) *Wing nut safety*
15) *Secondary sear reset*

The reset plunger (1) pokes the lever (4) which then locks the nut (2) in the correct position to hold the bow string. Pushing down on the secondary sear reset (15) depresses secondary sear (7) to its illustrated position. Tertiary sear (6) can be secured in position by a wing nut safety (14) on the bottom of the crossbow hull. The bow string is then cranked into position by an external cranequin or coffee grinder which hooks over the cranequin lug (5). When the bow string catches in the notch on nut (2) the mechanism is ready to be used.

This is the way the crossbow is carried when hunting. When the quarry is sighted pulling the reset wire (11) sets the hair tricker (12). The wing nut safety (14) is turned and the mechanism is free to function.

Pulling tricker (12) releases stricker (10) which knocks primary sear (8) out of the way of the secondary sear (7) and releases the rest of the chain allowing the nut to rotate and releasing the bow string. This series of leverages is necessary to make a one ounce pull on the tricker, release the bow string under as much as 1000 lbs. tension (see single set trigger mechanism on page 163).

MACHINES BEFORE GUNS

more fortress walls succumbed to inside treachery than were reduced to rubble by onager or trebucket.

"If ever the witte of man went beyond it selfe, it was in the invention of Artillarie or Engines of warre.

"Some kind of Bricol it seemed which the English & Scots called an Espringold the shot where of *K. Edward* the first escaped faire at the siege of Striuelin wher he with an other Engine named the Warwolfe pierced with one stone, and cut as even as a thred, two vauntmures, as he did before at the siege of Brehin; where Thomas Maile the Scots man scoffed at the English Artillarie with wiping the walle with his handkercher, until both hee and the walle were wiped away with a shot . . . the Sow [Vineae] is yet usuall in Ireland, and was in the time of *King Edward* the third used in the seige of Dunbarr, which when the Countess who defended the Castle saw, she said merily, that unlesse the English men kept their Sow the better, she would make her to cast her pigs.

". . . at the battaile of Hastings where England was conquored were slaine at the least 47,944 English, at Cressi 30,000 French. In that of Palme Sunday 360,700 when as since the commo used (common use) of gunnes, at Flodden feilde were slaine but 8,000."[2]

The crossbow, however, really worked, and over the years of the twelfth, thirteenth and fourteenth centuries the trains of escapements and cams were perfected to provide the shooter with a dependably cocked weapon to hold while aiming and a hair-trigger action on release.

The currently popular "miracle trigger," a short movement trigger used on some of Winchester's target guns, is a patent which Harry Sefried, the inventor, frankly admits was largely inspired by his study of fourteenth-century crossbow escapement mechanisms.

Leonardo da Vinci, in his compilation of sketches published as the *Codex Atlanticus,* illustrates some fantastic weapons, many of which are, and still belong, on the drawing board. Among them, amusingly enough, is the reinvention

Römisch Kaiserlicher Majestät Kriegsvölker im Zeitalter der Landshnechte, *Jacob von Falke, August Johann Graf Breunner-Enkevoerth, Vienna, 1883.*

[2] *William Camden,* Remaines/concerning/Britanie:/But especially England and the Inhabitants thereof: Artillarie, *(John Legall, London, 1614), p. 238.*

Feuerwerksbuchs der Frankfurt am Main *redrawn in Zeitschrift (see biblio.). Da Vinci illustrates a somewhat similar engine (trebuchet) in the Codex Atlanticus.*

of the ancestor of the crossbow. In da Vinci's sketch the cross-bow has been scaled up to the size of a siege weapon, with men in scale only as tall as the thickness of the bow. More practical designs are included in this interesting exhibition because, among other undertakings, da Vinci was chief of engineers for both Lodovico il Moro, Duke of Milan, Sforza and later, Cesare Borgia. His employment extended over a period of fifteen years and his knowledge of weapons and fortifications was extensive; he made sketches for what may possibly have been the first wheel lock action.

By da Vinci's time (1500) guns were very much of a reality, and the skills and experience of the armorers were being employed in the new art of gunsmithing. However, there is a recurring traditionality about weapons. Despite David's success with his slingshot, men kept on hacking each other up with swords and axes. So it was with guns . . . men were reluctant to depend wholly upon the new weaponry. This led to the wildest combination of lethal nonsense. In the armor collections at the Metropolitan Museum of Art in New York, and in museums around the world, there can be found rooms full of improbable—and impractical—combinations of guns and earlier, more primitive weapons. There are crossbows with gun barrels tucked into the stock; swords and daggers of all shapes and sizes with stubby pistol barrels sticking through the pommels; shields with gun barrels in the middle. Edward Tunis, in his book *Weapons*, sketches a "Holy Water Sprinkle"—an old-fashioned mace which is actually a multibarrel hand cannon with four holes drilled in the shaft in which the spikes are embedded.

Actually the less fanciful guns did work. Not perfectly at first, and not without casualties among the gunners; but the days of the knight in his poniard-proof suit of armor were numbered. (Armor was to get heavier, but to no effect.) In time, those beautiful ribbed suits of Maximillian armor now seen in museums and textbook illustrations came to be designed for wear in parades and at coronations, but never in combat. The story of the Gun, or Gonne, in the next chapter, might carry the subtitle, "The Death of Chivalry."

Römisch Kaiserlicher Majestät Kriegsvölker im Zeitalter der Landshnechte, *Jacob von Falke, August Johann Graf Breunner-Enkevoerth, Vienna, 1883.*

Off-hand shooting *with hand cannon and a matchlock from a picture by M. Feselen, 1533, in the Munich Art Museum.*

CHAPTER III

THE GONNE *Being a*
Summary of The Earliest Weapons Using Gunpowder,
Including Cannon, Hand Cannon, Pot De Fer, And Totenorgel

THE EARLIEST PICTURES, descriptions and surviving examples of guns date from around 1300. By and large early guns were not held in the hand. The first hand-held guns were attached to pikes or sticks and held away from the shooter as far as possible. There was excellent reason for this, as the early weapons were made with so little skill and knowledge that they sometimes functioned more as hand grenades than as guns.

These prototype weapons ran to extremes in size. The largest among them, the Ghent Cannon, the Belgrade and Constantinople cannons and Mons Meg in Edinburgh, had bores of twenty to twenty-five inches and shot granite cannon balls weighing six to seven hundred pounds. An eighteenth-century Scottish rumor has it that a child was conceived in the barrel of Mons Meg. Smaller surviving pieces such as a breech loading cannon rescued from a swamp near Madrid, and an early Swedish piece similarly preserved, from the town of Loshult, have bores, some of them tapered, of a couple of inches. They were used to shoot stone cannon balls in addition to iron, lead, and even brass balls, as well as assorted pebbles and scrap metal. Still smaller bores were employed in handheld cannon. Fire pots and beer stein breech loaders (so called from their approximate shapes) sometimes expelled arrows or crossbow quarrels.

What a fancy lot of names were given to these early pieces: Bombard, Basilisk, Serpentin or Musket, Cannon, Culverin, Falcon or Falconet. (The names are derived from animals in a descending scale to Musket, which is a young male sparrow hawk and also the name for the smallest gun of the period, a hand cannon with a bore of approximately one inch.)

These firearms can be divided into two general groups, cannon and mortars. The generic word cannon is derived from the Latin word *canna,* meaning a pipe or tube; mortar comes from the Latin *mortarium,* which originally meant the kind of mortar used by druggists to mix dry powders. Early

mortars were solid cast pots of metal which were filled nearly to the brim with powder and capped with a round stone or metal ball barely seated in the muzzle. Obviously very little aim was imparted by the position of the barrel. Cannon were longer tubes, which when properly loaded—the barrel not quite full of powder—could not only be pointed in the general direction of the enemy, but could be elevated at the muzzle like our present day mortars to give the ball greater range, or to lob it over a high place. Cannon were a problem to build, as the equipment to make big castings didn't exist.

Although the Egyptians had carried on smelting operations, and King Solomon's brass (copper) reduction furnaces have recently been uncovered by archeologists, metallurgical technology in the Middle Ages commenced all over again. Primitive cannon seem to have been constructed by beer and wine barrel coopers, who used the same techniques and sometimes the same materials. Barrels were made of oak staves banded with iron hoops—one of these at a Lindsay castle in Scotland survived far enough into the eighteenth century to be sketched and used as a book illustration. Oak, it turned out, made better whisky barrels than gun barrels, and the bravest men, fortified with the supernatural strength of St. Barbara, patron saint of gunners, trembled when they held the hot coal or iron to an early cannon's touchhole.

Soon the wooden staves or ribs were replaced with iron ribs or strips placed side by side around a tubular form or mandrel. The strips were welded together as solidly as they could be in the blacksmith's small fire with its hand-worked bellows. Next, iron bands—like beer barrel hoops—were shrunk on. This was done by heating an already forged ring to expand it, then driving it over the welded barrel and letting it cool and shrink. The more hoops used, the stronger the barrel was supposed to be.

Early gunsmithing had hit on the principle of autofrettage. The shrinking iron bands, later to become steel sleeves, put external compression on the internal ribs, giving them greater-than-normal resistance to the pressure of the gases created by the burning gunpowder. The Krupp masterpieces

Earliest known picture *of a hand gunner from the manuscript of Schems-Eddin-Mohammed. No# C. 686, Institute of the Peoples of Asia, Leningrad. Guttmann says the original was drawn c. 1320.*

RIGHT **Ancient Guns,** *Rudimentum Noviciorum, Lubeck, 1475.*

THE GONNE

of two world wars, the atomic cannon of the present day, zip guns made by delinquent juveniles, and Philippine Moro guns made of water pipe—the latter two, with string wound tightly around the tubes, are modern employments of the principle of autofrettage.

Some of the early cannon worked, and some blew up in the faces of their crews. In the early days, the professionals, whether they practiced their trade for the English, Spanish or Italians, seem to have been Nurembergers or Dutch. Edward the Third hired a team of German experts who were employed to operate cannon (presumably cast in Germany) against the Scots in 1327, according to the *Annals of Scotland*, by D. D. Hailes and also John Barbour, Archdeacon of Aberdeen, in his book, *The Bruce*, written in 1375. They were referred to as Crakys of War. Crakys have come down to us in the word "firecracker," in the sense of crack—an explosion. Shakespeare uses the phrase "Cannons overcharged with double cracks."

These early English pieces were cannon or hand cannon or bombards—the names seem to have been used indiscriminately—of small size or bore. One gets the idea that they were fired from the ground, resting on a rock, or sometimes on a wooden framework such as can be seen in a reconstruction in New York's Metropolitan Museum. There was no provision for recoil. Cannon were used by Edward the Third at Cambrai in 1339, and Froissart, in his *Chronicles,* mentions the same monarch's use of bombards in 1340 and at Crecy in 1346. Hand gunners on the royal payroll at Crecy were presumably shooting the pole type of hand cannon with the stick attachment held under the arm, the butt extending back of the armpit, or, and more likely, with the butt stuck in the ground. The barrels were two pipes of different diameters, the smaller to the rear holding the powder. The forward pipe, attached by a weld or screwed or sweated on, received the ball. Being of small bore they shot metal bullets, and the daily allowance for twenty gunners—about all there were—was 60 ounces of powder, 204 lead shot and twelve

pieces of lead. It is no wonder that the French totally ignored the English bombardiers. They attributed their defeat both to the fact that the early morning sun shone in the eyes of the Genovese mercenary crossbowmen, who fled, or later in the morning, to the devastation of their armored knights by the English longbowmen with their armor-piercing arrows.

Cannon, or gonnes, were slow to evolve. The monsters lacked mobility, the little bombards, or muskets, or arquebuses, shot a weak charge, and both took a long time to fire —clean the bore, clean the touchhole, pour powder down a reasonably cool barrel, ram the ball and fire the charge by means of a burning stick or a hot iron, which meant keeping a little campfire burning between every couple of gunners. This last was useful for maintaining morale and providing the basis for a "coffee break," but did not contribute to the mobility required when cavalry charged.

Greater speed and firepower was the idea behind the totenorgel of the Germans and the ribauldequin of the Veronese. These were primitive multibarrel weapons which fired all at once. A line of barrels of increasing length was strapped upon a two-wheel cart for mobility. The barrels looked like a giant Panpipe. When the monster was shot, or more literally "fired," one barrel ignited the charge in the next, as holes were bored between the barrels. Totenorgel with 33 pipes were not uncommon. The ribauldequin had barrels not only in rows, but tiers of rows. The Veronese model was fired by men on staging, and hundreds of barrels went off more or less at once. Of course it was unwieldy and impractical unless they had the good fortune to have it preaimed at massed groups of charging infantrymen or cavalry.

In time cannon did improve. Barrels with obvious flaws were discarded before becoming bombs. Proofing came into fashion. Guns were shot to see that they would not blow up and they were shot against armor, both horse and human, which had been strengthened to resist bullets. Proof marks begin to be used, the earliest surviving being on armor—a mark or a letter of the alphabet next to the dent of the bullet which hadn't penetrated the suit.

Armorers proof-shooting hand cannon *from an Aquarelle by Georg Költerer* Die Zeügbucher des Kaisers Maximilian I *(1504). See Boeheim,* J.D.K.S., *vol. 15, p. 295-391, Vienna, 1894.*

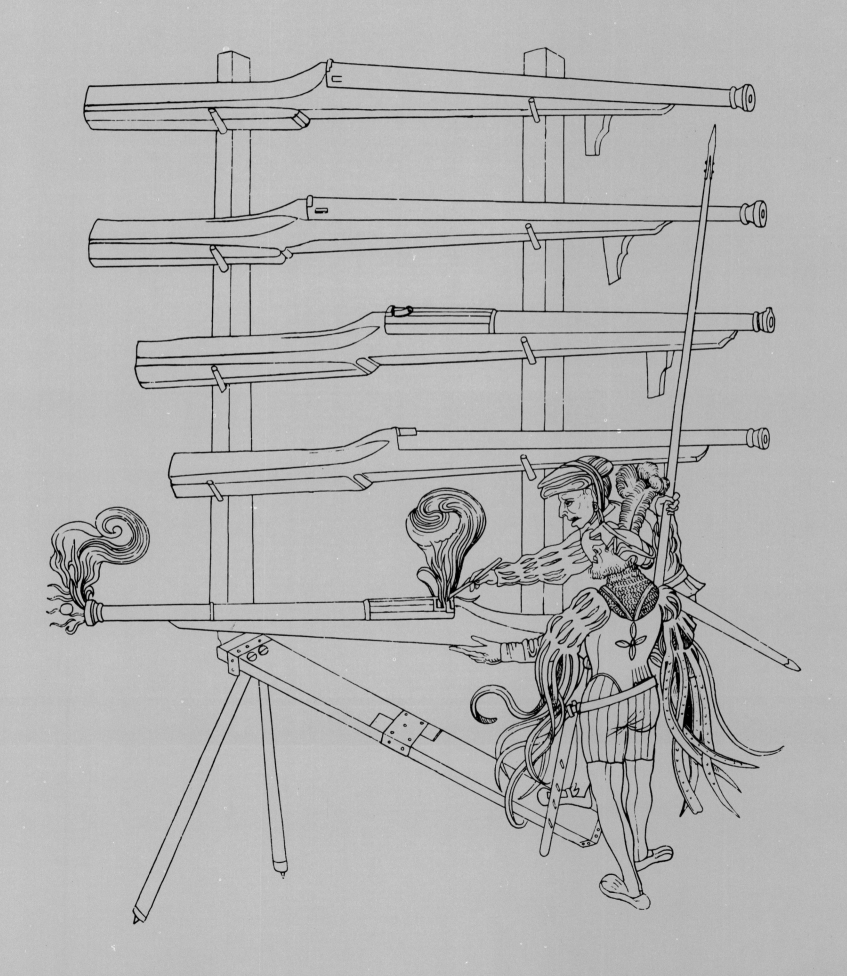

THE GONNE

While we can trace the existence of guns to around or before 1300, their coming into military significance took time. Part of this was undoubtedly due to the conservative nature of the military mind, which could not get itself out of a suit of armor, and part to the slowly developing practicality of the new weapons. It took years before some genius figured out that the touchhole belonged on the side, not the top, of the musket. The hole on top, with its open ring to hold loose priming powder, collected rain as well, and if the water didn't put the musketeer out of business, sometimes a breeze would.

A couple of dates help to show the transition from invention and experiment to practical use. There is a receipt for gunpowder in the library of El Escorial dating from 1250—one pound of live sulphur, two of charcoal of willow and six of saltpeter, reduced to a fine powder and mixed in a marble mortar. Cannon were used, as noted in Chapter One, in the land action at Seville in 1247, but it was a century later, in 1351, in a naval action between the Moors and the Spanish that ships' cannon won the battle. The Moors were recorded as using guns against the Christian defenders of the Alcazar in 1343. Venetians are supposed to have employed guns against the Genovese in 1380.

The complete absence of knowledge of the bursting strength of barrels led to making them very heavy. Gustave Adolphus, who was king of Sweden between 1611 and 1632, solved the problem of lightening field pieces for mobility with his famous leather guns. Actually they were made of copper tubes hooped with iron and wrapped with rawhide.

Furnaces increased in size, and skills improved through practice, so that by the mid-sixteenth century, gun barrels were cast complete with trunnions, eliminating the older trough carriages. As late as the mid-eighteenth century this event was celebrated by inscriptions on the ends of a British naval cannon's trunnions. On the butt of one cannon is the abbreviation for Vauxhall Foundry, Birmingham, and on the other, the word "SOLID" meaning that barrel and trunnions were cast in one piece.

Surviving European hand cannon are very rare. Knowledge of them has come down to us largely from descriptions and pictures. There are, however, a number of Indian and Japanese hand cannon in existence, as they were made from the fifteenth century until the mid-nineteenth century, along with matchlocks and flintlocks. Some of the Oriental pieces have handsome inlays in both stock and barrel, which undoubtedly led to their preservation as works of art. The earliest western weapons were crude and functional and were allowed to rust out between wars. Thus, most of the early European hand cannon suffered the same fate as chain mail armor, which often wound up as scouring pads, despite sovereigns' admonitions to the contrary.

This chapter has been about cannon in general, because of their interchangeable role with the earliest hand-held weapons. At almost this same time the matchlock made its appearance. The improvement of the matchlock over the hand cannon will be the subject of the next chapter.

Soldiers with hand cannon *from the picture book of the Hauslab Library (1430-1440).*

Swiss hand cannon, *14th century (Bern type) stock reconstruction according to Clephan and Alm. Author's Collection.*

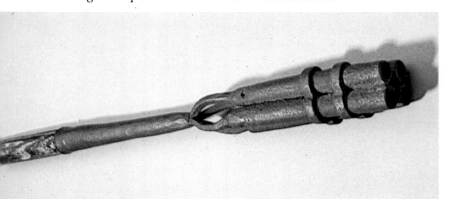

Four-barrel hand cannon *with wooden stock. Probably European, provenance unknown. The Winchester Gun Museum. New Haven. Conn.*

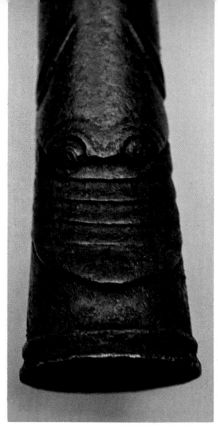

Muzzle of a hand cannon barrel
c. 1400 (Sclopeta) bbl. 22", loa. 37½", cal. .80". Smooth bore. Museo Storico Nazionale d'Artiglieria, Turin.

15th-century cavalry hand cannon.
This escopette, 48" long with a bore at the muzzle of 1⅛", comes from the Chateau de Horst at Rhode Saint Pierre. No. X/10, Musée de la Porte de Hal, Brussels.

Earliest dateable hand cannon *Vedelspang gun, found under the ruins of a castle in South Schleswig destroyed in 1426. bbl. to touchhole 7¼", loa. 32", bore tapered from 18 to 27mm. No.# B 1 Tøjhus Museet, Copenhagen.*

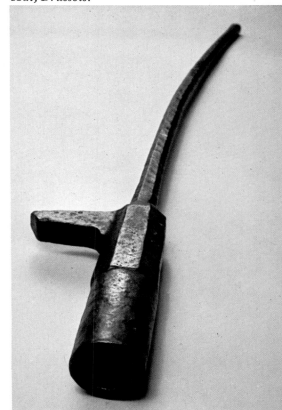

14th century, 3 barrel handcannon *with ramrod and sliding pan covers, loa. 17", bbls 8⅜", bore .38", cal. .40". No.# 5917, Musée de l'Armée, Paris.*

Muzzle of hand cannon *found in the ruins of the castle of Bouvigres c. 1500. No.# 5069, Musée de la Porte de Hal, Brussels.*

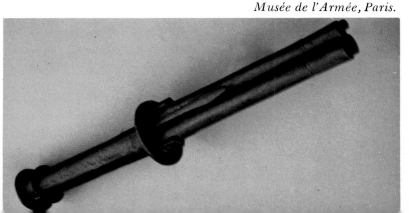

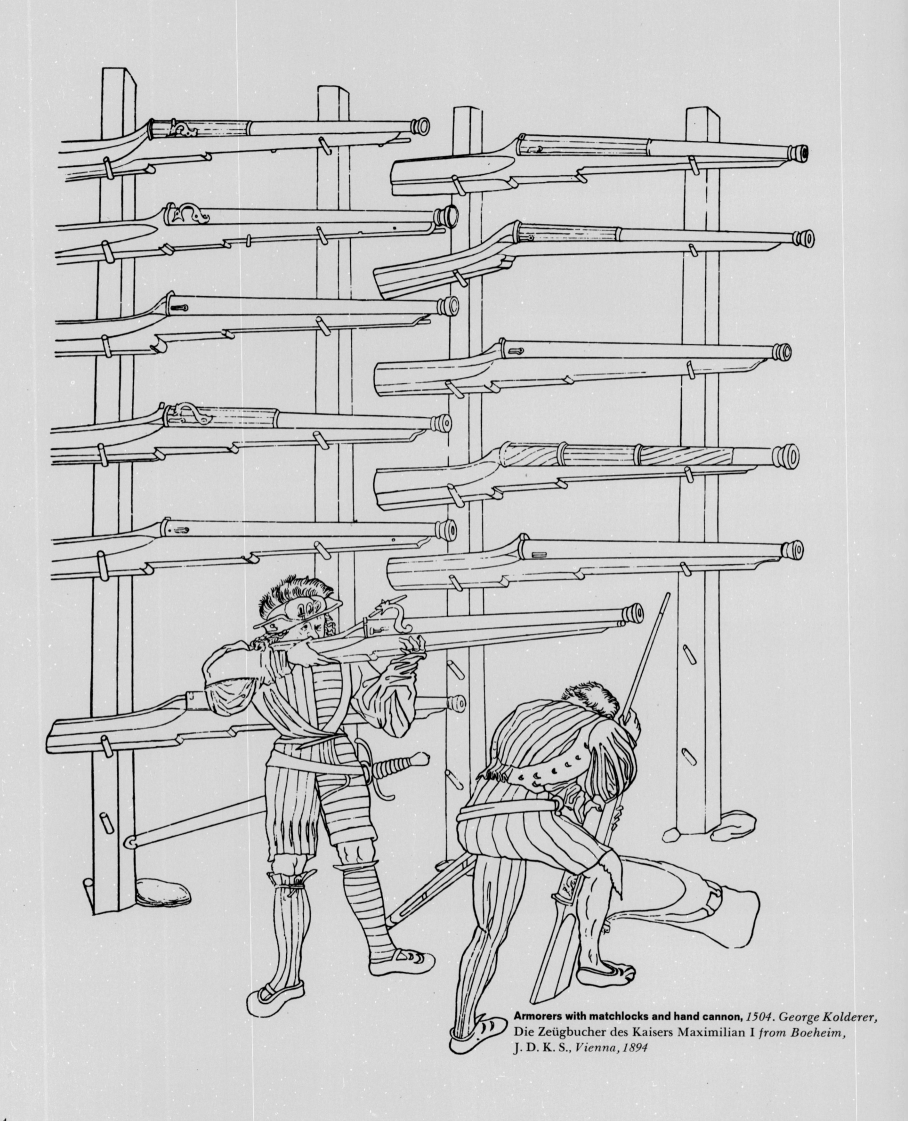

Armorers with matchlocks and hand cannon, *1504. George Kolderer,*
Die Zeügbucher des Kaisers Maximilian I *from Boeheim,*
J. D. K. S., *Vienna, 1894*

CHAPTER IV

THE MATCHLOCK– THE ARQUEBUS

THE RAMPARTS and battlements of medieval castles, with slits in walls three feet deep overlooking the one road that led to the gate, were ideal perches for the first hand gunners. They were close to a fire for their necessary hot coal or wire. They had a hook on the underside of the barrel which they could hold against the lower edge of the firing port to absorb the recoil of the cannon. Best of all, they had the wall as protection between themselves and an enemy charging on a plowhorse, in case the hand cannon didn't go off. Examples of this may be seen in the remains of the walled hill castles near Avignon in Provence. Overlooking village and church are walled terraces level with the tops of the houses and the steeple of the church.

The evolution from tenth- and eleventh-century defensive architecture points out the arrival of the gun. In the days of bows and crossbows, the firing ports were smallest on the outside of the wall—sometimes no more than a couple of inches wide. From the aperture to the inside face of the wall the hole grew bigger and bigger like a square-topped funnel, so that it would accommodate the head, shoulders and weapon of the archer.

With the advent of hand cannon, about the fourteenth century, the funnel was reversed to give the gunner scope to swing his barrel from side to side and up and down and also to provide him with a ledge or lip to rest his piece on. Examples of this transition may be seen at Oppide Le Vieux and La Coste, which castle later became the aerie of the Marquis de Sade.

In the field, the hand gonner was at such a miserable disadvantage that he needed bodyguards to protect him while he went through the processes of loading and firing. The job had so uncertain a life expectancy that applicants were all but impossible to find, and more than one early record shows that gonners were forcibly recruited from jails and escorted to their station in the field by armed guards, who kept them from running away.

Between 1400 and 1450, the matchlock improvement,

possibly a European invention, was carried eastward over the ancient caravan routes through Persia and Afghanistan and down the Khyber pass into Kashmir. From there, on the caravan shuttle, it found its way through India to Indonesia, China, and Japan. Arab traders took matchlocks to Africa during these same years and it may well be that the Arabs, who invented the Medfaa,[1] and not the Europeans, were responsible for the matchlock.

In any event, the matchlock got first-rate distribution throughout the Orient at this early date, and without the helping hand of the Europeans. How is this known? The evidence is strong. Marco Polo and others of his family travelled the length and breadth of the Near and Far East for more than thirty years and never saw guns or gunpowder, and Marco Polo died in 1374. Nevertheless, when the first Portuguese sailors touched at ports in India, Ceylon and what is now Thailand, they were greeted by natives bearing arms.

So far, so good, but here comes the rub. The Orientals knew a good matchlock when they saw it, and for four hundred and fifty years they never lost sight of it. Matchlocks just like the ones grandfather used to make were still being made for business in the mid-nineteenth century. They are still being made, but now their market is found among curiosity- and souvenir-hunting foreigners. There is a sort of poetic justice about all this, and not a little confusion.

Most of the matchlocks we have today, and all existing matchlock pistols, are of Oriental origin. Some of them are magnificent specimens of damascening and metal inlay on metal, especially the later Japanese pieces. The Japanese refined the essentially clumsy European prototype, and became, with practice, so expert in handling the Tanegashima (named for the island where the Portuguese first landed in 1543) that they could correlate the slow ignition of the matchlock to coincide with the quick movements of a bird. The well-nigh impossibility of this can easily be understood by anyone who has learned the much simpler trick of leading a gamebird in flight with an instantaneously firing modern

[1] *The Medfaa was an early form of hand cannon—a barrel on a stick—which is illustrated throwing a ball, but may have been used as a fireworks display to scare horses and country boys. Early guns were not always used to propel bullets—sometimes they just went "bang."*

THE MATCHLOCK

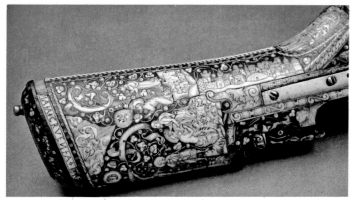

Club-butted matchlock. *Dated 1582, the rifle is decorated with bone inlays of mythological scenes, inscriptions, and inlays of crests in brass. 56¼" loa., bbl. 46" rifled, 6-groove, no twist. Land cal. .57", groove cal. .67". No. # W 1446, Bayerisches Armeemuseum, Munich.*

Popinjay (target) matchlock *with heavy carved wooden fore end, barrel square to octagonal, set triggers, signed F. VAN DER HOVE. loa. 60", bbl. 42⅝", cal. .60". Albert Van Zuylen Collection, Liège.*

Petronel matchlock, *c. 1550. Wooden stock carved in scale design. Two-shot superimposed load (forward lock removed) attributed to Cornelius Klett. loa. 50". bbl. 37", cal. .58". No.# 1449, Bayerisches Armeemuseum, Munich.*

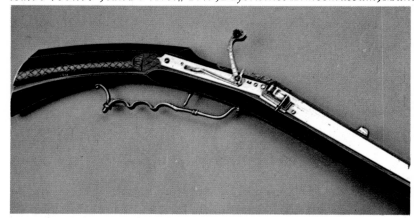

Detail of breech *of above, showing barrel-maker's mark and close-up of inlay and scale carving.*

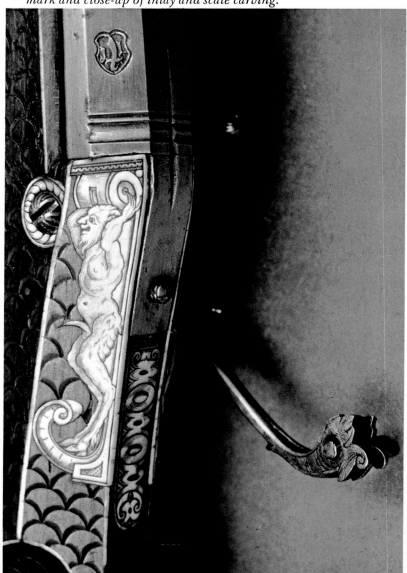

French arquebus, *c. 1600. Double-crowned muzzle. Brass orthoptic sight in the form of a Turk's head. Inscribed:*
POUR MAINTENIR LA FOI, SUIS BELLE ET FIDEL ET AUX ENEMIS DU ROI, SUIS REBELLE ET CRUEL.
loa. 62", bbl. 47⅝", cal. .78" or 8-bore. No.# M-10, Musée de l'Armée, Paris.

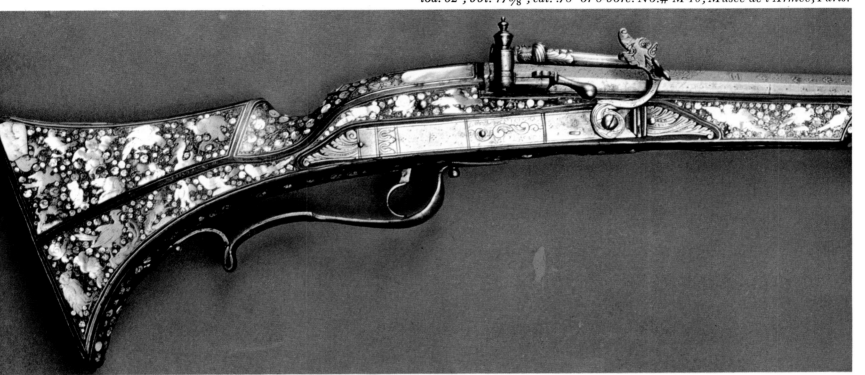

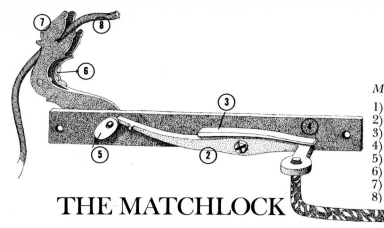

Upward pressure on the tricker (1) against the trigger spring (3) pushes down on the sear (2), rotating the cam (5). This brings the match holder (6) containing the live, burning match (8) to the open pan containing gun powder on the outside of the lock plate (4) (not illustrated).

THE MATCHLOCK

shotgun. Praiseworthy as this dexterity may be, it is no recommendation for matchlock skeet. It is a dubious venture at best to purchase an old Oriental matchlock that has not been validated by being in a recognized collection since the approximate period of its manufacture.[2]

Some time in the first quarter of the fifteenth century, the matchlock made its appearance in western Europe. There is an early example of one at the Germanische Museum in Nuremberg, dated or identified as having been made in 1423. (Military historians are not as positive of these early dates as they were a hundred years ago.) However, within seventy-five years the matchlock had made its way to Persia, India, and Japan, and was on its way to the New World. For several hundred years, because of its low cost and easy repair, it was retained by European armies alongside more sophisticated wheel locks and flintlocks. Matchlocks were still being used in Japan and Burma for serious shooting until the mid-nineteenth century.

The best description of a matchlock—outside of the illustrations—is that it is the "Earliest mechanical form of firing." It freed hand and eye, and let the shooter look at the target instead of the gun at the moment of shooting. Instead of holding the gun under the arm or over the shoulder, supported forward by the left hand, and maneuvering a hot wire or coal into a small touchhole with the right hand, the shooter now could use both hands to support the gun while the fingers of the right hand squeezed the outsized trigger (tricker) up toward the stock. This turned the other end of the serpentine holding the burning wick (the match) into a cup of finely ground powder outside the touchhole.

Match is cotton, linen, or woolen cord or tow soaked in a solution of wet gunpowder or saltpeter or other oxidizer and dried. The match was often lit at both ends as a precaution against going out, and varying needs led to the development of both slow- and fast-burning matches.

The original matchlocks had no springs. They operated with a serpentine—a hinged, weighted, "S" shaped piece of metal—with the match holder at one end and the trigger at the weighted end. The serpentine was attached to the stock by a center pin which served as a pivot. The weighted end kept the match-holding end upright by gravity and out of the way of the powder until a pull brought the match in contact—pulling the tail end of the "S" toward the shooter and dipping the top of the "S" holding the match into the pan.

Later on, a spring-operated trigger kept the match out of harm's way, and the serpentine was reversed so that the shooter could better see the lit end of the match and the priming powder when it started to burn. After sighting along the barrel it was customary for the shooter to remove his face for the second or two that intervened before the gun fired.

Gun author Harold Peterson has discovered a description of the proper military handling of the matchlock from a document of military law of the Virginia colony in 1611:

"He shall shoulder his piece, both ends of his match being alight and his piece charged and primed, and bullets in his mouth, there to stand with a careful and waking eye, until such time as his corporall shall relieve him."

An excellent manual had just preceded this and had been translated into English within a year of its publication in Holland. Pages of copper engravings done by the author illustrate the successive steps of employing the matchlock, which by this time and for years to come was the basic weapon of the foot soldier. Exercises with the pike were still practiced by the English in the eighteenth century, but wars were fought with massed blocks of infantry firing matchlocks. The book's full title was: *THE EXERCISE OF ARMES For Calivres, Muskettes, and Pikes After the order of his Excellence Maurits Prince of Orange . . . Sett forthe in figures by Jacob de Gheyn. With written Instructions for the service of all Captaines and Comaundours. For to shewe hereout the better unto their yong or untrayned souldiers the playne and perfett maner to handle these Armes. They are toe bye at Amsterdam by Robert de Boudous 1607/8.*

By de Gheyn's time the cavalry was armed with wheel lock pistols. Shooting a matchlock with its two ends of burning rope from a horse is a bit of a trick. As a matter of fact,

[2] *Unless the purchaser has the good fortune to be able to get some outstanding authority such as Randolph Bullock, the Curator of Arms at the Metropolitan Museum of Art in New York and an authority on Oriental weapons, to pass on it.*

Early armored car
from Vegetius, De Re Militari, *page 93, Paris, 1553.*

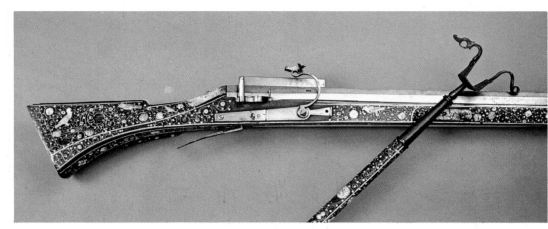

Matchlock rampart gun *with matching inlaid musket fork. German, dated 1656. Joe Kindig Jr. Collection.*

Butt detail *of matchlock* (above) *showing date and crest. Joe Kindig Jr. Collection.*

French matchlock petronel, *c. 1550. Head of an Indian inlaid in ivory on the top of the stock. Note the large trigger or tiller and square-headed screws. loa. 47", bbl. 38½", cal. .66". Smooth bore, No.# IX/6, Musée de la Porte de Hal, Brussels.*

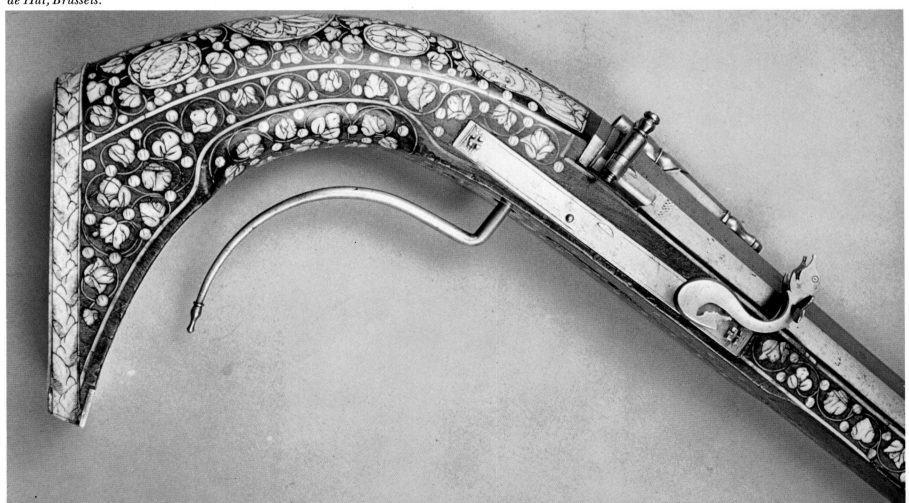

THE MATCHLOCK

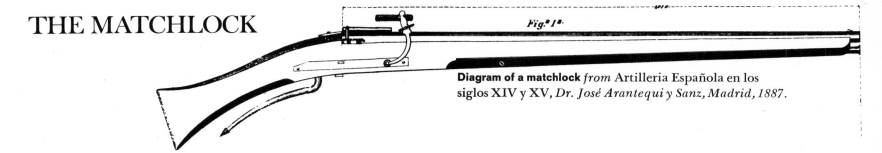

Diagram of a matchlock *from* Artilleria Española en los siglos XIV y XV, *Dr. José Arantequi y Sanz, Madrid, 1887.*

shooting a matchlock from the shoulder of a forked rest at a quickly moving target was not the easiest thing in the world, as we learn from the diaries and records kept by the early Spanish explorers.

Alvar Núñez, Cabeza de Vaca, a singularly unsuccessful sixteenth-century explorer of the American Southwest, says in his *Relacion,* published in Zamora in 1542, about fighting Indians:

> "The method they have of fighting is bending low to the earth, and whilst shot at they move about, speaking and leaping from one point to another, thus avoiding the shafts of their enemies. So effectual is their manouvering that they can receive very little injury from crossbow or arquebus; they rather scoff at them; for these arms are of little value employed in open field where the Indians move nimbly about . . ."

And from the *Expedition of Hernandez de Soto* published in Evora in Portugal in 1557:

> "Before a Christian can make a single shot (with crossbow or arquebuss) an Indian will discharge three or four arrows and he seldom misses his object. Where the arrow meets with no armour, it pierces as deeply as the shaft from a crossbow—when they strike upon armour, break at the place where the parts are put together; those of cane split and enter a shirt of mail doing more injury than when armed."

There was not much question of the superiority of a skilled longbowman over a hackbut handler,[3] and the English were fully aware of this, as in edict after edict they urged practice with the longbow and threatened punishment for failure to exercise with this weapon. Children were to be furnished with bows according to their strength, and employers were to furnish their employees with bows, arrows and quivers and time off to practice. Nothing worked; the supply of skilled bowmen who had won the battle of Agincourt ran out. To shoot a bow with skill takes practice from childhood, and to draw a bow that would pierce armor takes the muscles of an athlete. Crossbowmen or arquebusiers could be trained from raw recruits in short time.

A great disadvantage of the matchlock, however, was the necessity of the ever-present burning match. This meant a fire burning somewhere near at hand, or a supply of dry tinder, fuel, steel and flint. Rain put out the fires of the men who were serving with Hendrick Hudson, and the Indians surprised a boatload of them on the banks of the river that would later be named after him.[4] When an early French explorer—it may have been Cartier—had worked his way down from the Grand Banks to what sounds like present day Cuttyhunk in the Elisabeth Islands, he decided to take home a couple of Indians as a surprise to the King. The Indians had heard about this one from previous visitors and weren't having any. While the ship's longboat was being prepared and launched, the Indians danced and sang on the shore. When the longboat headed for them with their matchlocks, matches and tinder box, the Indians swam out with baskets of fish, fruit and vegetables. Once alongside, the baskets were used to scoop water into the longboat, extinguishing the fire and the matches. From there on it was easy for the Indians to ensure that the French went home without captives, as well as without a longboat and a part of her crew.

Throughout the early years of the use of gunpowder, its bark was much worse than its bite, although gunshot wounds were supposed to be fatal, and the report of the guns themselves had a startling effect when first heard. But there is always something alarming about a new secret weapon. That the principles involved were not well understood is profusely demonstrated in Valturius (Roberto Valturio), who wrote the book *De Re Militari* in Verona in 1483. It has pages of illustrations of "Miraculous Instruments"—so he called them—cannon that shot in all directions at once, cannon that had a full 90-degree bend in the middle of the barrel, and cannon with ice cream cone-shaped barrels.[5] Some of these illustrations were being reproduced centuries after. Francis Grose, in his *History of the English Army,* first published in 1786, who says that he has not seen the original Latin edition and is quoting the translation of a French Author, Joly de Maizeroy, reproduces Valturius' right-angle cannon and other mechanical impossibilities, with the com-

---

[3] *A hackbut was an arquebus with a bent-down butt that could be rested against the shoulder for a steadier aim.*

[4] *. . . our Master (Henry Hudson, ed.) sent John Colman with foure other men in our Boate over to the North-side to sound the other River (the Narrows, ed.). Being foure leagues from us—so they went in Two leagues and saw an open Sea (Upper New York Bay, ed.) and returned: and as they came backe, They were set upon by Two Canoes, The one having twelve, the other fourteene men. The night came on, and it begun to rayne, so that their Match went out; and they had one man slaine in the fight, which was an English-man named John Colman, with an arrow shot into his throat, and two more hurt Robert Juot,* The Third Voyage of Master Henry Hudson, *1610.*

[5] *Vedelspang gun in the Tøjhus Museum in Copenhagen.*

Try your match.	*Guard your pan.*	*Present.*	*Give Fire.*	*Come up to your Musket.*

ment that he questions the practicality of Valturius' arsenal.

That excellent writer and analyst of the very beginning of firearms, Dr. Jose Arantegui y Sanz, in 1887, after arguing learnedly about the probable origin of European firearms from the Medfaa, which were gun barrels on sticks,[6] reproduces Valturius' drawings alongside such authenticated primitive weapons as the beer stein breech loaders from Madrid and the early strapped weapons from Majorca.

Perhaps one of the truest commentaries on the effectiveness of early firearms can be deduced from the text on surgery by Guy de Chauliac entitled *On Wounds and Fractures* written in 1363 (years after Crecy and the naval battle of the Spanish and Saracen forces). In an edition of de Chauliac published in Venice in 1546, this physician to the Popes at Avignon devotes a part of the text to the treatment of wounds caused by specific weapons. There are headings for wounds inflicted to all parts of the body caused by:

"iron, others of thorn, others of bone . . . Besides some are plain and others barbed. Moreover some have a socket in which the shaft is set; others have a nail driven into the shaft. Besides this, some are poisonous, others not."

De Chauliac goes on to illustrate cannulated teneculae for the removal of barbed arrows, reversed augers to seize the iron sockets of lances or pole weapons, scissors to dilate the flesh in order that the arrows may be more easily extracted, and surgical arbalests whose use I will leave to the imagination except to quote de Chauliac again, "and the patient being well fortified," etc.[7]

Nowhere in this important text is there a mention of the treatment of gunshot wounds. Unless all gunshot wounds were fatal, a hardly plausible conclusion, their effect would seem to have been largely psychological. As a decisive factor in warfare, guns in the thirteenth and early fourteenth centuries were on a par with balloons in the U. S. Civil War or heavier-than-air aircraft in World War I. Nevertheless, the invention of the matchlock had a civilizing influence that was to be felt around the world. To quote Grose:

"This invention, although by Milton, and other

poets and writers, ascribed to the devil, was, without doubt, a most fortunate discovery for mankind, and has greatly lessened the slaughter and miseries of war. Formerly when men engaged hand to hand, they were so intermingled that the only criterion of victory was the having no more of the enemy to kill; the duration of sieges has also been shortened since the use of gunpowder and artillery, by which the lives of millions have been saved, who would have otherwise perished by hardship or disease, commonly in the sieges more fatal than the sword."

After reading Gibbon on the sieges and sacking of Italy from the time of the Visigoths, Grose's statement does not seem completely cynical.

In any event, another "most fortunate discovery for mankind" is just around the corner, and this time there is even a clue to who invented it. The wheel lock might have been independently invented by Johann Kiefuss of Nuremberg about 1517, although Leonardo da Vinci drew pictures of a wheel lock mechanism before 1507. Here we go again.

Return your match.

Manual of Arms
for the musket, caliver and pike, by Jacob de Gheyn, Amsterdam, 1607-8.

Take up your rest.

Trail your rest & open your cha...

Blow of your loose Powder and cast about your Musket.

[6] *Later substantiated by Oscar Guttman in* Monumental Pulveris Pyrii *(London, 1906) who rediscovered a copy of a manuscript on Arabian guns in the Musée Asiatique in St. Petersburg compiled by Schems Eddin-Mohammed probably around 1474, illustrating these pieces, or Medfaa.*

[7] *From the translation of W. A. Brennan, (Chicago, 1923)*

1548 wheel lock rifle. *Oldest dated firearm in Tøjhus museum, "L.S." on barrel, date on stock. Rifle exhibits early external spring wheel retainer. Augsburg. loa. 39¼", bbl. 28½", cal. .56". No.# B.35 Tøjhus Museet, Copenhagen.*

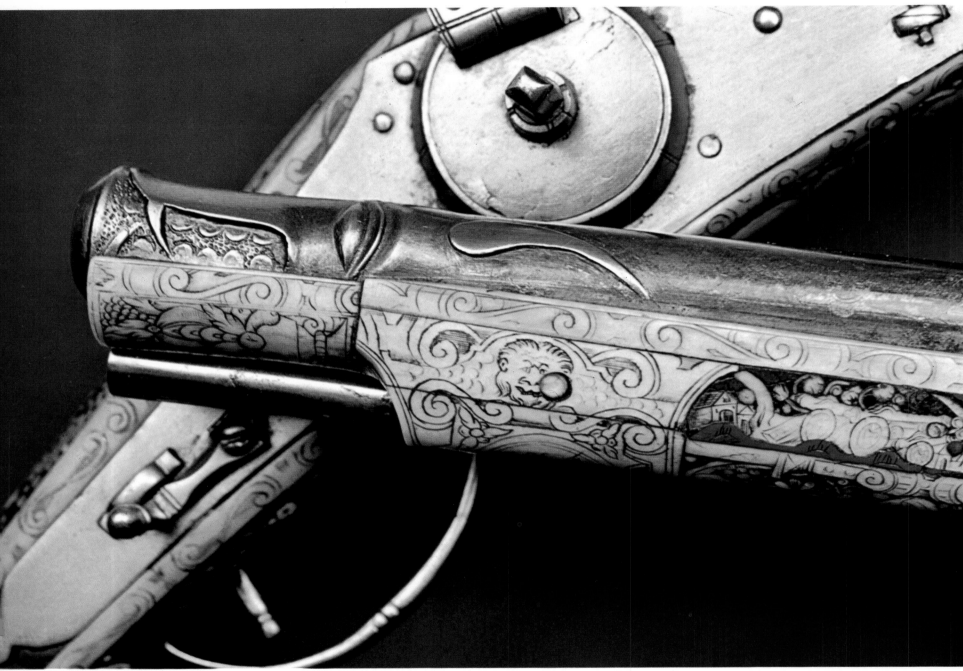

Saxon ball-butt pistols, *c. 1585. loa. 25", bbl. 14½", cal. 68". No. # B.128-129, Tøjhus Museet, Copenhagen.*

All-iron wheel lock pistol, *1575, belonged to Julius II and Hedwig of Brunswick. Trapdoor on butt has identifying crest, provenance Magniac Collection. Scissor mark and initials on barrel breech. 23" long, s.b. No.# 14.25 .1424, Metropolitan Museum of Art, New York, gift of William H. Riggs, 1913.*

CHAPTER V

THE WHEEL LOCK

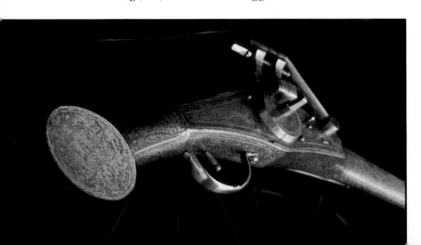

Detail *of 1600 all-metal Nuremberg dag showing Nuremberg control stamp on barrel and lock, also maker's stamp (see Behr). cal. .64". No.# 14.25.1406A, Metropolitan Museum of Art, New York, gift of William H. Riggs, 1913.*

WHEN HENRY VIII came to the throne of England in 1509 Germans in Nuremberg had begun to build the first wheel locks. This new gun mechanism was a logical evolution from the mechanical fire lighters of the day and clock mechanisms with spring, crank and chain. Da Vinci had sketched a prototype wheel lock between 1482 and 1499, and signed pieces are in existence dating from the early years of the sixteenth century. Many of these pieces were made by watchmakers.[1]

The invention of the wheel lock made pistols practical and provided a hunting weapon to rival the crossbow. Mobility, firepower, speed of fire and control of the time of firing were increased, as was the element of surprise and concealment, as soldier, hunter, and assassin could move around with a loaded gun with no telltale bonfire or burning match. Proof of the effectiveness of the new weapon is to be seen in the edict of the Emperor Maximillian I who forbade the manufacture of the gun in 1517. Wheel locks were banned within the city limits of Ferrara in 1522 and similar bans ensued at Modena, Milan and Florence.

The bans on wheel locks were no more effective than the Papal bull outlawing crossbows. Fine wheel locks and petronels found their way to England where Henry VIII was painted with one at his side, and a number of pieces turn up in contemporaneous inventories of weapons at the Tower of London. In France the *système rouet* appears in the *Ordonnances de Chasse* of Francis I, and in Italy, Pablo del Fucar wrote a book on hunting called *Ballestes Mosauetas y Arcabuces* in Naples in 1535.

The wheel lock of course made a fine cavalry weapon, and before the end of the century the German *Reiters* with their disciplined caracole horses and their ball-butted wheel lock horse pistols were the first of the dreaded panzer units.[2]

Perhaps nowhere, however, were wheel locks of as much value as in the new colonies in North America. Although they were expensive, they were worth their price to the settlers in the New World, for whom the matchlock was useless against the speed and mobility of the Indians. Captain

[1] *Giovanni Capobianco of Schio, an early 16th-century goldsmith, designer, and mathematician, made an alarm clock gun for Consul General Andrea Alciati and Cardinal Matteo Schnier (1511) which also lit a candle. Dizionario degli Orologiani Italiani, (E. Morpurgo, Rome).*

[2] *Marian Kujawski, "The Battle of Kircholm: A Masterpiece of Early XVII Century Military Tactics," The Polish Review, Vol. XI, No. 1, winter 1966.*

THE WHEEL LOCK

John Smith in his *Generall Historie of the Virginia Colony* says, "Captain Yearly had a Salvage or two so well trined up to their peeces, they were as expert as any of the English, and one hee kept purposly to kill him fowle." Captain Yearly was taking chances both with the Indians and the settlers as in the proceedings of the Virginia Assembly the following law was in the record:

"That no man do sell or give any Indian any piece shott or poulder, or any other armes, offensive or defensive upon paine of being held a Traytor to the Colony, and of being hanged as soon as the fact is proved, without all redemption."

The importance of the new guns is spelled out by Bradford in his *History of Plymouth Plantation* when he writes about Thomas Morton:

". . . Morton, thinking himselfe lawless, and hearing what gaine the French and fisher-men made by trading of peeces, powder, and shotts to the Indeans, he, as the head of this consortship, begane the practise of the same in these parts; and first he taught them how to use them, to charge, and discharge, and what proportion of powder to give the peece, according to the sise or bignes of the same; and what shotte to use for foule, and what for deare. And having thus instructed them, he imployed some of them to hunte and fowle for him, so they became farr more active in that imployment than any of the English, by reason of their swiftness of foote, and nimbleness of body, being also quick-sighted, and by continuall exercise well knowing the hants of all sorts of game. So as when they saw the execution that a peece would doe, and the benefite that might come by the same, they became madd, as it were, after them, and would not stick to give any prise they could attain too for them; accounting their bowes and arrows but baubles in comparison of them."

Bradford goes on to say that the Indians had fowling pieces, muskets, pistols, "moulds to make shotte, of all sorts, as muskett bulletts, pistoll bulletts, swane and gose shote, and of smaller sorts . . ."

According to many of the older histories of firearms, the wheel lock had a precise historical span from 1517 (the date of its invention by Kiefuss of Nuremburg) to slightly over three hundred years later, when LePage in Paris built a wheel lock on special order, probably for a German customer, in 1829. But there is more to the story than dates. The wheel lock was an invention that stemmed logically from skills and crafts already existent in Germany, and over a period of hundreds of years the Germans continued to prefer the wheel lock for hunting and as a cavalry weapon —long after the arrival of the snaphaunce and the flintlock.

Even today, looking at their wonderful workmanship, ingenuity, and their variety, one cannot fail to be impressed. Some of the wheel locks, the earliest, were combined with matchlock systems. Many were equipped with double ignition systems. Over-and-under wheel locks were built, so were graceful three-barreled models, with barrels apart at the breech and close together at the muzzle, so that as the barrels revolved the top one would be in the shooter's proper line of sight. Wheel lock revolvers still exist, as do splendid examples of semi-automatic wheel locks which wound themselves when the cock was drawn back.

Surviving wheel locks are mostly works of art, as the plainer weapons went to the scrap heap or were allowed to rust away, and no one thought of collecting obsolete weapons for their own sake until the early nineteenth century. Even the most primitive specimens of those guns we still have show highly developed skills. The glass-hard wheels could only have been made by armorers who were already making "proof" armor and had a good working knowledge of metallurgy. The same armorers needed skills of a high order to whittle the precisely fitted moving and butting parts, for the wheel lock was far from a simple piece of machinery. They always were expensive and they required no little skill to repair. It is a matter of conjecture whether the English ever learned to build wheel locks. Henry VIII imported German gunsmiths, as had his predecessor Edward III, and Caspar Kalthoff came to London with the family patents in 1658.

The very concept of such a weapon as a wheel lock must have come from men who had developed mechanical skills and practical knowledge from building clocks. We do know of more than one instance where the gunmaker came from a family of clockmakers, and of several examples where clock-

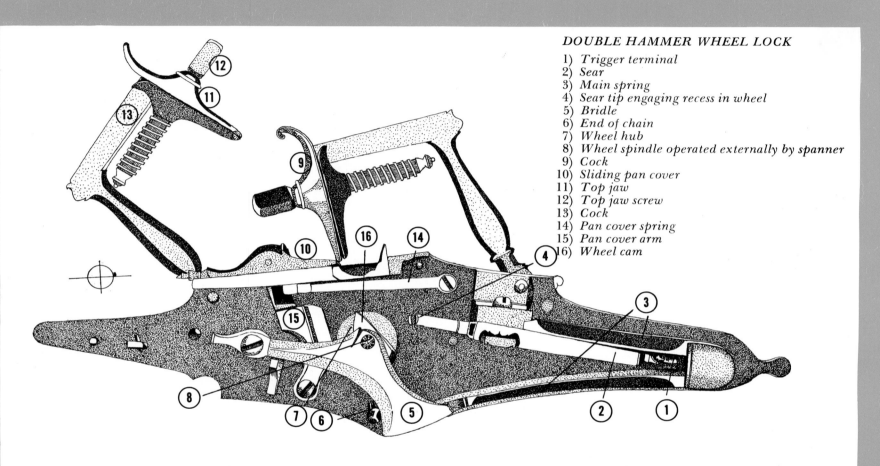

DOUBLE HAMMER WHEEL LOCK

1) *Trigger terminal*
2) *Sear*
3) *Main spring*
4) *Sear tip engaging recess in wheel*
5) *Bridle*
6) *End of chain*
7) *Wheel hub*
8) *Wheel spindle operated externally by* **spanner**
9) *Cock*
10) *Sliding pan cover*
11) *Top jaw*
12) *Top jaw screw*
13) *Cock*
14) *Pan cover spring*
15) *Pan cover arm*
16) *Wheel cam*

This wheel lock is equipped with two cocks as a safety factor in case the pyrites should break in either one. Only one cock is used at a time. The rear one (9) is illustrated (without pyrites), lowered into position. Prior to lowering the cock the primer pan is filled with powder and the sliding pan cover (10) is pushed to the rear to keep the powder from spilling. The firing sequence is as follows: Pressure on the trigger moves trigger terminal (1) moving the rear end of sear (2) sideways. This retracts the tip (4) from a cavity in the wheel plate (external). This allows main spring (3) to exert a downward force on chain (6) which is barely visible behind the bridle (5). The force of the main spring causes the rapid rotation of the wheel (7) and the serrated steel edge of the wheel rubbing on the pyrites on cock (9) throws a shower of sparks into the pan. In early wheel locks, it was necessary to push the pan forward by hand. In later models such as this, the pan cover is automatically pushed forward by an arm (15) activated by a cam (16) attached to the wheel hub.

THE WHEEL LOCK

type flat coil springs were used in a wheel lock instead of the usual long, cut springs. At an exposition of automata brought to the United States by the Pestalozzi Foundation in 1950 there were two interesting examples of the close ties between the crafts. One automaton was a crude sixteenth-century alarm clock. A clockwork mechanism fired a blank charge at the preset time (this was the alarm) and the sparks from the priming charge lit an attached candle. Another much later example was a little gold double-barreled pistol decorated with pearls and diamonds. Instead of flints, the cocks held polished moonstones. A pull on the trigger caused a clockwork mechanism to project a jewelled bird from the muzzles. The bird perched on the front sight and "sang" with the aid of a music box concealed in the weapon's stock.

In addition to armorers and mechanics, woodworkers, ivory carvers and inlayers and engravers lent their skills to wheel locks. The workmanship of wheel locks of all periods is a joy to examine. Cut steel and silver filigree decoration, sculptured butt plates, carved and engraved ivory, bone and mother-of-pearl stocks and carved steel receivers with hammered-in-gold and inlaid barrels exist on guns made in the sixteenth and seventeenth centuries. Among the most familiar, some of whom signed their work, some of whom used their initials and some of whom are unknown, are: the Sadelers, ironworkers who worked with Borstorffer in 1635, Meister H. S. in 1555, Jost Amman, and Virgil Solis were making their designs in 1570's. The list of artists and craftsmen includes the unknown Meister der Tierkopfranken, Hieronymus Borstorffer's successor Adam Vischer, and Caspar Spät, successor to Emanuel Sadeler; Etienne Delaune, Conrad Tornier in France and Acqua Fresca in Italy.

Cut steel, gold inlay and overlay, brilliant enamelwork and inlays of staghorn, superb wood carving and marquetry, sculptured and colored ivory, (a favorite color was green), made these single pieces miniature museums of the arts and crafts of the periods during which they were created. Subject matter of the decorations run a full gamut from pornography, scenes of the hunt, classical gods and goddesses, geo-

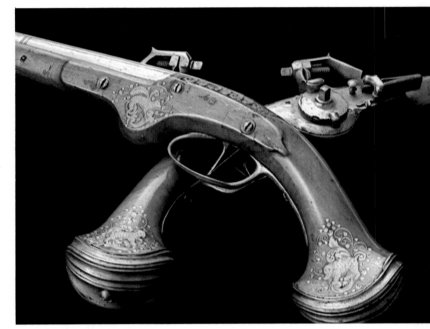

Pair of wheel lock pistols *with pear-wood stocks, steel butt plates, Joe Kindig Jr. Collection.*

Swiss wheel lock pistols *made by Felix Werder in Zurich, c. 1640. Russell Aitken Collection.*

Gilt mask butt plate, *detail of Werders,* above.

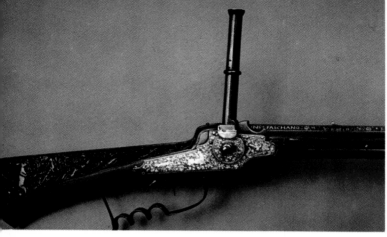

Wheel lock with smokestack *from the Emperor of Austria's hunting cabinet. Dated "1638", "Hanns Faschang" on the barrel in gold. The stock is by the Meister der Tierkopfranken. loa. 40½", cal. .50". No.# D-101, Kunsthistorische Museum, Vienna.*

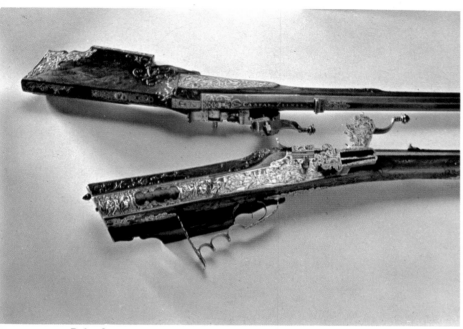

Pair of wheel lock target rifles *signed CASPAR ZELNER, Vienna, c. 1720. Made for Charles VI of Austria. Cat. no. 658, Kretzschmar von Kienbusch Collection.*

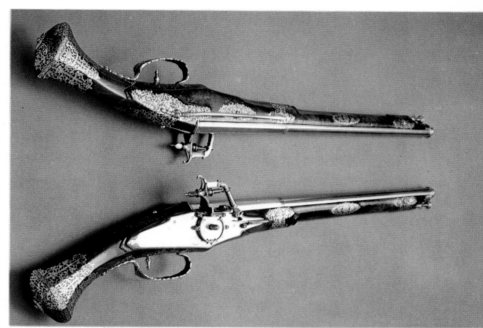

ANTONIO FRANCINO signed *pair of Brescian pistols, c. 1630-60. Cut and pierced steel. Russell Aitken Collection.*

Waterproof two-shot wheel lock pistols. *Made by Bergier in Grenoble c. 1635 for Louis XIII. loa. 21½", bbl. 14⅞", cal. 56". No.# 1659-60 Musée de l'Armée, Paris.*

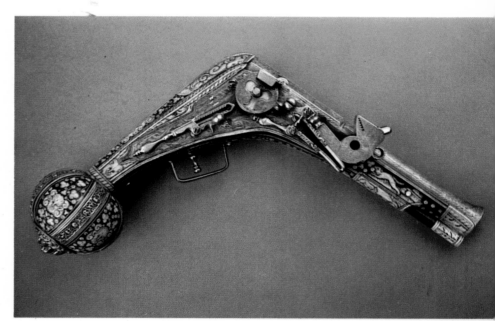

Right-angle ball butt *Nuremberg dag c. 1580. Russell Aitken Collection.*

THE WHEEL LOCK

metric and foliage filigree, to Biblical tableaux in ivory.

The workmanship of many of these weapons shows the same dedication that caused medieval sculptors to finish the backs of church carvings with the same detail as the fronts, though they would never be seen. Inside the guns the steel of parts and springs is often carved and engraved to match the external decoration. From the north of Italy came the superb examples of Lazarino Cominazzo and the Brescian barrel makers, with finely chiseled steel work and strong, yet light, barrels. In the Tøjhus Museet in Copenhagen there is a magazine repeater wheel lock built by Peter Kalthoff in 1645. This gun worked, since the presence of some fifty like it still in the Royal Danish Arsenal Museum testifies that it was an issue made to elite troops. The Kalthoff family took its invention as far away as England and Russia, where different members of the family built wheel locks employing the repeater system for three generations. In 1519 Peter (Pedro) and Simon Macuarte (Markwordt) were brought from Augsburg, Germany to Madrid by the Emperor Charles V. They introduced the wheel lock and stayed in Spain to found the Spanish arms industry—destined to produce fine steel barrels with signatures of Esquibel, Bis and Zegarra.

During the long period of time that the wheel lock was an important weapon, there were identifying evolutions in design. The earliest wheel locks had an external wheel guarded around the edges by a spring holding the dog against the rotating wheel. Later, but still early wheel locks, had a domed plate over the wheel. Next, the wheel was fitted into a well made in the lock plate, and finally, it was moved inside the lock. This is, of course, oversimplified, and exceptions and variations can easily be found. Examples of such exceptions are the Tschinkes, where the springs and chain remain outside, and in Brescian pistols where the wheel cover is skeletonized.[3] By and large, the evolutionary changes were made with one objective. That was to make the gun as weather- and waterproof as possible. By covering the working parts or by putting them inside the lock plate, the hazards of rust and breakage were reduced. One invention of the wheel

lock era—the double set or hair trigger, was mechanically perfect from its inception, and was used, unchanged in match weapons as late as the Creedmore match rifles of the 1870's.

While the wheel locks will work with a piece of flint in the jaws of the cock, they were designed for a softer abrasive to produce the spark. Iron disulphide, in the form of pyrites, gave off an even flow of sparks while doing the least damage to the hardened wheel. The same iron disulphide, which came from German mines, provided the spark for the wheel lock, the iron and steel for its construction, and the sulphur used in making the gunpowder. Agricola[4] illustrates and describes every step in detail for the student mining engineer and metallurgist.

The wheel lock is another fine example of mankind doing everything the hard way. Later weapons were much simpler just as effective, and cheaper to build and maintain. Had the wheel lock survived till today, it undoubtedly would be mechanically assembled from a group of plastic extrusions. The nylon dog would hold a Carborundum-impregnated plastic "flint" which would abrade on a high-impact styrene wheel with a metallized spray-on surface.

So that the reader may not be confused, or attempt to pigeonhole wheel locks or any other type of ignition system, let it be pointed out that just as there were steel-bladed daggers discovered in King Tutankhamen's tomb, in a period of time classified by historian and Egyptologists as the Bronze Age, similarly there were rockets, grenades, and flintlock guns during most of the wheel lock period, and they competed with matchlocks, crossbows, and bows and arrows. Witness this description of an encounter of Sir Francis Drake's off Quito, Ecuador, in 1578:[5]

". . . the night wind rose and the water began to ripple under the *Pelican's* bows. The *Cacafuego* was swiftly overtaken, and when within a cable's length a voice hailed her to put her head into the wind. The Spanish commander, not understanding so strange an order, held on his course. A broadside brought down her mainyard and a flight of arrows rattled on his deck."

[3] *Early Austrian wheel locks most often had exposed wheels held in place with two screws overlapping the wheel.*

[4] De Re Metallica, *(Basle, 1556).*

[5] *J. A. Froude,* English Seamen in the 16th Century, *p. 60.*

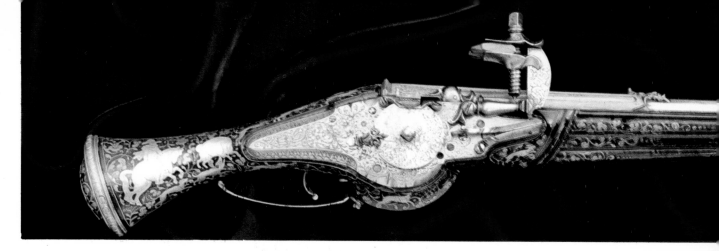

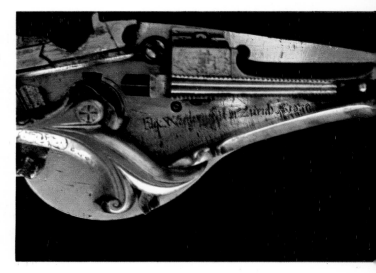

Felix Werder wheel lock pistol *may have belonged to Charles I of England. Signed and dated inside lock plate. Cavalier figures engraved on the face of the lock and inlaid in the stock and on the butt. No.# 10.42, Metropolitan Museum of Art, New York, Rogers Fund, 1910.*

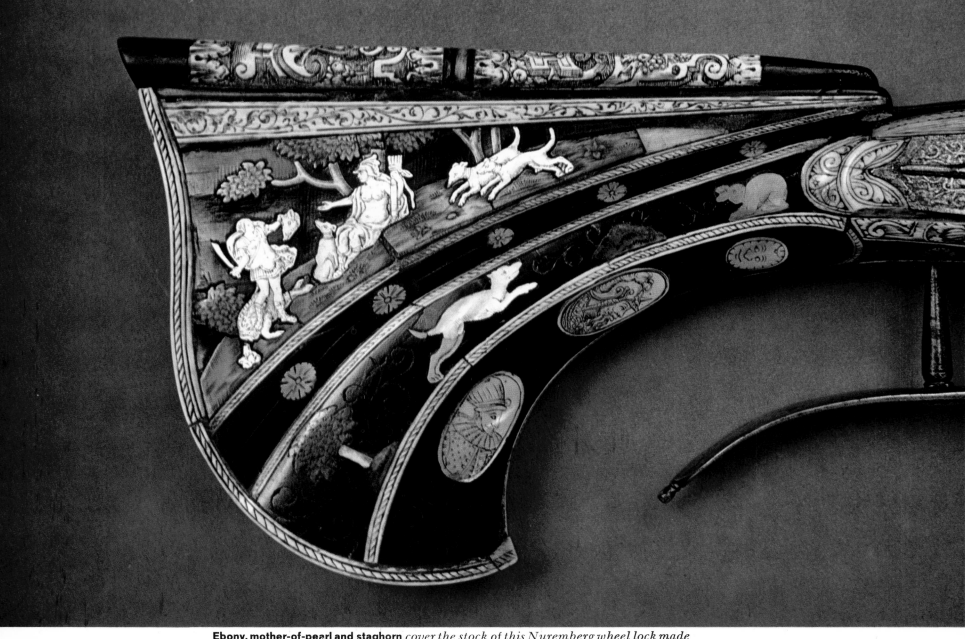

Ebony, mother-of-pearl and staghorn *cover the stock of this Nuremberg wheel lock made around 1600 from the designs of Jost Amman. Joe Kindig Jr. Collection.*

Almost a pair *of South German wheel lock pistols. Augsburg control marks on the barrels. Nuremberg control mark on one lock and Regensburg or Liegnitz mark on the other. One lock has the master's mark "G.H." c. 1590. loa. 20", bbl. 12", cal. .52", smooth bore. Nos. #51/126 & 51/125, Bayerisches Armeemuseum, Munich.*

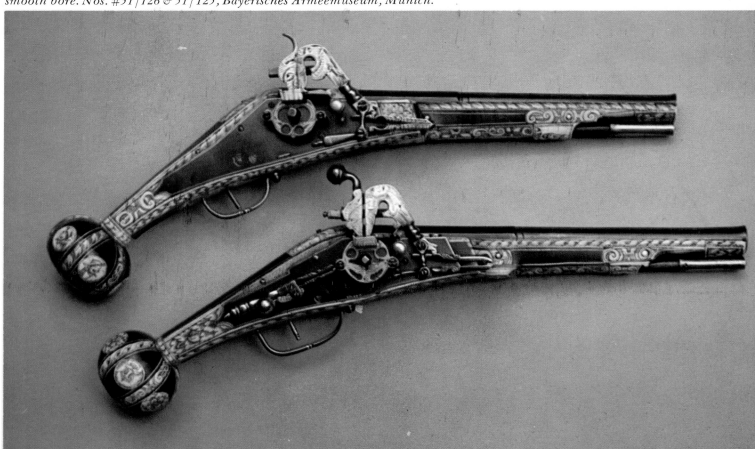

French wheel lock *dated 1621. Both the barrel and the plate under the pan cover are signed by Jean Hennequin of Metz. The rear sight is the devil's horns protruding from the mask. The cock is in the form of Atlas and the stock is inlaid with swirls of gold wire. loa. 59", bbl. 43¾", cal. .60", smooth bore. No.# 1933, Bayerisches Armeemuseum, Munich.*

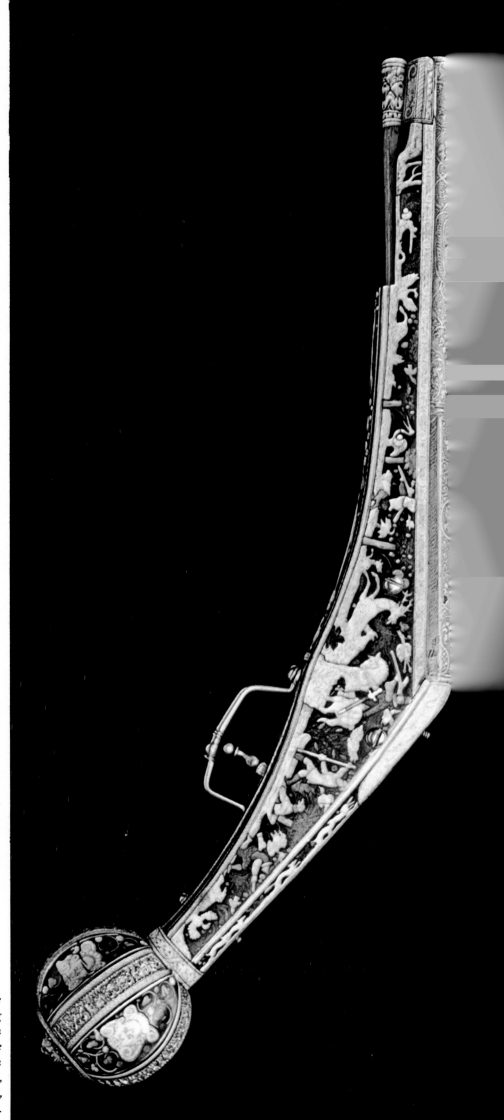

Peter Daner *or Peter Dauer (the same gunsmith) made this jewelled, ball butt dag in Nuremberg c. 1590. It has "P.D." on the barrel divided by the snake and eagle stamps. There is a lion in a shield with an "M" on the lock. Cal. .52". No.# 14.25.1419, Metropolitan Museum of Art, New York, gift of William H. Riggs, 1913.*

Ivory powder flask, *German, c. 1750. This and the flask on the opposite page show signs of having been done by the same sculptor or at least in the same school. Russell Aitken Collection.*

Ivory carving of *Adam and Eve. Powder flask from the Tyrol, with the Welsperg coat of arms, c. 1550. Gilt cap, rings, and spout with the ivory cut through to show a brown field of wood. 10" high by 5¼" wide. No.# 234-1854, Victoria and Albert Museum, London.*

Circular ivory hunting flask, *c. 1750. No.# R 4960 Bayerisches Armeemuseum, Munich.*

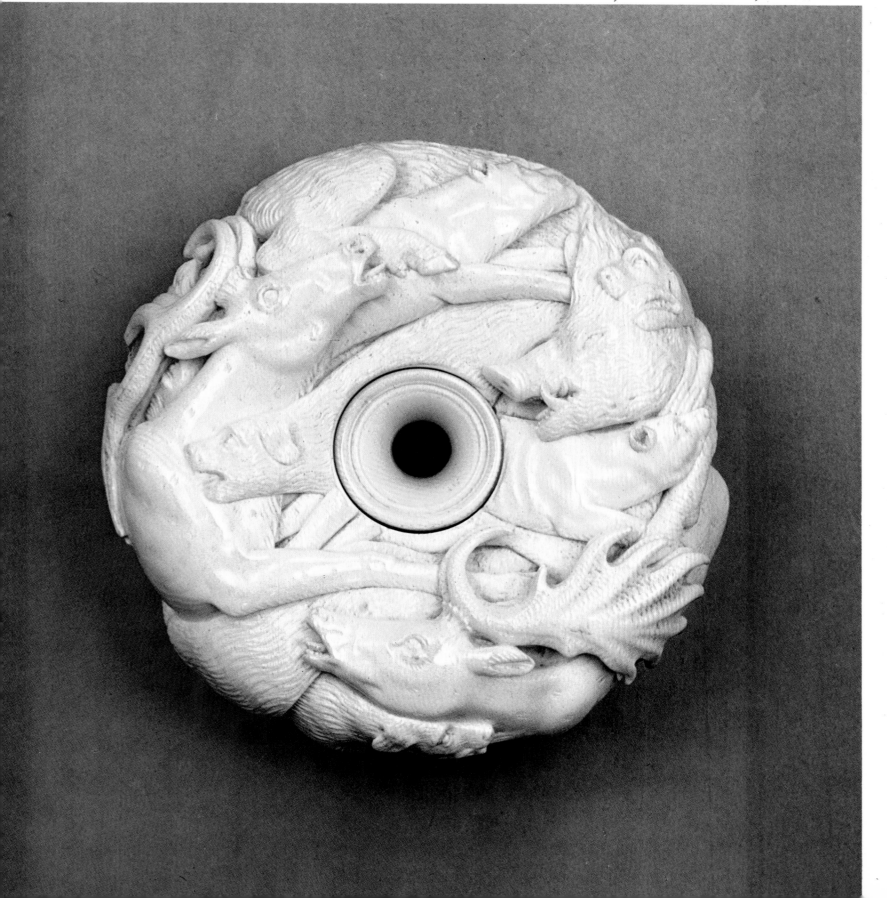

90 views of the Old Testament cover the stock of this wheel lock rifle which came from the Hearst collection. The Amsterdam mark on the metal dates it c. 1665. Joe Kindig Jr. Collection.

Goddess gun from Munich c. 1605. Steel carving by Emanuel Sadeler. Stocking and ivory inlaid panels by Adam Vischer. The delicate drawing on ivory is reminiscent of Fragonard. No.# B 308, Tøjhus Museet, Copenhagen.

Pierced and engraved brass inlays on this wheel lock gun show two reiters shooting flintlock pistols. Late 17th century, the shape of the butt shows the French influence. No.# 652 Kretzschmar von Kienbusch Collection.

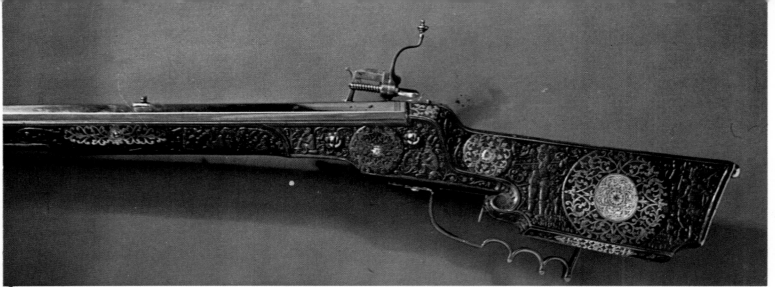

Meister der Tierkopfranken *stocked wheel lock dated 1659 on the barrel. Was in the Hearst collection, now No.# A 13, Russell Aitken Collection.*

Combined wheel lock and matchlock. *Made by Emanuel Sadeler and Adam Vischer in Munich ("A.V." on stock behind the barrel tang). One of the many classical scenes in ivory along both sides of the foreend, Vulcan with his work. The portion of the lock shows Neptune carved out of steel swimming through a sea of beaten gold. Made for Maximilian of Bavaria c. 1600. loa. 65½", bbl 50.4", cal. .71". No.# M/12 Armeria Reale, Turin.*

57

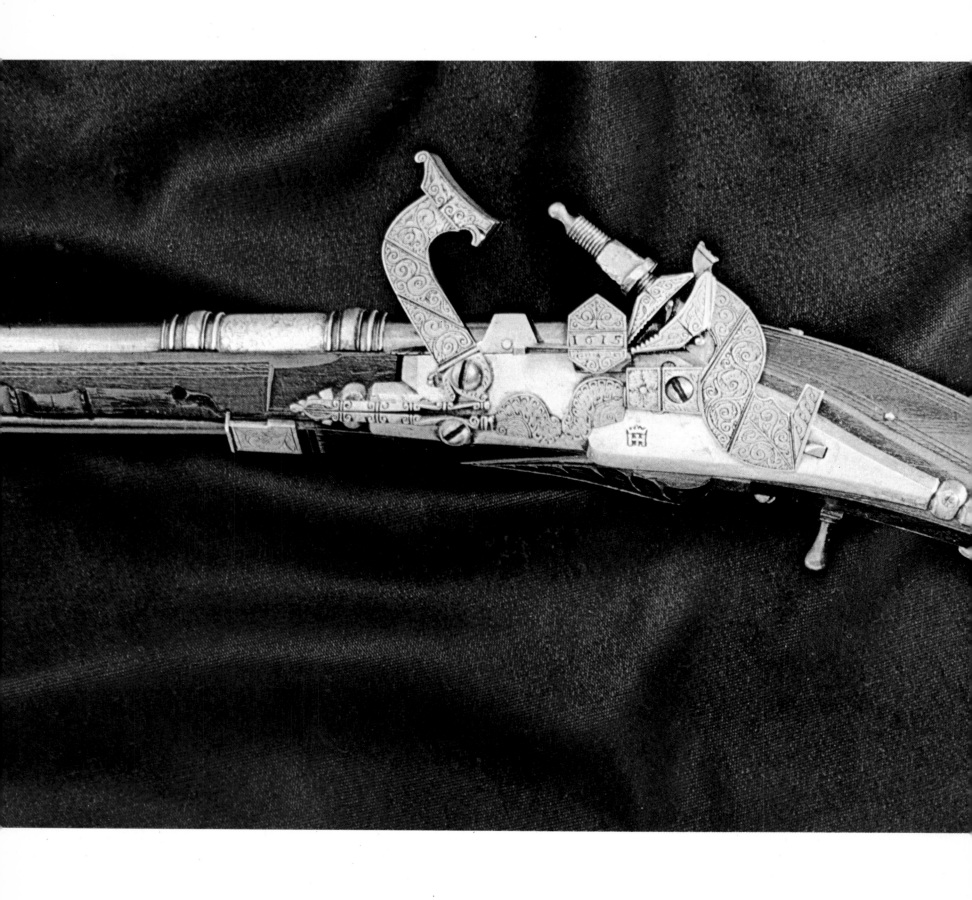

CHAPTER VI

THE SNAPHAUNCE

THE STORY goes that Pieter deVroom, a Dutch bulb grower on the outskirts of Zutphen, was asleep in his little cottage one July night in 1551. The windows were open, as it was a warm evening and Pieter, a light sleeper, heard a noise back of the house. Picking up his new fowling piece, he hushed his wife Hilda and crept to the little window overlooking the chicken house. The moonlight glinted on the diamond paned casement which was swung open out over the window box. Soon his eyes became adjusted to shadows cast by the house in the path of the bright moonlight. There he saw a crouching figure slipping out of the door of the roost. Sliding forward the pan cover of his gun and cocking it slowly so that there was only the tiniest click, he rested the barrel on the far edge of the geranium box, aimed, and pulled the trigger.

In court, for Pieter's bench shot was accurate, the dead man was found to be a runaway Moorish mercenary by the name of Swartje Tomas, who had probably deserted from the Spanish field army just across the border. The army was commanded by Charles V's general, the future Duke of Alba. At the inquest, the Dutch authorities, who were inclined to view the shooting as justifiable homicide, accepted Pieter's version that the black man had died of wounds inflicted by pecking hens—*Snaphaan* in Dutch. From that day, the kind of gun he was shooting, a Dutch invention, was called a snaphance, or snaphaunce.

This story is, of course, palpably untrue, for while the court records of the town of Zutphen have some understandable hiatii, there is no record whatsoever of the employment by Charles V of Spain of any Moorish mercenaries.

The wheel lock, which made its appearance in South Germany about 1500, was a complicated and expensive piece of machinery. Not only costly to build, it was difficult to maintain and service and required the attention of a skilled gunsmith if anything went wrong. This is the reason why the wheel lock never wholly supplanted the crude and less effective matchlock. The wheel lock was too costly to supply

Left-handed German snaphaunce *of Scottish design dated 1615. Both barrel and lock have a stamp of an "H" with an "I" superimposed, surmounted with a crown. Chased steel stock, silver and brass furniture, vivid blue barrel with gold and silver bands on the barrel, silver fishtail butt. Made for William Herzog zu Curland. Metropolitan Museum of Art, New York, No.# 46.105, Alexander McMillan Welch Bequest.*

THE SNAPHAUNCE

to masses of infantry and was too sensitive an instrument to function without service. In colonial campaigns—with the exception of North America—there weren't mechanics around to keep them firing. Nonetheless, the advantages of the wheel lock, or fire lock as it was often called, were apparent to every one who was familiar with the use of weapons.

The need for a less complicated and expensive weapon with the advantages of the wheel lock led to the development of the snaphaunce. The snaphaunce does everything that the wheel lock could do. The snaphaunce can be loaded and primed in advance. Once loaded, with the pan cover closed to retain the primer charge and keep out moisture, the weapon is ready for instant use. The burning match, need for fire, telltale smoke and glow of the match—all are eliminated.

Guesses as to the date of invention have run from 1500 to 1600, but study of existing pieces identified by actual dating, maker's initials or cartouche, historical association, and owner's insignia, have narrowed the date of initial manufacture to somewhere between 1540 and 1550.

Holland seems to have been where they were first built, with the second possibility northern Italy, but the name "snaphaunce" being derived from the Dutch favors the Netherlands, despite the few surviving examples.

Historically, the snaphaunce probably preceded the miquelet by ten or twenty years, yet it is likely that their development was independent rather than derivative. This is speculation as Charles I of Spain became Charles V of the Holy Roman Empire (Germany) and the Netherlands were politically part of Spain, where the miquelet originated.

Whether the invention of the snaphaunce influenced that of the miquelet or not is anyone's guess, but what makes more exciting speculation is: How did the snaphaunce turn up in such far apart places as Morocco, Scotland, Sweden and

Italy? The Scottish snaphaunces, among the earliest guns made in Scotland, have a curiously Moorish appearance but do not look like the Dutch model. The Italian snaphaunce doesn't look like the Scottish ones at all, nor does it have the circular shield at the end of the primer pan. The problem seems really to be one of nomenclature. By definition, a snaphaunce has a separate striking steel independent of the primer pan cover, unlike the one-piece frizzen and pan covers of both miquelet and true flintlock. The snaphaunce is descended from the wheel lock mechanism to the extent that the separate pan cover is connected to the base of the cock tumbler by a lever. When the hammer goes forward, the pan cover also slides forward, exposing the powder in the flash pan to the spark from the face of the separate steel. This mechanical detail does not necessarily make all snaphaunces in existence related.

The pinning down of the definition "snaphaunce" is a recent one. Only a century or so ago, snaphaunce, or *chena-pan*—the French version of the name—was any kind of a gun with a gun lock mechanism that went "snap." More recent attempts at definition seem to have put some strange fellows in bed together.

As for the dates of the ancestor of the flintlock—there are snaplocks in the Royal Swedish Armory dated 1547. There is a left- and right-handed pair of Scotch snaphaunces—Scottish pairs are usually left- and right-handed—in the Tøjhus Museet in Copenhagen dated 1602. Italian snaphaunces are distinguished from wheel locks by Cosimo di Medici, in his edict prohibiting concealed weapons issued in Florence in 1547. Finally, Moorish and Arabian snaphaunces were made from the very early period until at least as late as 1875. After that date the manufacture moved back to Liège in Belgium where the modern manufacturing facilities were used to supply the Near Eastern market and the tourist trade. Kitchener's men were shot at with these Arab snaphaunces in his campaign against the dervishes in 1898.

While the simple snaphaunce was being made for hundreds of years, the Germans never really took to the new invention, preferring their wheel locks right through 1700

SNAPHAUNCE
1) Sear
2) Tumbler
3) Main Spring
4) Bridle
5) Lock plate
6) Cock
7) Top jaw screw
8) Sliding pan cover
9) Pan cover spring
10) Hen, demi-battery (steel) or frizzen

The snaphaunce is cocked by bringing the cock (6) back to the rear until it clicks open held by a tumbler indent, and swinging down the battery (10). Pressure on the trigger (not illustrated) tips the sear (1) which releases the tumbler (2), dropping the cock (6) with some force against the battery (10). At the same time a spur on the tumbler pushes forward a rod connected to the pan cover opening the pan (8) to receive the spark. The illustration shows the battery (10) in a raised or safety position and the sliding pan cover (8) pushed to the rear to cover the priming powder pan.

THE SNAPHAUNCE

when the perfected flintlocks gradually superseded the wheel locks. Each broad statement like this, of course, brings an exception to mind. The two revolving snaphaunce carbines at the Tøjhus Museet, one dated 1597, were made at Nuremberg, and Balzac describes the Parisians arming themselves in 1879 with ancient wheel locks for use on the barricades. Incidentally, the revolving snaphaunce carbines from Nuremberg are the oldest dated revolvers in existence, and will be of interest to compare with the Colt and Collier revolvers.

Other variants of the snaphaunce are the Gønge guns, named for the Danish partisan troops who used them in a war with Sweden; the Swedish snaplock already noted; and a more delicate version of the snaphaunce, the Baltic snaplock with a big eye at the top of the thumb screw similar to the Spanish miquelet, and the upper jaw of the cock wrapping around the lower arm.

While J. N. George, in his definitive book *English Pistols and Revolvers*, first published in 1938, illustrates a snaphaunce revolving pistol of the 1650 period, the snaphaunce pistol had long been superseded in England by the English dog lock, which is really a flintlock because the frizzen and pan are one piece. As has been noted, the English were early to cast cannon and may have been among the first to use brass, bellmetal, or bronze, they were slow to take to handguns and slower in developing an industry to build them.

We have complete records of the smuggling of European handguns into London during the reign of Elizabeth I—they were brought in as bolts of cloth. Wheel locks were thus imported in some quantity, so much so that it was felt necessary by Robert Ward in his *Animadversions of Warre*, published in 1639, to instruct the officers of the Trained Bands, "Now in regard our English Pistolls differ from the firelocke (wheel lock), Pistoll, I will briefly touch two or three postures that are heterogeneall to the former." And he goes on to describe the steps of cocking and firing what must have been an English dog lock as there is no mention of covering or uncovering the primer pan, which would have been necessary had the weapon being described been a snaphaunce.

By 1631 the English were building their own guns, as is shown from an excerpt of a commission granted by Charles I to a committee of armorers, gunsmiths, pikemakers and bandolier makers of London.

	L.	s.	d.
For a new musket, with mould, worm, and scowrer		15	6
For a pair of firelock pistols, with a key, mould scowrer, worm, flask, and cases of leather, of a length and boar according to the allowance of the Council of War	3	0	0
For a pair of horseman's pistols furnished with snaphaunces, moulds, worms, scowrer, flask, a charger, and cases	2	0	0
For a harque-buze with a firelock and belte, swivell, flask, key, moulde, worme and scowrer	1	16	0
For a carabine with a snaphance, belt, swivell and flask, Etcetera, as aforesaid	1	0	0

As can be seen by this document, snaphaunces were cheaper than "firelocks". Also, English gunsmithing was not all that could be desired. The commission required that an apprenticeship be established and that weapons be proofed "because divers cutlers, smyths, tynkers, and other botchers of armes, by their unskilfullness have utterly spoiled many armes..."[1] In 1637 a charter was granted to the Gunmakers Company of London. Their proofmarks were a capital "V" beneath a crown, meaning that the barrel had passed the first "Viewing" inspection, and the letters "GP" under a crown meaning that the gun had been proof shot.

The few Scottish firearms which were made at this period at Doun have survived in better shape than their English counterparts. This is often because they were all metal, including their grips, which were made of brass or an iron alloy which has rust-resisting properties resembling modern stainless steel. However, Scottish firearms are rare and valuable as the English collected and destroyed all of the weapons that they could lay their hands on after the uprising in support of Bonnie Prince Charlie.

[1] *Grose, Francis,* A Treatise of Ancient Armour and Weapons, *(1786).*

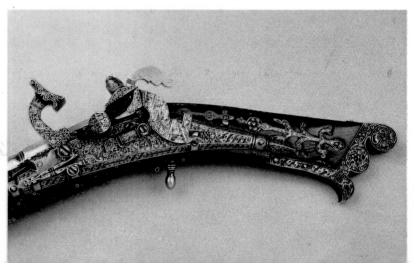

Left-handed Scottish pistol, *one of a pair of snaphaunces. They are initialed "C.A." on the locks, dated 1619 on the end of the pan. Pan covers linked with cocks. loa. 16⅝", bbl 11", cal. 36". No.# XII/737, Tower of London.*

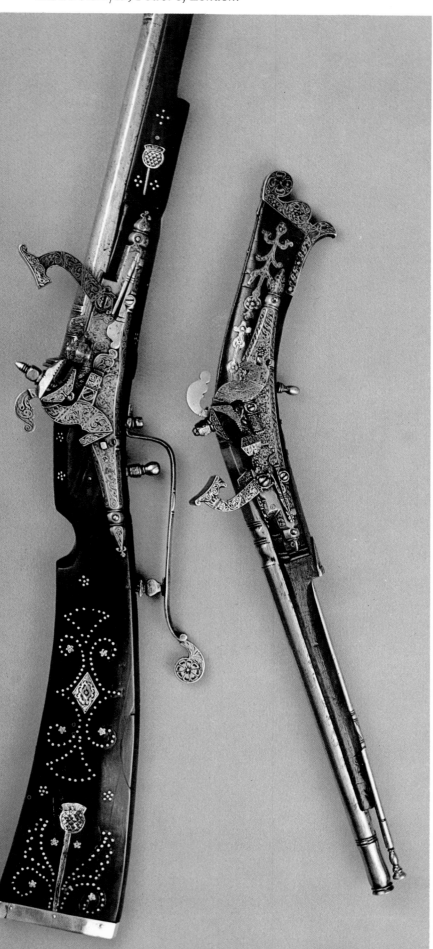

Ancient Scottish *snaphaunce garniture. Long gun dated 1614 on barrel and lock, with the initials "R.A." on the lock. Traces of gold in the barrel engraving, silver nails in the stock. Tudor rose and Scotch thistle design in stock. loa. 50½", bbl 38", cal .48". XII/63, Tower of London.*

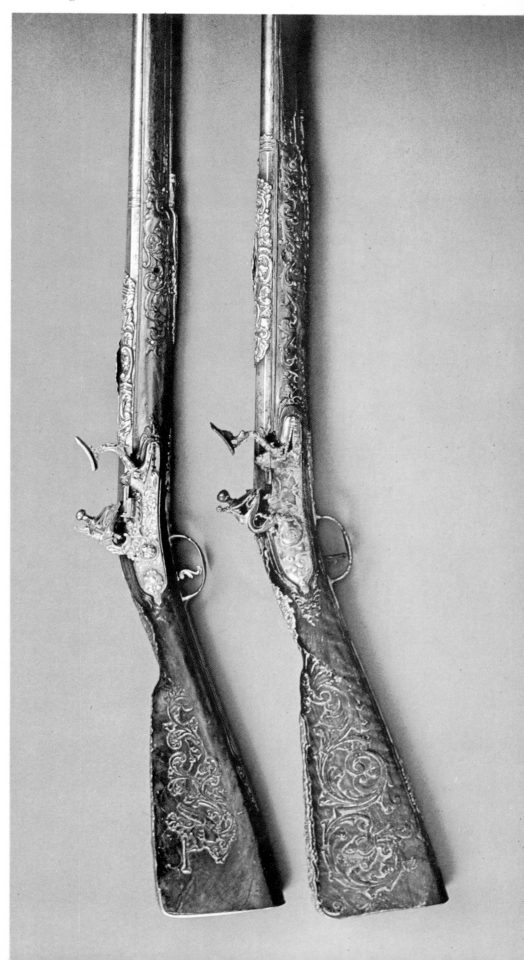

Italian snaphaunce guns, *not a pair. Left gun Tuscan, c. 1750. Gun on right is signed Bartolomeo Caltrani (c. 1750 also). Tuscany. Joe Kindig Jr. Collection.*

THE SNAPHAUNCE

While the Scottish pistols illustrated in this chapter are true snaphaunce types, it may well be possible that the term snaphaunce was being used by the British to mean a flintlock, as opposed to a wheel lock. J. N. George thinks so and Pollard,[2] who was an important collector as well as a writer, says that he has "yet to see a English made snaphaunce"—this was written in the 1920's.

Looking at an ancient snaphaunce today makes one want to rush out and invent the flintlock. The logic of the development seems so obvious today that one wonders why the Brescian gunsmiths took to making snaphaunces at a time when flintlocks were being built in France and even England. 20/20 hindsight is a virtue which many possess. As a matter of fact, there is neither much logic nor time sequence to the building of the Italian snaphaunces. Agostino Gaibi[3] says that: "L'acciarino alla fiorentina (the snaphaunce)" . . . "fabbricate nel Bolognese e in Toscana circa 1600-1630." The dates seem a little early and may reflect a bit of misplaced nationalistic pride. In any event, there are signed survivors in Italian museums from Andrea Rossi di Parma (1620-1680) and "Acqua Fresca" (Bastiano Cecchi di Bargi, 1619-1692), as well as the famous Michael Lorenzonus (Michele Lorenzoni) snaphaunce built between 1660 and 1670, and then, wonder of wonders, "Piastre alle fiorentina dell' Italia Centrale" made by another Cecchi about 1780.[4]

These are all true examples of snaphaunces—guns with frizzens separated from flash pan covers and quite different from the Mediterranean lock or miquelet, which was a Spanish improvement antedating the flintlock. It is curious that the Italians continued to build the archaic and awkward snaphaunce locks right along side of some of the greatest locksmithing and barrel making of the flintlock period. Lorenzoni, for example, was making a repeating magazine flintlock rifle during the same years that he was building snaphaunces. This typifies what makes firearms fascinating, and makes every effort to classify by dates just a little silly.

[2] *Major H. B. C. Pollard,* A History of Firearms, *(Butler & Tanner, London, 1933).*

[3] *Agostino Gaibi,* Le Armi da Fuoco Portatili Italiane, *(Bramante Editrice, s.p.a., Milano, 1962).*

[4] *Few dated Italian snaphaunces were made after 1800.*

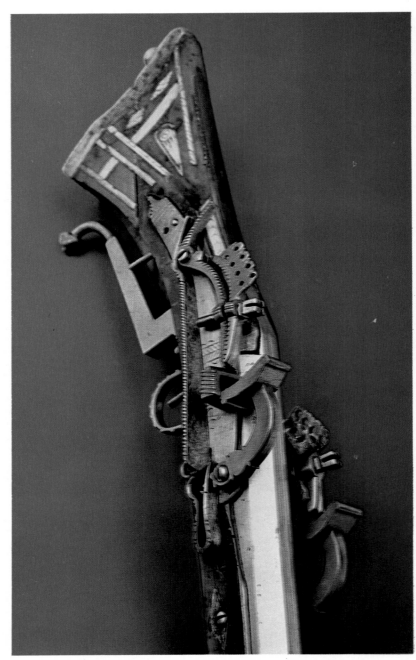

Single barrel, *two-shot Gønge gun. Superimposed load Danish-Swedish (Scania) snaplock dated from 1650 to 1660. Touch holes are on opposite sides 2½" apart. loa. 49", bbl 40", cal. .42", s.b. No.# B 505, Tøjhus Museet, Copenhagen.*

Baltic snaplock *with primitive inlays of faces, hearts, etc in mother-of-pearl. Joe Kindig Jr. Collection.*

18th-century Italian de luxe hunting guns. *The top snaphaunce belonged to Francesco I, Grand Duke of Tuscany, later king of Austria and Hungary. The lower "arma di lusso" is signed "Acqua Fresca", perhaps Matteo Cecchi of Bargi (1651-1738). Nos.# 2811-M82 and 2787-M57, Museo Storico Nazionale d'Artiglieria, Turin.*

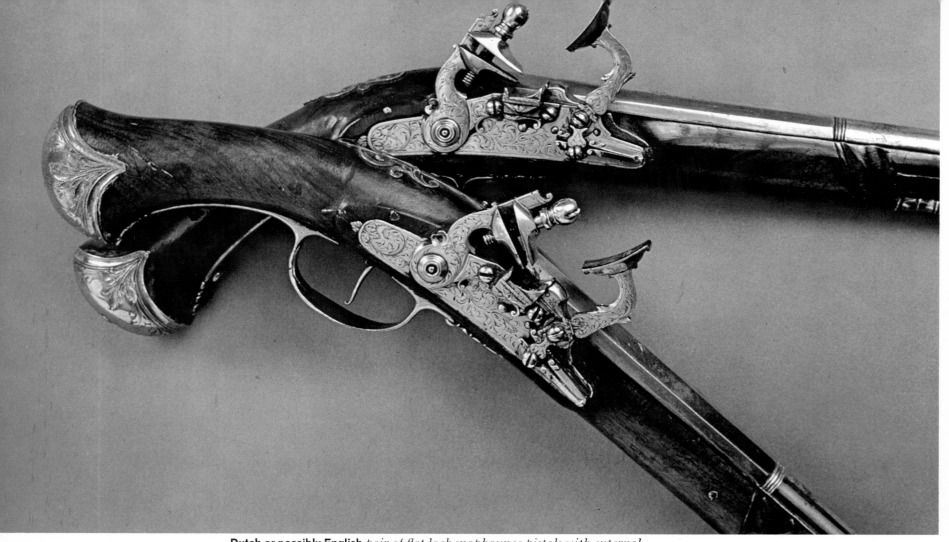

Dutch or possibly English *pair of flat-lock snaphaunce pistols with external buffers. c. 1660-1670. Joe Kindig Jr. Collection.*

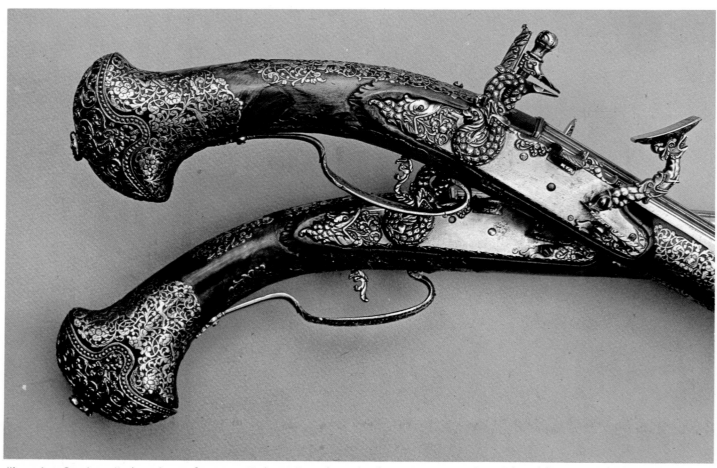

"Lazarino Cominazo" *signed snaphaunces. Pair of Brescian pistols from c. 1645 signed by either Angelo or his nephew Jacomo. The locks are signed "V.F.", probably Vincenzo Filipino of Brescia. loa. 21", bbl 13⅝", cal. .52". No.# 2242 and 2242A—1855, Victorian and Albert Museum, London.*

THE SNAPHAUNCE

Acqua Fresca snaphaunce *dated 1675. Gun barrel inscribed "Bielke Ao 1675". loa. 47¾",*
cal. land .56", groove .60", 8-groove. No.# B.1004, Tøjhus Museet, Copenhagen.

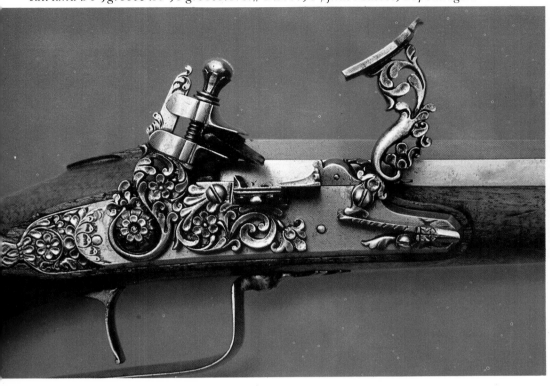

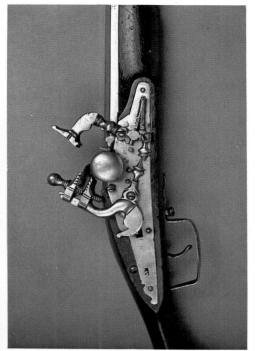

Externally buffered *Dutch snaphaunce*
c. 1615, loa. 26", barrel 17½",
Geoffrey Jenkinson Collection.

Wheel lock shaped *early Dutch snaphaunce. Note the lock shape and the sliding pan cover which works with the cock. c. 1630. Joe Kindig Jr. Collection.*

CHAPTER VII

THE MIQUELET OR MEDITERRANEAN LOCK

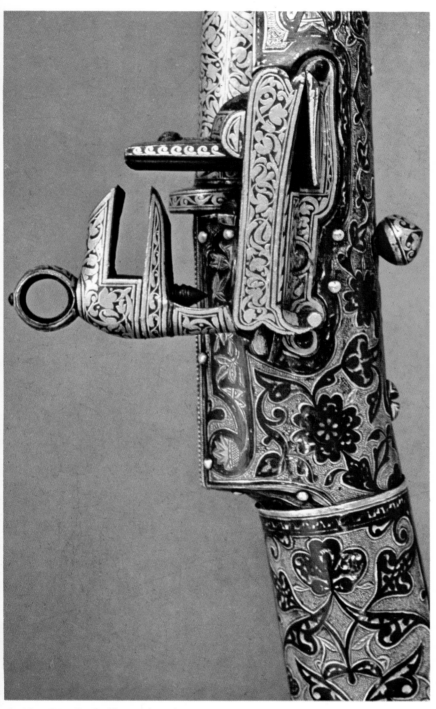

Gold and Niello *Balkan miquelet, made in 1825, signed Aba Muslem Khan, Sham-khal (a town in Daghestan). No.# 31.35.2, Metropolitan Museum of Art, New York, Rogers Fund, 1931.*

No TYPE OF GUN would be complete without a charming fairy tale to explain how it got its name. In the case of the snaphaunce, the name came from a chicken thief, the miquelet, in turn, from Spanish or Portuguese waterfront gangsters who were called Miquelites. Now while it is true that "Marsh" Williams built the prototype of the Williams M-I Carbine, a subcalibre .22, gas-operated machine gun, while serving a term in the North Carolina pokey for shooting a revenuer, it remains doubtful that very many gun designs can be attributed to the Ancient and Honorable Company of Chicken Thieves—or the cosa nostra of the Miquelites.

In the case of the miquelet, or Spanish lock, or demi-battery, as it used to be called, the development of the action is pretty well documented both by surviving examples in the Armeria Real in Madrid and in the *Compendio Historico de los arcabuceros de Madrid,*[1] by a famous Spanish gunsmith, Isodoro Solér. Charles V of the Holy Roman Empire (Germany), originally Charles I of Spain, was brought up and educated in the Spanish colony of the Netherlands and observed the skilled workmanship of the armorers of Augsberg and Nuremberg. When he was elected Holy Roman Emperor his interest in weaponry led him to take the opportunity to send a couple of his loyal subjects, Simon and Peter from Augsberg to Madrid to build weapons and establish the craft.

And this is just what they did. At first, as can be imagined, they built wheel locks after the popular German style, and may, as did the foreign gunsmiths in London, have imported some locks from Germany or brought them along with them. This was in the year 1530. The brothers continued to make guns in Spain and to instruct the Spanish armorers in the art, and about thirty years later, Simon Marquarte (Macuarte—Markwordt), Jr., is said to have produced the first "Spanish" lock during the reign of Philip II (1556-1598). He probably did, as contemporary sources credit him with having produced more miquelets—as opposed to wheel or matchlocks— than any other gunsmith. Simon, Jr. lived to be a very old

[1] *Isodoro Solér, gunmaker to our Lord the King,* Historical Account of the Gunmakers of Madrid from their origin until the present Day, with two Plates on which are engraved The Marks and Countermarks which they used in their works, *Pantaleon Mellizo, Madrid, MDCCXCV.*

Cominazzo monkey *on the ramrod belies the Neapolitan look of this miquelet which was built in Brescia for export in the mid 17th century. All the little figures are carved out of steel. loa. 35⅞", bbl 23⁹⁄₁₆", cal. .44". No.# 23, loaned by the Hon. Gavin Astor to the Victoria and Albert Museum, London.*

THE MIQUELET

man, and before his death he had seen the establishment of a healthy new industry that was rapidly making Spanish arms known world-wide.

No nation has enjoyed a reputation for quality workmanship and fine materials, especially in the steel used in barrels, for a longer span of time than the Spanish. The gunsmiths of Madrid, and later of Ripoll, were very proud of their work and signed their barrels unmistakably. The first mark, that of Marquarte, was a sickle (hoze in Spanish) which led the Spanish to refer to the original German gunsmiths as "de Hozes". After that the barrels are signed by name and dated. The marks of the more famous makers were published in 1795 as a guide to avoiding imitations and fakes.

The locks are signed on the better guns and the name of the maker appears boldly along the top of the barrels in many cases, but the most positive identification was a deep die stamp on the receiver or breech, hammered in before hardening, over which a thin sheet of gold was laid and more gently hit with the same die.

The makers were proud of their work, and instead of making a craft mystery of their skill, they told the world how they made barrels, as they had not the slightest doubt that they could not and would not be bettered and were annoyed with cheap copies with the names of the famous makers forged on them. Spanish barrels were so good that dozens of imitators copied them in lesser materials and signed them Belén, Bis, García, Santos, Esquibel, Lopez, Zegarra, and Solér. (Some of these famous makers and their marks will be found in the index of this book.) Even in the heyday of British arms manufacture, the best London makers did not hesitate to use Spanish barrels with their original markings. They even re-mounted and re-used old Spanish barrels with new stocks and locks. In all probability, the English sportsmen who patronized the London gun trade knew and demanded Spanish barrels.

Solér wrote his book to protect the Madrid trade from imitators as had Espinar a hundred and fifty years before Solér. Espinar compared the plight of the Spanish gunsmith with Cominazzo and his imitators.

"There was a craftsman who worked at one time in Italy, and he was called Lazari Cominaz;[2] he made very good barrels, but when they heard of the demand for these barrels many others set to work and made very bad barrels and they put the name Lazari Cominaz on them as did the real one, and these counterfeits a great many have burst and caused serious accidents."

The reputation of the real Cominazzo barrels had spread as far as England even back in 1646, as we learn from this entry in John Evelyn's diary:

"We came this evening to Brescia, which next morning we traverst according to our custom in search of antiquities and new sights. Here I purchased of old Lazarino Cominazzo my fine carbine, which cost me 9 pistoles and that workman Jo. Bap. Franco, the best esteemed."

The open secret about the superiority of Spanish guns and especially Spanish barrels was first described by Espinar in 1644. He attributes the innovation of forging barrels to Juan Sanchez de Miruena who was brought to Madrid during the minority of the Infante Don Fernando before 1558.[3] He forged his barrels from six or seven pieces of iron which could be worked better than a single bar—the old procedure. Nicolás Bis (1692-1726) took the process a step further when he put horses to work for him by using worn our horseshoes which had been made of ductile Biscayan iron. The shoes, of course, were being cold forged as they were hammered on rocky roads and paved streets by the horses. The old horseshoes were collected from blacksmiths, washed in the Manzanares river to remove not only the dirt but to "discover the quality of the iron, for there are some horseshoes which, not being Biscayan, are made of rough and brittle iron, and one alone is more than sufficient to spoil a whole gun."[4]

Fifty pounds of chopped horseshoes made a forging that weighed fourteen pounds in the rough, and machined out as a finished barrel weighing just under six pounds. The final tube shape was heated thirty-two times not counting the initial forging from one flat sheet or shovel, and the folding and forming to achieve a tough cross-graining.

[2] *Cominazzo is the family name of the most famous line of Brescian gunsmiths, predominantly barrel makers. The first, Lazarino Cominazzo, was building guns in 1600 and the same family was still at work in 1780. Lazarino, Lorenzo and others of the family signed their work in the language or dialect of the purchaser; hence we find their barrels signed Comminazzo, Commazzo, Cominaco, and Cominaz (for the Neopolitan trade and Spain).*

[3] *1503-1564.*

[4] *Solér's* Compendio Historico.

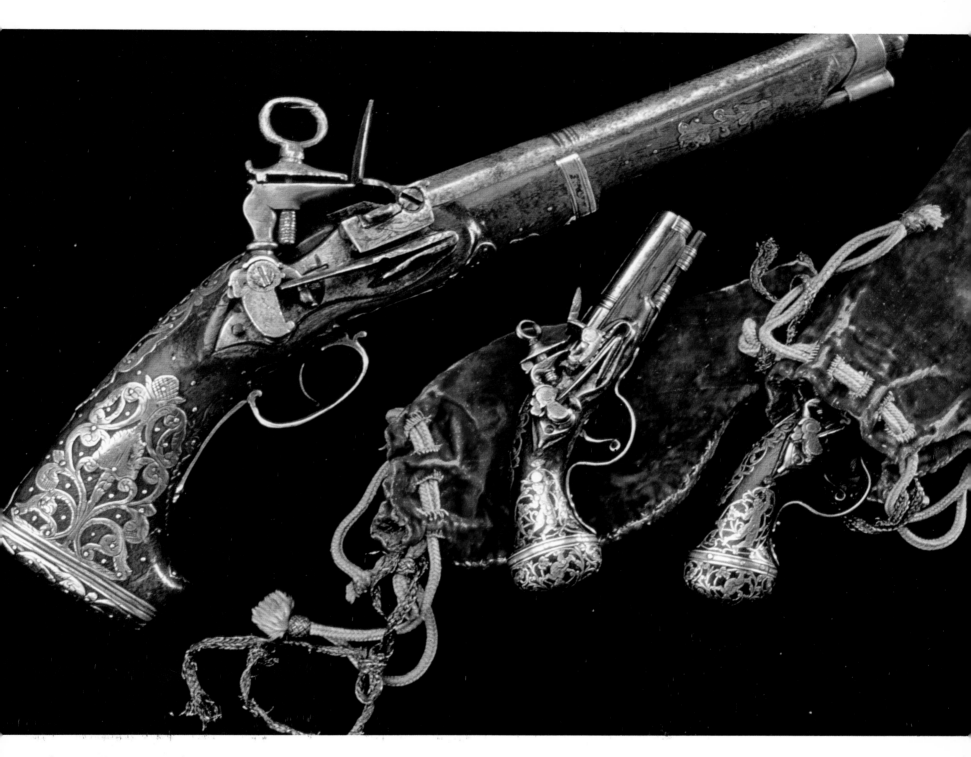

Three Ripoll miquelets. *Miniature pair of kit pistols have grooved and fluted barrels. The stock inlays are silver with a rampant lion and scroll design. The little pistols (about 5" long) are miniatures of the heavy horseman's pistol of the same 1670 era. Joe Kindig Jr. Collection.*

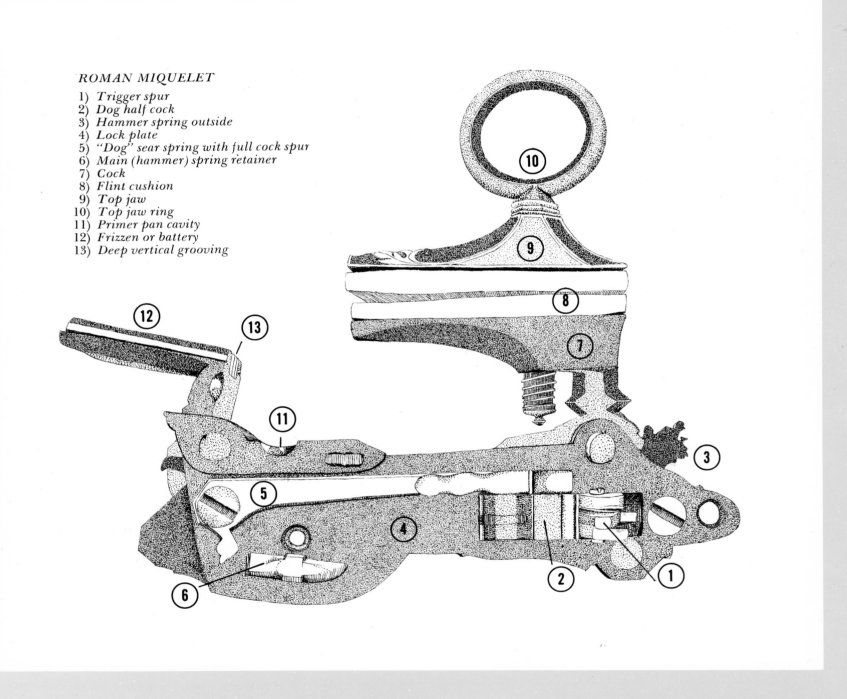

ROMAN MIQUELET

1) Trigger spur
2) Dog half cock
3) Hammer spring outside
4) Lock plate
5) "Dog" sear spring with full cock spur
6) Main (hammer) spring retainer
7) Cock
8) Flint cushion
9) Top jaw
10) Top jaw ring
11) Primer pan cavity
12) Frizzen or battery
13) Deep vertical grooving

The miquelet is cocked by pushing the cock (7) to the rear by the ring (10). The gun is primed at (11) and the frizzen (12) is flipped back to cover the pan. The gun is fired by pulling the trigger which engages the trigger spur on the sear (1) throwing the hammer forward. The flint in the hammer jaw (not illustrated) throws sparks into the pan which is uncovered as the frizzen is driven forward. The miquelet lock has a half cock position which is a bar extending through the lock (2). The heavy hammer spring (3) is external.

The final fanatical extreme in Spanish barrel making was achieved by Alonzo Martinez (circa 1740) who forged a gun from horseshoe nails. Nobody tried to beat that record, so Martinez dusted off his hands and went to Portugal where he became official gunmaker to King John V. He was later picked up as a prisoner-of-war by the Spanish (he was with the Catalonians) who, having no patience for such virtuosity, sentenced him to death. A gun collector, Captain General Prince Pio, "regretting that such skill should perish" freed him and set him to work as the Master of Arms of Majorca.

While Spanish gun barrels became the desiderata of shooters who preferred guns that did not blow up, the typically Spanish, or miquelet, lock became the standard for the Arab Empire, parts of Italy, and, of course, the Spanish Empire. Miquelet locks found their way to the Crimea and for generations the south Russians and the Cossack tribes were armed with Near Eastern or homemade versions of the miquelet. Many a finely decorated Russian miquelet survives in the Kremlin Armory.[5]

There exists a curious similarity between the early Spanish lock of 1610, a Ripoll miquelet of 1630, another miquelet from 1660, all illustrated in Keith Neal's excellent *Spanish Guns and Pistols,* and the completely indigenous and unique English dog locks of the Cromwellian period.

Just as there are a thousand variations to each broad classification of weapons, similarly there are simple identifying characteristics. Regardless of its nationality or period, the miquelet lock can be identified by its large and strong exterior main spring. Sometimes the spring bears on the heel of the cock—it does in the earliest Spanish examples—and sometimes on the toe—as in the case of certain Neapolitan and Sicilian examples. In any event, the sturdy external "V" spring is the identifying thing to look for. Another thing to look for, but not always present, is a wide, heavy battery or steel. These were most commonly grooved vertically, the ridges being hit by the flint and the valleys guiding the sparks into the priming pan.

There was no nonsense about the miquelet lock, it was sturdily built, and the strong main spring provided plenty of wallop to the cock's forward motion, producing a shower of sparks and positive ignition. The deep-grooved heavy battery weighed enough so that it would function even if its return spring were broken or missing. Both springs being on the outside of the lock plate were easily accessible for replacement if broken. Finally, when the half cock was evolved, an end of the sear stuck through a hole in the lock plate, preventing an accidental discharge. In the case of Ripoll weapons, as distinguished from those made in Madrid, the safety device was an external hook or dog functioning like the hook on a screen door.

Political ties—the kingdoms of Spain and Naples, Sicily and Sardinia were united—and the emulation of the military quickly spread the use and then the manufacture of the miquelet to Italy and Morocco, leading to the earlier name of Mediterranean lock.

Neapolitan, Sardinian, Spanish or Moorish, the miquelet was the father of the flintlock, and the first weapon to simplify and combine the frizzen or battery in one piece with the flash pan cover. The practicality of the lock, the ductile toughness of Biscayan iron and the patient craftsmanship of the Spanish gunsmiths of Madrid and Ripoll produced a superior weapon.[6]

While the first and the finest guns were made in Madrid, Ripoll soon won a reputation for quality and the typical lines of the Ripoll stock—a miniature of a modern rifle stock—were often copied in the Near Eastern versions. Ripoll had the misfortune to be in a geographical location that was continually contested, and the additional prize of the local gun industry was an inducement to conquest. Ripoll was occupied and reclaimed innumerable times until, in the early 19th century, the French razed this tiny industrial community on the Spanish side of the Pyrenees.[7] Survivors of the decimation of the town and industry went west along the mountain ridges and joined the gun manufacturing center

---

[5] Der Moskaur Kreml—Die Rüstkammer, *(Rybakow, Prague, 1962). Plates 27 and 28 and p. 122.*

[6] *Madrid and Ripoll claim the lion's share of attention of the collector of Spanish weapons, but fine guns were also made in Cadiz, Cordova, Malaga, Salamanca, and Seville and in then Spanish influenced Naples and Sardinia.*

[7] *This strip of land, now dividing Spain and France, has constantly received more than its share of attention from the military. The coastal route, of course, attached Spain to her Italian possessions or pretentions, and north west of Ripoll, the mid-millenium state of Roussillon stuck painfully into the France of the Louis'.*

THE MIQUELET

in the Basque country at Eibar near the Atlantic. Unfortunately, the skills and pride of craftsmanship had burned out at Ripoll. While Eibar-made guns—mostly percussion weapons—are fairly common, they are a far cry from the finest of Spanish workmanship.

In Eibar, percussion weapons were being made into the mid-nineteenth century with the characteristic large exterior spring working on the heel of the hammer and the sear tip protruding through a hole in the lockplate at half cock.[8]

From Ceylon, where it was taken by the Portuguese, to Spanish New Orleans[9] the miquelet was aimed and shot at a lot of Indians. In his *Mississippi voyage of Jolliet and Marquette*, in 1673, Marquette, in the neighborhood of "Naché" and "Naodiches", "saw plainly that we were not in a condition to resist savages allied to the Europeans (Spanish), who were numerous, and expert in firing guns, and who continually infested the lower part of the (Mississippi) river." Henry de Tonty in his *Memoir on La Salle's discoveries* talks of Indians with pistols and leather horse armor "a proof that they are not very far from the Spaniards." The Indians had Spanish pistols, and they were miquelets.

As the prestige of Spanish arms diminished so did the leadership of their armor. The rise of France and the invention of the true flintlock pistol are hardly coincidental.

[8] *The author's percussion Eibar pistol is dated 1834.*

[9] *Becoming French New Orleans in 1718; ceded to Spain in 1762 by a collapsing and impoverished France; and repossessed by Napoleon in 1801 for the sole purpose of raising money for guns by sale of the Louisiana territory to the United States in 1803 for $15,000,-000; as every schoolboy knows.*

Flat butt shape *dates these miniature miquelet pistols at around 1780. They probably come from Ripoll, are 7¾" long with 3¾" barrels, cal. .67". Silver bands hold the barrels to the stocks. XII/1303-1304, Tower of London.*

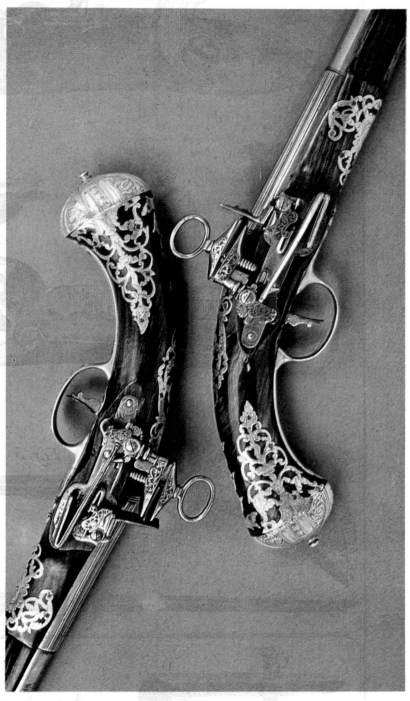

Brescian miquelets *signed "Schiazzano" on the lock plates (Støckel: c. 1700). Gold-mounted casque-butts with open foliate pattern-book gold inlays. Russell Aitken Collection.*

Strange bed fellows. *Russian and Turkish miquelet pistols. The Russian (Caucasian) pistol on the left is 18th-century. It is entirely metal sheathed except for its fire gilt barrel. The Turkish pistol on the right has a jade stock, gold inlays, and is decorated with garnets and emeralds. While the decoration is 19th-century, the barrel is dated 1140 A.H. (1728 A.D.) and signed Hassan. No.# 23.232.9, Metropolitan Museum of Art, New York, Morosini Collection, 1923. The gun on the left is No.# 36.25.2241, also Metropolitan Museum of Art, Bequest of George C. Stone, 1936.*

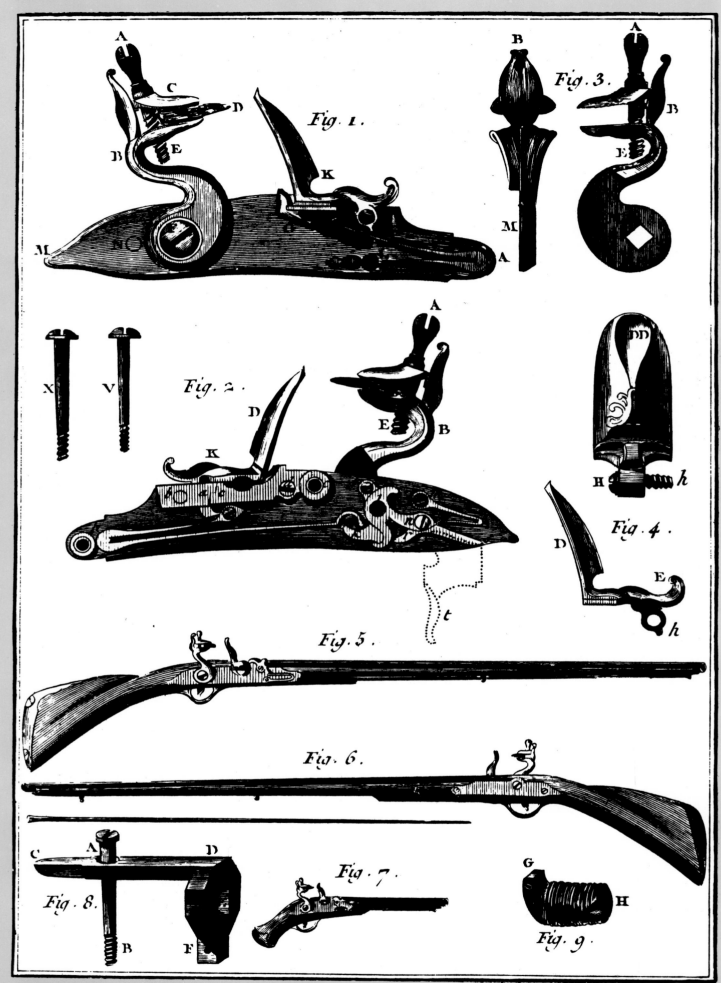

Diderot and D'Alembert *Encyclopédie 1751*

CHAPTER VIII

THE TRUE FLINTLOCK OR THE FRENCH LOCK

"Nothing could be smarter, more splendid, more brilliant, better drawn up than the two armies. Trumpets, fifes, hautboys, drums, cannons formed a harmony such as has never been heard of even in hell. The cannons first of all laid flat about six thousand men on each side; then the musketry removed from the best of worlds some nine or ten thousand blackguards who infested its surface. The bayonet also was the sufficient reason for the death of some thousands of men. Candide, who trembled like a philosopher, hid himself as well as he could during this heroic butchery".[1]

While Voltaire's story is an allegory and his setting a mythical Balkan kingdom, his description of the pitched battles of the seventeenth and eighteenth centuries is a contemporary if not an eyewitness account. France's day of glory on the battlefield and the invention of the flintlock went hand in hand. The battles which Louis XIII and Louis XIV fought could not have been won by the French soldier whom Richelieu describes in his *Memoirs:* "Musket on shoulder, his bandolier slung around his neck, his musket rest in his right hand, a long walking stick in his left . . . thus do we see the foot soldier in the engravings of Abraham Bosse or Callot. When he fired his weapon he had to light his match, load his musket, take his match again, twist it around the cock, and then take aim. He can hardly have had time to discharge his piece more than once at the attacking force, for his fire did not carry much further than sixty-nine yards. Thus, as a further defense against the enemy's charge, each company contained a certain proportion of pikemen, who opposed the advance of the cavalry by crossing their heavy weapons, fourteen feet long. As for the cavalry, it consisted of musketeers (dragoons, they called themselves); mounted infantry, which dismounted before firing; light horse; gendarmes in armor; and carbiniers, who acted as scouts and skirmishers.

"Uniforms there were none, save for certain picked troops; no special marks distinguished officers from their men. Colours (so huge, for the infantry, that the material dragged along the ground if the men carrying each had not kept a corner under his arm) and the small standards used by the cavalry, all differed from each other. So much so that the troops on one side frequently found their only method of mutual recognition was that every man should pull his shirt out of his hose, or else put it over his doublet."[2]

During the reign of Henri IV (1399-1413), the Treasury of France was replenished by Henri's avarice and the careful husbanding of his treasurer, Sully. With the aid of Sully a national treasury of 60 to 70 million livres was collected—6,000,000 livres in cash was packed in bags, boxes and barrels, in the tower of the Bastille.

Henri built his treasury in other ways, as well. He established the workshops of the Louvre, to which craftsmen were encouraged to come by special grants and subsidies which accompanied the official appointment of the King.

Among the master craftsmen—jewelers, artists, gunsmiths, furniture builders and tapestry weavers—to be appointed was Marin Le Bourgeoys to whom is attributed the invention of the flintlock.[3] Until the revolution, craftsmen of all kinds—the Gobelins, jewelers and goldsmiths like Jean Henequin, the cabinet makers who furnished Versailles, all thrived under official patronage and created the forms of art and decoration which we cherish as Louis Treize and Louis Quartorze.

When the future Louis XIII was a child of seven or eight, he used to play in the courtyard of the Louvre, and a contemporary writer noted his normal childlike interest in cannons and weapons—an interest that followed him through life.

While his mother, Marie de Medici, was stringing magic beads and compounding philtres with her constant companion, Leonore Dori, the future king was dragging a toy cannon on a string across the paved courtyard of the Louvre. Le Bourgeoys may well have been working at the forge with his brother Jean and the noise and the smoke attracted the prince.

It can easily be imagined that the conversations between the child and the master craftsman may have inspired Louis' lifelong interest in hand weapons.[4] In any event, he was an ardent collector of handguns and armor, and the record of Louis XIII's *Cabinet d'Armes* compiled by Du Metz de

---

[1] *Voltaire,* Candide, *(Random House, New York, 1929), Chapter three. English trans. Charles E. Merrill, Jr.*

[2] *Jacques Boulenger,* The Seventeenth Century. *Tr. from the French. (Heinemann, London, 1920).*

[3] Brevets de logements sous la grande galerie du Louvre. *Archives de l'art Francais. (T.I., Paris, 1851-52), pp. 193-258.*

[4] *Torsten Lenk,* The Flintlock, *(Holland Press, London, 1965).*

THE FLINTLOCK

Rosnay[5] and first published by Jules Guiffrey in his *Inventaire general du mobilier de la couronne* in Paris in 1886 provides us with one of the few authentic contemporary documents from which existing guns can be identified. The scholarly Dr. Torsten Lenk in his work, *The Flintlock* in 1939, noted the then locations of arms known to be from the Louis XIII collection. In Hayward's English translation of Lenk an astonishing 70 items of the original 455 are listed as existing in private collections and museums. Many are preserved in the Musee de l'Armee in Paris. Others are scattered from the Hermitage in Leningrad to the Renwick collection in Arizona. The most important private collection of these early French weapons is a part of the arms collection of W. Keith Neal in Wiltshire, England.

Among the surviving examples from the *Cabinet* collection of weapons, (some having belonged to previous French kings), are the first true flintlocks designed and made by Marin le Bourgeoys. The steel and pan cover have become one well-shaped piece, performing both functions. The cock and half cock positions of the hammer are controlled inside the gun by a vertically acting sear which catches in notches cut into an interior tumbler or steel disc. The simplicity of the mechanism is extraordinary compared with the wheel lock, even in its most basic form, or with the self-spanning snaphaunce. For instance, the working parts, the springs, and the locks which protruded through the lock plate of the miquelet or the English dog lock have been eliminated. The result was simpler manufacture, function and weatherproofing.

The invention of the flintlock, and the putting of working parts into the gun's interior, made it possible to streamline weapons. Dr. Lenk holds that the flintlock was invented in Germany and that le Bourgeoys never left his watchmaking, locksmithing family in Lesieux, Normandy. But all quibbles aside, guns and pistols began to assume the shapes which are now familiar. The "French" stock which could be rested on the shoulder, the pistol grip which made the handgun balance and hang in the hand, made their appearance.

The effect of these new designs was so impressive that not only the shapes, but the styles of the decorators became popular and were applied to earlier styles of mechanisms.

For this reason late wheel locks look like lumpy flintlocks to the casual observer. The "German" stock with its truncated triangular appearance from the back, gave away—knob and all—to the more humane and person-fitting stocks of the French gunmakers, who went so far as to upholster the cheekpieces with leather or velvet.

Few gunsmiths of any period made complete guns. Cominazzo, for example, was a fine barrel maker who shipped bundles of his barrels to gunsmiths in Germany to have locks and stocks fitted to them. Augsberg and Nuremberg, Germany, were famous for the manufacture of wheel lock mechanisms, and stock makers such as Johannes Sadeler and Heironymus Borstorffer the Elder in Munich signed the stocks which the iron carvers had engraved and decorated.

The average gunsmith, whether he made all or part of a gun, was of necessity more of a mechanic than an artist. To be sure, when he made his masterpiece, the *chef d'oeuvre* by which he was judged by the masters of the guild to have completed his apprenticeship, he may have made a complete weapon as a *tour de force*. In his day-to-day operation, the gunsmith was and is a lock fittter, a barrel bedder and gun assembler. If today's gunsmith has an order for a particularly fine piece, he calls on the services of a jeweler and engraver. So it was with early gunsmiths.

The engraver, the goldsmith and stock decorator needed a design. The first things at hand and the easiest to come by were the coats of arms of the intended owner. This was a sure fire hit.[6] Next, of course, were scenes of the chase. Some pretty stumpy, stiff-legged deer, elk and boar decorate stocks of green and natural colored bone-ivory stocks of the wheel lock period. For pure design, outside inspiration was called for, and to fill this need came the rubbings and pattern books of the master engravers and artists. Some of these pattern books were done by famous gunstock decorators and steel

---

[5] *"Intendant et controleur general du mobilier de la couronne" to the Kings of France until 1673.*

[6] *Of course, every good thing can be overdone. Felix Fuchs cast a cannon for Count Anton Gunther of Oldenburg, which traced his ancestry back to Charlemagne via 512 coats of arms, covering every square inch of its ten-foot-long barrel. The cannon, cast in 1633, can be seen today in the Tøjhus Museet in Copenhagen.*

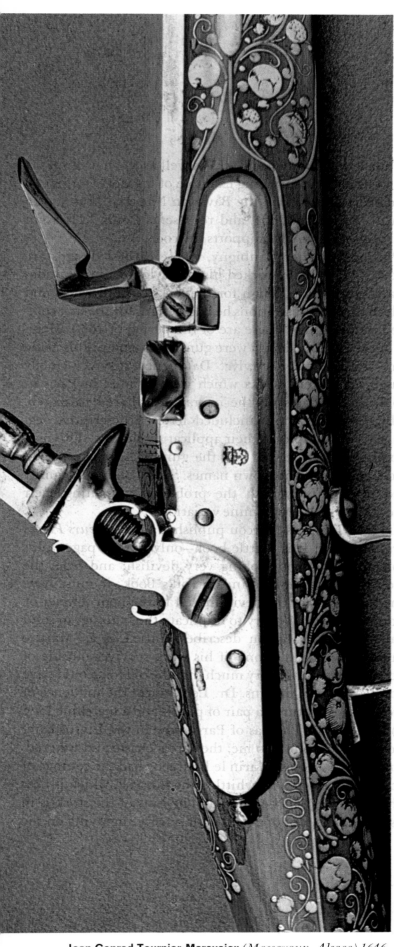

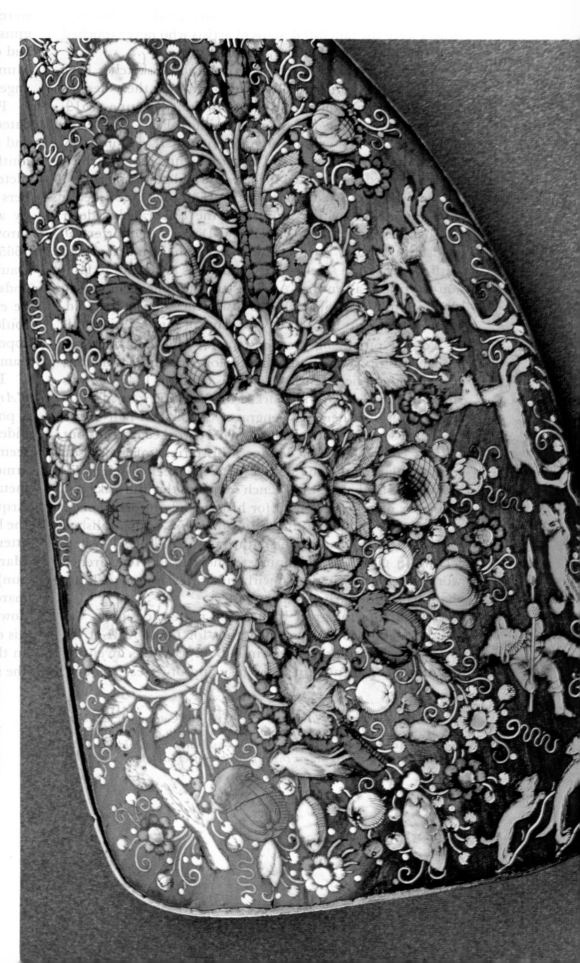

Jean Conrad Tournier-Marevaicx *(Massevaux, Alsace) 1646.*
If the gun were not dated, the shape of the lock, the stiff action and
the tall barrel top-jaw screw would serve to identify this among
the earliest flintlock guns. Kennard and Schedelmann have both
written monographs on it. The stock inlay material is green
and white staghorn and brass wire. loa. 59¼", bbl 42⅝",
cal. .40". No.# XII/1549, Tower of London.

THE FLINTLOCK

engravers, others were the work of court jewelers, while still others were the fanciful designs of artists who never touched a cutting tool or handled the action of a gun.

There were a few early designers whose sketches have survived, and examples of the adaptation of their designs have also survived on finished guns. Etienne Delaune (1519-1588) was an engraver at the royal mint in Paris. At the age of fifty he traveled extensively in Germany. It was probably during this period that he did the ornamental designs which were engraved and printed for jewelers and gun makers.

Jan van der Straet (Stradanus) 1530-1605 published a guide to design which influenced the celebrated Sadeler brothers, Emanuel and Daniel, and David Allenstatter the goldsmith, who in turn set the style for the Munich school with its carving in steel[7]—a style that was to remain in fashion for nearly a century. And we still find fine examples in the work of Caspar Spät who was using the same by-then old-fashioned designs until nearly the time of his death in 1691.

Peter Flötner engraved designs for wheel locks, using Roman history and classical mythology for subject matter, in Nuremberg between 1523 and his death in 1546. He was succeeded by his son, who worked in Nuremberg until 1618. Virgil Solis, another artist engraver of this first half of the sixteenth century, does not seem to have worked on guns but left his contribution of designs, illustrations of goddesses, for the inlayers of bone plaques and the steel chiselers. Finally, and still before the French school of the flintlock, Jost Amman's designs were used for bronze and gilt ornamental casting. His compendium, *Kunstbüchlein*, was published after his death and at the end of the period, in 1599. The new feeling in guns was beginning to show itself. The French work, particularly in design without figures, is more delicate than that of the early German masters.

The first of the great French gun pattern designers was Jean Henequin, who decorated guns for Louis XIII at the same time that goldsmith Marin le Bourgeoys was inventing the flintlock. Henequin's designs, appropriately enough,

were made for both wheel locks as well as the new flintlock guns. The earliest surviving example of his work is a signed and dated wheel lock in the Bavarian National Museum in Munich. It is dated 1621, and represents Louis XIII as an angel with wings; Atlas supports the cock.

Philippe Cordier Daubigny, whose earliest designs are dated 1634 and 1635, worked his gargoyles, reclining nudes and arabesques into design for the locks of both wheel and flintlocks. In his illustrations he had designs for the first complete flintlock guns. These are of the period of 1630. Members of the Cordier family were gunsmiths, and pistols made by an Isaac Cordier survive. Daubigney survives chiefly through his pattern books which were printed in Paris in 1665 with the dates on the engravings altered to match. Daubigney's engravings included lettered descriptive legends, but no examples of their application survive. This may be explained by the fact that the gunsmiths of the period could barely spell their own names. The Cominazzo family coped imaginatively with the problem by spelling their name with at least twenty-nine variations.

In 1657 Francois Marcou published his *Plusieurs Pieces d'Arquebuzerie*. It is a little book—only sixteen pages, plus a portrait of Marcou looking very devilish; and from the hideously ornate designs in Marcou's book, it must have seemed the work of the devil himself to the poor jeweler or armorer who set out to try to duplicate the fantasies in solid metal. Although Marcou describes himself as a "Maistre Arquebuzier à Paris" none of his work survives outside of the book, and I doubt very much that the old fox would have attempted his own designs. Dr. Lenk traces the influence of Marcou to a garniture (a pair of pistols and a matching long gun) made by P. Thomas of Paris, now in the Livrustkammaren in Stockholm. To me, they are a chaste and watered-down version. At least Marin le Bourgeoy had the courage of his convictions when he whittled the flintlock which is now in the Hermitage in Leningrad. The butt of the stock is in the shape of the foot of a deer with tracery engraving on the

[7] *J. F. Hayward, in his book,* The Art of the Gunmaker, *explains the Munich craftsmen's work, which amounted to dedication. They carved in iron; heat treated the surfaces, and then had gold inlaid on the flat, instead of carving or casting in the softer metal.*

Solid silver barrel *on this gun (probably the only one in the world) signed by "Bertrand Paraube" and dated 1685. This powder-puff flintlock sporter was presented by Louis XIV to Charles Lennox, 1st Duke of Richmond, the bastard son of Charles II. loa. 51", bbl 42", 20 gauge. No.# XII/1690, Tower of London.*

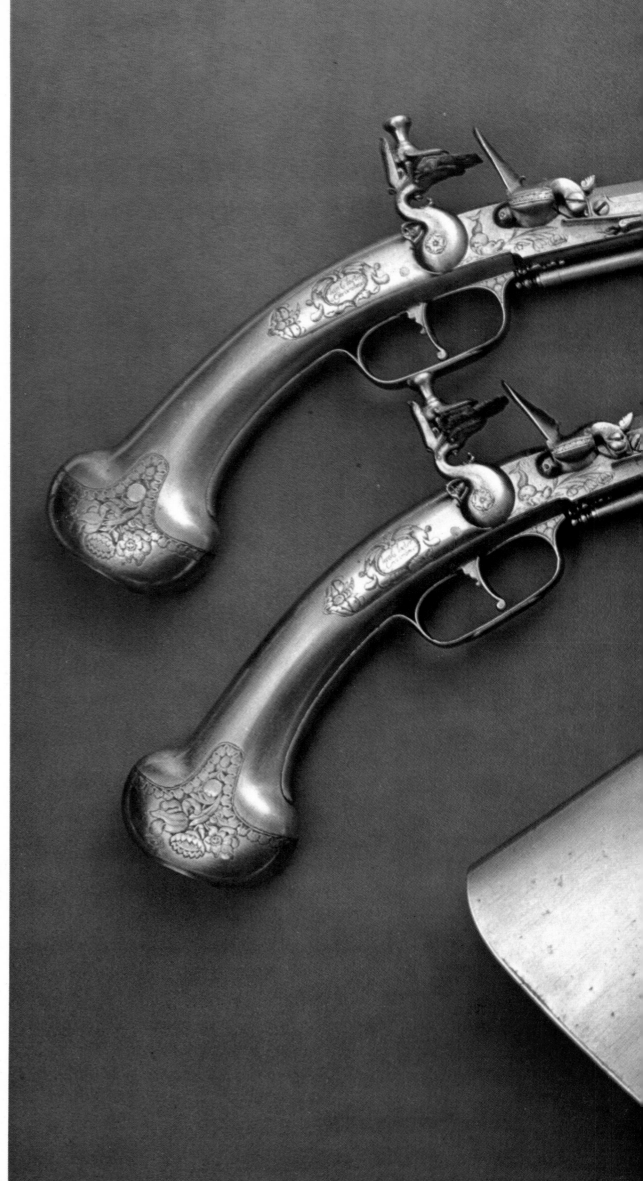

THE FLINTLOCK

All iron and steel garniture. *A flintlock rifle with two pistols made and signed on the pistol locks, behind the hammers, "Ian Cloeter a Grevenbrock". These guns with their hollow stocks of iron plate were made about 1680. The rifle is a breech loader with a turn-off barrel. The pistols are 23½" long with 16" barrels, in .55" calibre. The rifle, which has an interrupted thread take-down and a barrel release in front of the trigger guard, is 44¼" long with a 31¾" barrel, .66" caliber with multi-groove twist rifling. Nos.# B903, 904, 905, Tøhus Museet, Copenhagen.*

82

THE FLINTLOCK

hoof. The cheekpiece is a reclining warrior in armor. The last ten inches of the breech end of the barrel are deeply carved in bas-relief scroll designs, a cupid sports in a garden of arabesques on the face plate opposite the lock, and the fore end is inlaid with swirls of silver wire.

Jean Berain, who published pattern books in 1659 and 1667, not only drew pictures, but also decorated one of the most beautifully ornate guns to survive to this day. It is a double-barreled (Wender type—the barrels turn over or revolve) presentation piece made by the famous French court gunmaker Le Conte—an impressive present from Louis XIV to Charles XI of Sweden in 1673. From the horsemen on top of the barrel to the owl on the back of the lock, the metal parts are damascened in gold against a rich blue field and the stock shows a little wood for contrast through the engraved sheets and wires of silver. Berain "illustrated" only flintlocks.

Finally, there was Jacquinet, who had been the actual engraver for Marcou's book. In 1660 he published *Plusiers models des plus nouvelles manieres qui sont en usage en l'art d'arquebuzerie* from the works of Thuraine and Le Hollandois, who were gunmakers by appointment, but not in the work shops of the Louvre.[8] While his book consists of ornaments for flintlock guns, he also includes sketches of a contemporary gunmaker's shop where, curiously enough, the workmen are making wheel locks and matchlocks.

Two individual guns and a garniture of Thuraine and Le Hollandois survive in the Tøjhus Museet in Copenhagen. The garniture is gracefully made but shows nowhere the richness of design of Jacquinet's pattern book. A pair of pistols in the Musée d'Armes in Liège are better examples, and item M 601 in the Musée d'Armes looks like one of Marcou's designs in richness. A few other guns survive signed either by Thuraine or Le Hollandois, (whose real name was Adrian Reynier—he came from Holland), but they seem to have had an in-and-out partnership and Thuraine finally took in his own son as "Les Thuraines à Paris" in 1685.

The earliest French flintlock guns, made by Marin le

[8] *Only one gunmaker at a time had occupancy of the Louvre workshops.*

Roman designs *including deep carving on the barrel of this Le Hollandois gun date it according to Dr. Lenk in the 1660's. loa. 60½", bbl 45¼", cal. .60" (20 gauge). No.# M 601, Musée de l'Armée, Paris.*

European flintlock, *1650. Heavy black bluing, loa. 66¾", bbl 51⅝", .66" calibre (16 gauge smooth bore). No.# B 660, Tøhus Museet Copenhagen*

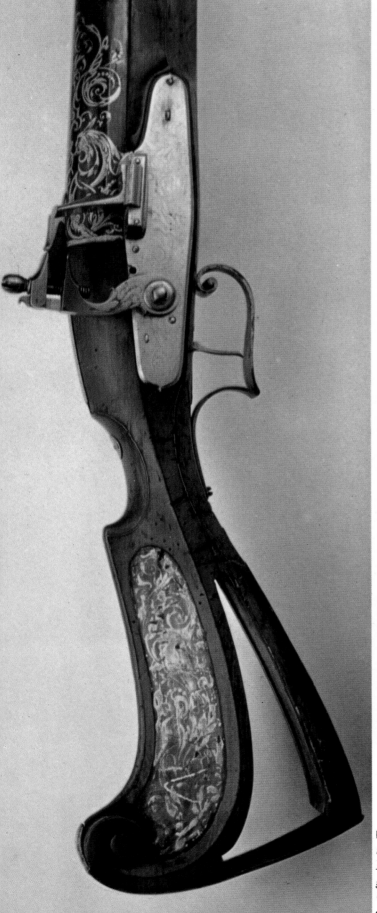

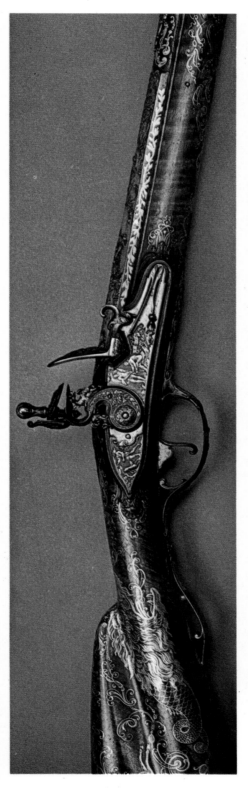

"Arault à Versailles," *flintlock gun completely ornamented with designs from de Lacollombe worked in gold wire inlay and gold bas relief, chiselled lock face, fire gilt barrel. c. 1740 loa. 56", bbl 42", cal .64" or 16 ga. No.# WR 2890, Bayerisches Armeemuseum, Munich.*

Louis XIII's gun *made by Marin le Bourgeoys in the 1620's. This and the Bourgeoys gun in the Hermitage are possibly the two oldest flintlock guns surviving. Painted stock, tube rear sight. Cabinet d'Armes No. 122. loa. 50½", bbl 42", calibre 1½". No.# M-435, Musée de l'Armée, Paris.*

THE FLINTLOCK

Bourgeoys or his brother Jean Bourgeois, Le Conte, Bernard Piraube, Chasteau à Paris, Le Languedoc, Thuraine and Le Hollandois;[9] as well as the decorators with their pattern books, Henequin, Daubigny, Marcou, Berain and Jacquinet, set a new style in gun design and decoration. They provided the patterns and models that were copied and sometimes improved on not only in the provinces of France, but also throughout most of the gunmaking world for 200 years.

In the eighteenth century, while the French were continuing with their rich designs, turning out masterpieces signed by de Lacollombe, La Roche, Boutet and Le Page, the English were refining the action of the flintlock. Griffin, Manton, Egg, Nock and Wogdon built guns which were undecorated by French and European standards. The stocks were plain and simply shaped, the checkering fine and sharp but conservative, the barrels brown and undecorated except for a tube of gold or platinum at the touchhole and around the breech to prevent corrosion at these points. The explanation given for this conservatism is that these guns were used for dueling and were designed neither to reflect light into the eye of the shooter or make too bright a target for an adversary to shoot at. Inasmuch as duels were fought in daylight and the duelers usually faced each other at point-blank range stripped to their white shirts, the gun decoration couldn't have added much to the visibility of the target.

(9) *Work by Piraube can be seen at the Tower of London; that of Chasteau and of Thuraine and Le Hollandois at the Tøjhus Museet, Copenhagen; and of Le Languedoc at the Victoria and Albert Museum, London.*

Combination matchlock and flintlock *from Louis XIII's Cabinet d'Armes. Made by F. DuClos who also made a wheel lock pistol now in the Metropolitan Museum of Art, New York. This two-shot superimposed load gun works the match with a tiller and the flint with a trigger. Cabinet number 151, dated 1636, the gun has an ebony stock decorated with silver and a gilt bronze atlanta under the shooter's chin. loa. 59½", bbl 41-7/16", cal. .70". No.# M-410, Musée de l'Armée, Paris.*

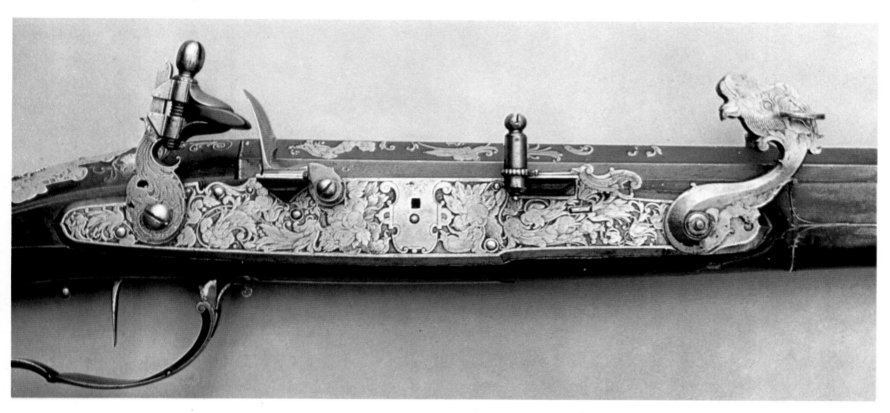

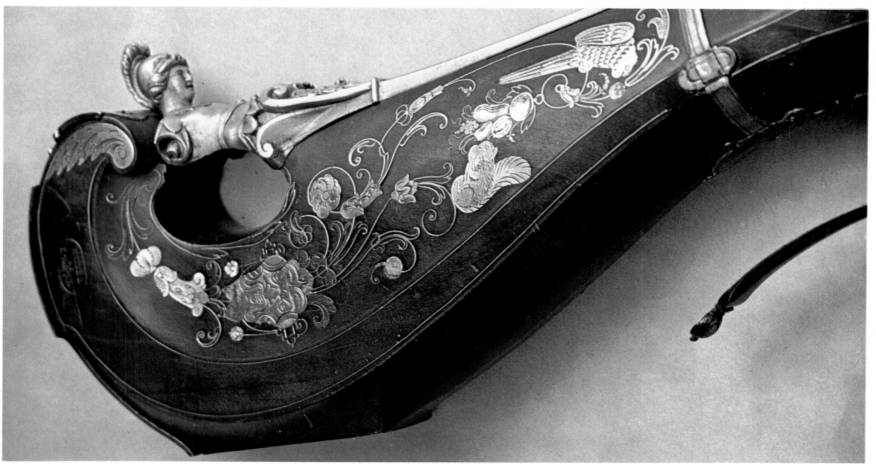

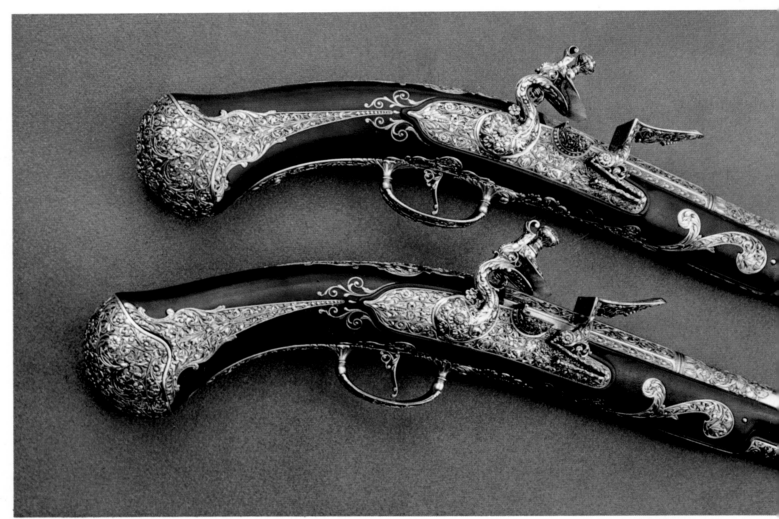

Pair of flintlock pistols. *Made by Acqua Fresca (Luigi or Matteo Cecchi) and signed "Aqua Fresca à Bargi—1681". Even the ramrod tips are chiselled steel. loa. 20", bbl 13-3/32", cal. .50", No.# 14958, Musée de l'Armée, Paris.*

Heavy gold-inlaid *pocket pistols made by "LaRoche à Paris" in 1734. The red velvet sheaths have the royal fleur-de-lis embroidered in silver thread. The decoration includes gold wire stock inlay, fire gilt and gold and silver inlay in the blued steel of the barrels. loa. 10½", bbls 5⅜", cal. approx. .48" (bore flares out at the muzzle). No.# M1729 and 16958, Musée de l'Armée, Paris.*

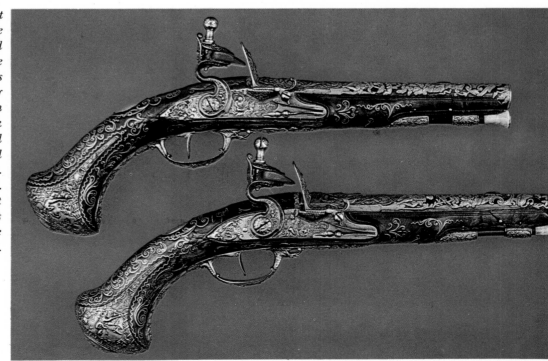

THE FLINTLOCK

The simplest explanation is that the British gunsmiths were building guns for British gentlemen, and the gentlemen liked their guns that way. The total number of duels fought would break the heart of a romanticist.

The real interest of the British gunmaker lay not in decoration but in the perfection of the mechanical function of the flintlock. First off, take apart an Egg, a Manton or a Nock. The finish of the woodwork and the metalwork of the lock's hidden parts is as good as the exterior—which is more than can be said for some of the chased and engraved and gold-plated Boutet guns. Secondly, the British gunmakers introduced refinements to make the basic flintlock work more smoothly, with fewer misfires. An anti-friction roller on the steel spring provided a smoother, quicker spark. Additional bridles helped to maintain the correct angles and positional relationship between the cock and the steel, and precision fitting made the pan cover part of the steel fit so closely that it was watertight against even complete immersion.[10] These beautiful English guns functioned so well in the field that celebrated sportsmen, usually interested in any gadget to improve their shooting, stuck to flint long after it was made obsolete by the percussion cap. Colonel Peter Hawker, who was a great hunter and a fine shot, kept his flintlocks in the field even though in his *Instructions to Young Sportsmen* he takes credit for suggesting the percussion cap to Joe Manton.

The flintlock type of ignition invented by Le Bourgeoys or at least at the time of Le Bourgeoys around 1610 was the best there was for nearly 200 years. There were, however, disadvantages. The flint could break, and often did; after seven or eight shots the face of the flint became worn or chipped and ignition became more uncertain, and finally the flash of the sparks from the flint occurred a perceptible part of a second before the gun went off—just time enough to alert or scare off wild game. The next major advance in guns was to come from an unlikely source—a Scottish divine who had taught himself chemistry.

[10] *Joseph Egg made a flintlock in 1816 with an airtight slide protecting the touchhold which was fired on test after repeated dunking in water.*

THE FLINTLOCK

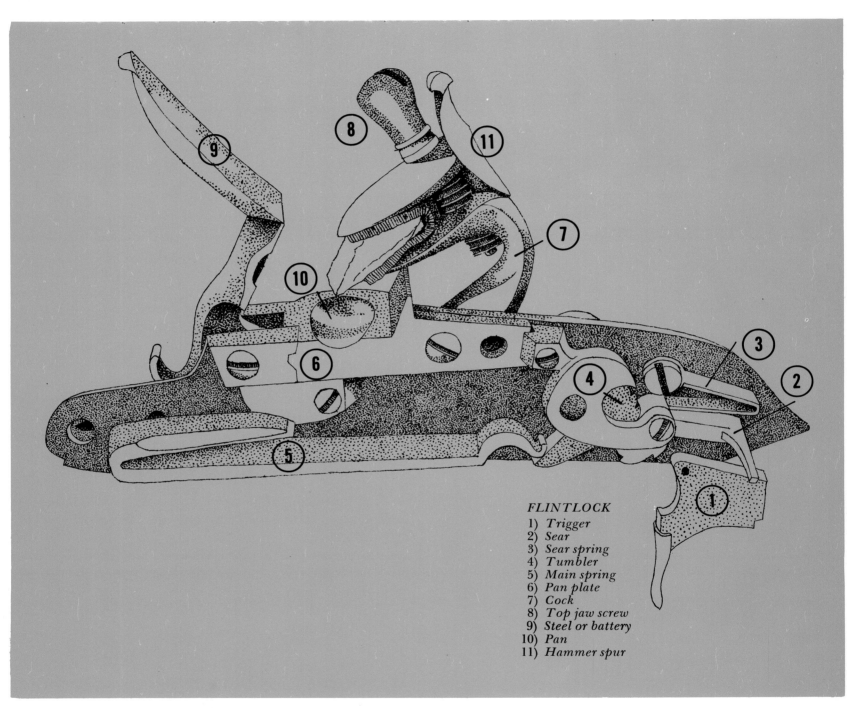

FLINTLOCK
1) *Trigger*
2) *Sear*
3) *Sear spring*
4) *Tumbler*
5) *Main spring*
6) *Pan plate*
7) *Cock*
8) *Top jaw screw*
9) *Steel or battery*
10) *Pan*
11) *Hammer spur*

Rearward pressure on trigger (1) lifts sear
                (2) against the pressure of the sear spring
                (3) releasing tumbler
                (4) which allows cock
                (7) to fall.
The previously cocked hammer or cock (7) flies forward striking battery
                (9) and showers sparks in pan
                (10) which has been uncovered by the blow.

Details of the interior *of a gunmaker's shop in Paris in the mid-1600's, and a typical flintlock lock design. It is of interest to note that the gunmakers in the shop are busy building wheel locks. Illustrations from* Jacquinet's Plusieurs Models *which was published in 1660.*

Lock Details *from Jacquinet,* Plusieurs Models.

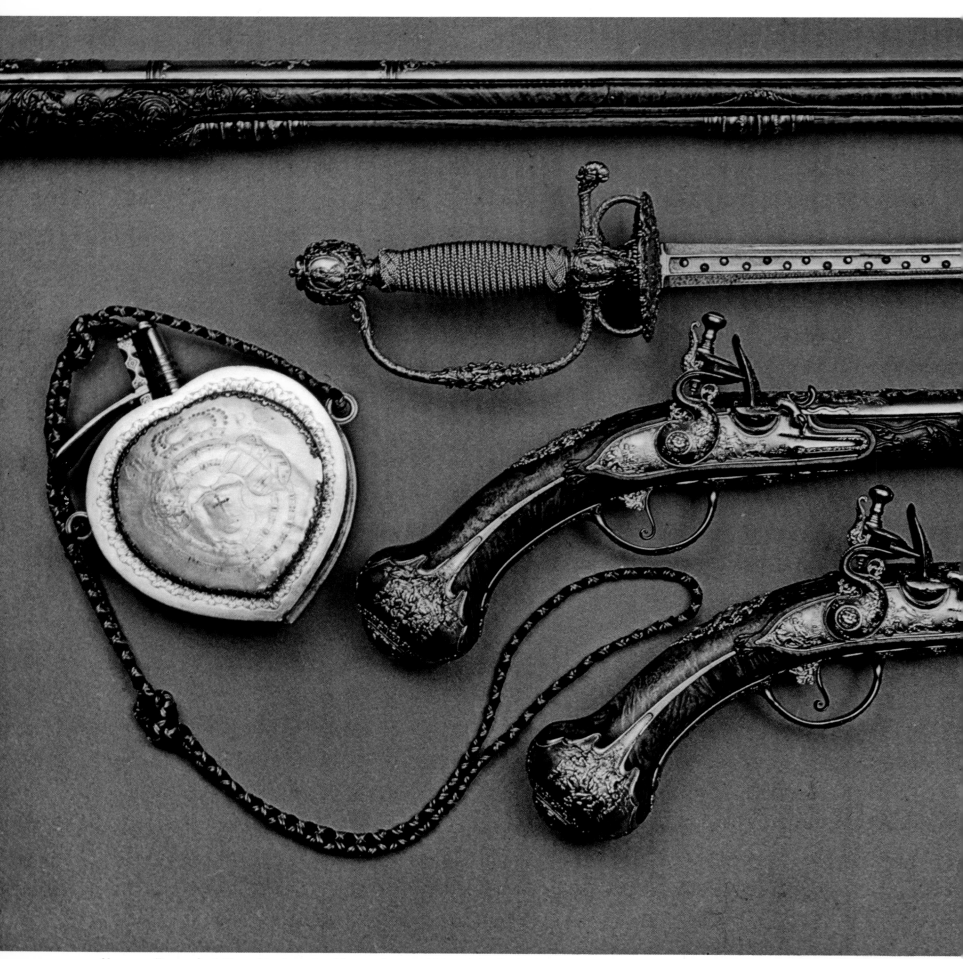

Hermann Bongard *of Dusseldorf made this garniture which originally included a cane, for the Elector Johann Wilhelm of Pfalz in Zwei-brücken between 1680 and 1689. A traveller, Zacharias von Uffenbach, admired the garniture and described it in 1709. He says that he put on his gloves to examine them. The pistols are 21½" long, barrels 14", cal. .60". The shotgun is 60" long, bbl 46", bore 14 gauge. The powder flask is gold and mother-of-pearl, Nos. gun—13/583; pistols—13/1031 and 13/1032; the sword—13/1291; the flask—W-2896. Bayerische Armeemuseum, Munich.*

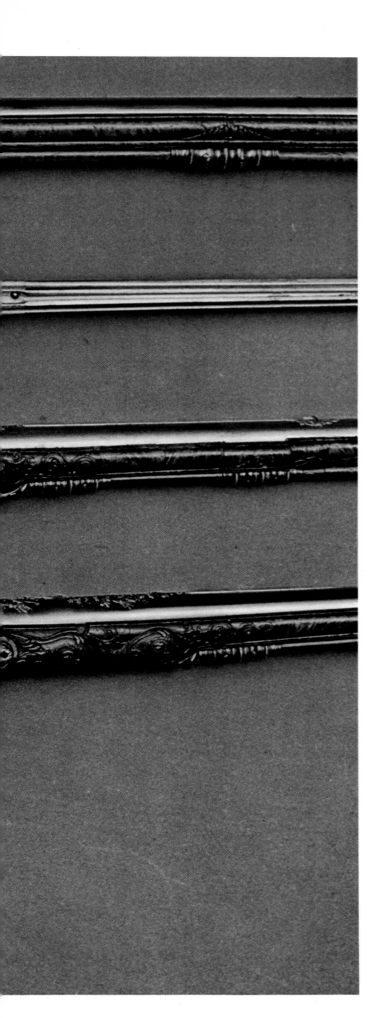

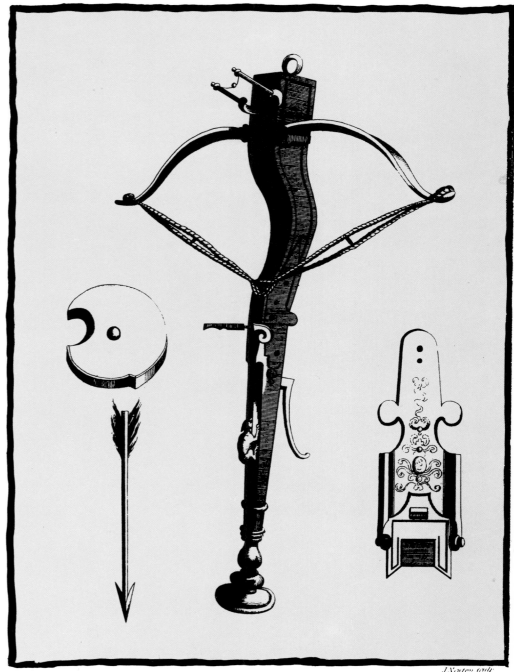

CROSSE BOWE.

J. Newton fecit

Diderot and D'Alembert *Encyclopédie 1751*

Fabrique des Ar

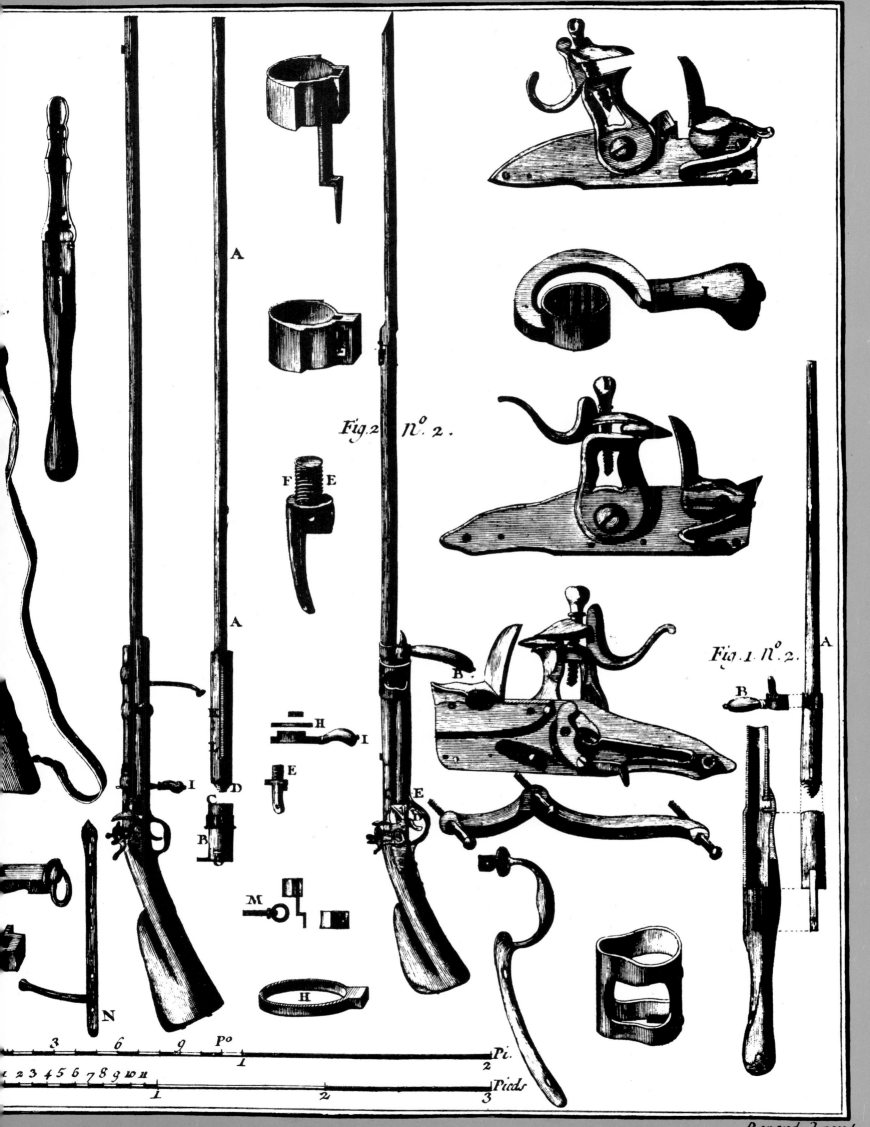

Fig. 2. N.º 2.

F E

A

A

H

I

E

D

C

B

I

M

N

B

E

B

Fig. 1. N.º 2.

A

B

H

3   6   9   Po.

Pi.

1   2

1 2 3 4 5 6 7 8 9 10 11

1   2   Pieds

3

Fusil de Munition

THE FLINTLOCK

Boutet's finest boxed pistols. *Made for Napoleon to celebrate the Egyptian campaign (1798-99), the designs include sphinxes, Libyan lions, pyramids, and Cleopatra's asp. On the little pocket pistol at the right, there is a tired French cavalry-man in a pose reminiscent of Remington's cowboys. The engraving may have been done by Montigny. Pocket pistols, 5½" long with 1" barrels. The duellers are 18⅜" long with multi-groove rifling cal. .60". Each gun barrel of the duellers has 291 gold stars inlaid in the blued field. The effect of the guns is a silvery lightness despite their excessive ornamentation. No.# N. 05876, Musée de l'Armée, Paris.*

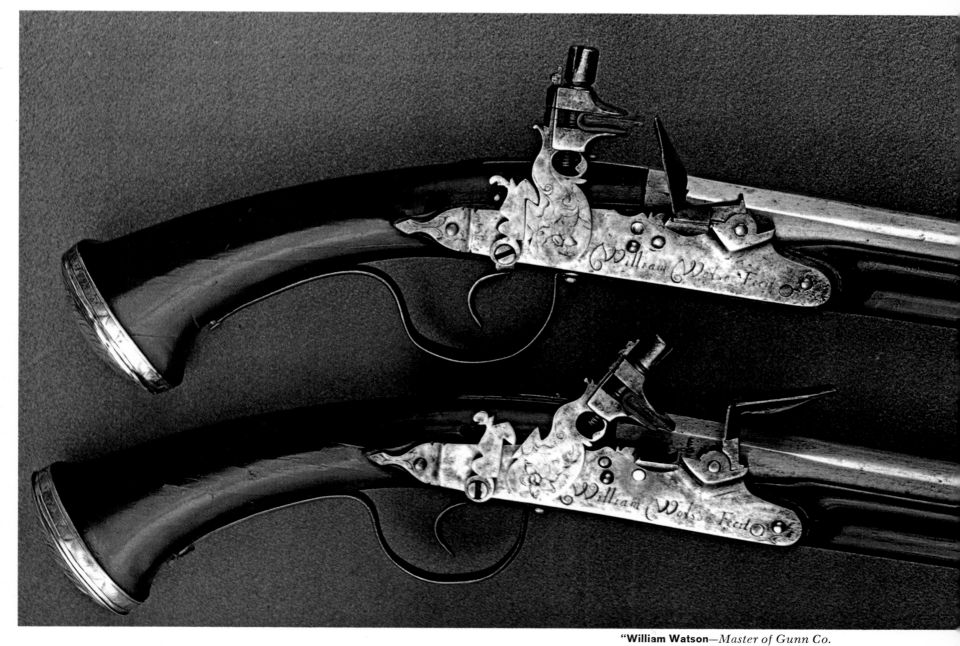

"**William Watson**—*Master of Gunn Co. 1646-1649" made these dog-lock pistols between 1649 and 1650. Ebony stocked with silver furniture, these English cavalry pistols are of exceptional quality. loa. 20¾", bbls 13⅝", cal. .60". Nos.# XII/1495-1496, Tower of London.*

CHAPTER IX

FULMINATING POWDERS AND TRANSITIONAL WEAPONS

"LA REPUBLIQUE N'A PAS besoin de savants." This was the decision of the tribunal which led Lavoisier to the guillotine in the Place de la Revolution. The judges were not only historically incorrect, they didn't even have hindsight. The man whose head they had chopped off could have helped to avert the disastrous gunpowder shortage which handicapped the revolutionists. Fortunately for the French, one of his pupils was spared by oversight. Otherwise, neither might the revolution have succeeded nor Napoleon won his first battle.

Antoine Laurent Lavoisier (1743-1794) had already done more to load the French guns than any other man. As a geologist, he had found new sources for that vital ingredient of black powder—saltpeter. As a chemist, he was able to increase the efficiency and improve the quality of gunpowder, and as "Regisseur des Poudres" in 1775, he did away with an abuse that had existed in France for hundreds of years—almost since the invention of gunpowder—which allowed government employees to enter and search the cellars of private homes for deposits of nitre (saltpeter), on stone foundations. In 1777 he published *Sur la combustion en general,* and two years before the revolution, he published a text on the nomenclature of chemistry with Berthollet, who was later to carry on experiments with the highly explosive fulminating powders.

To Lavoisier, fulminating powders were just one more kind of explosive; an explosive which perhaps would be more effective than gunpowder as it was more violent. Guns had, since their intention, been fired most successfully with gunpowder, although Leonardo da Vinci had invented and sketched a steam gun, and surviving airguns date back as far as 1650.[1] Gunpowder, as has been described in Chapter I, had improved over the centuries from a weak and uncertain propellant to a substance which could be pretty well controlled in manufacture to perform a specific job. First came the corning of powders which gave a more uniform explosion. This provided a control of the size of the particles and eliminated the chunks which burned slowly, and the powder

or dust which flashed. Next, powder was glazed with powdered graphite, which increased its moisture resistance and kept it in usable condition longer.

By the 1600's corned powders were good enough so that it was possible to figure out how long it took a certain batch of powder to burn, and by the end of the seventeenth century special quick-burning pistol powders existed. Gunmakers then were busy sawing off the ends of the old long-barreled pistols, as a long barrel was no longer necessary to allow for complete combustion. Powders continued to be refined, and in addition to very coarse powders for cannon, there were two sizes of powder used by hand gunners, plus a fine powder used for priming. The priming powder worked well, burning rapidly, and detonating the coarser powder in the barrel; unless, of course, the flint failed, or the spark missed the pan of powder, or the wind hit it, or the shooter clumsily spilled the priming powder before the shot, or unless it got wet.

Waterproof pans to hold the priming powder were devised, drain holes were drilled in the bottom of pans, and pan covers were hitched mechanically to the cocks so that the protective cover stayed in place until the trigger had been pulled and the flint in the cock was already travelling toward the pan. Neither loose priming powder nor loose fulminate were dependable, but at least the fulminate took up so little space that it could be protected from water more easily, and the intensity of the flash that it gave off made it practically certain to ignite the black powder of either pistol or long gun.

What are fulminates and what are they good for? The *Encyclopedia Brittanica* says: "Fulminic Acid. HCNO—$H_2C_2N_2O_2$—an organic isomeric with cyanic and cyanuric acids—its salts, termed fulminates, are very explosive and are much employed as detonators."

The old *Brittanica* article goes on to add that the free acid is explosive and the vapor poisonous. This was all discovered the hard way by the contemporaries and successors to Benjamin Franklin, who, between their periods of pre-

[1]*An air gun survives which belonged to Queen Christina, daughter of Gustav Adolphus of Sweden, who reigned between 1644 and 1654. The gun is in the Livrustkammaren in Stockholm. The copper barrel is inscribed "Macht michs Hans Köler von Kitzing anno 1644."*

Officer and Sergeant *from a Highland regiment from Francis Grose's* Military Antiquities, *London, 1802.*

TRANSITIONAL WEAPONS

occupation with the causes of lightning and thunder, were mixing fulminates on the back of the stove. Progress and explosions went hand in hand. First Berthollet got a big bang by mixing ammonia with precipitated silver oxide (1788). In 1798 Brugnatelli improved silver fulminate by dissolving silver in nitric acid and adding a hooker of brandy.

Mercury based fulminates were invented, or at least demonstrated, the following year by Edward Charles Howard who blew himself up in public as he demonstrated the new salts to the Royal Society in London in 1799. Howard's amateur enthusiasm for chemistry was diverted into other channels—his comment: "I am more disposed to prosecute other chemical subjects"—and it was left to the more thorough and painstaking researches of Von Liebig (1832) to perfect the safer mercuric fulminates which have been used since.[2]

So much for chemistry and science. Who was going to be the Thomas Edison and make a practical application of the new fulminates? The idea was that the new explosive could replace gunpowder. It didn't because it was so powerful that it blew up the guns. How it could be used, and in very small quantities, was in detonating the slower burning gunpowder, which continued to provide the propelling charge.

The use of fulminating powders for the detonation of firearms, and the mechanical inventions to control the priming of handguns and cannon came from an unexpected source. Far away from the Royal Societies and the scientific seminars of London, Paris, Philadelphia, and Turin, a Scottish clergyman, Alexander John Forsyth, put two and two together. Only 22 years after bloody Culloden, on December 28, 1786 (not quite 90 miles from Scotland's last battleground) Forsyth was born in the village of Belhelvie, Aberdeenshire. A pastoral life, and a peaceful one—he never gave up his Presbyterian parish and the call lasted for fifty-two years—were conducive to shooting wildfowl and thinking. The flash in the pan of Forsyth's old flintlock scared away the few birds that the pastor encountered on his shooting walks. Being an inventor, he first made a crude shield to cover the

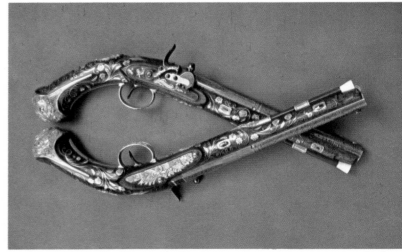

2nd model Forsyth pistols *with automatic self primers. Locks by Beckwith. These London-made guns were obviously made for a rich or royal person. They are far too highly decorated for the English taste of the period. The picture at the right shows the lock and hammer action. Russell Aitken Collection.*

LePage cased pair of pill locks. *The pills were loaded in the urn-shaped container on the top of the touch-holes. A spring-loaded firing pin was placed on top and the cap screwed down. The hammer, smooth on the face, drove the firing pin into the percussion pellet. Russell Aitken Collection.*

[2] *Von Liebig heated a mixture of alcohol, nitric acid, and mercuric nitrate which produced a salt less explosive than silver salt. Although discarded today by commercial ammunition makers because of its corrosive action on steel, mercuric primers are still used by the U.S. and British armies because of their dependability and lasting qualities.*

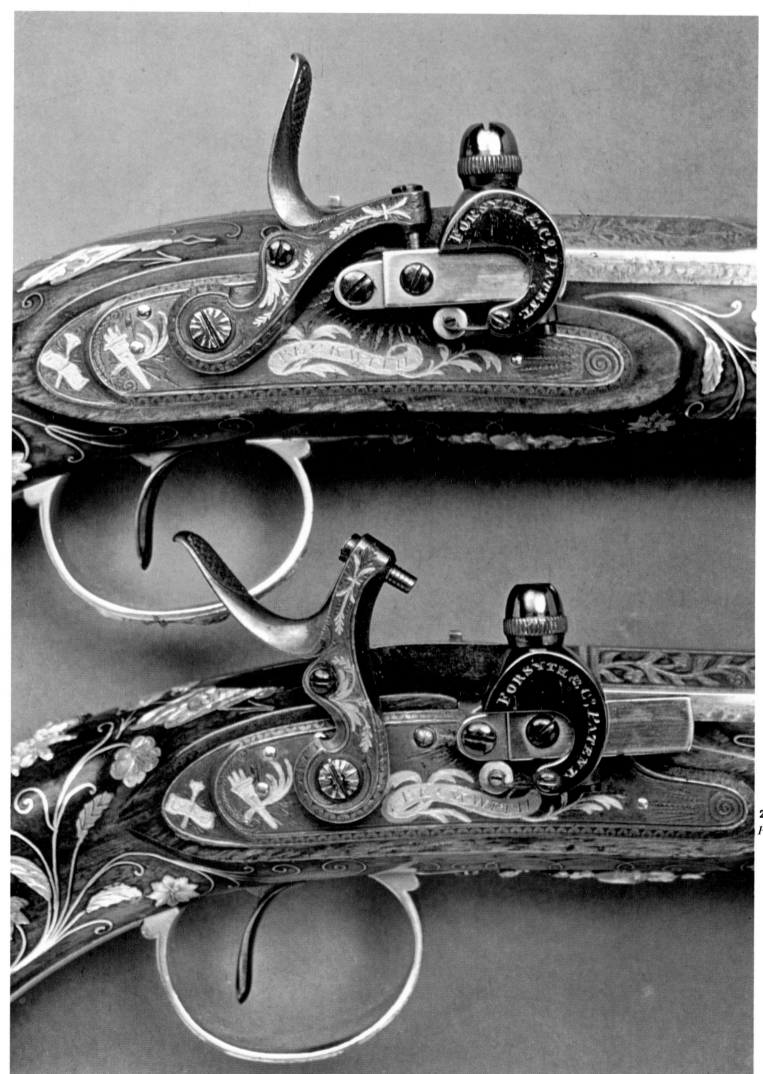

2nd model Forsyth pistols
Russell Aitken Collection.

TRANSITIONAL WEAPONS

flash pan, thus reinventing the enclosed flintlock which the Augsberg locksmiths and Stanislaus Paczelt[3] (in Kuttenberg, Bohemia in 1738) had perfected before 1750.

As an amateur chemist, he experimented with the new fulminating powders. This in turn led him to experiment with "almost every form of hammer and pan that has yet been devised".[4] In 1805 he had a combination that worked. He shot with a fowling piece equipped with this new lock during the hunting season of 1805, and took the new invention to London in 1806. After a frustrating bout with the military, he applied for a patent for the scent-bottle lock in 1807. He developed a lock for a three pounder (cannon) and later improved on his scent-bottle with a primer dispenser that slid back and forth, synchronized with the cock, dispensing primer mix in the pan on each journey.

Forsyth was a canny man who never gave up his living in the church and was not about to go it alone as an inventor before his time. He set up in business in London with James Watt, the successful inventor of the steam engine, and he had his patent guns built by James Purdy, one of London's finest gunmakers. All surviving Forsyth guns are very well made.

In 1809, the famous French gunmaker, LePage, demonstrated a percussion lock to the "Societe pour l'Encouragement de l'Industrie Nationale". It was successfully demonstrated by firing over 300 times without a misfire. In 1810 Prelat, a patent-conscious Paris gunmaker, took out a patent on Forsyth's system, and in 1812, Pauly, the Swiss balloonist, patented a breechloader with a firing pin which detonated fulminate imbedded in the center of the cartridge.

All Europe at this time was at war. After the British dismissed Forsyth's invention (they were busy building up an inventory of flintlocks that lasted until the 1840's), Napoleon's agents are supposed to have offered Forsyth £20,000 for it, but Forsyth is reputed to have turned them down, perhaps remembering the last time the French had helped a Scotsman, namely Bonnie Prince Charlie at Culloden. However, when Pauly demonstrated his system, which performed

perfectly to one of Napoleon's generals, Napoleon had no time for new gimmicks.

At this point a vast upsurge of invention started. Nobody really knew what he was doing, but here was a new device that needed refinement. There were pellet locks, pill locks, tube locks (by the redoubtable Joe Manton), cap locks, rolls of caps (later made practical by a Philadelphia dentist, Dr. Maynard) and finally, Pauly, who had a really good idea in the first place, came back with a hot air detonating system which seemed to sum up the whole matter.

There was really only one tiny thing missing. What was needed was a simple, safe way to contain a correct amount of detonating powder. Detonating powder can be very nervous, and a small amount safely encased is the best package to turn loose to the fool who knows nothing but wants to shoot a gun. Loose fulminating powder, such as was contained in Forsyth's scent-bottle (enough for 20 charges) could be very unpleasant if it decided to explode when given a sharp rap. This was partially protected against by having an expendable cork in the powder end of the scent-bottle, but that end was not a good place to hold your hand. In the last war, whole buildings have disappeared when an inexperienced factory hand ran a little hand truck full of "safe" percussion caps into a brick wall, thus producing just the right jolt.

Between the years 1805 and 1825 there were lots of inventions, many patents and much patent litigation. Joe Manton invented both the pellet and the tube lock. Forsyth sued him successfully for violation or infringement. Prelat's invention was a direct steal, but there was nothing that Forsyth could do with England and France at war, nor were there any international patent agreements. In Denmark, an inventor-gunsmith, Lobnitz, engineered a couple of detonating locks before building his underhammer percussion pieces. Good French guns by Le Page and Pauly with detonating systems found their way to England and the United States. Although the percussion cap had been invented simultaneously by a half-dozen people in 1816, Durs Egg was still able to sell a Pauly detonator to George IV in 1824.

---

[3] *Paczelt, dated, Tower of London, No. XII-627. Double-barreled fowling piece from the collection, Gewerrkammer, of the Electors of Bavaria, the Bavarian National Museum, Munich, No. 13/589.*

[4] *Sir Alexander John Forsyth Reid,* Alexander John Forsyth.

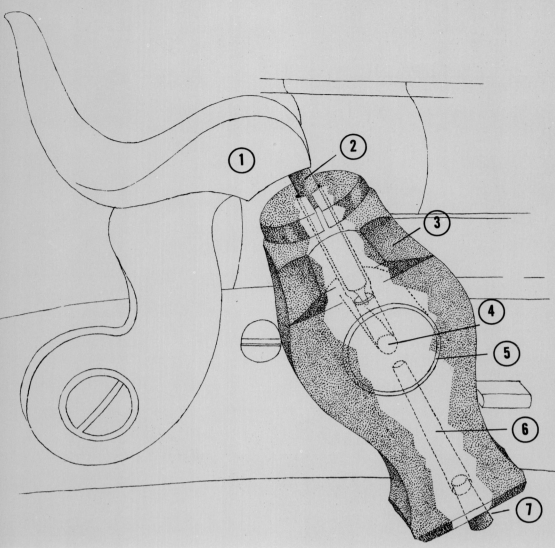

The scent bottle revolves on a hollow tapered axle or pin (4). It is illustrated in fired position with the hammer down. The firing sequence is as follows: Cock hammer (1), rotate the scent bottle 180 degrees so that priming magazine (6) is in an upright position. This allows a small amount of fulminate to drop into the hole of the axle (4). The scent bottle is then brought back to the illustrated position. When the trigger is pulled the hammer hits the firing pin (2), driving the pin into the percusive powder. This explodes the fulminate and ignites the charge in the barrel.

While Joe Manton was easily the most active experimenter with new systems for detonating the percussive fulminating powders, there are many other half forgotten names of gunmakers whose systems and variations have come down to us in examples of their works. Joseph Contriner in Vienna built some fine guns which survive despite their transitory usefulness. Bruneel in Lyon, de l'Etrange in Versailles and Pottet in Paris, all produced improvements on Prelat's and Le Page's guns. In England, Webster, Westley Richards, and Charles Moore made ingenious variations. The most important of the subvarieties of fulminating firearms, loose powder, pellets, tubes, and tapes are illustrated. The rest, which are well described by Blackmore,[5] Reid,[6] Winant,[7] and Hoff,[8] would make a solid subject for some young man's Ph.D. thesis.

Pellet locks, pill locks, tube locks and cap locks were essentially what their names implied; all were an attempt to employ fulminate material in a safe and positive manner.

Pellet locks held a pellet of fulminate in the flash pan until the instant the hammer hit it, detonating it against the anvil of the pan. Joseph Egg even invented a gravity pellet feed which attached to the top of the barrel and fed one pellet after another into the pan. The pill lock was a wax coated pill of fulminate of mercury which fitted into a specially drilled hole in the hammer itself. A tube was inserted after the pill. When the gun was fired the tube was driven against the pill causing the flame to shoot down the tube and in through the touchhole. Tube locks worked with a copper tube of fulminate, open at one end, which was inserted directly into an enlarged touchhole. The hammer struck the tube a smart blow, which caused the fulminate to explode and the flash to go down the touch hole with great intensity. The lock system worked so well that Joe Manton was able to keep building tube locks long after the percussion cap had taken over. The strong flash worked especially well for heavy punt guns and hand-held four- and eight-bores which had a

[5] *Edward L. Blackmore,* British Military Firearms *and* Guns And Rifles of the World.
[6] *William Reid,* Journal of the Arms and Armour Society, *Vol. II, p. 181-210.*
[7] *Lewis Winant,* Early Percussion Firearms.
[8] *Dr. Arne Hoff,* Danske Perkussionsbøsser.

Five-barrel volley gun. *First model Forsyth detonator with scent bottle, serial no. 3235, probably made around 1820 although the Forsyth patent was issued in 1806. The primer flash discharged all barrels simultaneously when it entered the platinum-lined false breech. loa. 41", bbl including false breech 24⅛", each barrel .410" gauge. No.# XII/1589, Tower of London.*

William Moore's pill lock pistols. *Platinum plugged with safety vents. A patented rocker, which was removed by the action of the teat on the hammer, held the pill or pellet safely in place until the gun was fired. These guns, made in London in 1820, belonged to the 2nd Marquis of Clanricard. loa. 14⅝", bbls 9¼", cal. .50", smooth bore. Tower of London.*

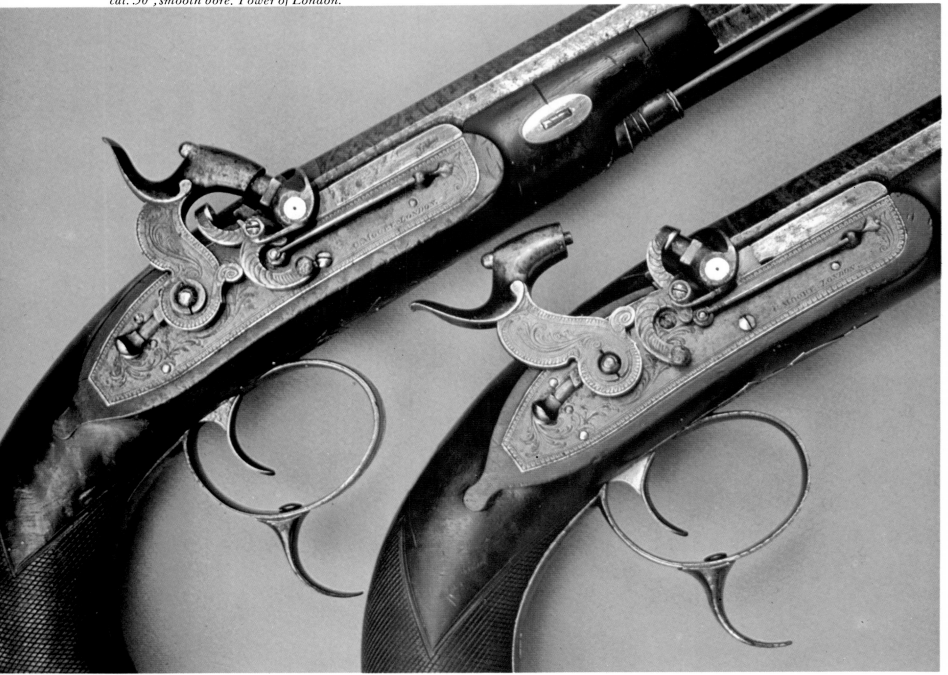

huge powder capacity. Cap and pellet guns were both popular on the continent and were built by LePage and others.

Sometimes the little waxed pellets were put between two pieces of paper just like our present cap for a cap pistol. This gave rise to Maynard's invention—a roll of caps which fed from a magazine in the body of the gun. These caps were varnished to keep them waterproof. The caps were smaller and the tape or roll narrower than a roll of toy caps but the fulminate mix was much stronger. Maynard's caps worked so well that he was able to secure U. S. Army contracts in a relatively short time after developing the ignition system and building a model gun. Many old guns, including flintlocks were converted to the Maynard system. It was used on the Jenks and Sharps carbines, and the U. S. Army incorporated the Maynard tapes in their issue weapon of 1855. The advent of primed breech-loading cartridges made the system obsolete, but fine cased sporting Maynards such as the one illustrated were used by sportsmen for many years.

Once again, Maynard's invention was an evolution from an earlier effort. The Maynard patent was issued in 1845, while back in 1831 a French inventor, Leboeuf de Valdehon, patented a gun which was detonated by a straw filled with fulminate. Pieces of straw were chopped off by an underhammer which at the same time detonated the cut-off piece by impact. This proved to be nothing but a straw in the wind and none seem to have been built. It was, however, the idea which inspired a French urologist, Dr. Heurteloup (Baron Charles Louis Stanislaus), to make the tube of soft pewter (half zinc and half tin) in 1834. The tube filled with fulminate was fed into the primer anvil from the breech when the gun was cocked. The tube was chopped and the piece chopped off was detonated in much the same fashion as the Valdehon straw. A Greek name for the action was given to it by the scholarly Dr. Heurteloup. It was named the *koptiteur*, which is a French version of the Greek stems of the verbs to slice and hit. Despite the name, *koptiteur* actions were successful for a time in France and Belgium. A Swedish version came out of Husqvarna, and a Russian example survives in the Paris Musée de l'Armée.

This was the nineteenth century, a period when the most important people in the gun business were patent attorneys instead of master gunsmiths and artists. The warm-up legal tangles of the detonating period were a foretaste of an avalanche of patent suits to come. Patents were issued for drilling a hole *all* the way through a block of steel; for the ratchet principle of the revolver, examples of which had been around for three hundred years; and for a thousand re-applications of earlier gun design. *A History of the Colt Revolver* by Haven and Belden will give any interested reader a sufficient example. W. Keith Neal has a detonator miquelet built by Joseph Gutirrez in Seville in 1820 which has a hound for a hammer forever chasing a wary rabbit perched on top of the touchhole. I don't know which animal Gutirrez intended to represent the patent lawyer and which the inventor, but then, the time has come to go into who *really* invented the percussion cap.

Joe Manton's double tube lock. *Note the knife on the hammer. Manton patented this action in 1818. This gun was built in 1820, signed "Joseph Manton, Hanover Square, London" on the barrels. loa. 46", bbls 29¾", 14 gauge. No.# XII/1589, Tower of London.*

CHAPTER X

TRUE PERCUSSION

IF THERE WERE any justice in this world, there would be an inventor to go with each invention. This would be neat and tidy and the historian would have easy going in relating the facts. In the case of the invention of the percussion cap there are too many facts, and far too many inventors.

In the previous chapter some of the many ingenious detonating devices are described. These existed before, during, and after the era of the percussion cap and some, like the tape primer, had advantages over the percussion cap. But first, what is a percussion cap? If you take a thin piece of soft metal—copper is the most popular—and shape it on a press into a cup about the size of a midget's thimble, then pour into the bottom of the cup a tiny bit of your favorite fulminate you have a percussion cap. What do you do with it? You fit it over a nipple, which in turn has a hole in it that leads to the firing chamber of the gun, where the charge of powder is. Then you pull the trigger, after cocking the hammer; the hammer hits the percussion cap a sharp rap, the fulminate material in the cap explodes, shooting a jet of flame down the nipple's touchhole into the black powder in the breech and the gun goes off—you hope.

Of the many claims, there are two contemporary eyewitness accounts of the invention of percussion. Both authorities are reliable and the accounts of the invention were recorded at the time and not too many years later.

"The copper cap is now in general use all over the world; and therefore many gunmakers attempt to claim the invention as their own. I do not mean to say that I was the inventor of it—probably not; but this I must beg leave to state:—when Joe first brought out his detonators, in Davies Street (those which were discarded from giving so much trouble), he made me the most perfect gun I ever saw; and doubting whether such another could be got, I set my wits to work in order to simplify the invention. At last the plan of a perforated nipple, and the detonating powder in the crown of a small cap occurred to me. I made a drawing of it, which I took to Joe. After having this explained, he said he would show me something in a few weeks time; when, lo and behold! there was

a rough gun altered precisely on my own plan! His factotum, poor old Asell, assured me that the whole job was done from my drawing. Thus Joe, who led the fashion for all the world, sent out a few copper-cap guns, and I know, with some degree of reluctance. The trade, finding that he had then deviated from his patent, adopted this plan; and it proved to answer so well that we now see it in general circulation. So much, and no more, have I to say about the wished-for discovery of the copper cap inventor."[1]

Colonel Hawker sketched it and had Joe Manton build it against his better judgment. Joshua Shaw, an English artist, without an assist from any one, made a steel cap coated on the inside with a paste of fulminate or a pellet of the same substance. He had a gun which would function with the new invention made up by a country gunmaker named Roantree in Durham, England. The steel cap was reloadable. In successive years, Shaw invented a non-returnable pewter cap, and a copper cap.[2]

Shaw's perfected invention preceded the Manton-Hawker invention by two years. Manton didn't patent the tube lock until 1818, and continued to build tube lock sporting guns for many years after. According to Hawker's account, 1818 was the year of his inspiration. Purdy, who had been building guns for Forsyth, also thought that he had invented the percussion cap. It came to him in a flash as he sat at a restaurant table waiting for the waiter to bring a menu. His eye focused on an inverted tumbler on the table and, voila!

Joseph Egg might have gotten the same inspiration if he had joined Purdy for lunch, but that day he had only a few pennies in his pocket, so he took the economic course and made a copper cap out of a copper, all the while Purdy was presumably waiting for the check.

Egg settled the whole matter of priority of invention to his own satisfaction by the simple expedient of printing a label which he pasted on his gun cases. It read simply: "INVENTOR OF THE PERCUSSION CAP".

In all probability Shaw brought the cap idea to Egg. J. N. George, in his classic *English Guns and Rifles,* shrewdly sus-

[1] Instructions to Young Sportsmen, *Colonel Peter Hawker.*

[2] A Sketch or History of the Copper Cap, *Joshua Shaw, Bordentown, N.J., 1847.*

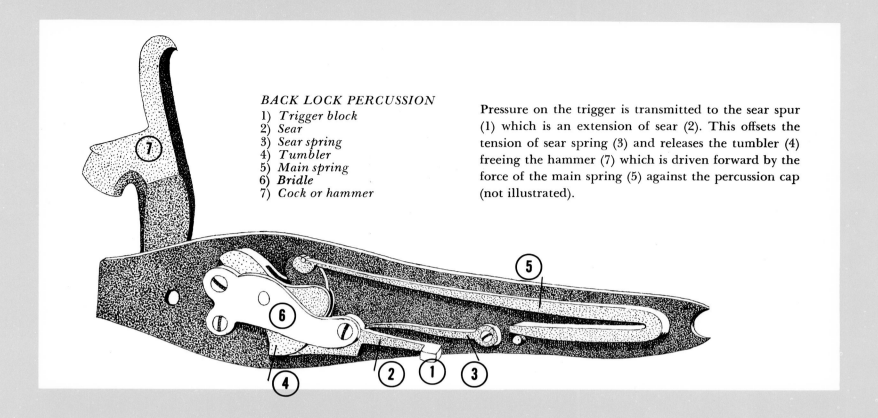

BACK LOCK PERCUSSION
1) *Trigger block*
2) *Sear*
3) *Sear spring*
4) *Tumbler*
5) *Main spring*
6) *Bridle*
7) *Cock or hammer*

Pressure on the trigger is transmitted to the sear spur (1) which is an extension of sear (2). This offsets the tension of sear spring (3) and releases the tumbler (4) freeing the hammer (7) which is driven forward by the force of the main spring (5) against the percussion cap (not illustrated).

pects that Manton encouraged Hawker in his opinion that the idea was his in order to avoid the onus of having stolen the Egg cup. This opinion is pretty well borne out by Manton's advertisement which accompanied his first percussion gun, stating "Made from the Original Design of Colonel Peter Hawker."

Shaw, on the other hand, came to Philadelphia in 1817 but did not bother to take out a patent for the percussion cap until 1822. He could not have taken out a patent for a year or so after his arrival as he was an alien, but for reasons unknown he forgot to apply until three years after that.

These are only a few versions of the story of the invention. There is a complete French version with a huge new cast of characters, the most noteworthy being Francois Prelat, of the Parisian gunmaking family, who took out a French patent, or brevet, in 1820, replacing an ingenious system for using fulminate which he had developed and patented in 1816. Shortly, both LePage and Boutet were making handsome percussion double guns and pistols. A particularly beautiful pair of percussion shotgun barrels were added to an already magnificent flintlock double-barreled shotgun which had inlaid gold sunbursts underlighting the sights. This gun, with its two sets of barrels, has found a home in the Metropolitan Museum of Art in New York. In England, by 1825, John and Joe Manton, Purdy, Parker, Mortimer, Greener and Joseph Egg were turning out fine percussion shotguns and elegant pairs of boxed percussion pistols.

In the United States, through the self-interested efforts of Joshua Shaw, and the need for weapons to make the West safe for the army, the new percussion guns swept the flintlock into total eclipse. All the new guns, such as the now famous Deringers, were percussions. Simeon North's protégé in Middletown, Connecticut, Henry Aston, was to build thousands of the new percussion pistols for both the U.S. Army and Navy (for $6.25 each, for which he was later investigated for war profiteering), and scarcely a flintlock escaped the converters, who hacked off the steel and steel-spring, plugged the hole that was left in the lock plate, brazed a hunk of iron onto the side of the barrel, drilled and tapped it for a percussion nipple, and replaced the flint cock with a percussion hammer. Beautiful flintlock Kentucky rifles, Norths, military and commercial guns alike—everything was made over into percussion. And ever since, collectors have been trying to make the better pieces over again—this time back to flint.

At the end of the Napoleonic wars, both the British and

Commissioned by the French government *as a bribe for Abd el Kadir, the Algerian nationalist, these savagely ornate guns were built by Perrin LePage before the Kadir was captured by the French in 1847. LePage kept the guns. Russell Aitken Collection.*

Devillers boxed percussion pistols. *(Une boîte-nécessaire en acajou). A gentleman's cased set of gold damascened duellers and pocket pistols mounted with ivory. The pistols are signed "J. Devillers, Liège, 1829". loa. duellers 15¾", bbls 8⅜", cal. .50", multi-groove rifling. The double-barrel pocket pistols have folding single triggers. The single selective trigger fires first the right and then the left barrel. Pocket pistols, loa. 9¼", bbls 4", cal. .44", Box, 26¾" by 11¼", is inscribed "Made in 1829 for Prince Guillaume des Pays Bas". No.# A.H. 30, (EK. 29-2/8403) Musée d'Armes, Liège.*

TRUE PERCUSSION

the French had vast stores of flintlock weapons—so many, in fact, that they could not afford to modernize their small ordinance (hand-held weapons). England, for example, had two million flintlocks left over from the war, plus three million flintlock replacement actions and one million replacement barrels. It was no wonder that even after a convincing demonstration of the superiority of the percussion system, the British Army Ordinance Department chose to stay with the flintlock. The test, however, was a convincing and exhaustive demonstration of the superiority, dependability, and speed of handling of percussion caps versus flintlocks and loose powder. The test only confirmed what sportsmen and hunters already knew.

In 1834 a shoot-off was arranged at the Woolwich Arsenal proving grounds. Six thousand rounds were fired from six guns of each type of lock. The flintlocks malfunctioned nearly a thousand times while the percussion arms misfired 36 times. In 1848 the 1st Battalion, Royal Sussex Regiment, was issued its first percussion arms. It took 14 years, and a fire in the Tower of London to prod the British military mind. J. N. George comments mildly that "The whole procedure—was carried out at—an incredibly leisure pace." [3]

On the continent there was civil war in Spain, revolution in Portugal, Greece and the Balkan states were rising up against the Turks, and Metternich was cautioning King Frederick William of Prussia about the evils of democracy, universities, and the press. With possible trouble so near, the French army adopted percussion in 1829 and the troops had all been issued percussion weapons by 1840. Sweden started in 1833 and completed her conversion of weapons in the same year that France did. Prussia switched in 1839, but by that time was already deep at work on her secret project at Sommerda under the direction of Dreyse, Pauly's pupil from his Paris workshop.

In the United States recourse to guns was constant. Besides the normal belligerency of a frontier society, with Indians in the way of colonization and settlement, there were two ominous political actions. Florida was ceded to the U.S. by Spain in 1818 which led down the path to the Seminole War, and Daniel Webster forced through Congress the Tariff of 1828 to encourage Northern industry with the highest protective tax thus far. This was the day the division between the North and South began.

No sooner was the Seminole War a part of history, than the United States went to war with Mexico—a series of engagements from Mexico City to Santa Fe to Sacramento, California. While General Kearney was on the march from Leavenworth, Kansas, to California, General Scott was besieging the heights and fortifications of Mexico City.

Whatever the U. S. Ordnance Department thought of the percussion system—and they were as dilatory as their European counterparts—North Americans wanted the new guns. While Henry Deringer had commenced building his pocket percussion pistols in 1825, the U. S. Army didn't issue its first percussion rifles and muskets to the troops until 1833, and percussion arms were not standard in the U. S. Infantry Manual until 1841. Colt, however, grasped the new idea and applied it practically to the old concept of a revolver in 1836, and if it hadn't been for Christian Sharps' fine breech-loading percussion rifle patented in 1848, "Bleeding Kansas" might have been bloodier still.

John Brown's son had been killed and his house burned to the ground when, half-crazed, he seized a supply of Beecher's Bibles (Sharps' Rifles) and made his futile attempt to free the slaves at Harpers Ferry. Henry Ward Beecher had said that one Sharps' had more moral effect on slave owners and the evils of slavery than one hundred Bibles.

More percussion arms, from single-shot muskets, and cheap double-barreled percussion shotguns to the sophisticated Colt's and Sharps' poured into the Kansas battleground. Here they were known as Kansas Bibles, as they had been sent west by the New England Emigrant Aid Company through the enemy territory of Missouri in wooden cases labelled "Bibles." Beset on the east by small armies of armed

---

[3] *J. N. George,* English Guns and Rifles, *(Samwirth, Harrisburg, Pa., 1947).*

thugs from Missouri who attacked the tiny plains settlements with cannon, burning the roofs off the sod homes and murdering the new settlers, and attacked on the west by plains Indians who were in cahoots with the Missourians, Kansas hardly needed a pro-slavery army outfitted by the Federal Government which appeared on its doorstep in 1856 commanded by a Buford at the head of a force of Georgians and South Carolinians.[4]

It is no wonder that a settler of two years in Washington County, Kansas, wrote this letter back to his friend in Haddam, Connecticut:

"Well as far as crops is here they look spleandid corn crop especially it goes far ahead of any I have ever seen and wheat has done verry well it is all harvested and I have got mine stacked I had one hundred shock so I dont expect to have to live on corn meal another year unless the Indians burns it up and if they do I will get me a horse and a sharps rifle and hunt Indians and secessionasts for the next six months and shoot every one I get my eye on."

Later on he writes to his same friend:

"If we could only get arms and ammunition here we could take care of our selves powder is worth two Dolars per pound and the one third of the men hasent got guns we have applied to the governor for arms but he says he hasnt got any."[5]

Percussion guns were the order of the day up and down the new continent. Duels were fought with them in New York, and riverboat gamblers carried little pocket derringers in their sleeves and vest pockets. Red-necked farmers from Illinois lugged old heavy single-shot muskets from the farm in Urbana across the mountains and deserts to fight Mexicans in Santa Fe. Stagecoach drivers, emigrants with wagon teams, and marauding plains Indians all carried short, smoothbore percussion carbines. The Indians, who were apt to have come by longer barreled trade guns, sawed off the barrels, front sights and all, in order to have handier saddle guns. Some of these have been preserved in dilapidated condition and studded with brass nails. Not many survived, as the Indians used their guns and didn't take care of them.

Of course, the United States did not have exclusive rights to the percussion idea. They simply had an immediate and a vast need for them. There were other events going on in the world, in which the new percussion weapons saw action. There was a revolution in Poland during this period. Revolution in Spain saw the English land at the mouth of the Tagus river in Portugal. The Sepoy mutiny, the Crimean War, and the Opium Wars in China were all fought by the British with percussion-capped Brunswick rifles, Minies, and Enfield rifles made with tools supplied by Yankees in Windsor, Vermont, and Chicopee Falls, Mass.

The Armeria Reale in Turin has an interesting collection of the percussion pistols and occasional weapons which were used against the Austrians by Garibaldi and sometimes against other Italians by Cavour, Victor Emmanuel or Ferdinand.

Fine percussion weapons were built in Copenhagen and Liège, and examples can still be seen in the Musée d'Armes and the Tøjhus Museet. Løbnitz in Copenhagen was an active inventor during the early eighteen-thirties and built several original designs of underhammer guns. These had the double advantage of providing a clean sighting plane as well as protecting the shooter from the bits and pieces of copper from an exploding cap. Percussion weapons in Liège were often of the finest quality and the Musée d'Armes has a collection of twist or damascus barrel, hard-soldered double guns which are as fine as any made anywhere.

The percussion cap has been considered in this chapter as a separate entity. It was slipped over a nipple and when struck, threw a hot flame down the touchhole into the barrel of a gun. Percussion caps are still very much in use today, only they are imbedded in the head of center-fire cartridges where they perform the same function. That is where they belonged in the first place.

[4] *Edwin Emerson, Jr.,* A History of the Nineteenth Century, *(Collier, New York, 1901), p. 1217.*

[5] Letters of John Ferguson, *(1943), Kansas Historical Quarterly,* **Vol. 12.**

TRUE PERCUSSION

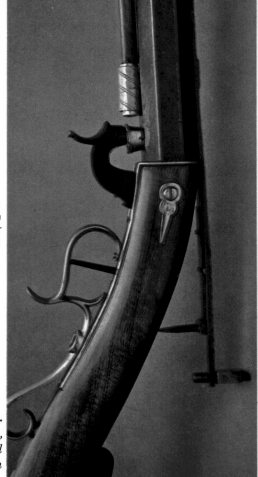

Underhammer percussion carbine.
*Made by D.H. Hilliard, Cornish,
New Hampshire, in 1860, bbl
24", cal .38", Winchester Gun
Museum, New Haven, Conn.*

Richly decorated shotgun. *Made by J. Tinlot in Liège in 1860,
the gold decoration inlaid in the damascened twist barrels, and
the vignette on the lock plate are Victorian. The barrels were
made by "Haaken-Plomdeur". loa. 48¾", bbls 31¾", 12-gauge.
Barrels full (right) and modified (left) No.# Ah 41/6038,
Musée d'Armes, Liège.*

Fine target rifle *with 'scope. Made by Wm. Billinghurst in
Rochester, N.Y., in 1868, the bull barrel pistol has a rifle stock
extension, a false muzzle and telescope. Cal .32".
Dr. Harman Leonard Collection.*

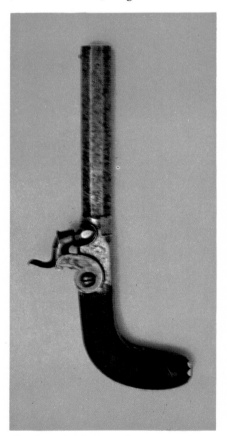

Bootleg pistol. *Fine damascened
barrels and folding trigger made
this bootleg pistol popular with
Americans. Imported from
Liège, it is stamped with the
importer's name, "H. Spies" of
New York. It dates from the river
boat period just prior to the
Civil War. Author's Collection.*

Cased percussion pepperbox. *Thi
mint gun is signed "J. Collins,
London". It is ivory stocked with
silver nails decorating the ivory.
Hinged butt plate holds caps.
Collins was the successor to
Wilson. Russell Aitken Collectio*

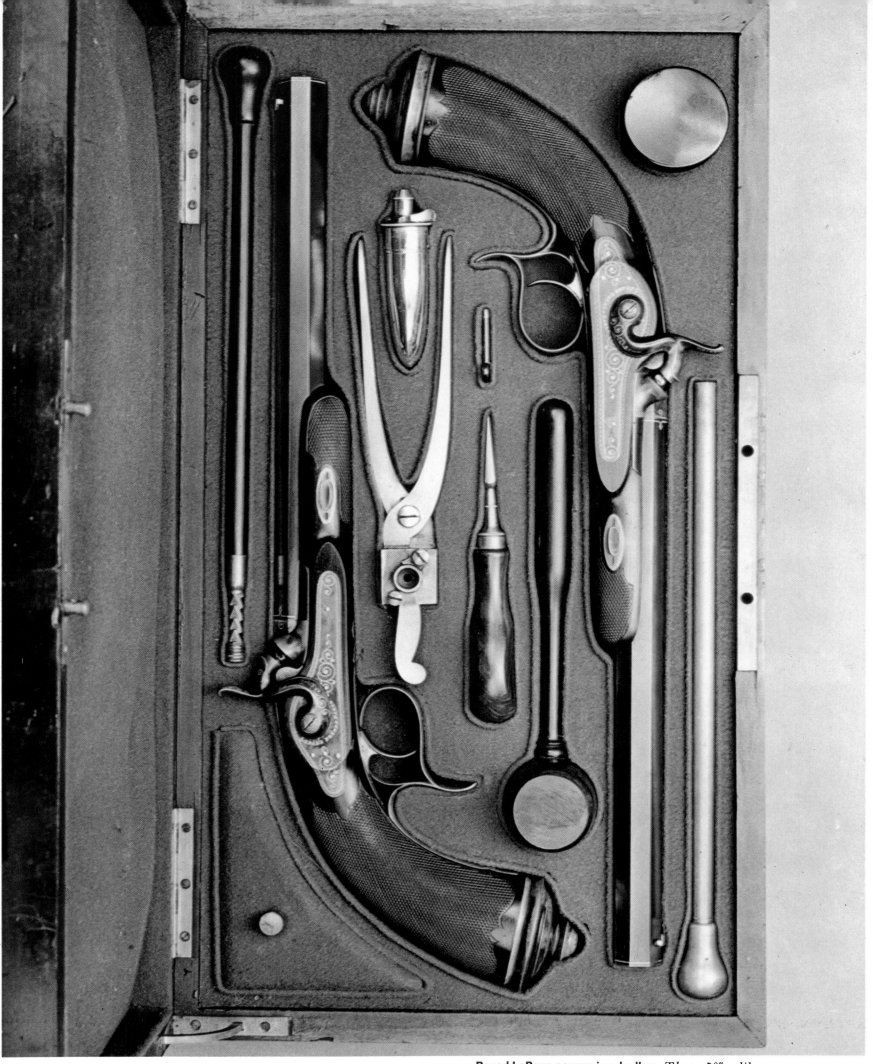

Boxed LePage percussion duellers. *These .50" calibre rifled pistols are stocked in ebony and inlaid with gold. The set belongs to George Vitt, Jr., whose great-grandfather bought them new from LePage.*

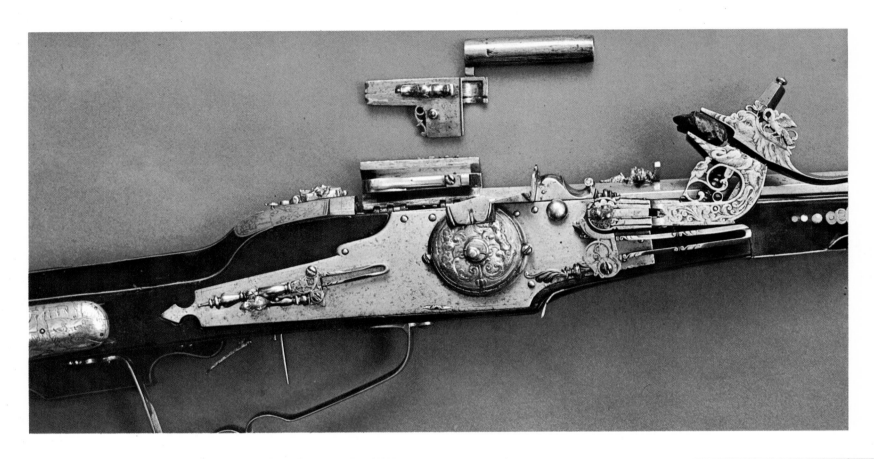

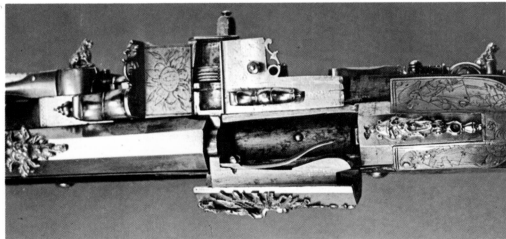

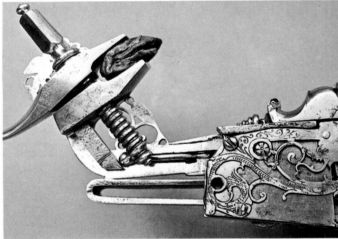

Breech-loading wheel lock. *This cartridge gun from the early or mid 17th century is loaded wth a steel cartridge which has its own pan and pan cover attached. The hinged breech is opened by lifting up and pulling back the gold mask on the barrel tang. A hunting rifle, it is South German in styling, and is decorated with applied trophies, a knight in tilting helm, halberds, helmet with panache, gauntlets, etc. Russell Aitken Collection.*

CHAPTER XI

BREECH LOADING

Even the inside of the lock is elaborately engraved and decorated. While probably never seen by the owner, and only on occasion by another locksmith, the engraving and carving of the spring terminals and the bridles which support the moving parts is as fine as the outside decoration. On the left, a sea serpent holds the cock spring in place. On the right, the bridle supporting the chain axle is carved into a bird-headed dragon looking over his shoulder at a rabbit munching a carrot. Russell Aitken Collection.

"THE CHIEF difficulty in running buffalo, as it seems to me, is that of loading the gun or pistol at full gallop. Many hunters for convenience sake carry three or four bullets in the mouth; the powder is poured down the muzzle of the piece, the bullet dropped in after it, the stock struck hard upon the pommel of the saddle, and the work is done. The danger of this is obvious. Should the blow on the pommel fail to send the bullet home, or should the bullet in the act of aiming, start from its place and roll towards the muzzle, the gun would probably burst in discharging. Many a shattered hand and worse casualties besides have been the result of such an accident. To obviate it, some hunters make use of a ramrod, usually hung by a string from the neck, but this materially increases the difficulty of loading. The bows and arrows which the Indians use in running buffalo have many advantages over firearms, and even white men occasionally employ them."

Then later:

"I—shot into her with both pistols in succession. My fire arms were all empty and I had in my pouch nothing but rifle bullets too large for the pistols and too small for the gun. I loaded the gun however, but as often as I leveled it to fire, the bullets would roll out of the muzzle and the gun returned only a report like a squib, as the powder harmlessly exploded. I rode in front of the buffalo and tried to turn her back but her eyes glared, her mane bristled, and, lowering her head she rushed at me with the utmost fierceness. . . . Riding to a little distance, I dismounted thinking to gather a handful of dry grass to serve the purpose of wadding, and load the gun at my leisure. No sooner were my feet on the ground than the buffalo came bounding in such a rage toward me that I jumped back again into the saddle with all dispatch. . . . At length bethinking me of the fringes at the seams of my buckskin trousers, I jerked off a few of them, and, reloading the gun, forced them down the

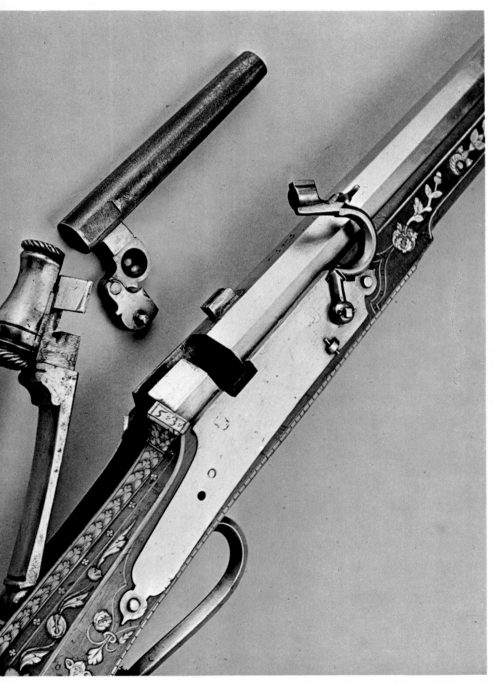

Peter Peck of Munich *made this scroll-butted breech-loading matchlock in 1553. The steel cartridge with attached pan and pan cover is removed from the breech for reloading by pressing back on the spring loaded orthoptic (tubular) rear sight. In addition to the date "'53" on the barrel and Peck's initials "P.P.", the coat-of-arms of Charles V, Holy Roman Emperor, is inlaid on the cheek of the stock. loa. 55¾", bbl 41½", cal. .60", smooth bore. The trigger is the large tiller visible in the picture. No.# W 1445, Bayerisches Nationalmuseum, Munich.*

barrel to keep the bullet in its place: then approaching, I shot the wounded buffalo through the heart. Sinking to her knees, she rolled over lifeless on the prairie."

This account appeared in Parkman's *The Oregon Trail* published first in 1847, describing his trip west in 1846. This was before the day of the breech-loading Sharps' rifle which accounted for so many buffalo that one model of the Sharps' rifle was identified as THE Buffalo Gun.

Having learned at first hand the disadvantages of a muzzle loader on horseback, Parkman was an enthusiastic reporter when his company of hunters on their return trip eastward ran into an army detachment. Parkman had gone west from Fort Leavenworth, up through what are now the Dakotas and Wyoming, along the trail to Oregon and the Pacific. His band of hunters and Astor trappers had then gone south through the eastern foothills of the Rockies and picked up the Santa Fe Trail heading east. When the party left Leavenworth they had avoided the fort as it was the westernmost outpost of the U.S. Army, and the Army disapproved of civilians wandering unprotected through sometimes hostile Cheyenne and Crow Indian territory. During Parkman's long trip, the U.S. went to war with Mexico. General Kearny set out from Fort Leavenworth with, among others, a company of St. Louis volunteers. These were the civilian soldiers whom Parkman encountered, on their way to take Santa Fe, and relieve the settlers in California.

Parkman describes the St. Louis volunteers' motley mixture of civilian clothing and military uniform and goes on: "Besides their swords and holster pistols, they carried slung from their saddles the excellent Springfield carbines, loaded at the breech." These cavalry carbines must have been Hall's rifled breechloaders made at Harpers Ferry arsenal. John W. Hall and William Thornton had patented a flintlock breechloader with a removable self-contained chamber in 1811. This gun was modernized with a percussion chamber, and a few thousand Hall rifles were manufactured at Harpers Ferry arsenal. It was at the Harpers Ferry arsenal

BREECH LOADING

that John Brown directed his famous raid, and at this same arsenal Christian Sharps learned his trade under Hall. The Sharps' breech-loading rifle did not appear until 1848, two years after Parkman's trip.

Breech loading, however, had been around for a long time. The earliest dateable guns that we know of, the Anholt Find guns in the Tøjhus Museet in Copenhagen, which antedate the death of Queen Margrethe in 1412, are stocked, wrought iron, breech-loading hand cannon or wall pieces, with separate chambers. An iron ball was loaded into the breech end of the barrel and an iron chamber loaded with powder was placed behind the breech containing the ball. Barrel and breech block were embedded in a heavy crude oak stock and the separate breech (which had a handle and looked like a rough iron beer mug) was held in place snug to the barrel by wedges driven in at the rear. Breech-loading small cannon similar to these are to be seen in the Metropolitan Museum in New York—one from Madrid—and tacked to the walls of the Musée de l'Armée in Paris. The latter are attributed to the British, but no one really knows. They have been on the Musée de l'Armée walls for hundreds of years.

The guns in the cannon hall of the Tøjhus are pretty well dated, as they came out of the wreck of a ship which was discovered north and east of Anholt in the Cattegut. The ship belonged to Queen Margrethe, the Semiramis of the North, Queen of Denmark, Norway and Sweden.

Breech loading is a necessity when the muzzle of a gun is exposed to enemy fire and the gun too heavy to move. Similarly, breech loading was the solution to Henry VIII's gun shields, some of which still survive in the Tower of London and the Victoria and Albert Museum. Obviously it would have been a poor piece of business to lay down your shield, walk around in front of it in order to pour powder and ram down a ball, then walk back around and resume fighting. These shield breechloaders, from what is left of them, seem to have been matchlocks. There are two other breech-loading guns of Henry's in the White Tower. This is not surprising

Royal Gunmaker *to the Saxon Court. Valentin Rewer in Dresden built this eight-groove, tip-down breech-loading flintlock sometime between 1703 and 1737. The gun is opened by pushing the convenient lever in front of the trigger guard to the left with the index finger. The cartridge, shown to the right of the open breech, is made of steel and has its own primer pan and steel. Cartridges like this were expensive to make and were never thrown away. The barrel is .60" calibre. Russell Aitken Collection.*

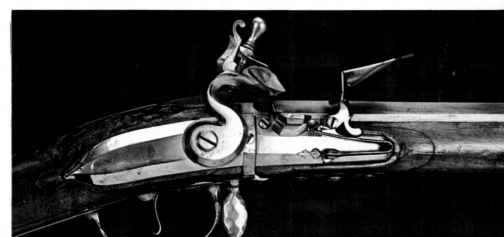

as they were German made wheel locks, originally, and the Germans and the Austrians had been making breech-loading wheel locks for a long time.

Fine dated or datable wheel lock breechloaders are to be seen today in the Kunsthistorisches Museum in Vienna and in the Armeria Reale in Turin. In the Vienna collection there is a case of self-spanning wheel lock petronels, six guns in all (vitrine number 11), which are breechloaders with iron cartridges. In addition to these fairly early examples, there is a three-shot revolving breechloader signed by Paolo Appiano, who was building guns in 1660. Two more breech-loading pieces are in the Vienna gallery. Both were made by an ingenious Viennese gunmaker, Michael Gull. One is a wheel lock built in the 1650's, with a barrel threaded to the receiver, similar in operation to the later Queen Anne turn-off barrel pistols. The wheel lock cock is reversed and comes up from behind the wheel in order to leave the turn-off barrel free. The other is a breech-loading flintlock which the same Michael Gull built around 1670. It has a hinged breech block with a steel cartridge or chamber which is fitted with a lug that slides into a slot in the barrel. The lug in the slot keeps the touchhole in the barrel and the cartridge in alignment. There are, however, many flintlock guns which employed breech loading in one or another form before the Hall rifle.

In the Armeria Reale in Turin, there is a beautiful little saddle carbine breechloader which is profusely decorated, engraved and inlaid with ivory. It was built around 1550, and works with a hinged breech and steel cartridges. Gen. Agostino Gaibi illustrates the little gun in his impressive book *Le Armi da Fuoco Portitali Italiane*. He describes the "Pistoletto" as being "selfloading"—a bit much, but the carbine is self-spanning, i.e., the wheel spring is wound without a key by the action of lowering the cock, which is interestingly behind instead of in front of the wheel.

The Armeria Reale also displays one of the finer collections of magazine breech-loading systems. They are of the Lorenzoni-Berselli-Chalembron-Cookson type which are loaded from two magazines, one containing lead balls, the other, powder. They all load by turning the gun up or down,

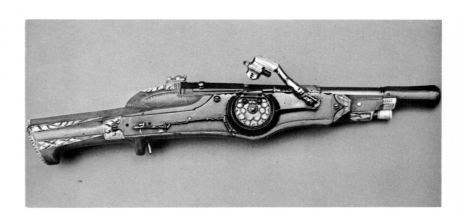

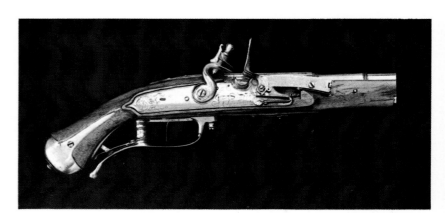

TOP: **Breech loading** *bell-mouth wheel lock pistol: .48" cal. s.b. 18" long with belt hook. The steel cartridge has a positioning lug which lines up the hole in the cartridge with the touch hole in the breech of the pistol. May have belonged to Ferdinand I, South German, 1540-50. No.# A 603, Kunsthistorisches Museum, Vienna.*

MIDDLE: **Louis Barbar of London** *made this turn-off barrel all-metal breech loader around 1700. The key twisted off the threaded barrel for loading. loa. 6", bbl 1¼", cal. .42". No.# 810, Musée de la Porte de Hal, Brussels.*

BOTTOM: **23³/₄" long breech-loading** *pistol with automatic priming was made in Hanover, Germany by Jan Sander between 1670 and 1715. Worked by swinging the trigger guard, it anticipated Fergusson by nearly a century. Joe Kindig Jr. Collection.*

Miquelet breech loader. *Made in Vienna around 1650 by Franz Jeradtel, this rifle employs the Spanish miquelet system with the heavy external main spring reversed to keep it out of the way. Signed "Jeiadtel yn Wien" the gun is 40¼" long with a 28¼" barrel. Deep grooved quick twist rifling. Land-to-land, bore .52", groove-to-groove, .58". No.# B 570, Tøjhus Museet, Copenhagen.*

Two-shot breech-loading *flintlock.*
Made by Thomerat in Paris for
Louis XIV c. 1670. The breech, shown
open, rotated in a pivot. It is incribed on
the barrel, "Magazin Royal". loa. 20",
bbl 14¹³⁄₁₆", cal. .46". No.# M 1768,
Musée de l'Armée, Paris.

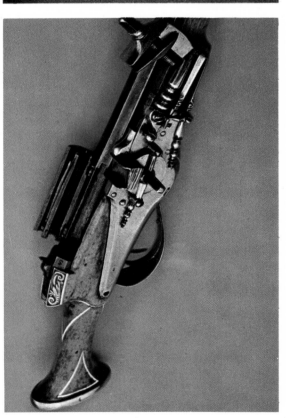

Pair of top-loading *flintlock pistols. Ornately decorated Carlsbad pistols which loaded*
by dropping the breech plug. The plug is lowered with a detachable crank handle. The
barrel is inscribed "Johann Adam Knod". The inscription around the loading
port; "G. E. SCHWIND BISTOHLL". Støckel lists a gunmaker "Schwend" who worked
in Germany in 1715. Knod was born in Carlsbad in 1690. Joe Kindig Jr. Collection.

TOP: **Hans Stockman hinged-breech** *wheel*
lock pistol was made in Dresden in 1610.
The sturdy, bone-inlaid pistol is 27¾"
long, barrel and breech, 21⁹⁄₁₆", cal. .62",
s.b. No.# M641-1927, Victoria
and Albert Museum, London.

John Hall's Harpers Ferry
breech-loading military flintlock
was patented in 1811 and used
in the Seminole Indian wars
(1818). Winchester Gun Museum,
New Haven, Conn.

BREECH LOADING

depending on whether the magazines are in front of the breech or in back, and rotating a side lever. The side lever is attached to a cylinder with recesses which picked up the ball and powder by gravity feed from their magazines and dropped them in proper order in the breech. The drum also served as a solid breech block, thereby requiring that it be fitted very closely, to prevent gas leakage and fouling and, more seriously, the ignition flash from starting the powder magazine. Many of these guns have or had priming magazines, which operated with the loading lever which also raised the cock. They were complicated pieces of machinery and required great mechanical precision in manufacture. However they did provide a rapid rate of fire especially when they were new and tightly fitted. When they wore, the insurance rates went up. The guns in Turin are signed Giacomo Berselli, Michael Lorenzonus (Lorenzoni), and Gio Pietro Callin. Berselli probably invented the system, although Lorenzoni got the credit. Cookson, in London, was a few years later than Lorenzoni—1686 versus 1684; Cookson in Boston around 1703 and Chalembron, (Chelembron, Cholambron—the experts all spell it differently and so perhaps did Chalembron), built his guns in Pondicherry, India around 1780.

Other examples of the Lorenzoni systems are in the Tower of London, the Musée de l'Armée and in private collections such as Joe Kindig's in York, Pa., and the Renwick collection in Arizona. Keith Neal, at Bishopstrode, has a hinged breechloader with steel cartridges, which was built in London in 1710. Like so many of its German counterparts, it is rifled. The Neal collection also contains several German and Austrian breechloaders from the 1600's including a drop-down action similar to a modern shotgun or double rifle, which was built for the Duke of Saxe Weimar around 1680, and a breech-loading miquelet built by Michael Gull. Howard Blackmore describes the rifle at some length and illustrates it in his book, *Guns and Rifles of the World*. Its most interesting feature is a rifled steel cartridge with the flash pan attached which screws into corresponding rifling in the barrel.

In another area entirely, but similar in method of operation to the Lorenzoni systems, are the many weapons built by the Kalthoff family of Copenhagen gunsmiths. In the Tøjhus Museet Armory Hall, alongside a German steel cartridge breech-loading rifle built in 1585, there are racks of Kalthoff breech-auto-loading wheel and flintlocks. The oldest, dated 1645, and inscribed *Das Erste* was built by Peter Kalthoff, gunmaker to the Danish King Frederik III. The powder magazine is in the wooden butt stock and the bullets in a magazine in the forestock under the barrel. Other Kalthoffs emigrated to England and Russia where they, too, built auto-loading rifles which vary somewhat in design but all have the characteristic Kalthoff profile of the breech-loading rifle illustrated here. They were a very prolific family and Støckel, in his directory of gunmakers, devotes three pages to the different members of the family and their marks, usually a knight standing at attention holding a halberd. The Kalthoff guns, while they suffered from the problems occasioned by wear, and had the hazard of a loose powder magazine in the stock of the gun, were easy guns to shoot rapidly. They had such military advantage over either muzzle- or breech-loading wheel or flintlocks that they were issued to special troops in the Danish army and are known to have been used in battle. Caspar Kalthoff, the brother of Peter who was in London, built a horizontally operating repeater. This design for a gun may well have been the inspiration for Abraham Hill's patent application in 1664 which refers to "A gun or pistol for small shott carying seven or eight charges of the same in the stock of the gun."

Which invention is remarked upon by Pepys in his *Diary* who says he saw: "a gun to discharge seven times, the best of all devices I ever saw, and very servicable and not a bawble." This, two years before Hill's patent. In Salzburg, Sigmund Klett was building Kalthoff type repeaters a few years after *Das Erste* (in 1652). Other versions of the Kalthoff were built by gunmakers in Gottorp and Utrecht.

The last of the breechloaders prior to the invention of the expanding cartridge were the guns designed by La Chau-

BREECH LOADING

mette and Ferguson on the La Chaumette principle. (Ignoring revolvers, as they will have a chapter of their own.) These guns had a large hole drilled in either the top, side, or through from top to bottom of an otherwise solid breech. The holes were threaded for a screw with a very steep pitch. The screw most logically attached to a moveable trigger guard which in one turn or more dropped the screw out of the barrel about an inch. Top loaders and side loaders of course worked differently. If the screw went down, as it did in the La Chaumette guns, the ball went in first and the gun then tipped down to seat the ball and make room for the powder charge which was then poured in. If too much powder was poured in, it was forced up and out of the gun when the screw was elevated. Chaumette started his gun design on paper in 1700, but he was one of the many good Huguenot craftsmen who found it healthier to emigrate from France after the revocation of the Edict of Nantes made life and property ownership a bit uncertain under Louis XIV. A fellow countryman, Bidet, who did not invent the bidet, built several fine guns on the La Chaumette principle, including one presentation piece for George I of England.

A romantic character, Major Patrick Ferguson, improved on the Chaumette system in two ways: he put vertical cuts on his screw in addition to the steep twist thread to cut out the fouling that formed after every shot, and he had a smooth rounded recess cut in the screw which formed the back of the breech when the gun was closed. In a Woolwich test, in the rain, Ferguson, who was a crack shot, was able to get off as many as six aimed shots a minute. He averaged four shots even while in motion walking toward the target. The story about Ferguson is worth telling. He came to North America with a company of one hundred riflemen equipped and trained with his rifle. The very fact that it was a rifle made it shoot farther and more accurately than the smoothbore Brown Bess musket of the regular British troops or even the heavy but crude, rifled *scheutzens* of the Hessians.

Ferguson wrote a prophetic letter home telling of the range and accuracy of the Pennsylvania squirrel rifles in the hands of the frontier hunter-soldiers with the Continentals. Ferguson was wounded badly at Brandywine in a British effort to flank a body of American troops at Chadd's Ford. Returned to active duty two years later, but without his company of expert riflemen, he stopped a bullet from one of the squirrel rifles that he had admired, at the battle of King's Mountain. He was thirty-two years old when he demonstrated his rifle at Woolwich and thirty-six when he was killed at King's Mountain in 1780. Of the hundred or more guns which were built, and there must have been more, to equip a company of men, only one original Military Ferguson survives. It is now in Morristown National Historical Park in New Jersey. How it got there nobody knows. Probably it was picked up on the battlefield by an American who used it through the rest of his term of enlistment and brought it home as a war trophy. Durs Egg, the fine London gunsmith, however, built several commercial models of the Ferguson. Keith Neal has one in his collection which is almost brand new. It has a curious flat wood checkering of large squares. The silver furniture has a hall-mark for the year 1777, and it is inscribed "The Gift of Bryan Scotney Esquire to Major General Hector Munro." Other Durs Egg Fergusons are in the Tøjhus, the Smithsonian, Windsor Castle, West Point and various private collections.

Breech-loading cannon. *Capo Bianco.* Corona e Palma militare.

Breech-loading wheel lock petronel. *Caspar Spät? or Elias Becker? made the stag and ivory inlaid stock in Augsburg around 1668. The pistol is cocked by moving the cock backward and then lowering it again. loa. 22½", cal. .60", rifled. No.# A584. Kunsthistorisches Museum, Vienna.*

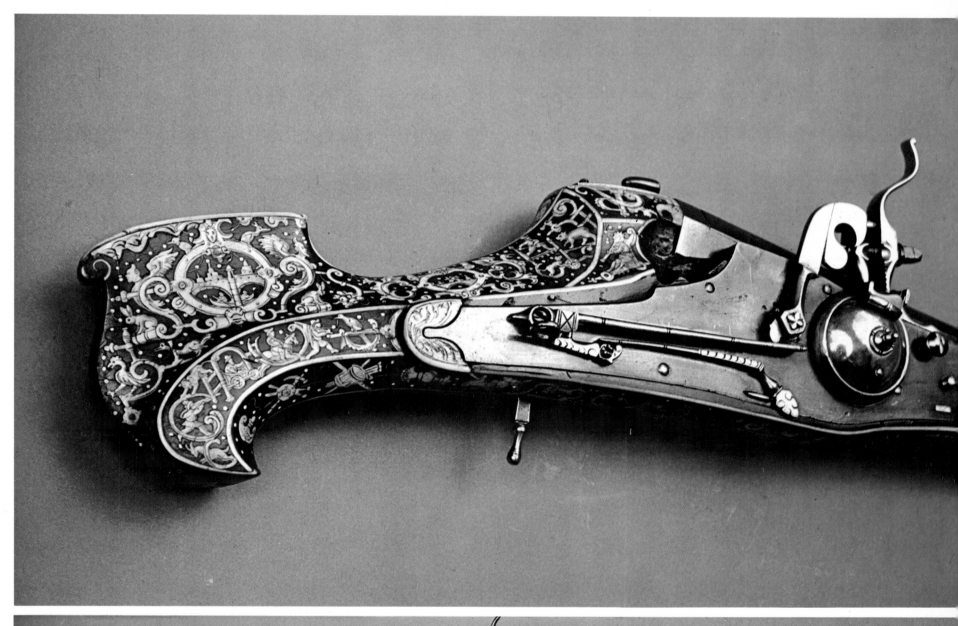

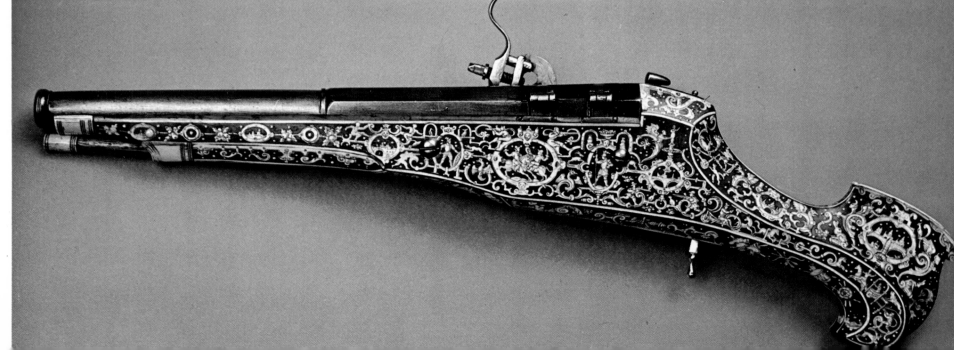

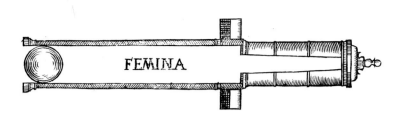

CHAPTER XII

THE COMIC HISTORY OF BULLETS

WHAT WITH one thing and another, it took all of the traditional stolidity of the Flemish national character to light the fuse of a hollow iron cannon ball filled with black gunpowder. These cast iron monster grenades were loaded into the barrels of siege cannon, in front of their charge of propellant powder, whereupon an expert standing in front of the cannon stuck a stick of burning pitch pine down the barrel. In theory, when the cannon ball fuse was so ignited, it would explode over enemy territory. In practice, it led to a drastic reduction of the number of experts, cannoneers, and weak-at-the-joint cannon, giving the whole sport a bad name.

Later on some coward discovered that unlit, powder-filled cannon balls exploded on impact, and the job of recruiting artillery experts became less arduous.

Very little, as a matter of fact, was known about projectiles until the eighteenth century when the noble science of ballistics was invented. Newton had previously made some observations about gravitational effects on falling objects, in 1740 the first ballistic pendulum was constructed to measure the velocity of projectiles, and in 1742 one Benjamin Robins published a treatise on the theory of rifling. Up to this time the chief scientific instrument of the cannoneer was the gunner's quadrant which, when hung from the mouth of the gun with one angle flush on the bottom of the barrel hole, gave the operator his angle of elevation. With this knowledge the correct angle could be maintained once the cannon had been zeroed in by trial-and-error.

One of the earliest projectiles in written history is David's sling stone with which he killed Goliath. The author has seen little ceramic pellets which were purportedly sling stones made by the ancients out of clay in areas where suitable pebbles were not available.

Arrows are of course a form of projectile, and since ancient times they have been feathered to give them a spinning flight. In Egyptian and Babylonian carvings of war and hunting bows, it is hard to see whether the feathering was angled,

but fletched, or feathered, arrows made to give the shaft a rotating flight were found in the large supply buried with Tutankhamen. Crossbow bolts or quarrels were fletched, sometimes with leather, wood or metal instead of feathers, at a very slight angle to the shaft in order to impart a slow rotation. The earliest illustrated cannon shot an adaptation of the crossbow bolt. Garros or arrows were standard equipment along with other types of projectiles for use in cannon and handguns as late as the sixteenth century. Quarrel guns are mentioned in a treasury report of Henry IV (1399-1413), and the Tower of London lists musket arrows, 892 of them, in 1595. In 1599, fifty-six of them needed new feathers. The missiles themselves were variously called quarriaux, carreauz, garros, garroks and musket arrows. Some of these, according to a 1356 arsenal list, quoted in Napoleon's *Etudes,* were winged with brass for cannon and differentiated in the early inventory from other heavy arrows, which were used with espringales and ballistas.

Arrows fired from guns were still being used in naval actions around 1600. Usually they were fire arrows, with a wad of burning tow around the shaft designed to set fire to an enemy's sails and rigging. In 1588 Sir Francis Drake ordered 500 muskets and 1,000 arrows for the muskets. The Privy Council gave him 200.

While it is true that the Venetian, Nicolo Tartaglia, recommended the use of geometry in estimating target distances in 1537, and in England in 1672 Captain Thomas Venn explained the use of the gunner's quadrant and a system for estimating distance in his book, *Military and Maritime Discipline,* the truth was that most artillerymen couldn't read or write. Except for the gunnery school which Louis XIV set up in Douai in 1679, artillerymen matriculated from taverns with press gang sergeants for tutors.

The projectiles of the mechanical monsters, the ballista, onager, springal and trebucket, were the bullets of the new cannon. With the exception of dead horses, which are too big, practically everything has been shot out of cannons, in-

Military Antiquities, *Francis Grose, London, 1786.*

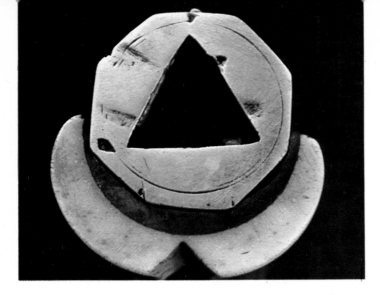

THE COMIC HISTORY OF BULLETS

cluding captured enemy truce emissaries returning rejected peace overtures. The favorite early projectiles were stone balls, and piles of these still survive in Rome's Castel Sant' Angelo, where they were neatly quarried from classic Roman sculpture. Stone cannon balls were fashionable for a long time and for good reason. They were the only material available for such giant cannon as the Constantinople cannon and the Ehrenbreitstein casting, which shot 800- and 600-pound granite balls. Also, they made a fine kind of gritty shrapnel when they hit the paving blocks of a medieval guildhall square. The Amberg bombard and Mons Meg in Edinburgh both shot stone bullets, and the North Italians, who have always had both an affinity for stone and a good steady supply, had a business which was a profitable sideline for the pupils of Michaelangelo and Donatello—whittling ammunition.

The two disadvantages of stone—its abrasive effect on gun barrels and its crumbly quality when it struck something really solid, led the French to start using iron cannon balls against the Italians when they invaded Italy in the sixteenth century. The Condottieri, who had not been playing for keeps, took this very badly and complained about the violation of the rules of war. That the Italians lost was no news, but this time they blamed it on the superior firepower of the French, whose iron cannon balls went farther and hit harder than the more artistic carved stone ones. At least this is what Gibbon says in *The Decline and Fall*.

Once the art of casting reasonably round balls out of metal had been perfected, the casting of lead balls for the smaller-bore handguns was a cinch. As a matter of fact, lead being the easier material to melt, it may have been the first bullet material, and is listed in the inventories of the fourteenth century British arsenal.

Thus far the shape of the bullet was round and the barrel of the gun was smooth. Firing a gun was like throwing a ball, and the trajectory of the small lead ball was erratic and precipitous. However, as soon as the making of guns became as skilled a craft as the making of crossbows—some time around

TOP: **"Augustinus Kotter, 1627"** *Augsburg, loa. 44½"
bbl 33½" No.# B 279, Tøjhus Museet, Copenhagen.*
MIDDLE: **Also Kotter,** *1632. loa. 38¾" bbl 28½"
No.# B 280, Tøjhus Museet, Copenhagen.*
BOTTOM TWO: **Andreas Neidhardt of Elsinore,** *made
these cookie cutter barrels for the King of Denmark
between 1631 and 1653. bbls from 38" to 40". Nos.
B 164, and B 163, Tøjhus Museet, Copenhagen.*

Italian cannon projectile. *It whistled as it went. The turbine buckets on the side of the projectile made a screaming noise as the iron projectile churned along on a vertical axis toward its target. The cannon that shot it was designed by S. Robert in Naples in 1873. The name of the cannon, Paolo. No.# 1635-Q 101, Museo Storico Nazionale d'Artiglieria, Turin.*

Wheel lock rifle *by Daniel Fitsholsky (c. 1730) has two barrels, one inside the other. This was an invention of Cornelius Klett, in 1653. This finely decorated gun has silver and rhinoceros horn inlay, gilt ramrod and pipes. loa. 46", bbls 34" plus. The inner barrel is .35" calibre, multi-groove; the outer barrel is .60" cal. with 9 deep grooves. The rifling makes ⅞ths of turn in the 34 inches. No.# 1394, Tøjhus Museet, Copenhagen.*

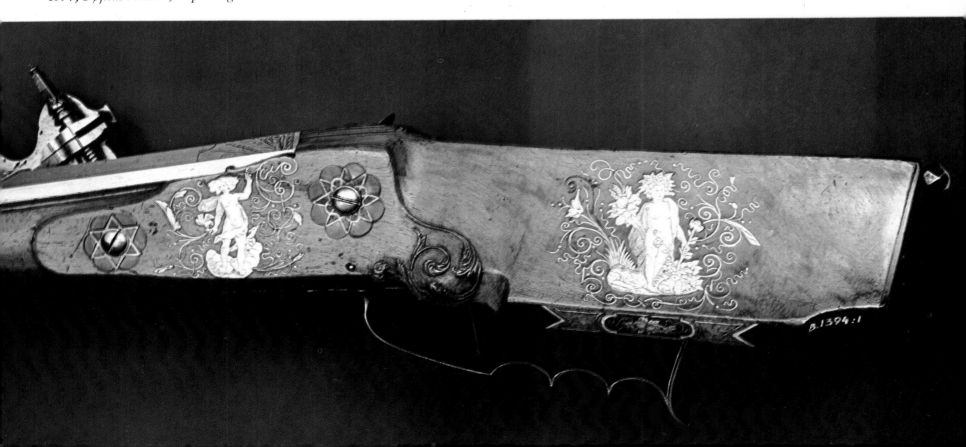

1500—gunsmiths began trying to design guns that would be effective at more than point-blank range. Rifled barrels and bullet-shaped bullets came hand in hand. Surviving sixteenth century wheel lock guns built in Germany had either slow or quick twists. Some, it is true, are smoothbore and some had straight rifling which did no good, but the majority of those that have come down to us are rifled correctly. While rifling improved the flight accuracy of a round bullet or ball, a cylindrically-shaped bullet with a conical point benefitted more from rifling, as it took up more twist from the rifling, besides traveling faster than a ball, because of decreased wind resistance. This was learned by gunmakers and shooters early in the sixteenth century. Bullet molds for shaped bullets survive, as do Leonardo da Vinci sketches of modern-looking projectiles. It's hard, though, to tell from the mirror-written caption how much of these designs was inspired by art and how much by a knowledge of ballistics.

The science of ballistics as applied to handguns is not very complicated. Interior ballistics refer to what happens to the bullet inside the gun barrel, and exterior ballistics tell what happens when gravity and wind resistance change the direction and velocity of the bullet after it emerges from the barrel. Wind resistance and the pull of gravity were calculated by firing at targets at measured distances such as 100, 200, 500 and a thousand yards, and measuring the distance that the bullet dropped from the center of the bull's-eye at progressive ranges. In this way it was easy to calculate the curve of drop of different sizes and weights of bullets propelled by different amounts of powder. Here it was discovered that the shape of the bullet mattered. The bullet with the best streamlining had the least wind resistance and traveled farther before the constant pull of gravity downed it. Two other factors help to stabilize the flight of the bullet. One was the twist given to the bullet by rifling in the barrel. The other was the sectional density. The longer and narrower the bullet—the more arrow-shaped—the greater the stability in flight; just as a long, narrow boat creates less of a bow wave than a short, chunky one.

In the last half of the 18th century, theoretical science began to speculate on wind resistance, leading to the shape of modern projectiles up to, and including, rockets to the moon. Simple turbulence caused by the air rushing in to fill the void behind the backs of square-ended bullets was partially cured by the boattail bullet shapes of the U. S. .30 caliber and the British .303 caliber military cartridges. The old bullets, with their black powder charges, didn't travel so fast or so far that they created very complicated problems. A round-nosed heavy slug such as the bullet for the .44/40 Winchester, or even the celebrated Minie ball of Civil War fame, traveled with sufficient accuracy for the distance that a black powder charge would push it. Such a slug, however, needed the stability of the spin that rifling gave it, and this was a lesson that gunmakers kept forgetting. Although some of the earliest guns, such as wheel locks of the sixteenth century, were rifled, many later later weapons were not. Rifling, like breechloading, was invented and forgotten many times. The increased accuracy of a rifled gun was demonstrated time after time, yet military weapons continued to be predominately smoothbore till the mid-nineteenth century, partially on a basis of economy and partially because of the belief that the individual foot soldier could not hit anything with a rifle anyway, and all that counted was the group fire of closely massed infantry. This theory was thoroughly disproved by an American demonstration of selective, aimed fire at British soldiers in the late 1770's. But the Americans hadn't remembered their lessons either. Despite the fact that the Pennsylvania squirrel rifle descended from the German *Jaeger,* which was almost always rifled, six out of seven of the finest Kentucky's in existence in Joe Kindig's collection in York, Pennsylvania, are smoothbore. Their straight, well-made barrels will shoot right along with the best modern Winchester at ranges up to fifty yards, as would a fine smoothbore English duelling pistol, but it would take an awfully unlucky elephant on the downhill side to get hit at 200 yards. Those man-dropping shots from the Kentucky woodsman's deadly homebrewed smoothbore at 500 yards were made before the ruler was invented.

In between forgetting to rifle the barrel of otherwise well-made guns, gunsmiths turned out some pretty interesting shapes and styles. If it wasn't science, it was fun. Valterius started the fun with his gun that shot around corners. The barrel took a sharp 90-degree turn right in the middle. Of course, nobody ever built or fired one of these, but they kept turning up in gun illustrations for hundreds of years.

Then there are the square-bored guns. One is in the Metropolitan Museum, undoubtedly drilled by a square Arab, and several samples of another are in the New Armoury of the Tower of London. The latter are the work of a gun designer and promoter by the name of James Puckle, who patented a hand-cranked flintlock gatling gun in 1718. It had square bullets to be shot through a square barrel at heathens, and an interchangeable barrel and cylinder to shoot round bullets at Christians. Before and since, imagination has run riot. The Tøjhus Museet in Copenhagen has a selection of weapons which have barrel bores in cookie-cutter shapes and apparently shot bullets with three, five or seven scallops, as the bullet moulds survive along with the guns. These cookie cutters were built by a Danish gunsmith from Elsinore, Andreas Neidhardt, who worked between 1631 and 1653. A century later, a fine German gunmaker, Joseph Mons, built sporting rifles with an inside and outside barrel in the sectional shape of a three-leaf clover. It is doubtful, however, whether this design was intended for a clover-shaped bullet. Probably a round ball rode on the lands and the patch fitted into the clover-shaped grooves: at least this was the professional opinion of its owner, Leonard Heinrich, the former armorer of the Metropolitan Museum. And, rounding up the better known examples of non-round experiments, the Tøjhus Museet in Copenhagen has a gun with a heart-shaped bore, and the Museo d'Artiglieria in Turin has a cannon of World War I vintage which fired a lens-shaped projectile edgewise from a parabolic or elliptical smoothbore barrel. The projectile has turbine buckets, or air scoops on both flattish sides to make it howl as it churns through the air. Finally, a cousin not too far removed from the Puckle gun is the Dardic pistol, whose promoter conceived the idea that the world needed a three-sided cartridge. He chickened out, however, and had a round-sectioned bullet coming out of a three-sided cartridge.

Even with a perfectly round hole in the barrel of a gun, it is still possible to shoot some pretty bizarre junk out of the end. Chain shot, bar shot, cannister and grape shot were designed to mangle people or tear out the rigging of a man-of-war. Pointed-nosed steel bullets with or without an explosive charge in the projectile have been made to pierce armor. High explosive bullets explode on impact, tearing big holes in people or things, and tracers spew out a trail of burning magnesium so that the gunner can see where his bullet went.

At the beginning of the use of guns in warfare, bullet wounds were considered to be invariably fatal, and often they were, especially if they took bits of dirty clothing into the wound with them. Today's military cartridges have jacketed bullets which make neat clean holes through you. This makes for neater corpses.

French inventors C. Pottet in 1829, and C. E. Minie in 1859, designed soft-lead cylindro-conical bullets with anvils at the base to force the lead into the grooves of the rifling. In the meantime, Greener and Needham patented similar devices in England, and the British experimented with a muzzle-loading belted ball which fitted into the two grooves of the Brunswick rifle. In 1867, Boxer used a baked clay plug at the base of the bullet to force expansion against the lands, and the predecessor of the Winchester, the Volcanic rifles and pistols, used a propelling charge of fulminate in the base of the lead bullet which was not only supposed to propel the bullet out of the gun, but force the sides of the bullet into the grooves. It didn't.

While a lot has been learned over the past hundred years about the behavior of bullets, it is only since the Second World War that X-ray and high-speed photography have been combined to photograph the bullet in flight and even as it makes its quick trip down the barrel of the rifle. Even today, however, as was done a hundred and two hundred years ago, individual bullets are weighed on delicate scales

THE COMIC
HISTORY OF
BULLETS

to make sure that there are no hidden air holes in the lead castings which would unbalance the bullet in flight and send it lobbing in the wrong direction.

When soft lead bullets of whatever shape were rammed down the barrels of muzzle loaders, they were inevitably hammered out of shape, and they flew from the barrel like the lopsided slugs that they were. In order to correct this, undersized balls were used with patches of cloth or chamois. If the patch stayed with the ball on its way out the barrel and separated from the ball after leaving the muzzle of the gun (much as a spent rocket section falls away in flight), the bullet had a chance to make an accurate trip. If the patch was shot or burned through and the ball went ahead, the ball would make a couple of rapid ricochets off the sides of the bore and head in the direction imparted by the last bounce. The British in the seventeenth century came closest to solving this problem with their breech-loading, screw-barrel, Queen Anne pistols. A wrench twisted off the rifled barrel and a slightly oversized ball was dropped into a close-fitting chamber, powder poured in back of the ball, and the gun reassembled. This was the best shooting gun of its period. The burning powder built pressure before forcing the ball to accept the rifling, the ball was not deformed by being hammered down the muzzle, nor was it too loose for the rifling to do any good. Once loaded, with the pan cover closed, a Queen Anne pistol was pretty weatherproof. It would deliver one well-aimed shot whenever needed, and could be unloaded safely by twisting off the barrel.

These guns, too, went out of style, and the smoothbore muzzle loader held the field until Pauly invented the self-obdurating (flexible, expanding mouth) cartridge, which sealed the gases from the breech and made the breech-loading gun with fixed cartridge and ammunition a practical reality.

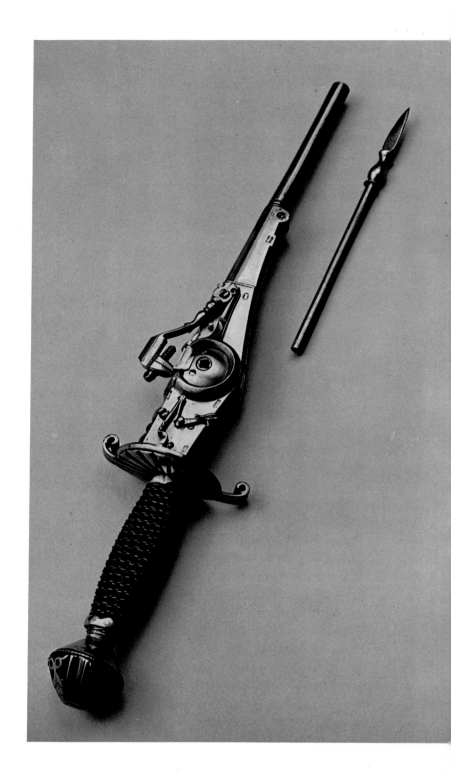

French-designed dagger-shaped pistol. *Made around 1550, this wheel lock pistol shot arrows. loa. 16", bbl 9½", cal. .29". No.# IX/95 (795), Musée de la Porte de Hal Brussels.*

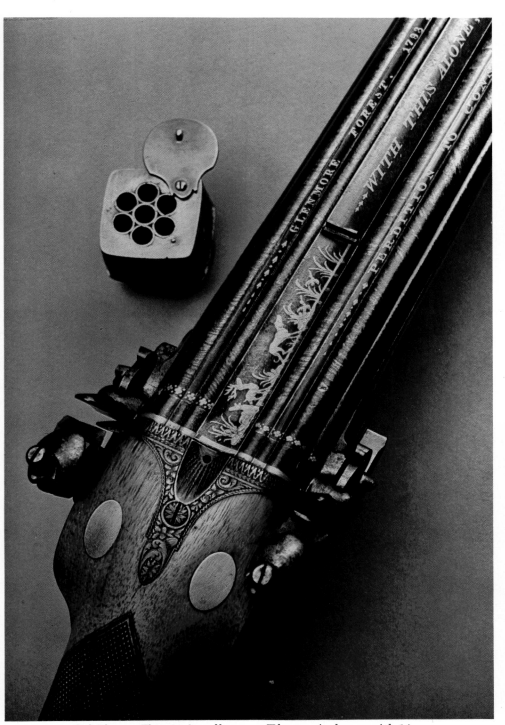

Three-barrel revolver *which shoots darts. This pistol was made in Nuremberg around 1530 for Charles V. May have been worked on by Charles V. The barrels are rotated by turning a wing nut on the butt. The breech of the barrel cluster has the double eagles with the motto of Charles V, "Plus Ultra". loa. 16¼", bbls 8", cal. .29". The arrows or darts, split and slightly sprung at the back to keep them from sliding out of the barrel, are identical to the darts with the Porte de Hal museum pistol illustrated here. No.# N/49, Armeria Reale, Turin.*

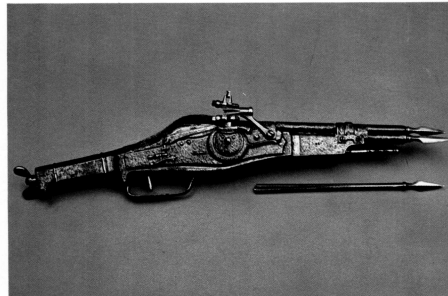

Col. Thomas Thornton's *volley gun. The gun is shown with 14 barrels. It could also be converted to shoot only seven barrels at a time. The gun is inscribed variously: "Dupe & Co." "Perdition to Conspirators", "Glenmore Forest 1793", and "With this alone I'll defend Robro Camp, 1795". Each of the 14 barrels has seven flat sides. Smooth bore. The bore of each barrel is approximately .30" cal. loa. 34¾", bbls (all 14) 20⁵⁄₁₆". No. Ae 1 (5866), Musée d'Armes, Liège.*

Benin Relief. *Bronze plaque cast in Benin, Nigeria in 1525 of a Portuguese marine wearing body armour and carrying a matchlock.*

Monumenta Pulveris Pyrii
Cannon founders shop with a portrait of Berthold Schwartz hanging in the right hand arch. Engraved by Philip Galle, circa 1570.

Field Cannon. *Field cannon with elevating mechanism from the Munich Codex, Manuscript 600, circa 1390-1400.*

CHAPTER XIII

THE SEALED BREECH: PINFIRE, NEEDLEFIRE, RIMFIRE, CENTER FIRE

IN 1812, SAMUEL JOHANNES PAULY was issued a French patent for the first breech-loading gun which fired an expanding (self-obdurating) center-fire cartridge. The cartridge sealed the breech of the gun at the moment the powder exploded. The soft-brass and paper case was pushed into the sides of the breech wall, keeping the hot gases from escaping to the rear. This simple device made breech loading a practicality. All of the previous breechloaders had worked with loose powder and ball, or had employed a solid iron cartridge which had no flexibility and sealed the breech only as well as it was exactly machined to fit. After burning gas had corroded the breech closure, the iron cartridge no longer provided a seal. Pauly's brass-headed cardboard case swelled at the moment of explosion and then contracted enough to allow extraction. The Pauly tubes were not intended to be reloaded.

Pauly had made another small but important step. He observed the detonating powders and lock which Forsyth had invented and Prelat had patented in France in 1810. Pauly put the detonating powder into a primer rosette within the cartridge itself. This eliminated the fulminate holder, the fulminate dispenser, the ingenious automatic primer feeds, the pellet pockets with their spring-loaded firing pins, and a host of unnecessary external gadgetry. Only one or two persons, including Dreyse, who was then one of Pauly's workmen, realized the importance of what Pauly had done. Brillat de Savarin, as the head of a committee commissioned to test the system, missed the point completely. He reported to the Society for the Encouragement of National Industry, that Pauly's guns did not hang fire, burned less powder, could not be double-loaded, were waterproof against either rain or fog, and eliminated the need for a ramrod. All these points were true, but secondary to the importance of the invention itself.

Someone else who missed the point, but shouldn't have, was Napoleon. It was after Moscow and perhaps the Emperor was too cold to think. In 1813 Pauly demonstrated his gun and the new cartridges to one of Napoleon's generals, the Duc de Rovigo. It was a sight to gladden the heart of any ammunition manufacturer. Pauly, firing his own weapon which shot brass-based center-fire shot shell with green (for ball) and yellow (for shot) cardboard sleeves, burned up twenty-two rounds in just under two minutes. He should never have demonstrated the gun's consumption of ammunition to a logistics expert who had lost his baggage trains.

Despite Rovigo's enthusiastic recommendation, the Emperor hammer-headedly made a comment worthy of all army ordnance chiefs of all time: "The trials have not convinced me..."

Waterloo was only a year away.

Dreyse got the point, however. He returned to Germany and set up an arms manufactory in his home town of Sommerda where, shortly after Waterloo, he began the experiments which led to his invention of the first bolt-action cartridge breechloader, the Prussian needle gun. While Pauly's gun worked with a split receiver, the top of which hinged upward (as did the "Robert à Paris" pinfire shotgun which succeeded it), Dreyse's needle gun had a much more compact action, which was better suited for military use. Pauly's gun is a delightfully balanced lightweight shotgun which is a pleasure to bring to the shoulder. Dreyse's military rifle, which was not perfected until 1841, had a straight bolt which drew back the breech in a line with the barrel. The spring-loaded needle firing pin traveled through a channel in the breech and drove through the entire length of the body of the cartridge containing the powder charge until it hit and detonated the primer. The primer, for no good reason, was placed far forward in the cartridge, just behind the bullet and wad. The needle was, therefore, right in the middle of the cartridge at the moment of explosion, and the heat, after repeated firing, crystallized the firing pin (or needle) which became brittle as glass and eventually broke off. While the needle gun was a military success and was imitated by other countries (including the Italians who built a needle gun called the Carcano in 1868), the surviving needle guns with needles intact are as scarce as hens' teeth. The French finally,

Dr. Edward Maynard's *own cap-lock gun. Built in 1845 to support his patent application, the cased gun has three sets of barrels, all sorts of loading and take-down tools, spare parts in a package with notes in the doctor's handwriting. Rolls of the original Maynard caps and reloadable brass cases with a hole in the back to admit the flash from the external cap primer make this cased set complete. George Rowbottom Collection.*

THE SEALED BREECH

despite Napoleon's verdict, came up with an improved version named after its inventor, the Chassepot. The Chassepot had a great advantage over the Dreyse. The primer was in the rear of the cartridge, so the needle was not subjected to the heat of the explosion.

When the Prussian military learned of the Dreyse needle fire, they made such a well-kept secret of it that the Danes, the Austrians, and the French never knew what hit them. Muzzle loading died hard. The British Ordnance kept reviving it as though it were the King James Version, and only in 1866 dismissed their muzzle loaders and adapted the breech-loading Snider single shot rifle. Thouvenin[1] in France and N. S. Jessen [2] in Denmark attracted the attention of the military mind and set guns back fifty years by the invention of the Tige, or pillar breech—a muzzle loader with a fixed bolt or bar extending into the chamber. These guns were loaded with loose powder and the bullet rammed home in the old way, but when the hollow-based bullet hit the pillar it was forced to expand into the grooves by blows on the ramrod. This slowed military firepower down to a most satisfactory snail's pace.

In the United States at the time of the Civil War there were a number of breech-loading guns which fired cartridges. Some of the guns had cartridges with holes in the breech which admitted the flash from a separate primer. These were the Burnside, fired with a conventional percussion cap, and the Maynard, which was detonated by caps in rolls, which Dr. Maynard fed over a percussion nipple from a magazine in the lock plate. Others working with a separate primer were the Smith, with a rubber cartridge, the Starr, the Allen and the Perry. The British shipped some side-gate Needham guns to the U.S. built on modified needle gun principle. Rimfire guns were made by both Sharps and Spencer and some of the European pinfires found their way to the U.S., but the demand for arms was so great that percussion muzzle loaders were the standard. In *U.S. Infantry and Rifle Tactics* published in 1863, the drill instruction is entirely for muzzle loaders. It reads: "Take the (paper) cartridge in the thumb

and first two fingers, and place the end of it in the teeth." And for four pages of small type the manual continues: "Tear, charge (pour), draw (ramrod), ram (cartridge), return (rammer), halfcock, prime, shoulder, aim, fire."

In the meantime, back in France, where the breech-loading cartridge was invented, patents had been issued to Lefaucheux for a center-fire pinfire cartridge, and a year or so before that, Flobert of Paris was producing the first rimfire cartridges. The ordinary pinfire, with the pin sticking out the side of the cartridge, was invented by Robert. The pinfires worked well and were the most popular sporting cartridge outside of England and the United States for forty years. Fine pinfire rifles, shotguns, and pistols were made in both France and Germany, including so many by Lefacheaux's factories that he, not Robert, is generally credited with the invention. The pinfire principle, by the way, survives today in the tiny Austrian and Japanese charm pistols.

The rimfire cartridge, which evolved out of the percussion cap, originally contained nothing but the percussion mix, no actual gunpowder, and its use was in saloon or gallery guns where a very small bullet was fired indoors at targets only a few feet away. This was similar to present-day BB and CB caps. The only rimfire cartridges which survive today are the .22 short, long and long-rifle cartridges. These have a primer mixture around the inside of the rim, applied as a wet paste which is allowed to dry before the little case is filled with powder. Rimfire cartridges during the 19th century were made in a variety of sizes: .22, .32, .38, .44, .50, .52, and .56 calibers. The first successful repeating arms and breech-loading revolvers all shot rimfire cartridges. The .44 rimfire was the first of the big-bore cartridges and was the ammunition for both the original Winchester and the Smith & Wesson revolver, while the popular Spencer shot a .56-caliber slug.

Center-fire cartridges, the kind we shoot today, arrived with the Snider in 1866 and the Winchester in 1873. The Snider was a single-shot rifle invented by a New Yorker and adopted by the British as a military weapon. While it was

[1] *J. Schon,* Modern System Of Small Arms, *(Dresden: 1855). Plates No. 35, 40 and 44.*

[2] *There is a pillar-breech presentation rifle made for the Tøjhus Museet signed by Niels Staal Jessen and dated 1852 which can be seen in the Tøjhus Armor Hall today. (B. 2598)*

the first breechloader generally issued to the troops and did see service in India, it was a poor composite cartridge made of iron, tin and paper in .577 caliber. It was replaced by the Martini-Henry, rechristened the Enfield, in five years.

The Snider and the Winchester typify the difference of opinion between the Europeans and the Americans. While the Americans were concentrating on weapons which would provide a succession of firing and a flexible personal defense weapon, the Europeans were concerned chiefly with developing the best single-shot gun for the infantryman. Also, there was a tradition of large-bore guns among the European armies. This was a hangover from the round ball of the muzzle loader. When bullets became bullet-shaped, they were cast to fit the bore of the older rifles designed for round ball. When the bullet became twice as long, it was twice as heavy, and the mid-nineteenth century military ammunition was heavier than that needed to kill elephants. Sporting guns and ammunition which were designed to kill elephants, lions, and tigers were not needed in the Americas, hence the concentration by American designers on smaller-caliber repeaters.

Summing up the European pinfire and needle guns with their many variants: They were chiefly significant, not for their mechanical improvements, but for making practical for the first time a breech-loading weapon which shot a fixed cartridge. The cartridge, usually of thin copper or brass alloy, often combined with a cardboard tube like our present shot shell case, expanded to close the breech tightly and keep the explosive gases from escaping. The shooter could concentrate on aiming and hitting his target. He no longer had to contend with loose powder in a flask, a bag full of balls, a box of priming caps, patches, ramrod and cleaning tips—bits and pieces for which he had too few hands. Now for the first time, he could load the gun with a single motion, hold the gun calmly to his shoulder, aim it, and gently squeeze off the trigger.

Breech-loading fixed ammunition was quicker, and gave the infantry greater firepower without the hazard and expense of multishot weapons.

Cartridges with projections, such as the pinfires, or cartridges which had to be penetrated with delicate needles, did not lend themselves to magazine loading. When the Yankee mechanics turned their inventiveness to the development of the repeating and magazine rifle in the 1840's, they went back to the tiny Flobert cartridge, which was little but a primer cap inserted directly into the barrel. One of the first ideas, which turned out to be a dismal dud, was employed by Walter Hunt and Lewis Jennings with their Rocket Ball cartridge-bullet. This shortly became the cartridge which Horace Smith and Daniel B. Wesson employed in the predecessor to the Winchester—the Volcanic pistol and rifle.

The Rocket Ball was a conical lead bullet with the back end hollowed out for powder. A disc in the base held the powder and a hole in the center of the disc admitted the primer flash. The original Volcanic version had the bullet cavity filled with primer mix, thus making it a complete cartridge, but it was a cartridge that didn't go anywhere. Sometimes the bullet stayed in the barrel, and sometimes it emerged tired, landing on the ground a few feet in front of the intrepid shooter. Detractors said that an agile catcher could snag the bullet in mid-flight without a mitt.

All of a sudden, Winchester (Benjamin Tyler Henry) in New Haven, Triplett and Scott in Meriden, Peabody (The Providence Tool Company), Spencer in Boston, and Sharps in Hartford began to think in terms of a complete, metal encased, rimfire cartridge.

Christian Sharps, who had learned his trade from John Hall at Harpers Ferry, had been building a breechloader which took a paper cartridge. When the Sharps breechloader was closed, the sharp knife edge of the breech block sheared off the back of the cartridge, leaving the loose powder in the breech exposed to the primer flash. Sharps converted these guns to rimfire and later to center fire without losing the strong, solid breechlock system.

Daniel Wesson and B. Tyler Henry worked together and separately on the idea of a rimfire cartridge. In addition to the .22 caliber, which was borrowed size and all from Flobert,

THE SEALED BREECH

Transitional needle-fire *Dreyse shotgun. While Dreyse of Sommerda, Germany, had already built breech-loading guns, he reverted to a muzzle-loading cartridge for this 20 gauge shotgun. The spring-loaded needles are cocked by rotating the handles on the barrels toward the rear. loa. 46¼", bbls 32¾". No.# 2438 (Vitrine No. 7, Ag. 107) Musée d'Armes, Liège.*

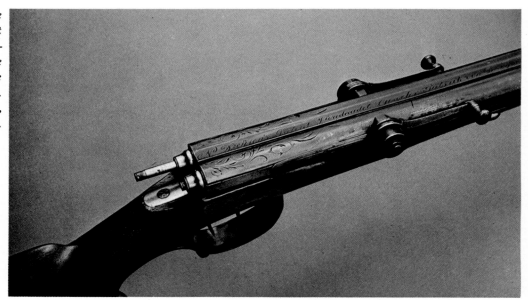

LeFacheaux pinfire *revolving military rifle. Chinese markings on the flat of the 12mm hexagonal barrel indicate that LeFacheaux had a contract to supply a Chinese warlord's private army. The gun was made in France in the mid 19th century. loa. 44", bbl 25¼". Bayonet fittings. Author's Collection.*

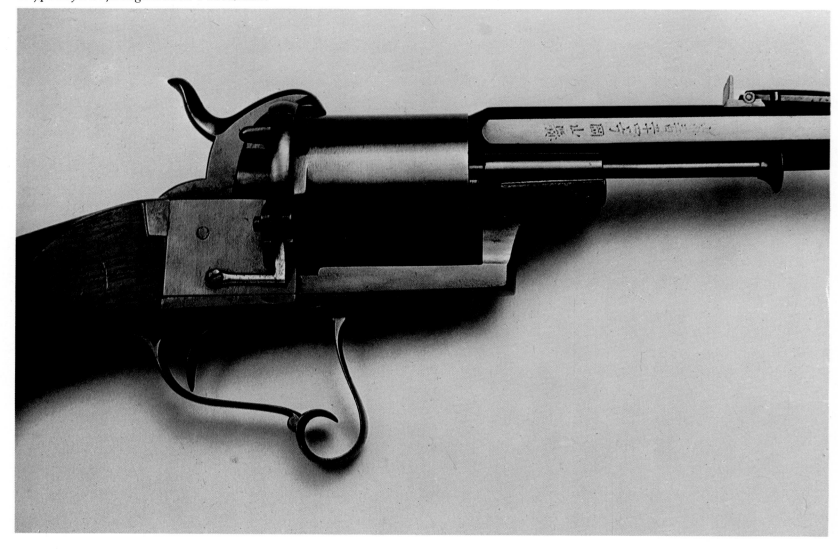

RIGHT: **Pauly double gun** *with the patent drawings in a special case at the Tower of London. loa. 47¼", bbls 29¹³⁄₁₆", 18 gauge.*

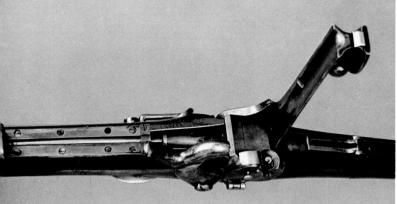

Merrill, Latrobe and Thomas *patented this monster in 1859. It was built by E. Remington in Ilion, New York. It used a Maynard tape primer and a paper cartridge which was sheared open by a knife in the breech. The tail of the cartridge was then supposed to drop out of a hole in the trigger guard. Cal. .54". No.# 2728 V 1, West Point Museum.*

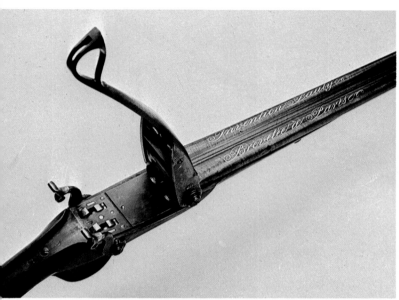

Pauly patent of 1812. *The browned twist and gold-inlaid barrels are inscribed "Invention Pauly Brèvetée à Paris". loa. 44", bbls 27" plus, 20 gauge. No.# Aj 1 (Vitrine 13), Musée d'Armes, Liège.*

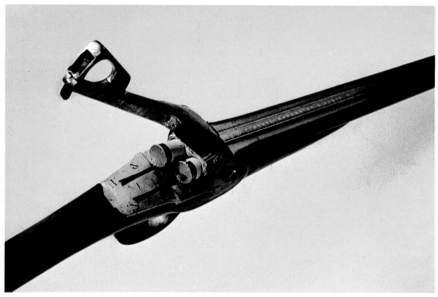

"Fusil Robert Bte à Paris." *Used paper-cased pinfire shot shell or ball. loa. 42¾", bbls 27⅜" bore 16 gauge. Author's Collection.*

but lengthened to hold gunpowder as well as primer mix, they doubled the bore diameter of Flobert's saloon gun and came up with the .44 caliber rimfire. Cartridge manufacture became a big business in the United States during Civil War days, and, in addition to pinfire cartridges for foreign guns, rimfire cartridges for the new guns of privately-equipped soldiers and plainsmen were made in quantity.

While Smith & Wesson and others made .22 caliber guns and varmint calibers that were hardly man-stoppers, the Sharps and the Spencer and the Allin trapdoor conversion of the Springfield rifled musket supplied the meat hunters who provisioned the pioneer transcontinental railroad crews with buffalo meat. These guns were of heavy enough caliber to stop an occasionally-encountered grizzly.

In 1862, Colonel Hiram Berdan's boys, equipped with Sharps at the Colonel's expense, went into action against one of the regiments of the South, the Richmond Howitzers. Before the Richmond cannon could be brought to bear on the Berdan militia, the defending unit had been cut to ribbons by the long-range rapid fire. A Confederate eyewitness said: "We went in a battery and came out a wreck." The Spencer received equal praise for its performance against odds at Gettysburg by Ordnance Captain Hurd describing a small number of General Geary's troops holding off a whole

United States Infantry Manual, *1863.*

division of the Confederate army under General Ewell. One Reb said mournfully that this Spencer rifle was loaded on Sunday and shot all week. A few copies of the Spencer were built in the South.

Hiram Berdan, who was a mechanical engineer in civilian life, having had first-hand experience proving the value of rapid and accurate rifle fire, set to work after the Civil War and came up with the primer and center-fire cartridge which bears his name.[3] The Berdan center-fire cartridge employs a primer cap with no anvil. It is detonated by impact with a bump in the bottom of the primer pocket. Two small holes on the side of the bump convey the flash to the powder.

At approximately the same time, Colonel Edward M. Boxer, who was superintendent of the laboratory of the British Army's Woolwich Arsenal, undertook to improve the Snider cartridge. In addition to the wood or clay plug which he introduced in the hollowed base of the bullet to make it expand into the grooves, he strengthened the cases of the Snider by substituting coiled sheet (shim) brass for the paper tubes used on the original Snider. Most importantly, he modified the Frenchman Pottet's[4] primer and came up with a good center-fire cartridge for the Snider. It was good enough to survive in the smaller caliber Enfield of 1871. Containing its own anvil, the Boxer primer is set in a recess in the back of the case. At the bottom of the recess is a large hole admitting the primer flash to the powder chamber. Because of the large hole in the head of the case it is easier to extract the Boxer primer for reloading. As the United States has always been a nation of do-it-yourself reloaders, the English Boxer primer became popular in the United States. The American Berdan primer, having first seen military service in both Remington breech-loading conversions and Colt-made Berdan rifles sold to Russia, became the favorite in Europe.

The new center-fire cartridge was made stronger, with thicker walls and tougher material than the rimfires. Cast, rolled and drawn brass was substituted for soft copper as the cartridges did not have to have the rims crushed in order to detonate. The primer is protected from all but a direct blow by being in the center of the brass head. These primers have remained in use for a century. With the advent of smokeless powders in the '90's, bores were reduced, twist increased, and the old center-fire calibers were reduced. The military .577 British, the .500's and the .450's and the American .45/70 became approximately .30 caliber. The greater twist and the higher velocities were blamed for rapid bore deterioration. Actually, the corrosion came not from the smokeless cordite powders but from the corrosive primer effect on the now-clean metal, no longer protected by the black powder fouling. Non-corrosive primer compounds, developed in Germany, have been in use in sporting ammunition since 1930. The newest and cleanest, lead styphnate, has even been accepted by the United States and British Armies. Hot water would always dissolve the primer salts, but few people ever bothered to clean out their gun barrels with it.

As late as the battle of Gettysburg, the muzzle loader was predominant. Twenty thousand muzzle-loading weapons were left on the battlefield. They had been jammed, double loaded, loaded with the ball first, and some had six or eight charges. The first primer hadn't worked, the charge was wet, the touchhole was clogged, the guns were simply abandoned by frightened, green recruits. Many of them probably didn't know that their gun had not fired, as they had gone through the motions and pulled the trigger when the command had been given for a volley.

A single-shot military needlefire gun saw action in the hands of both the French and the Germans in the Franco-Prussian War in 1871. The Snider, which went around the world with the British, was celebrated in a poem by Kipling describing jungle warfare in Burma.

> "A Snider squibbed in the jungle
> Somebody laughed and fled
> And the men of the first Shikaris
> Picked up their Subaltern dead,
> With a big blue mark in his forehead
> And the back blown out of his head."

[3] *Berdan was aware of the one shortcoming of the Spencer repeater. The sensitive rimfire cartridges jammed into one another when the gun was fired as they were end-to-end in a tubular stock magazine. Hundreds of soldiers had their heads blown off when the heavy cartridges jarred together on recoil. Berdan, knowing the defects as well as the advantages of the Spencer, took the idea of the center-fire pinfire and substituted a primer cap. Dr. Maynard in 1854 had built a pierced brass case for his carbine that lent itself to the new primer.*

[4] *Clement Pottet patented a stoppered cartridge with a removable base for fulminate in 1829 and a primer with an anvil in 1855. Pottet is credited with inventing the modern shotgun shell.*

Spanish revolving rifle *signed "Rovira—1702". loa. 60⅜", bbl 45¾", cyl. 3⁷⁄₁₆", cal. .60". No.# XII/1123, Tower of London.*

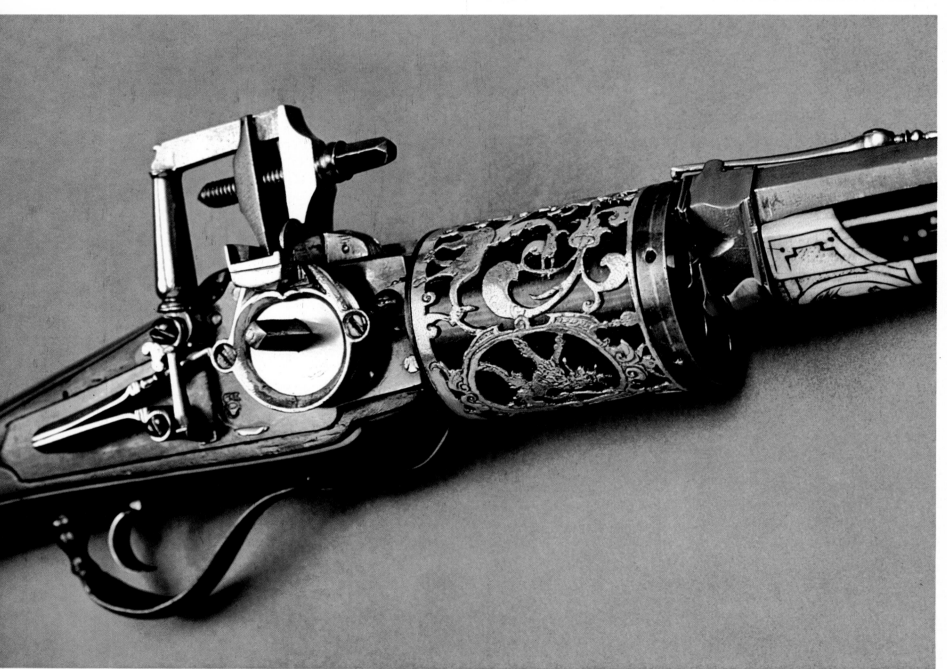

Oldest wheel lock revolver. *The two-tailed crowned lion in the gold lattice work on the cylinder is Bohemian. The six-shot smoothbore revolver probably belonged to Matthias before 1606 when he became King of Hungary. Barrel has a mark of a kettle with a handle and the initials "C-K". loa. 29½", cal. .40". No.# A-1145, Kunsthistorische Museum, Vienna.*

Oldest dated revolving firearm. *Snaphaunce revolver made in Nuremberg in 1597. The gun is rifled and has an 8-chambered cylinder. loa. 41¼", bbl 27.7", cal. .42". Illustrated gun is one of a pair; No.# 294-295. Tøjhus Museet, Copenhagen.*

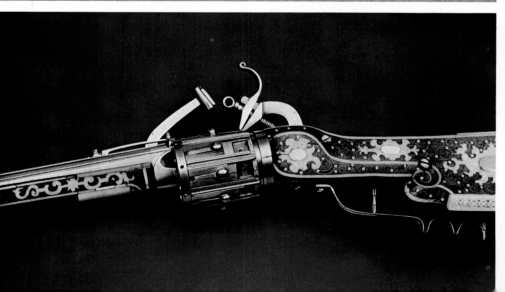

CHAPTER XIV

REVOLVERS

BELOW:
Inscription *on the tang, "Barcelona". The gun has four chambers in the cylinder and is hand rotated.*

THE SUN WAS making its quick exit from the Indian Ocean and the sordid smells of Calicut had disappeared along with the last small cloud over the Maldives when Captain Spaulding's voice boomed forth from the after house of the *Corlo*. "Colt! Who's at the helm?" "I, Sir" said the teen-aged Sam. "Well, why in bloody Hingham are we in irons, off course—and what are you doing lying on deck!" "I was just watching the wheel spin, Sir, noticing that every time it rights itself, one of the spokes of the wheel returns to an upright position."

This is a rather fanciful account of how young Sam came to have his vision. He would invent the revolver. The fact that he did so has come down to us through his version of history—the history of the trial of Samuel Colt versus the Massachusetts Arms Company, 21 years later. In this trial Sam's lawyer introduced an incontrovertible piece of evidence—the very cylinder, and other wooden parts, that Sam had whittled before the mast under the guidance of that kindly clipper master, Captain Spaulding. Of course, sixteen-year-old Sam had had some difficulty drilling six evenly-spaced holes through the piece of wood that he was whittling from one of the ship's ribbon blocks. That was when Sam was helped out by the kindly old captain. Sam had told him what to do, he had written in lead pencil on the end of the block "drill here."

The testimony in this lengthy and ludicrous trial sustained Colt's claim that he had independently invented the revolver despite the fact that revolvers have been built almost as long as guns have been made, and they have employed every known method of ignition. The earliest revolvers—hand cannons—fired when you brought a hot wire or punk to the touchhole of each barrel. The whole gun was revolved on its broomstick stock as the shooter brought one barrel after another into firing position.

Matchlock revolvers were made in Japan with separate pan covers to keep the priming powder from spilling out as the barrels revolved on a central spindle. An eighteenth-cen-

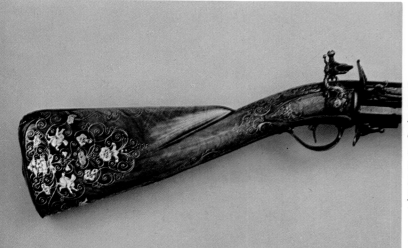

Three-shot revolving flintlock. *Made in France around 1670, the stocks are inlaid with silver sheet and wire after the patterns of Berain. The sculptured head on the cock is probably a portrait. loa. 52", bbl 31½", cal. .60". No.# XII/1553, Tower of London.*

REVOLVERS

tury Indian matchlock revolver wheel that belonged to Sam Colt has exhaust ports for its four chambered cylinders in case all the charges went off together.

Snaphaunce revolvers were fairly complicated mechanisms. Each time the snaphaunce hammer came forward, a tiny arm attached to the hammer pushed away the sliding cover of the individual pan. The snaphaunce is a revolver as we know it today, with a single barrel and a cylinder which rotates mechanically or by hand. The fine, unsigned and undated snaphaunce revolver in the Tower of London has a companion piece in the Hartford Atheneum, though missing its frizzen and the arm to open the primer pan covers. It is signed by John Dafte, London, and can be dated around 1680. Other snaphaunce revolvers can be seen in the Musée Royale de la Port de Hal in Brussels and in the Armory Hall of the Tøjhus Museet in Copenhagen.

The Tøjhus revolving snaphaunce rifle was made in Nuremberg and is dated 1597 on the stock—the oldest dated one in a collection. It is a well-made gun with ivory inlays on the stock, and is chambered for eight shots in the cylinder.

Strangely enough, there were even some revolving wheel locks made. A revolving wheel lock wasn't much use, as it had to be reprimed after each shot, but there is a revolving wheel lock that shoots darts—with the darts intact—in the Armeria Reale in Turin. It was made for Charles V in Nuremberg around 1530. In addition to the Vienna wheel lock illustrated, another revolving wheel lock dated 1612 is in the Musée de l'Armée in Paris, and a third one, a wheel lock carbine with a six-chambered cylinder is in the Tower of London. This one is of German make from around 1600. It is signed H. K. with a pair of spectacles. With the German gunsmiths' love of puns, the maker's name may well have been Kneifer, but more likely the initials stand for Hans Klett or Hans Kraus of Nuremberg. The Kletts were a famous family of gunmakers from Suhl, and Hans was known to have been making guns around 1600.

Hardly handguns, but utilizing the revolver principle, are two pieces in the Palazzo Ducale in Venice and the Puckle gun in the Tower of London. Both of the Venetian pieces are rampart guns. One is a five-shot revolver with a cylinder, the other is a twenty-barrel matchlock on a pedestal. Both guns are dated by Agostino Gaibi at about 1620. The Puckle invention of a century later has eleven chambers, works with a match or a flint, and is hand-cranked.

The Spanish started building really fine revolvers around 1650-1660. They are all equipped with the early heavy versions of the miquelet or Mediterranean locks. The oldest is a six-shot .28 caliber revolver-sword combination made around 1650, now in the Metropolitan Museum in New York. A three-barrel revolver with a Spanish lock, but apparently made in Milan, is in the Waffensammlung of the Kunsthistorisches Museum in Vienna. It is signed Paulo Appiano, and dates from the 1660's. Keith Neal has a four-shot revolving rifle from Spain dating from the early 1700's, and there is a signed Spanish miquelet rifle which is self-priming, in the Tower of London. It is signed Rovira and dated 1702. On the tang is the inscription "PERA CARBUNELL EN BARCELONA EN ANO 1702." Rovira is known to have worked both in Barcelona and in Ripoll.

By the time we get to the eighteenth century, well into the flintlock period, most European gunsmiths knew how to build revolvers. The author has seen Russian, Brescian, French, German and Austrian revolving flintlock rifles and pistols. Some are works of art, such as the three-shot French revolving flintlock in the Tower, which has silver wire inlaid in the stock after the pattern book designs of Berain. While the Russians may not have invented baseball, they preceded both Collier and Colt by approximately 50 years with handsome, well-built flintlock revolvers. A long gun in Munich and a pair of pistols with gold sleeves on the cylinders in the Aitken collection, were both made by B. Kalesnikow in Tula in 1780. Russian revolvers, both flintlock and snaphaunce, are in the Kremlin Armory, signed by Isay Pervushkin who was building guns between 1620 and 1630.

The modern revolver has its direct line of descent from

Fine revolving cannon *for use when completely surrounded; from Vegetius,* De Re Militari, *page 126, Paris, 1553.*

REVOLVERS

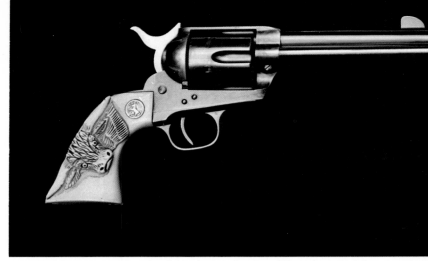

Andy Palmer's stunt gun. *Single action Colt .45 calibre Army with ivory grips and special hand-honed factory action. 4½" barrel. Author's Collection.*

Snaphaunce revolving carbine. *Signed "John Dafte, Londini" on the lock plate; this snaphaunce six-shot revolver, built c. 1680, is missing its steel. loa. 33", cal. .40". No.# 1905.1022, Wadsworth Atheneum, Hartford, Conn.*

the English pepperboxes of Gorgo and Barbar, both London makers. While the British were still building pepperboxes (Rigby and Nock) and seven-barrel volley guns (Dupe and Forsyth), three Americans, Captain Artemus Wheeler, Elisha Collier and Cornelius Coolidge, all Yankees from Massachusetts, built flintlock revolvers and patented them. Wheeler, in the U.S. in 1818, Collier, in England in 1818, and Coolidge in France in 1819. These guns were ingenious and well-built, especially the Collier, which besides having a fine finish and being well-fitted, had a primer magazine, as does the Russian revolver in the Bavarian National Museum in Munich.

It wasn't until 1836 that Colt produced his first percussion revolver in Paterson, New Jersey. The invention of the percussion cap in 1818—it was patented in the U.S. in 1823—made the manufacture of a cheap, mass-produced revolver a practical proposition. Colt did not originally claim to have invented the revolver. His patent was based on three claims which were granted. The first was his system for lining-up the barrel hole and locking it in position when the gun was fired. The second claim was for the safety device of isolating the nipples on the cylinder so that the flame from one percussion cap would not ignite the charges in the other chambers. The third part of the patent application covered the design of the ratchet which rotated the cylinder when the hammer was cocked. These patents were upheld in the United States, giving Colt the protection that he needed to survive the bankruptcy of his first company in Paterson, and the apathy which greeted his invention on the part of the U.S. Army. The fact that the Colt revolvers were crude by comparison with the Collier or the Kalesnikow arms made no difference in the United States, where few people had seen fine handmade arms and fewer still could afford them. That Colt's claims would have been laughed at by a European gunsmith also made no difference so long as Colt was protected by patents in his home market. Colt's problem was distribution of his product, and this he eventually overcame by sampling. There was hardly a commissioned officer in the U.S. Army who did not receive a "Presentation" Colt

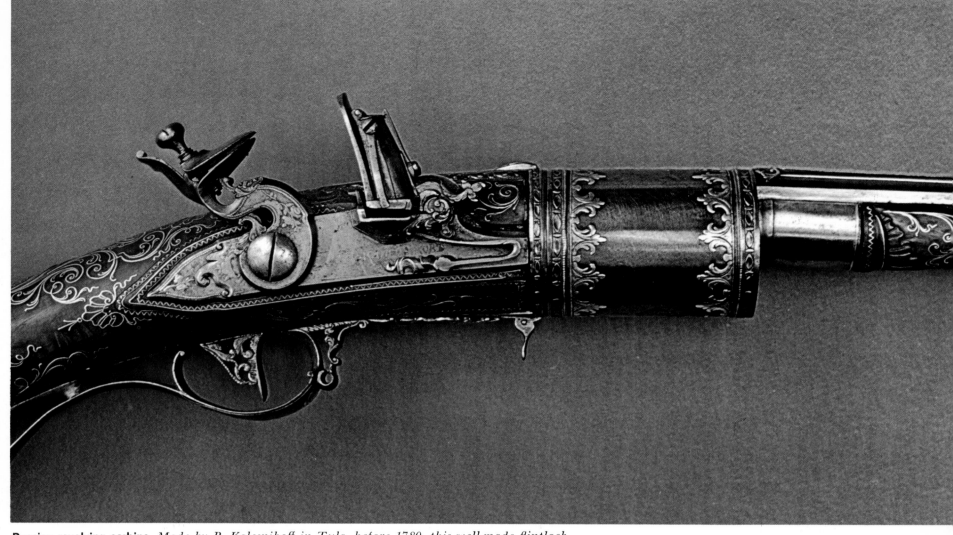

Russian revolving carbine. *Made by B. Kalesnikoff in Tula, before 1780, this well-made flintlock revolver has silver wire inlaid in the stock and gold and silver inlays in the blued cylinder and barrel. 6 shot, loa. 44½", bbl 26", smooth bore, cal. .58". No.# W 2843, Bayerisches Nationalmuseum, Munich.*

Pancho Villa's *.44" cal. Smith and Wesson. Engraved and ivory stock carved by L. D. Nimsch. in New York. Nickel plated, serial no. 2569, cal. .44 Henry. Harry Sefried Collection.*

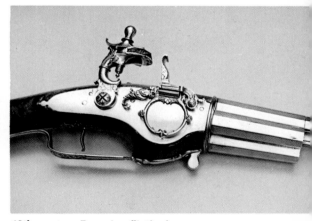

18th-century Brescian flintlock *revolver with wheel lock-appearing primer magazine. Tipping the gun over primed the pan. Four-shot, hand-rotated cylinder with catch under the barrel. loa. 24⅜", bbl with cylinder and false breech, 16¼" (cylinder, 2¹³⁄₁₆"), cal. .50". No.# 148, Musée de la Porte de Hal, Brussels.*

REVOLVERS

pistol decorated in keeping with the officer's station and influence. This forward-looking merchandising policy eventually paid off, although not in time to save the Paterson operation. Undeclared war with Mexico brought a Captain Walker to equip his Maryland contingents with a special heavy ball-and-cap revolver which Colt made at Walker's suggestion. Walker was killed in action only a few weeks after receiving the new Colt pistols, but the Walker Colts as well as some of the smaller caliber arms made in Paterson had a good workout before Santa Anna surrendered and Mexico City was captured. Colt's reputation was made.

Still, the Army would never have made Colt a success. Never before in history had so many civilians felt the need for a side arm. As thousands of Americans and Europeans flocked to the roughhouse West, they increased their feeling of security by buckling on one of Sam Colt's toys. Out there "The gun that won the West" came to be better known as "The gun that made the West safe for the Army".

While Colt's factory was humming, other Yankee inventors were not sitting on their hands. Ethan Allen, a modest cousin of the soldier after whom the fort was named, brought out a six-shot pepperbox percussion pistol. Starting with a patent granted him in 1837, Allen formed a partnership with a man by the name of Thurber. In Worcester, and later in Norwich, Connecticut, Allen and Thurber pepperboxes and some single-shot pistols poured out in profusion. Allen and Thurber sold more pepperboxes than Colt did revolvers during the Paterson and Walker days, and Allen and Thurber pepperboxes were carried in great numbers by soldiers on both sides during the War between the States. By this time, however, the clumsy .32 caliber solid six-guns, with their bow-heavy barrels, were running second to the lighter, larger caliber, more easily aimed revolvers. Allen and Thurber had a problem with their design. In the then-popular caliber .44 or .45, the block of steel up front would have made their gun too unwieldy to manage.

Colt's major competition was not just the pepperbox. Smith & Wesson, who had learned the gun trade working with Ethan Allen and with Benjamin Tyler Henry, were able to make a ridiculous patent stick from the time they bought it, in 1857, until it expired in 1869. This was the Rollin White "invention" of a cylinder "bored end to end" which was issued to White in 1855. Of course, there was no need for a cylinder bored end to end with a percussion arm, but White, who was working for Colt, foresaw the use of fixed ammunition in a revolver. Colt did not, so White took his baby to Horace Smith and Daniel Wesson, who did. They set up a little factory in Springfield, Massachusetts, and started manufacturing revolvers which would shoot the modified .22 caliber Flobert saloon gun cartridge. From this humble start, Smith and Wesson got a vise-like grip on the business of manufacturing breech-loading revolvers in the U.S. In this way they were able to keep the competition —Colt—out in the cold all through the vital Civil War years. Smith and Wesson had the good sense to build a precision weapon and finish it as cleanly as possible with mass production. Smith parts, by and large, were interchangeable on the same model of revolver while Colts often were not. Interchangeability, though bragged about by Colt, was not one of the lessons that he learned too well even though he had contracted for arms with the Eli Whitney plant in 1847, where the first Walkers were produced. Whitney, the father, had been a supplier of U.S. military muskets with interchangeable parts since 1809.

Colt's success lay to a great extent in the fact that he was a remarkable showman with a tremendous amount of energy. He exhibited at the Crystal Palace in London in 1851, and had the temerity to address the English Institute of Civil Engineers the same year. He was selling the idea of mass production, which was a novelty to the British, and the interchangeability of parts, at which he was only a so-so expert.

His brashness led him to start a factory in London which lasted from 1853 to 1857. Although Colt made over $5,000,000 between 1847, when he started in Hartford, until he died in 1862, he was barely literate, as the following quote from *The History Of The Colt Revolver* illustrates:

"I have been bothered to deth in endevering to lode the cillinders with the conical ball by means of the old fashioned leaver and have abandoned it as a bad job. There must be a leaver attached to the barrel on a new plan which will work purpindicular otherwise you never can get your balls strate in the cillinder."

This is from a letter to Walker on January 23, 1847, in reference to the 1847 model pistol. In this he was following, perhaps, the great tradition of illiteracy among gunsmiths which had persisted from the days of the Cominazzos. He was also inclined to distort chronology and historical fact when it would best suit his own ends, much to the confusion of his biographers and early writers on arms. Most of these fables were offered in testimony at the patent suit with the Massachusetts Arms Company. At the trial, Colt introduced a wooden model of a revolver cylinder, cylinder pin and trigger unit. He said that he had carved it as a boy of sixteen when he was a cabin boy, or an apprentice seaman on an American merchantman. Interestingly enough, just barely visible on one end of the cylinder are the noted penciled instructions "Drill here," which presumably were placed there to give the fatherly old captain a clue as to how to entertain his young crewman.

At this period Colt confused everyone by slipping the dates of his meeting with Walker and the building of the Walker pistol from 1847 to 1839, thus making it a product of the Paterson factory. Haven, in 1940 still had to go to a lot of work to prove that Walker and Colt did not meet before 1847, and that the Paterson factory never produced a Walker Colt. Finally, it was Colt's contention that while he may not have been the first to invent a revolver, he had arrived at the invention independently. This, too, is interesting, as his own collection at his home at Armsmear, in Hartford, contained not only the Dafte revolver, the 18th century Indian revolver, the fine Collier revolver illustrated here, but as great a collection of revolving weapons as existed in the United States in the first half of the nineteenth century. Incidentally, the Indian revolving matchlock may have

Paterson Colt *c. 1838, with wooden model parts, exhibited at the Mass. Arms Co. trial. Decorated with 10 silver bands. 9″ bbl, cal. .36″. Serial no. 984. Marked on the top of the barrel "Patent Arms M'g Co. Paterson, N.J.— Colts Pt.,". Wadsworth Atheneum, Hartford, Conn.*

Elisha Collier's revolver. *Flintlock with primer magazine made c. 1820. Frizzen engraved "E. H. Collier/71 Patent." loa. 13⅞″, bbl 6⁷/₁₆″, 5 shots, cal. .46″. Wadsworth Atheneum, Hartford, Conn.*

4-barrel, 8-shot revolvers. *Pair of superimposed load revolvers have double touch-holes leading from the primer pan. A button on the lock plate slides up and down. In the down position, the rear touch-hole is open. Signed "Cornelius Klett", Salzburg, Germany, c. 1660. loa. 21", bbl 13½". Joe Kindig Jr. Collection.*

King Christian IV of Denmark *owned these 1740 Austrian 3-shot flintlock revolvers. The cylinders are hand rotated. loa. 21¼", bbl 13⅜", cal. .52", s.b. No. B 1387 Tøjhus Museet, Copenhagen.*

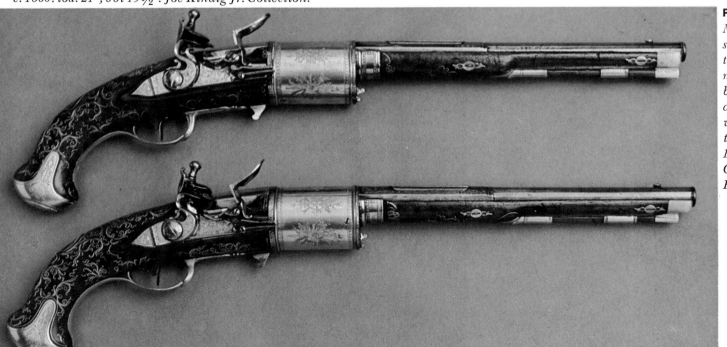

Pair of Kalesnikov revolvers. *Marked "Tula" these six-shot flintlocks, made by the Russian court gun-maker, have gold-plated bronze cylinders and cylinder caps, and silver wire, pattern-book inlay in the stocks. Made in the 1740's, they predate both Collier and Colt. Russell Aitken Collection.*

REVOLVERS

been seen by Colt on his voyage on the *Corlo*. His ship did touch at several Indian ports.

The reason Colt deserves the attention he has been accorded is the perfectly staggering number of ball-and-cap guns he did produce. Starting in 1849, 330,000 Old Model pocket revolvers; 255,000 Old Model Navy's after 1851; 200,000 New Model Army's in .44 caliber after 1860.[1] Some of these were produced after Colt's death, but by 1869 the Smith patents had expired and the Colt company was able to convert to cartridge loaders.

During the first half of the nineteenth century there were many experiments with percussion-capped multi-firing pistols. Cochran, an American, built a revolver and rifle with a wheel-shaped cylinder which rotated on its side, with the chambers bored in the position of spokes. The Cochran patent was issued in 1837. Several vertical-wheel cylinder guns were built, including one patented by E. W. Porter of New York in 1851. A Dane, Peder Rasmussen, built an eight-shot military revolving rifle in .62 caliber in 1845, and various chain rifles were built with the cartridges linked together, including a one-hundred-shot chain rifle, reputedly French, now in the Winchester Museum. Also in the Winchester Museum is the Harmonica gun illustrated. This little gun, with a fine built-in lack of balance, is signed "Jarré Brevete Paris" but has no date.

While the patent wars were being waged in the U.S.—and they were not restricted to revolvers, but covered all manner of mechanisms for discharging a gun—the French, and eventually all other European countries, were busily engaged in building percussion and pinfire arms. Fine pinfire revolving pistols and long arms were made by Lefaucheux in Paris from 1851. Lefaucheux built every conceivable type of arm, all employing the pinfire principal. There was hardly a market that the enterprising Lefaucheux did not invade, from finely made matching pairs of duelling pistols to shoot in the Bois de Bologne to 12 mm revolving rifles (one in the author's collection) with the markings neatly engraved in

Chinese. This rifle was one of a shipment made to equip Chinese warlords' private vest pocket armies.

In London, Colt was not successful for long, but he did succeed in stirring up the English gunmaking trade. Robert Adams, although not an exhibitor at the great industry show at the Crystal Palace, managed to take out his first English patent the same year—1851. It had two advantages over the Colt of the time. First, it had a solid frame with a metal strap *over* the top of the cylinder, and secondly, it was double action. Double action meant that it could be fired more quickly, although less accurately, by repeatedly pulling on the trigger. The Colt, being single action, needed to be cocked by the hammer, which rotated the cylinder, after each shot. The stronger frame of the Adams lent itself to the heavier British military cartridges, and eventually as the Deane-Adams, it replaced the Colt with the East India Company and became the service revolver in the British Colonies. Tranter, Webley, Lang, Rigby and Cooper all built revolvers in England during the period 1851-1863. Some were successfully manufactured for a time due to an excess of patriotism on the part of the British, and a flow of letters from Army types describing the success of the English-made pistols in the Crimea, and the Indian Mutiny. The only English pistol to survive into fairly recent times was the Webley and its ugly cousin, the Webley-Fosbery automatic revolver. The latter is a truly remarkable hybrid, mounting a criscrossed revolver cylinder way up in the air over a table containing a mechanism that makes the cylinder revolve automatically on recoil. Come to think of it, the Webley-Fosbery isn't much clumsier than some of the simple break-model predecessors.

While the British were building some tremendously heavy revolvers chambered for the .445 and even the man-killing .577 cartridge, they never had a competitive need to design for the civilian market. Ned Buntline, Wyatt Earp and Bat Masterson were a long way away (thank God) in some American cow town named Dodge City. So was the need for a quick draw revolver. For this reason, the British,

[1] *R. L. Wilson,* Samuel Colt Presents.

and for that matter most of the European revolvers, have an ugly look to American shooters. There are too many big bumps and sharp corners for an easy belt, pocket or holster draw.

There are, of course, exceptions to this generalization. LePage and his successor, Moutier-LePage built some good-looking, good-shooting revolvers using Collier's final improvement—the percussion pieces illustrated here. Even these pieces, however, are fitted, cased pistols, not primarily designed for holsters.

Smith and Wesson started, as has been noted, in 1857, the year when Colt's patent for locking the revolving cylinder in line with the barrel expired.

When the Smith & Wesson patents (actually the Rollin White patents) in turn expired in 1869, every American gunmaker worth his salt got into the act. Remington, which had been making rolling-block military rifles, as well as single-shot and percussion revolving pistols, came out with their first successful cartridge revolver designed for cartridges based on Smoot's patent in 1873. They had had a brief, unhappy bout with a rimfire that didn't work designed by William Mason in 1865, after having built sturdy percussion revolvers since 1856 based on the Fordyce Beals patents. Beals was a Remington employee who had come to Ilion, New York, ten years before, along with a contract to build Jenks breechloaders.

Hopkins and Allen, Joslyn, Manhattan, Marlin, Moore, Norwich, Prescott, Shattuck and Whitney are all names of American cartridge revolver manufacturers who bit the dust.

It took the Colt company until 1873 to come out with a practical breechloader chambered for the rimfire cartridge.[2] This is the same single action which is manufactured today to shoot center-fire cartridges, by both Colt and Sturm Ruger. In 1877, both Colt and Smith & Wesson obtained patents for double-action revolvers, thus incorporating the ideas of the Deane-Adams percussion revolver introduced in England in 1854. The double-action Colt Army revolver was introduced in 1878 with a solid frame and rod ejector. The Smith & Wesson was a break-open model with a top strap lock. It wasn't until 1889 that Colt brought out the present double action with swing-out cylinder and simultaneous ejection.

Revolvers are still popular in both North and South America because of their sturdy positive action, and because they are easier to check to see if they are loaded. There is no possibility of one cartridge being left in the chamber as with the older automatics. Also, there is a lot of sentiment, especially in the States, for the old single action, just as there is for shooting percussion weapons and flintlock Kentucky's. Double-action revolvers are still carried by most police forces, and the F.B.I. for years has had a little snub-nosed monster chambered for the .357 magnum cartridge, designed to shoot automobiles. It is reputed to punch a hole in the engine block if fired at right angles, and not too far from its target. The .357 magnum was a development of the Prohibition gangster era of the 1920's and '30's.

Within the last ten years, Smith & Wesson has introduced a still harder-hitting cartridge than the .357. This is a .44 magnum with a cartridge designed for both their revolver and the Sturm Ruger carbine, just as the old .44's could be used in both the Winchester rifles and the Colt and Smith revolvers. Today's shooter, like the cowboy of the '70's has to wear only one cartridge belt.

In 1966, Colt, Harrington & Richardson, High Standard, Iver Johnson, Smith & Wesson, and Sturm Ruger are still building revolvers. The old single action still survives largely because of the impetus given it by Westerns on television. Over a million .22-caliber Sentinel revolvers designed by Harry Sefried have been manufactured by High Standard since 1957, and thousands of revolvers are being built in Italy, Spain and West Germany for the American market. In the rest of the world, the revolver is pretty much of an anachronism.

[2] *The same year George Schofield's .44 caliber Smith & Wesson was introduced.*

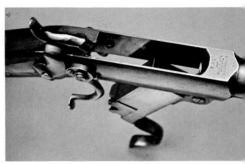

Burnside breech-loader. *.54" cal. carbine fires tapered metallic cartridge with external percussion caps. Pat. 1856. Ser. No. 164. No.# 2700, West Point Museum.*

Frank Wesson, *Worcester, Mass., single-shot .38" cal. extra long rim or center fire. Patented 1859 & '62. Harry Sefried Collection.*

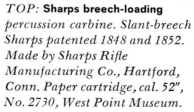

TOP: **Sharps breech-loading** *percussion carbine. Slant-breech Sharps patented 1848 and 1852. Made by Sharps Rifle Manufacturing Co., Hartford, Conn. Paper cartridge, cal. 52", No. 2730, West Point Museum.*

SECOND FROM TOP: **.52" calibre Sharps,** *paper-cartridge rifle with patch box. loa. 47", bbl 30", marked "C. Sharps Pat. Oct. 5 1852, R. S. Lawrence Pat. April 12, 1859." Serial no. 36,736. West Point Museum.*

SECOND FROM BOTTOM: **.50" calibre conversion** *to cartridge. "New Model" '63 carbine, barrel sleeved, still has disc primer magazine. No.# 2812, West Point Museum.*

BOTTOM: **Sharps-Borchardt** *cal. .45"-.70". "New Military Rifle Mdl. 1878" also known as "Old Reliable". Made in Bridgeport, Conn. No.# 2465, West Point Museum.*

Munich Mss. *Codex 222,*
c. 1500, State Library.

CHAPTER XV

THE SINGLE-SHOT RIFLE

O N JULY 8, 1876, the following account appeared in the newspaper, *Rod and Gun* which was published every Saturday at 33 Park Row in New York:

General Custer

The death of this brilliant and very popular officer is a public calamity, and especially in the manner of his untimely taking off in the very flower of his age (he was the *beau sabreur* of the American army) has fallen by the bullet of the redskin. The last time we saw him a merry jest was passed about his fine hair being sacrificed now that he was going against the scalp-raisers. He was an occasional contributor to the columns of this paper, and personally known to some of us. Our hope is that as the news needs further confirmation it may not be altogether true. The wretched mismanagement of our Indian affairs is a national dishonor. The government makes treaties with the savages which its agents break. We give them reservations and cancel the grants; we supply the enemy with arms and ammunition, and then send detachments where armies might find work. Altogether the Indian bureau is a stench and an opprobrium. Let us wipe out the Indian or treat him decently.

The publication, *Rod and Gun,* dedicated to "shooting, fishing, natural history, fish culture and the protection of fish and game," carries in the same issue ads for the Winchester repeating rifle, Parker Shotguns, Whitney breechloaders, Maynard's Patent Creedmoor Rifle, Military and Hunting Remington's, a very early ad for cigarettes "tenderly white and sweetly fragrant," and an ad for "Old Reliable" Sharps' Rifles, Military, Long-Range and Mid-Range.

There were so many single-shot rifles and so many patents for closing the breech issued by the U.S. Patent Office that it's a wonder that between 1851 and 1862 some New England mechanic was not issued a patent for a rifle that

only fired one shot. It would have been in keeping with the Rollin White patent for a "hole bored all the way through."[1] While there was, of course, nothing new about single-shot rifles, or even about breech-loading single-shot rifles, the spirit of invention had seized upon the Yankee gunmakers who foresaw the advent of the U.S. Civil War. It was in search of war contracts, rather than accurate target shooting, that brought about the Ballards, Remingtons, Sharps and Peabodys. They were to prove themselves in combat serving as military small arms in Denmark, England, Egypt, France, Rumania, Russia, Spain, Sweden, Switzerland and Turkey, as well as in the United States, Cuba and South America.

The host of fine single-shot breech-loading rifles produced before, during and after the Civil War ceased to be of military significance with the advent of the magazine breechloaders which were accepted by most European armies during the eighties. (The U.S. replaced the single-shot Springfield with the Krag-Jorgensen bolt action, box magazine rifle in 1892.)

But despite the initial intentions of the inventors of these American single-shot breechloaders, the resulting guns were refined to become the fine target rifles used in the Creedmoor matches in the United States. Prize money was won at Wimbledon, England, and Dollymount in Ireland by "Crackshot" Farrow, one of the first professional shooters, who was employed by Marlin to demonstrate the superiority of the Ballard rifle. This was in 1877, and target shooting with breech-loaded rifles had been practiced by Schuetzen Clubs since the 1860's.[2]

Having a diminishing military market between the Civil War and World War I, at least a dozen manufacturers in the U.S. built fine accurate single-shot pieces for target work, and several dozen more German and Swiss gunmakers built Schuetzen rifles using the various falling block actions of which modifications of the Martini-Henry (Peabody-Martini) were the most popular. While these fine single-shot target guns stopped being built in the U.S. by the beginning

---

[1] *But then Rollin White was working for the Sharps' Company in Hartford and had a patent on the shearing block.*

[2] *The first Schuetzen Fest in the U.S. took place at Highland, Illinois, in the '60's according to E. C. Lenz's* Muzzle Flashes, Standard Publ. 1944.

Target shooting *outside the city gate, Nuremberg Chronicle, first edition A. Koberger, 1493.*

of the First World War, and ceased being built in Europe at the time of the Second, there is today a great respect and affection for the old guns and their fine workmanship. Many of them have been converted to modern smokeless cartridges. This has been possible within reason, as the rolling blocks and the falling blocks were such strong actions that they are able to withstand the greater pressures of modern smokeless loads. Let it be repeated, *within reason*. It is unsafe to bore out a nice old Ballard for a .30 government cartridge. The pleasantest shooting, and some of the most accurate, comes from reloading the black powder cases that were designed to be shot originally in these guns. [3]

In alphabetical order, the first of the great single-shot actions was the Ballard. It was built continuously between 1861 and 1892. Although there were four different manufacturers, the Marlin Ballard achieved the greatest fame and was built in the largest quantities. Of 58,000 guns built, over 36,000 were built by J. M. Marlin between 1875 and 1881, and the Marlin Fire Arms Company between 1881 and 1892. The Ballard has a light, graceful action, perhaps not the strongest from the standpoint of conversion to smokeless powders, but strong enough to have been used in limited quantities as a military weapon in the Civil War. While the early military Ballards were rimfire, as were the Ballards made by the two other earlier manufacturers, the Creedmoor Match and the Schuetzen Ballards were primarily center fire. The Ballard action is of the falling block variety, operated by lowering the lever which is also the trigger guard. The block comes downward and away from the breech.

Edward Maynard, the American dentist whose invention of the tape primer is discussed in Chapter IX, was also the designer and manufacturer of some fine tip-up barrel sporting rifles with interchangeable barrels of different calibers. Again, Dr. Maynard probably did not plan it that way—like the others, he started off trying to get government contracts. But while the number of Maynard conversions of Sharps' and other rifles ran into the tens of thousands, Maynard himself had to be content with an order for a mere 400 carbines placed by the government in 1857. This necessitated Maynard's shift into the sporting field. In this area his gun was a success. The Maynard rifles were finely made and as a result of a lot of hand finishing, worked smoothly. Many stocks were made of selected walnut and were checkered and hand rubbed to perfection. A cased set of Maynards with several sets of barrels, loading tools and accessories such as the ones illustrated here, and these are only a little better than typical, would make any gunner's mouth water.

While Dr. Maynard was a dentist in Washington, D.C., his factory was located in Chicopee Falls, Massachusetts. That was where the good gun mechanics were. Fine Maynard single-shot sporters continued to be made in Chicopee Falls until some time in the 1890's, when the high cost of fine workmanship finally proved too much. During the forty years that Maynard was active, guns had progressed from tape primers to rimfire to center-fire, not to mention Maynard's own cartridge. Later Maynard guns were, of course, built to shoot these more modern loads as they evolved, and, while the shape of the gun illustrated is most typical of the Maynard sporting rifles and shotguns, the factory did build long-range Creedmoor types and a certain number of the more elaborately stocked Schuetzens.

Henry O. Peabody of Boston undoubtedly topped everyone in personal modesty, even in his own greatly understated town. He managed to be virtually unknown even after his invention turned into a world-wide success. Within six years from the time of his invention his gun became the Peabody-Martini and, three years later, he had succeeded in erasing his name entirely. His invention and its successors are best known to the world as the Martini-Henry rifles (after Friedrich von Martini of Frauenfeld, Switzerland, and Alexander Henry of Edinburgh, Scotland) and finally as the Enfield (after the place where it was made when it was adopted as the service rifle by the British). Such self-effacement is remarkable when one realizes that Peabody (this time disguised as the Providence Tool Company), took orders for 650,000 rifles from the Turkish government in between 1873

---

[3] *Without a doubt, the most exhaustive and informative series of texts on the single-shot rifle have been written by James J. Grant who has also contributed a definitive piece on the subject to the* Encyclopedia of Firearms. *Anyone owning a single-shot rifle should consult at least the first of Mr. Grant's four volumes entitled* Single Shot Rifles, *published by Morrow.*

THE SINGLE-SHOT

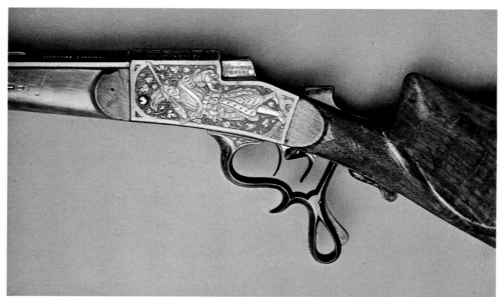

Sempert-Krieghoff *schuetzen rifle, system Marrkolbe, serial no. 7635, 815x46R (cal. .32") Author's Collection.*

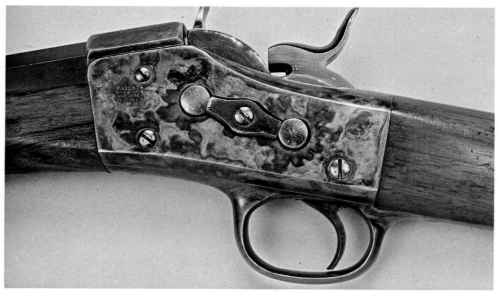

Single-shot rifle. *"I. D. Moritz-Sohn, Leipzig" on the receiver, "J. P. Sauer & Sohn, Suhl" on the barrel. .44" cal. magnum (11 x65R). Action opens with thumb lever. Serial no. 43124. Harry Sefried Collection.*

"E. Remington & Sons. *Ilion. N.Y." Mint rolling block with case-hardened receiver. Serial no. 11970, cal. .38", extra long center fire. Harry Sefried Collection.*

TOP: **Gibbs Farquharson,** *single-shot cal. .450", No. 2 W. R. "Medford's patent 1566, George Gibbs, Corn Street, Bristol" on bbl.*

MIDDLE: **"Jno Rigby & Co.,** *Dublin & London" on bbl and receiver. Calibre. 360", nitro express. Serial no. 15022.*

BOTTOM: **Single shot Holland and Holland** *rook rifle. Lyman sight fitted at the factory, cal. .295/350". Serial no. 21410. All three single-shot guns from the collection of George Rowbottom.*

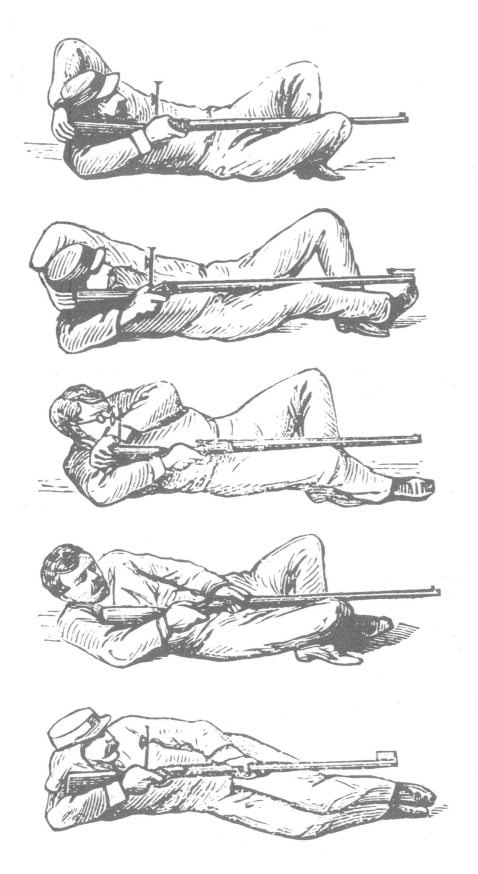

Prone positions *used at the Creedmore matches.*
Rod and Gun *and* American Sportsman, *1876, New York.*

and 1879, and Peabodys were still the official arm in the Balkan Army in 1912 and 1913. Sam Colt's ghost would have blanched at the very thought of such unassuming modesty.

The first Peabody gun and patent appeared in 1862, again inspired by the U.S. Civil War, and Henry's first orders for .50 caliber military rifles for the U.S. Army and the Connecticut State Militia. Canada bought some and so did the Rumanians and the Swiss. In 1868, Martini improved them by substituting an internal coil spring and striker for Peabody's external hammer.

The Scotsman Henry's patent improvement was for a change in the rifling. The original Peabody design was for a breech-loading rifle or carbine which worked by lowering the trigger guard, thus opening the breech and extracting the spent cartridge. Martini's improvement cocked the new striker which replaced the outside hammer. Many of the Peabodys and Peabody-Martinis were not only well made of excellent material, but were fancily engraved as sporters especially designed for the long-range target shooting of the Creedmoor matches. One of the cartridges for which the Peabody-Martini was chambered had the curious name of "What Cheer."[4] This black powder delight is a .40/90/500. A 500-grain, paper-patched bullet driven by 90 grains of black powder through a .40 caliber hole. What Cheer indeed.

The Remington-Rider patented single-shot rifle was not only original, but the strongest and the most successful of all of the nineteenth-century single-loaders. Patents were assigned to Joseph Rider and the Remington Company between 1858 and 1873 for breech-loading guns, but the basic rolling block, the most distinctive improvement in breech-loading of all of the single-shot guns, was patented in 1863 and first manufactured at Middletown, Connecticut, in 1865. It was the invention of Leonard Geiger who designed the basic mechanism and protected it with his patent No. 37501 in January 27, 1863. Rider did make subsequent contributions to the hammer design, but this was an afterthought to the basic idea of a hammer hung back of the breech block axis, supporting the block against the explosion force.[5]

[4] *Named for a rifle range in Providence, Rhode Island*

[5] *Charles and Carrol Karr,* Remington Handguns, *Military Pub. Co., p. 54.*

THE SINGLE-SHOT

The rolling block idea was so simple, safe and sturdy, that not only did Remington buy it from Geiger, but it became the most widely used military action in both pistols and rifles in the world. The U.S. Navy, Egypt, England, France, Russia, Spain, Sweden and Turkey got on the bandwagon. Several of these rolling blocks saw heavy action, as we can judge by the order that Turkey placed for ammunition with the old E. Remington and Sons, Co. It was for 210,000,000 rounds of ammunition, the largest single order for fixed ammunition to that date (1879).

The Remington rolling block sporting rifle was introduced in 1869, and the list of the cartridges for which it was chambered grew to 26 before the gun was discontinued in 1911. Deer rifles, buffalo rifles, and Creedmoor rifles were made in great profusion, and the finely stocked, hand finished Creedmoors sold for the astonishing price of $125.00 in 1883. In 1883 you could buy a fair horse for $1.00. Of course, Remington threw in a wind gauge front sight with a spirit level built in, and a vernier rear sight. These were standard equipment for long-range prone shooting. By 1905 Remington was even building a Schuetzen match rifle complete with set triggers, grapevine trigger guard and the works.

The most romantic gun of this period was the famous Sharps rifle, which had started out as a percussion breech-loader. This dropping breech block percussion arm was adapted shortly to the use of the Maynard tape primers, and a number of these were purchased by the U.S. Army, including those that were used by Colonel Hiram Berdan at Richmond. By 1865, after building over 90,000 rifles and carbines, the Sharps factory in Hartford brought out their first cartridge gun. After that, they brought out cartridge guns in enormous number, and in such a wide variety of calibers that it would seem that they never made two guns alike, which, of course, they did. The slanting-breech Sharps is the first design—the later model "Old Reliable" Sharps traveled the breech block on a nearly vertical elevation—and the Sharps Borchardt was a hammerless version which was very popular with target shooters during the brief period

that it was built—between 1877 and 1881. As the Sharps rifle was primarily intended for long-range power and accuracy, it was available with a long heavy barrel for buffalo shooting and with double set triggers. It is no wonder that it was easily adapted from a buffalo gun and a sharpshooter's piece to one of the best shooting target guns that was ever made. The action of the Sharps may well be as strong as the rolling block.

The Sharps-Borchardt rifles were the last of the long line of Sharps improvements, and their finest target gun. They were made at the Bridgeport plant of the Sharps Rifle Company by a group headed by circus man Phineas T. Barnum, who revived the bankrupt Sharps Rifle Manufacturing Company, which had been owned by Robbins and Lawrence in Hartford. Sharps himself died the year the new company was formed, and had nothing to do with it or with the Hartford Company after the first two years. The Sharps-Borchardt, the development of the same Hugo Borchardt who invented the Borchardt self-loading pistol, retained the strong falling block principle of the original action, but substituted an inside firing pin actuated by a coil spring for the big side hammer of the "Old Reliable."

Incidentally, good as the Sharps rifle was, the term sharpshooter did *not* come from the gun. The term has been used at least as long ago as the beginning of the nineteenth century. Beaufoy's *Scloppetaria*, printed in London in 1808, mentions "the Duke of Cumberland's Sharp Shooters" and in *The Book of the Rifle,* by Freemantle, there is a reproduction of an 1811 print depicting a rifle match between the Duke of Cumberland's Sharp Shooters and the Robin Hood Rifles.[6] Probably a sharp-eyed reader knows of an even earlier use of the expression.

Christian Sharps died in Vernon, Connecticut, in March of 1874. He was trying unsuccessfully to breed trout at the time, and the total value of his estate was set at $341.25. This was the man whose invention had been made famous as Beecher's Bibles. The inventor of the gun used by John Brown, Hiram Berdan, General Custer and a thousand buffalo hunters. At the time of his death there were factories

---

[6] *Winston O. Smith,* The Sharps Rifle, *(William Morrow, New York, 1943).*

THE SINGLE-SHOT

making Sharps rifles in Mill Creek, Pennsylvania, Hartford and Bridgeport, Connecticut, and in Philadelphia, and the British government had used Robbins and Lawrence (the Sharps manufacturers in Hartford and Windsor, Vermont) as a model and a source for special machinery for the new English arsenal at Enfield.

Far and away the greatest interest in shooting and in the perfection of fine single-shot rifles was stimulated by the Schuetzen Verein which sprang up in large numbers all over the United States in the wake of the post-Civil War immigration of Germans. The name that stands out singly, however, is that of the Creedmoor long-range matches. As every rifle manufacturer in the United States thought it worth his while to designate his finest made guns "Creedmoor Match," it will be of interest to have a first-hand view of the affair.

"Creedmoor is a camp covered with tents and canvas quarters of the various regiments and rifle organizations and military staffs. Banners and pennons are flying; thousands of visitors move to and fro, and it presents the 'tout ensemble' of an active energy at variance with its dull and placid appearance all the rest of the year. The effect will not compare for an instant with that of Wimbledon and Aldershot, but it is better, in all events, in the eyes of the strangers than in its ordinary condition, and is more in harmony with the exuberant vitality of our people. The field is in perfect order, and the tents, with their banners at mast-head, render a detailed description inadequate to the occasion. As the visitor enters he sees the long range of buttes in the distance, and a score or more at the firing point, where the work has commenced. This is all taken in at a glance, but he looks around and asks what in the world are all these thousand and one tents for?"

The Issue of *Rod and Gun* of Saturday, September 16, 1876 continues its page one lead article by describing what all those tents were for. Five housed the International teams; others, teams identified as being from New Haven; Goshen and Saratoga, New York; Jackson, Michigan; and Washington, D.C. The subsequent issue of *Rod and Gun* contains a brief history of the inception of the Creedmoor matches.

"The use of the rifle and the skill of our scouts and pioneers in its use, are familiar to all Americans, and the topic has for years been a staple with our story writers until the idea has arisen that the American boy is born with a natural gift, and takes to rifle shooting as the boys of older nations take to throwing stones. So far from any national or natural taste for the art, rifle practice as a part of military training or civilian recreation, is very recent. The impulse was given by the institution of the Hythe School of Musketry in England. Some of our American officers after the war, and as we believe, Colonel George W. Wingate, of the 22nd N.Y.S.N.G., in particular, took considerable interest in the Hythe practice, and thought it would be good to introduce similar schools of practice in the American army, and such practice, to some extent, was introduced in that regiment. The rapid growth of the Wimbledon meetings, and the favor with which those great gatherings were regarded by the English public, seemed to sustain the idea, and it was naturally thought that our militia system admitted of a school for improvement that had been found so satisfactory on the other side."

The article goes on to tell how Colonel Wingate had written letters published in the *Army and Navy Journal* in '69-'70. The National Guard formed an association in 1871 and General Burnside was elected president in November of that year. Messrs. Remington presented 25 rifles and the Gatling Gun Company, one gun. In 1872 the National Rifle Association, with funds from the New York State Legislature, New York City and private individuals, purchased the old Creed farm which belonged to a Mr. Conrad Poppenhuysen. "It was waste, unprofitable soil, and had to be levelled and cleared of stones and underbrush." Yet they paid $26,250 for this tract of Long Island real estate in the neighborhood of the two last New York World's Fairs.

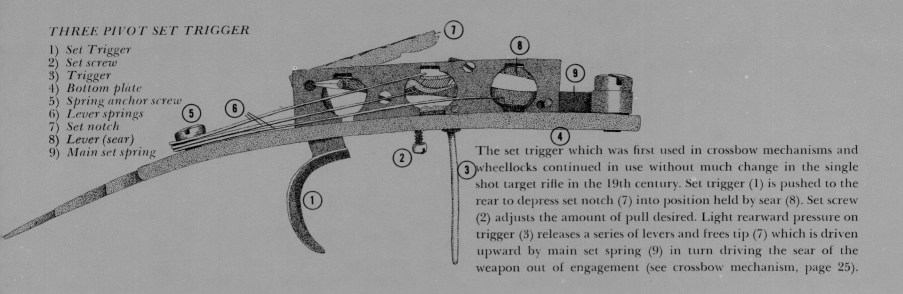

THREE PIVOT SET TRIGGER

1) *Set Trigger*
2) *Set screw*
3) *Trigger*
4) *Bottom plate*
5) *Spring anchor screw*
6) *Lever springs*
7) *Set notch*
8) *Lever (sear)*
9) *Main set spring*

The set trigger which was first used in crossbow mechanisms and wheellocks continued in use without much change in the single shot target rifle in the 19th century. Set trigger (1) is pushed to the rear to depress set notch (7) into position held by sear (8). Set screw (2) adjusts the amount of pull desired. Light rearward pressure on trigger (3) releases a series of levers and frees tip (7) which is driven upward by main set spring (9) in turn driving the sear of the weapon out of engagement (see crossbow mechanism, page 25).

The names associated with the first matches were Gildersleeve, Wingate, Fairbanks, Schermerhorn, Alford, Collins, Fulton and Bruce. The first match was won by Bodine, shooting a Sharps "Old Reliable" seven shots at 500 yards. This was in '73; by '76 the international competition was at 800, 900 and 1000 yards, and the prone shooting position, which is illustrated, had been established. According to Chris Roads, curator of military arms of the Imperial War Museum in London, and an active target shooter, the old backprone position has been revived and is being employed in extremely long-range shooting by the British at targets 1700 to 2000 yards away. While this position provides the maximum sighting radius and stability, there are attending disadvantages as discovered in this report on the Wimbledon meeting of 1875:

"... it was no common sight to see volunteers tramping off to the firing points to meet their engagements there, shoeless, with naked feet and trousers well rolled up, the only clothing visible being an all-embracing waterproof overcoat and rubber hat. To fire, it was necessary, when the throng was great, to lie down in some decidedly disagreeable looking spots, and the marksmen reminded one of porkers wallowing in the mire."

Hardly the picture one would imagine of a proper Victorian gentleman and officer!

Although the Americans came late to the international competition they brought good rifles and some natural ability as they cleaned up at Dollymount, Clandeboye, and Wimbledon in the summer of 1875.

In 1877, the U.S. team beat the British again at Creedmoor, which the *London Sporting Gazette* attributed to the Sharps-Borchardt rifles although admitting that someone did have to hold the rifles and that Americans were precocious.

Looking over the scores of these matches of nearly one hundred years ago, it is apparent that the most popular match rifles were the Sharps' and the Remingtons. While one occasionally sees a shooter listed as shooting a Maynard, or later on, a Ballard, the lists of shooters' guns usually reads like this one quoted:

> Remington
> Remington
> Remington
> Remington Military
> Remington
> Remington Military
> Remington Military
> Sharps
> Remington Military

Where diversification of arms proliferated, was in the Schuetzen Verein matches, and these went on all year long, indoors and outdoors and all over the country. In the same issue of *Rod and Gun* that announces the Creedmoor matches in 1876, there are notices of "Festivities"—beer drinking and rifle shooting—at the Baltimore Schuetzen Park, the Zettler Rifle Association at 207 Bowery, the Plattdeutsches Volkfest at Union Hill, New Jersey, Koch's Park in Brooklyn, and the Brooklyn Schuetzen Corps annual prize shoot at Myrtle Avenue Park (won by Mr. Zettler, who seems to have taken the ferry over from 207 Bowery).

Every kind of a single-shot rifle that you can imagine was tooled up and stocked for the Schuetzen matches: Ballards, Maynards, Peabody-Martinis, Remington-Riders, Sharps, Stevens, Frank Wessons, Winchesters ('though not 'till '85), and Whitneys, not to mention Büchels, Neumanns, Haenels,

THE SINGLE-SHOT

Aydts, Kolbes, Kesslers, Sempert and Kreighoffs, and Stahls plus at least 50 Peabody-Martinis, Martini-Henry variants which were being built in Germany, Austria and Switzerland, and imported into the United States. The imported guns were beautifully made, finely engraved, and the stocks elaborately carved. They made most of the American machine-made guns look crude by comparison. While the Middle European actions were, by and large, improvements and modifications of the original Providence Tool Company Peabody, the workmanship was obviously far superior.

The British, who had entered the earlier international competitions with fine muzzle loaders and the Irish with their Rigbys found themselves outclassed by the American breechloaders. Back to the drawing boards went the British and came up with the Farquharson, the B.S.A. Martini and a streamlined Farquharson type made by Westley Richards. All were falling block actions traceable back to the original Sharps and Peabody inventions. The Farquharson was the strongest action of the English, as it had to be in order to handle the king-sized black powder and cordite cartridges that the British preferred. At the other end of the scale were the graceful little Rook rifles. These neat and small single-shots were made by Greener, and Fraser in Edinburgh, among others. Their fine finish and lines make them very desirable collector's pieces.

Some few American makers who produced single-shot rifles deserve a word of identification.

Stevens, though perhaps best known for their falling-block Walnut Hill models and the bicycle guns which they made in great numbers, also produced fine falling-block target rifles made for match target shooting. Many were stocked at the factory with Schuetzen stocks and Swiss buttplates. In 1901, Stevens bought out Harry Pope, the famous barrel maker, with name and tools, and produced the Stevens-Pope—a gun that was fine enough to win the Palma Match at Bisley, England, in '03. The advertising people at Stevens were no match for their barrel maker. The best names that they could come up with for their very fine line of guns were:

"Ideal, Favorite, Hunters' Pet, and Reliable."

Frank Wesson was one of the earlier manufacturers of single-shot breechloaders, having built guns from 1859 'till 1886. He built a limited number of fine rifles and quit at the peak of the single-shot rage. While the typical Frank Wesson guns are finely finished light tip-up models stocked with figured walnut and often with heavy silver plate on the furniture, he also made a limited number of falling-block actions which were dutifully called the "Long Range Creedmoor Rifle." These guns, too, were better made than most American guns, with delicate English type scroll and line engraving. While multishot magazine rifles took the edge off of the single-shot market, Frank Wesson could not compete with *any* fully mass produced gun. During the Civil War bonanza, Frank, who was Daniel's brother, got an order for all of 150 carbines. The author James Grant, who knows more about single-shot rifles than anybody, and has been collecting them all of his life, had only seen four falling block Wesson rifles when he wrote his first book in 1947. Of the four, there were three distinct variations. This was like old-time custom gunsmithing, and had no place in competition with factory assembly lines. It was also a lot of fun.

Winchester got into the single-shot gun business, but not until 1885 when they bought the patent rights to a gun which had been designed by John Browning. Browning actually built a few of these guns himself before Winchester got interested. Perhaps it was a sales stunt to get Winchester's interest—anyway, something was necessary to get tough old T. G. Bennett, Winchester's boss, off balance, and Browning managed to do so for a number of years. When Winchester got into the single-shot business, they went whole hog: coming out with guns chambered for fifty-nine different cartridges. They built high-walls, low-walls, take-downs, and Schuetzens with double-set triggers. The high side-wall was the first model. It was built for medium velocity cartridges. The low-wall, which followed it, was designed for .22's and less powerful ammunition. Many Winchesters were built and many of them survive, including a surprising number from the black powder era. Despite the original fifty-nine factory-loaded cartridges for which the single-shot Winchester was chambered, a favorite indoor sport used to be for the amateur gunsmith to rechamber the guns for varmint cartridges. The high side-wall was preferred for these conversions as it made a stronger, safer gun.

The Whitney Rifle deserves mention here chiefly because it was the end of a long line of famous guns. The Whitneys, father and son and grandson, Eli, Eli Jr., and Eli III, had been building rifles and pistols in the little brick factory under the dam in New Haven since grandfather Whitney got his first government contract for 10,000 Charleville muskets at $13.40 each. That was in 1798. The last Whitneys to be built, outside of a line of cheap pistols, were rolling block rifles. A galloping horse could not tell the difference between the Remington rolling block and the Whitney. If you take them apart you still can't tell the difference. Nevertheless, Whitney modified the rolling block and got a patent in 1871, and others in '72, '74 and '75. The rolling-block Whitney was offered in the inevitable "Long Range Creedmoor" a "Mid Range Creedmoor," a military rifle and a military carbine, plus a variety of gallery and sporting rifles.

The Phoenix rifle made by Whitney around 1874 was an original gun. Describing it, Grant says that "the Phoenix system has the fewest parts and the simplest mechanism of any breechloader to my knowledge. The moving parts consist of a breechblock, firing pin, extractor, hammer and trigger." Later on he praised the gun again by saying: "It was just too simple and practical for the military mind to fathom." The Whitney Phoenix was built in both Creedmoor and Schuetzen styles and stocks, as well as in a military model. Whitney never got a military contract and the gun never proved a phoenix to the declining company.

What killed off the era of the splendid breech-loading single-shots was the magazine rifle, and that is almost solely traceable to the evolution of the Volcanic, the Henry, the Winchester '66, '73, '86, and all the rest, that is the subject of the next chapter.

Another day's *target shooting at Zurich during September, 1504.*

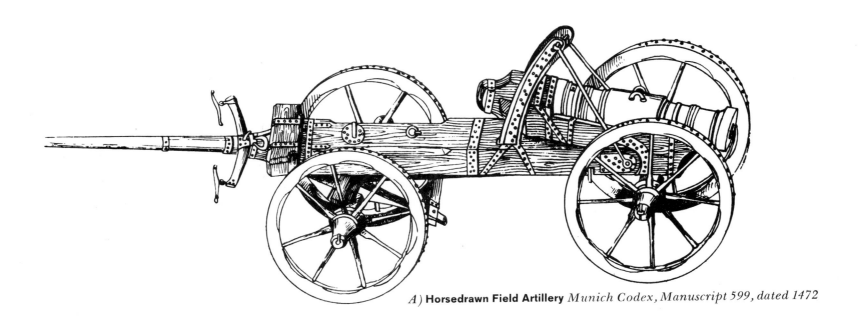

A) **Horsedrawn Field Artillery** *Munich Codex, Manuscript 599, dated 1472*

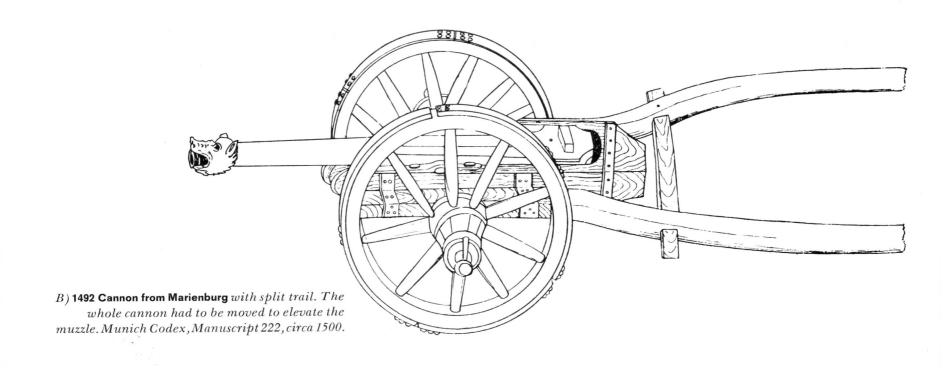

B) **1492 Cannon from Marienburg** *with split trail. The whole cannon had to be moved to elevate the muzzle. Munich Codex, Manuscript 222, circa 1500.*

C) **Split Level Field Artillery** *with ingenious elevating mechanism. Munich Codex, Manuscript 599, dated 1472.*

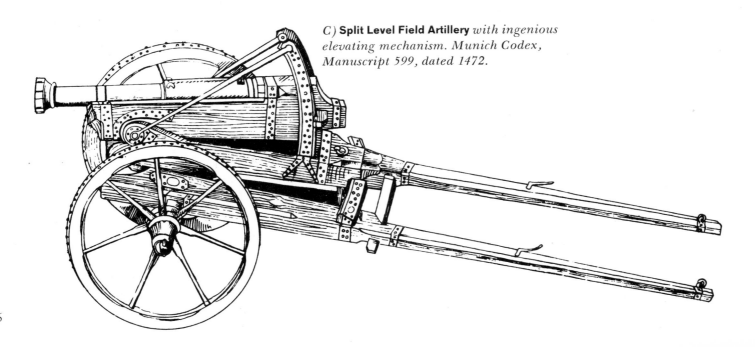

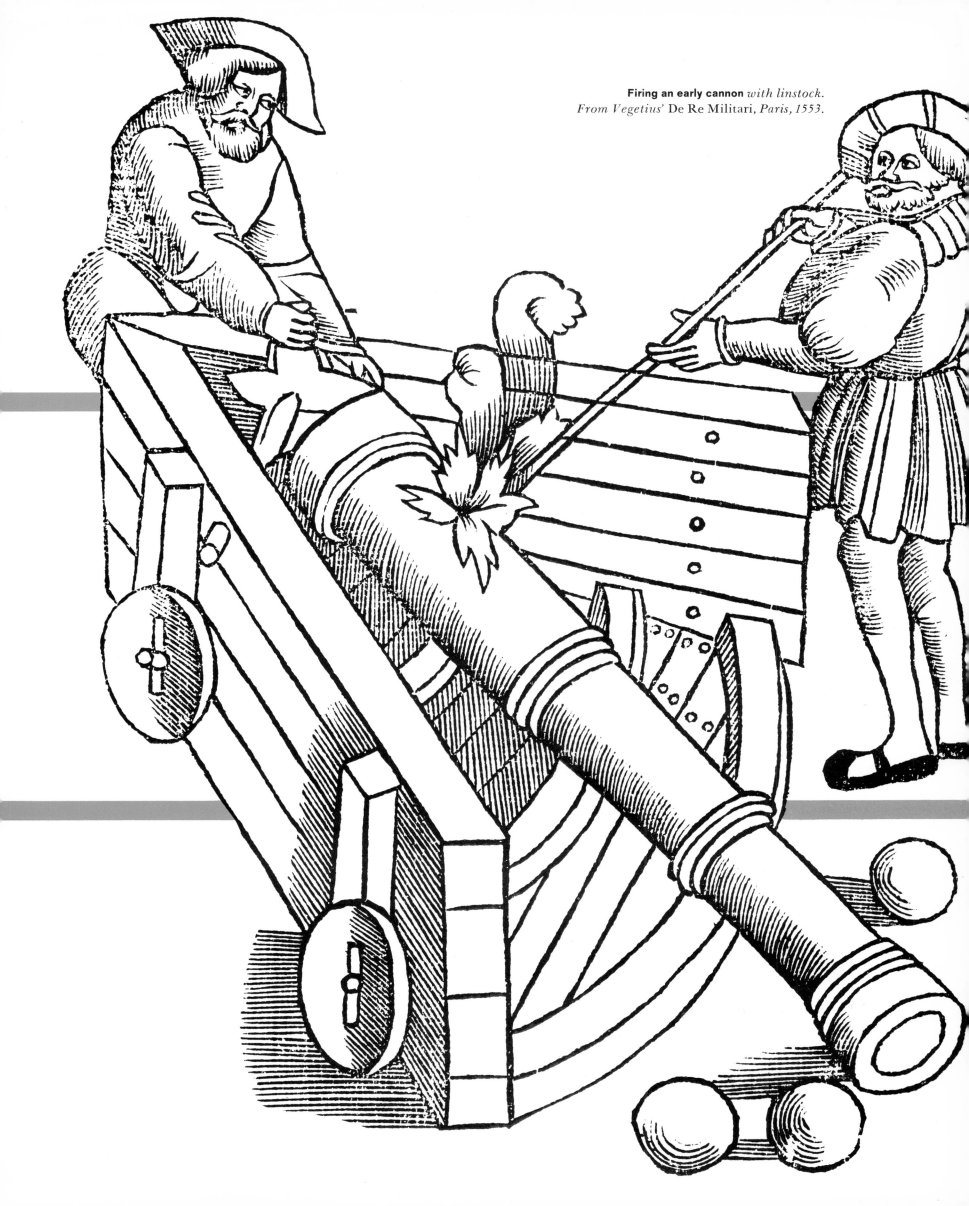

Firing an early cannon *with linstock.*
From Vegetius' De Re Militari, *Paris, 1553.*

CHAPTER XVI

MAGAZINE REPEATERS

MEN WHO ARE afraid of guns, or their own marksmanship, have always preferred multifiring weapons. There have been a variety of multifiring weapons built as a result of this ready market. Guns with several barrels were among the first, while revolvers were a close second. Hand weapons with superimposed charges—the magazine in the barrel—made their appearance as early as any of the systems. The first illustration of a five-shot magazine repeater, a superimposed load, appears in the Codex manuscript 3069 in the Vienna National Library. The manuscript, dating from the early 1400's, illustrates a five-shot Roman candle-operating hand-cannon. The drawing of this early repeater was specific enough to permit a reconstruction of the gun to be made for the study collection of the Waffensammlung of the Kunsthistorisches Museum in the Neue Berg. The enthusiastic museum man who labelled it calls it an automatic, and he may have a point there, for if one were to shoot the gun it would probably be a case of automatic death.

As a matter of fact, the principle of superimposed loads, while on a par with Russian Roulette, has survived the test of time admirably, which just goes to show how many fools there are with their heads still attached to their bodies.[1] In the Musée Royal de la Port de Hal in Brussels there is an early but undated four-shot military matchlock on the sliding lock system—its survival would seem to rest on the fact that it was never shot. The gun is in powder puff condition—just the way it left the gun maker's shop several centuries ago.

By 1565 there were a number of Nuremberg wheel lock pistols with two locks attached to the same barrel. This was an improvement over the pure Roman candle design. If the gun functioned correctly, and the forward charge was fired first *and if it did not detonate the charge behind it,* you still had a second shot. Double-locked double barrels with superimposed loads came along by 1600—there is an example in the Tower of London—and the chances for blowing your head off became practically limitless. Francisco Mambach,

with his four-barreled flintlock with Roman candle loads that shot a total of 29 shots (mostly unaimed), was the Richard Gatling of 1660.

The first Roman candle guns just kept right on shooting —just like a Roman candle—and once you lit or fired the thing there wasn't anything in the world that you could do to stop it. It kept going off until it was empty. You couldn't even drop it and run away as it would probably hop around and shoot you in the leg as you departed. People who dropped their guns tended to have fewer and fewer friends.

The next great step in superimposed loads was to supply more than one lock and separate the charges, in the pious hope that when you pulled the trigger, only one charge would go off at a time. Triple-lock wheel locks and quadruple flintlocks were not uncommon. Multiple locks got expensive and cumbersome, so the next great invention was a gun with a sliding lock and a series of touchholes. The one illustrated here, with a lock by Simeon North of Middletown, Connecticut, fired ten shots and had ten touchholes, each with its own hinged cover. It paid to remember in shooting it, to start with the lock all the way forward. The last man to prove that a bad idea dies hard was a J. P. Lindsay, who was granted a patent in 1860 for a two-shot single-barreled pistol and rifled musket with two hammers: two charges and one barrel. Just to prove that fools do not come singly, the U.S. Government gave him orders for one thousand of the muskets, which he obligingly built right down on Orange Street in New Haven. One thing that can be said for Lindsay is that he got the contract by demonstrating that the steel in the breech of his gun was so strong that the gun was safe even if both charges were fired simultaneously.

The basic idea of multiple charges in the barrel was unsafe at best. The pressure from the front charge was bound to push backward against the bullet of the next charge, even if the shooter were lucky and skillful enough to load his gun in such a way as to avoid the direct flash from igniting two or more charges.

[1] *Hayward,* Art Of The Gunmaker, *Vol. I: "According to a memorandum written by Duke Julius of Braunschweig (dating from 1573, and preserved in the Wolfenbuttel Landesarchiv) the superimposed load system was invented for the first time in the city of Goslar in Braunschweig in the year 1572. In the same memorandum the duke recommends the arming of his troops with such arms and mentions that two shots in succession can be fired rapidly out of such guns WITHOUT ANY DANGER.*

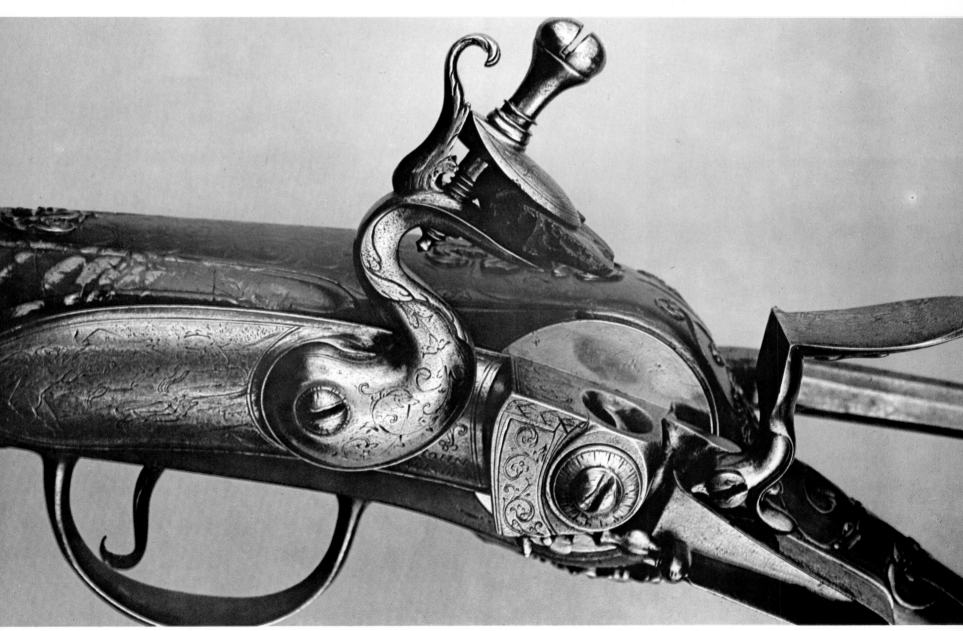

"John Cookson" *signature on the lock plate, although this magazine breech-loader looks very similar to the Berselli illustrated later in this chapter. loa. 50", bbl 33", cal. .54" No.# 77-1893, Victoria and Albert Museum, London.*

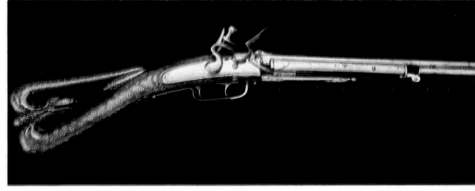

Lorenzoni System, *North Italian breech-loading, 14-shot, magazine flintlock, with ball and powder magazines on under side of the barrels. c. 1680-90, Joe Kindig Jr. Collection.*

Winchester Model 12,
12-gauge shotgun fitted with standard polychoke. Fugger engraved at Griffin & Howe. From drawings by Francis Lee Jacques. Russell Aitken Collection.

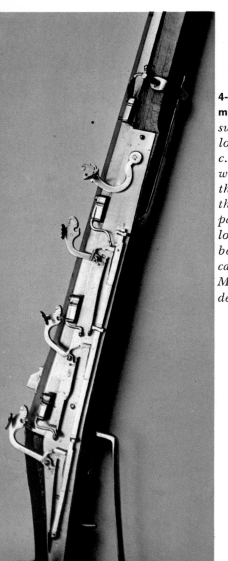

4-shot military matchlock *with superimposed loading. German, c. 1610. First shot was fired by tiller, the other three by the trigger in no particular order. loa. 61", bbl 46", bore (roughly) .84" cal. No.# IX/5 Musée de la Porte de Hal, Brussels.*

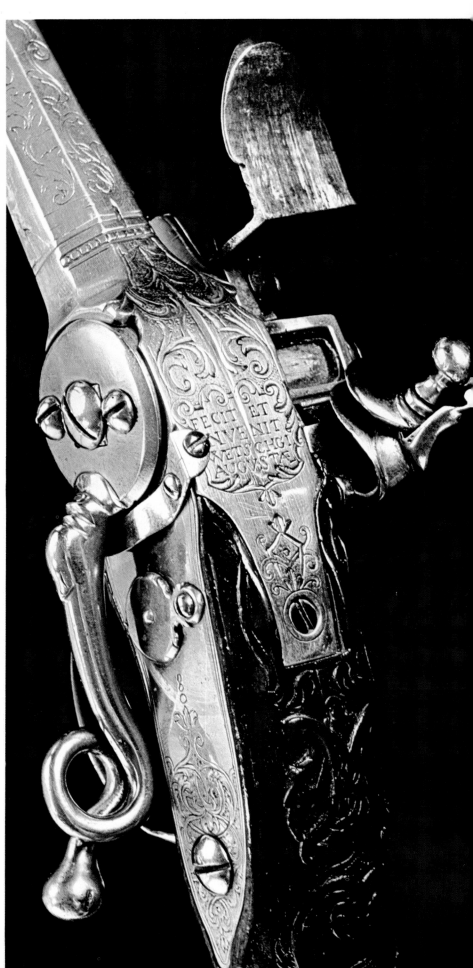

Despite the claim *on the barrel August Weschgi did not invent the Berselli repeater. This gun was made in Augsburg around 1690. The lever feeds in loose powder and ball. Joe Kindig Jr. Collection.*

Expendable as infantrymen were in 1645, the impressive invention of the Kalthoff family found a ready market in every country of Europe where members of the family took demonstration models. The Kalthoff systems, and there were several, were the first to transport loose powder and ball by gravity, through a series of ingenious gates, from magazines in the stock into the barrel. There the load was theoretically isolated safely from the rest of the loose powder when detonated. This was a great improvement over having successive loads in the barrel.

The first repeater made by any member of the Kalthoff family was a wheel lock built in 1645 by Peter Kalthoff in Copenhagen, Denmark. Very proud of the gun, he engraved on it the legend *Das Erste;* on another wheel lock from the same decade, he, or the owner, engraved the claim that it was capable of thirty shots. The 1645 gun had the bullet magazine in the fore end of the stock and the powder magazine back of the breech, very nearly under the shooter's chin. Subsequent versions of the Kalthoff had both magazines aft, and various types of loading gates were employed. The first one worked from a lateral movement of the trigger guard, a system that was to be used over and over again in breechloaders for a couple of hundred years, especially in the single-shot guns of Jan Sander of Hanover (1670-1715); La Chaumette in London (1725); and Ferguson (1776).

The Kalthoffs were a prolific and industrious clan. According to Dr. Arne Hoff, whose museum, the Tøjhus in Copenhagen, owns more Kalthoffs than anybody, the best known members of the family, which originated in Solingen, were William, in Paris; Peter, in Holland and Denmark; Caspar, in London; and Caspar's son, Caspar, in Moscow. The first Kalthoff repeater had a squarish breech block with three holes in it which moved sideways across the breech, depositing first the ball, then the powder in the barrel, and finally more powder in the pan to prime the gun. Caspar of London made guns with a vertically rotating cylindrical breech block, with suitable cavities for powder and ball. Shooting of any of these guns was rather like rocking a pin-ball machine. If the bullet magazine was in the forestock, you raised the muzzle to let a ball roll into the right hole in the breech block, then you depressed the muzzle so that the powder would run into the next hole out of the magazine in the stock. With the muzzle still depressed, you rotated the breech by means of a lever, pouring all the loose ingredients down the barrel except for a little powder that was wiped into the primer pan. This was the system that took hold and was adopted, improved and modified by a succession of European gunmakers. Within ten years of the first Kalthoff invention, Harman Barne, a Dutchman in London; Jan Flock in Utrecht; Henrich Habrecht, the Master of Gottorp; and the Kletts of Suhl among others, were making repeating breechloaders after the Kalthoff systems.

In 1664, Abraham Hill obtained Letters Patent for all manner of breech-loading guns. His patent application is an early and fine example of double talk, but he does, all in one enormous sentence, come up with this phrase: "another gun or pistoll for small shott, carrying seaven or eight charges of the same in the stocke of the gun, which is let into the gun by thrusting forward the sight. . . ." By 1690 there were a number of makers of magazine rifles and pistols. August Wetschli in Augsburg modestly inscribed his pair of pistols:

"FECIT ET
INVENIT
WETSCHGI
AUGUSTAE"

The name that stuck for the invention of the vertically rotating breech block, however, was neither Kalthoff or Wetschgi, but Michele Lorenzoni, of Florence. Guns signed by Lorenzoni survive in the Armeria Reale in Torino, alongside the guns of a number of other Italian and German makers of the same 1685-1700 period. The Tower of London has a Lorenzoni-system breech-loading flintlock from 1690 signed Bartolomeo Cotel. Turin has probably the finest collection of these guns. Three different ones in addition to two Lorenzonis are signed "Gio Pietro Callin à Genova," dated 1685; "Giacomo Berselli" (1666-1720), and "Perreaux à Verrue" (Turin) (1670-1730).

Justice is peeking *over her blindfold on this gold-plated, Ulrich-engraved model '66 Winchester. .44" cal. magazine rifle. Winchester Gun Museum, New Haven, Conn.*

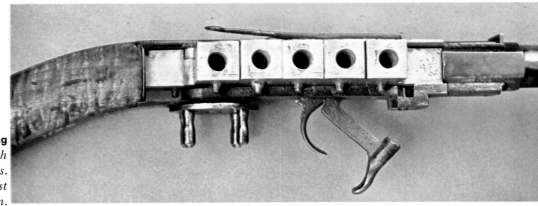

Bennett's breech-loading
*percussion chain rifle with
linked chamber blocks.
cal. .40". No.# 2240, West
Point Museum.*

The Winchester Idea. *TOP: Volcanic rifle patented in 1854, 25-shot lever action, tube magazine loa. 39", bbl 21", cal. .40". MIDDLE: Presentation engraved Henry rifle "Henry's patent Oct: 16, 1860"."Manufactured by the New Haven Arms Co., New Haven, Ct." serial no. #1443. loa. 43½", bbl 24", cal. .44", 16 shot. BOTTOM: Presentation '66 Winchester. Gold-plated receiver inscribed: "E. Reynolds, New Haven, Ct. Feb. 1st, 1872." serial no. #96020a. 15-shot. Harry Sefried Collection.*

In England, John Cookson built or signed some of the first Lorenzoni repeaters. (They look suspiciously like the Turin Berselli.) At least several of Cookson's versions survive, while there are no known examples of actual guns to substantiate Abraham Hill's patent claim.[2] Little is known of the Englishman Cookson, but either he or his son turned up in Boston to advertise a nine-shot breechloader in the *Boston Gazette* in 1756. By 1780 a Frenchman by the name of Chelembron was making some fine magazine breechloaders with both magazines under the barrel, in Pondicherry, India. A neighbor of his, in a manner of speaking, Major Claude Martin, a remarkable Englishman who spent his entire professional life in India, built magnificent guns at the Lucknow Arsenal, some of which are today in the Tower of London. They compare in quality to the finest London gunsmithing.

And, speaking of the finest London gunsmithing and summing up the whole subject of magazine guns which handled loose powder, there is a lever-type magazine pistol in the Smithsonian Institution in Washington, D.C. It was built

by one of England's famous gunmakers, H. Mortimer, during the period of the supremacy of the London gun trade. The whole side of the breech on the side of the shooter's face is blown out, and the once beautifully checkered stock is in splinters. This is what happened to the best made of the loose powder magazine breechloaders. When the guns were brand-new and the joints were tight, they worked fine—some of the Kalthoffs, as has been noted, saw action in the siege of Copenhagen in 1658—but they all suffered from the same basic defect. The powder magazine was almost always in the breech, just under the shooter's face, and when the gun had been shot enough to allow the parts to move freely, a tiny spark from the chamber could find its way back to the storage magazine of loose powder.

Finally, realizing the hazard of the Kalthoff-Lorenzoni guns, Francois Antoine Henry (no relation to Winchester's Henry) took out patents in Paris in 1837 for a magazine breechloader which had tubular magazines for both powder and ball out in the open on the top of the barrel. But by this time there was a safer and saner possibility in the offing. The invention of fixed cartridge ammunition made the magazine repeater not only practical, but safe. Who but the inventor of the safety pin, one Walter Hunt, of Brooklyn, should come up with the prototype of all cartridge magazine repeaters?

In 1848 Hunt got his patent for the Rocket Ball cartridge-bullet and the following year, a patent for The Volition Repeater, a gun designed to shoot the Rocket Ball. The Rocket Ball cartridge had the powder in the base of a conical lead bullet, but still required a separate primer. Hunt's gun was overly complicated, with a pair of levers, (one to elevate the cartridge from the magazine), and tiny parts that would have done credit to a watchmaker but that were too delicate for a gun. The priming mechanism of the Hunt was a major problem, because of the tiny parts that were required to feed pill-lock priming pellets to a primer firing chamber.

Anyway, Hunt was an inventor pure and simple, and the worst businessman in the world. While the Volition Repeater embodied most of the invention that was incorporated

[2] *Howard Blackmore,* British Military Firearms, *(Herbert Jenkins, London, 1961), page 256: "a pistol with this action, signed by the inventor (Hill) has been recorded." Blackmore does not say where, but does quote from the Marquis of Worcester's* Century of Inventions, *where Worcester mentions employing Caspar Kalthoff. Worcester patented guns, also presumably on the Lorenzoni system—Pat. No. 131—February 18, 1661.*

Map of fortified Turin *in 1684 from*
Les Travaux de Mars,
Mallet, Paris.

MAGAZINE REPEATERS

in the later successful Winchester—a straight-drive, spiral, spring-activated firing pin, and an under-barrel tubular cartridge magazine, it didn't remain long in Hunt's hands. Neither did the fountain pen or the sewing machine he also invented. Hunt assigned his patents to a promoter named Arrowsmith for a few dollars and a repeating magazine full of promises.

Arrowsmith found a supporter for the project, Courtland Palmer of Stonington, Connecticut, a financier whose ancestor, Nathaniel Palmer, had established that family's fame and fortune as a whaler and sealer as well as discoverer of Palmer Land in Antarctica. Palmer invested successive sums of money in the Hunt repeater, which had been simplified by Lewis Jennings, a machinist who worked for Arrowsmith. This all happened with great rapidity. Hunt's Volition Repeater patent was issued on August 21, 1849; Jennings' improvement, December 25th of the same year; and within the next month or so, Palmer had contracted with Robbins & Lawrence of Windsor, Vermont, to produce 5,000 repeating rifles on the Hunt-Jennings principle.

The guns did not work very well. It must be remembered that part of the work of the mechanism was engaged in the precarious proposition of pushing around loose primer pellets. Robbins & Lawrence, being practical Vermonters, solved part of the problem by making most of the Jennings' rifles as single-shot guns. Between 1851 and 1855 Smith and Wesson got into the act, first as individuals, and then as a team. They made two contributions to the repeater, both important, but not important enough to make the gun a success. The first improvement was a complete cartridge to replace the Rocket Ball. This cartridge, which has been described previously, was a lead bullet with fulminate and gun-

powder in the cavity.[3] The fulminate was supposed to detonate and the powder to propel the bullet. It did not do the Job well enough. The other Smith and Wesson contribution was the toggle-link lever action, which was a basic improvement, and was incorporated in the later successful Winchester and Marlin repeaters.

The combination of Palmer, Smith, and Wesson, with B. Tyler Henry working for them as an employee, produced guns in Norwich, Connecticut, first as the firm of Smith & Wesson, and then under the name of the Volcanic Repeater Arms Company. By 1856 the Volcanic company was broke and Smith, Wesson and Palmer had all departed. A new company emerged with Benjamin Tyler Henry in the mechanical and manufacturing end and Oliver Winchester, who had been a stockholder of the former company, in charge of the money. The new company produced the Henry rifle, using Frank Wesson's adaptation of the Flobert rimfire cartridge. Henry contributed his name to a .44 caliber cartridge as well as inventing a two-pronged firing pin and a rimfire extractor.

Between the years of 1857 and 1867 the company had the names of The New Haven Arms Company, Henry Repeating Arms Company and, finally, Winchester Repeating Arms Company. The breakthrough into a successful operation came after Henry's improvement, with the use of the rimfire cartridge, plus the introduction of the loading gate on the wall of the receiver. This feature first appeared on the model 1866 Winchester. Previously, both the Henry and the Volcanic had had to be loaded by taking apart the front end of the gun to get at the tubular magazine.

This 1866 Winchester was one of the first of the successful magazine repeaters, but while the evolution of the '66 was taking place between 1848 and 1866, other American in-

[3] *Rocket ball cartridge bullets were made: 1) with powder and separate primer bullets; 2) with percussion powder only; 3) with both gunpowder and percussion powder.*

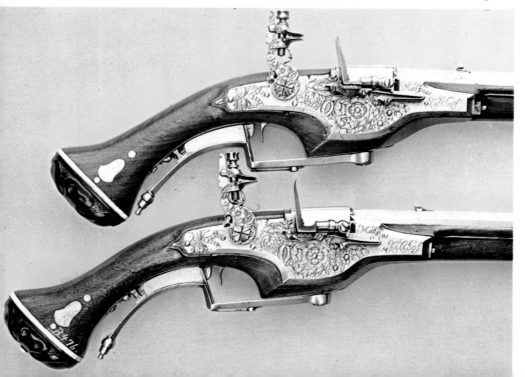

Pair of Kalthoff pistols. *Magazine under lever pistols, made by Mathias Kalthoff in Copenhagen around 1660. loa. 26", bbls 16", cal. .44". Nos.# B 475 & 476, Tøjhus Museet, Copenhagen.*

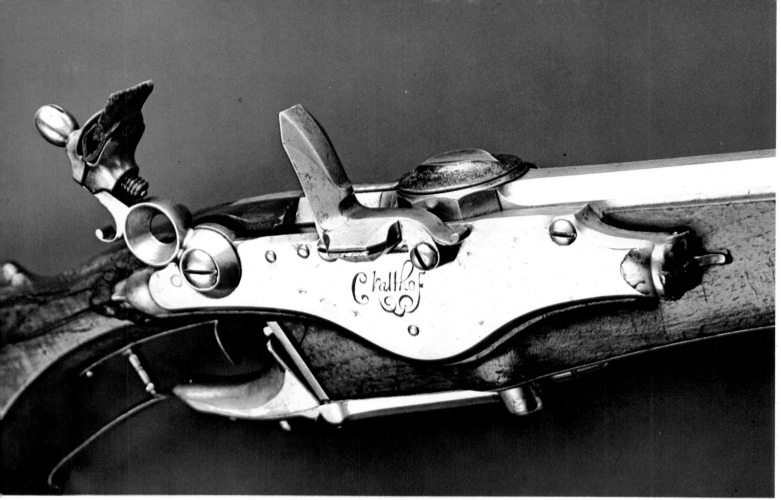

English-made magazine flintlock *rifle by Caspar Kalthoff of London. loa. 57¼", bbl 41½", cal. .64". No.# B 762, Tøjhus Museet, Copenhagen.*

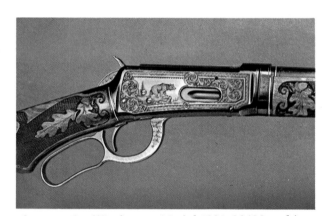

Lever-action Winchester. *Model 1894 .30/30 carbine engraved by John Ulrich. Winchester Gun Museum, New Haven, Conn.*

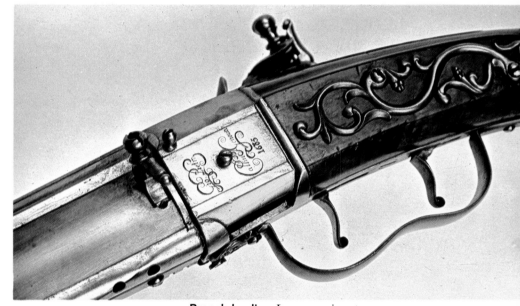

Breech-loading *Lorenzoni system tubular magazine repeater signed "Gio Pietro Callin a Genova, 1685". loa. 47", bbl 31¾", cal. .54", s.b. No.# M/62, Armeria Reale, Turin.*

Giacomo Berselli *(c. 1660-1720) magazine flintlock. Rotary mechanism with self priming and self cocking device. Berselli may have exported these guns to England and America. loa. 47", bbl 29", cal. .52", s.b. No.# M/65, Armeria Reale, Turin.*

175

MAGAZINE REPEATERS

ventors were already in business. Over 100,000 Spencer carbines and rifles had been made and delivered to the Union troops from the time that young Christopher Spencer had demonstrated his seven-shot rimfire repeater to Abraham Lincoln on the White House lawn in 1860. While the Sharps rifle remained a single shot during the Civil War and after, the Triplett and Scott turnover action, Ball's carbine, made by Lamson, in Windsor, Vermont, and even a few of Needham's needle guns with tubular magazines under the barrel, found their way to the fronts of the American Civil War.

None of these other early companies have survived, but the lever action Winchester has gone on for 100 years. In 1873, Winchester came out with a revised model for center-fire cartridges. The '73 had a forged iron frame which was stronger than the brass frame of the '66 and it also had a sliding lid on the top to close the ejection port and keep out dirt and rain. It was succeeded in 1876 by a still stronger, larger model for heavier charges. In 1886, Winchester manufactured its first model designed by John Browning with an improved feed and a much stronger locking mechanism than the previous models. Winchester continued to buy Browning's designs, including the model '94 which was (according to George Watrous)[4] the first lever action designed especially for smokeless powder. The success of the lever action can be judged by the fact that the 1,000,000th '94 was presented to Calvin Coolidge, and the 2,000,000th to Dwight D. Eisenhower. Nearly 100,000 gold plated "Centennial Models"—still lever actions—were made in 1966.

While there have been a lot of weird and wonderful variations of the repeating rifle, including the lop-sided Jarré and Kendall harmonica rifles, there are really only three surviving basic forms. Beside the lever action, there is a pump (or trombone) action, and a bolt action.

The pump gun seems to have been invented by W. Krutzch and patented in England in 1866. The gun looks like a pun on the maker's name. Anyway, it was barely more than another inventor's experimental model. The pump action did not begin to take hold until Colt came out with its Lightning model in 1890, and Winchester followed with John Browning's version of an earlier Spencer 12 gauge pump shotgun in 1893. The '93, the '97 (which was also made with a short barrel for trench and riot use), and the famous Model '12 without an external hammer, have been Winchester's most popular shotguns. Pump guns have been made in quantity from .22 short to practically all gauges.

While the first bolt actions—the Dreyse and later the Mauser, which was introduced in 1868—were single-shot rifles, they were a military success as they could most easily be reloaded in a prone position. Frederic Veterli of Switzerland added a magazine to the single-shot bolt action in 1874, and Benjamin Hotchkiss, who had a gun factory at St. Denis, near Paris, brought the idea to the United States in the form of the Hotchkiss rifle. It was introduced at the Centennial Exposition in Philadelphia in 1876. Winchester purchased the gun from Hotchkiss and began producing it in 1879. The first satisfactory bolt action sporter was the Winchester-Hotchkiss model of 1883. By this time Kropatschek and Lebel had brought out military bolt action rifles with magazines.

The built-in box magazine was the invention of James Lee in 1879 and the clip feed came along in 1885, invented by Ferdinand Mannlicher. Both the Lee straight-pull rifle (1893) and the Mannlicher were primarily designed as military weapons, as was the magazine Mauser, which did not appear until 1888. These guns, of course, like the single-shot rifles of the Civil War, have been modified into sporters by soldiers who brought home their military weapons and cut them down for hunting.

In 1892 the United States Army adopted the Norwegian Krag-Jorgensen bolt-action magazine-fed rifle in .30x40 caliber. It was a five-shot side-loader which, with variations, was the military arm for both Denmark and Norway. It was originally designed for smokeless powders. The Krag saw action

[4] George R. Watrous, Winchester Rifles and Shotguns, (second edition, 1950).

in the Spanish-American War but was gradually superseded by the Springfield. The Springfield bore the designation '03, from the date of its adaptation and first production at the Springfield Arsenal. It used a Mauser patent action, and had the advantage over the Krag of accepting a five-shot pre-loaded clip. This made for a slightly faster rate of fire than the Krag, which could only be hand loaded, one shot at a time. In adopting both the Krag and the Mauser, the Army Ordnance Corps was following a time-honored tradition of looking to Europe for their prototypes, much to the annoyance of American gun designers. Krag got a dollar apiece royalty for each gun that the United States built following his design. Nobody knows what Mauser was paid, as the Army still considers this to be classified information, but it is fair to assume that royalty payments stopped when we went to war with Germany in 1917.

The average man may learn to shoot only one gun well in his lifetime. The Sharps, the single-shot Civil War Springfield, the rolling-block Remington and the lever-action Winchester have all had their day as major hunting equipment. Except for the lever-action, which is still popular for white tail deer, the bolt action has taken over. The reason is obvious. During the First World War, masses of men were trained to shoot a bolt action as their first heavy gun. Once having gained skill in shooting it, they felt that they could work better with it in the field. Even today, with infantrymen being trained to shoot automatic weapons, the shortage of game, the feeling of sportsmanship, and the strength of the action and accuracy of the bolt action rifle all combine to keep the Mauser-Springfield rifles in demand for both hunting and target work. Only in big game country, primarily India and Africa, where the animals can fight back if they are wounded and mad enough, does the bolt action have a rival. This is the double rifle which has been developed and perfected by the British, starting in India over a century ago. The story of double guns is a chapter by itself.

Knight firing *a 15th century field piece with a hot poker. Knights usually delegated this job. Copper engraving collection, Berlin Art Museum.*

CHAPTER XVII

DOUBLE-BARRELED:

"He Raised His Double-Barreled gun, Fired and Killed the Two Monkeys." (Voltaire's Candide, *Paris, 1759)*

THE EARLIEST SURVIVING double guns are over-and-under wheel lock pistols and rifles. A fine example, with a pommel and shape of a *main gauche,* has silver wire wound over what looks like sharkskin, number IX 94 A in the Port de Hal in Brussels. While this wheel lock pistol is neither dated nor signed, it is of the same vintage as an ivory inlaid swirl-butt dagger-hilt double-barreled wheel lock pistol in the Metropolitan Museum in New York, which is documented. The one in the Metropolitan Museum was made for Charles V by Peter Peck in Munich around 1540. Both of its wheel lock wheel covers bear the insignia of Charles as well as the old imperial German double eagle—then the double eagle of the Holy Roman Empire. The initials P.P. on the barrel identify the maker. Other over-and-under wheel lock pistols and rifles dating from this same period—the middle of the sixteenth century—are to be found in the Bayerisches Armeemuseum in Munich and the Tøjhus Museet in Copenhagen.

Over-and-under guns came before side-by-side doubles, as they were the easier to make and did not present the problems of barrel alignment. If the barrels pointed in the same general direction that was all that was required of them, as the guns were turned over to fire the second shot. Aiming, on a take-it-or-leave-it basis, was done by looking down the top of the uppermost barrel. The gunmakers of Nuremberg complicated their own lives quite a bit by building true over-and-under guns, with two locks fired by a single trigger. These guns, usually all-metal, have a distinctly angled grip and were not designed to be turned over. Both barrels had to shoot in the same direction. A fine example in the Kienbusch collection shows that a lot of thought and work went into solving this problem of alignment. Between the barrels is a fitted and tapered iron rib, to which both barrels have been brazed. Undoubtedly these barrels were aligned by the same trial-and-error system that has obtained with double guns ever since—the two barrels are set up in rough position, held apart by clamped-on iron wedges, and

Miniature *over and under tap-action breech-loading flintlock pistols made by Auguste Francotte in Liège. loa. 5", bbls 1⅜", cal. .28". Author's Collection.*

W. J. Jeffery *double elephant rifle shot a 1365-grain patched bullet. loa. 41½", bbls 24", cal. .88". Wt. 16 lbs plus. Author's Collection.*

DOUBLE-BARRELED

shot to see what happens. Each barrel is shot independently until it groups accurately and vibration is balanced. This is done by moving the wedges up and down the barrel length. When both barrels group well independently of each other, they are then pushed together or pulled apart at the muzzle by driving in or pulling out a muzzle wedge until the two barrels shoot approximately to the same point at a given distance. When the barrels are being aligned, barrels, solder, wedges and all are tightly wrapped with iron wire. Then red hot iron rods are placed in the barrels until the barrels themselves are hot enough to melt the hard solder—thus acting as their own soldering irons. This process is repeated over and over with soldering and unsoldering until the alignment is perfect. Top and bottom ribs are then soldered in place, sights attached, and the barrels struck and polished. Simple as this whole description may sound to a contemporary reader accustomed to sophisticated hardware that goes to the moon, the alignment of barrels is a subtle and difficult job. There is no one in America today who is building a double rifle, and in England, where for nearly two centuries the finest double rifles and shotguns were built, there are only a handful of craftsmen left who can build you a two-barreled rifle that will place a bullet from both barrels in approximately the same spot at a specific distance.

The problem is not just the mechanical alignment of two perfectly straight tubes which are externally tapered. If this were all that there was to it, the life of the double gun maker would be a merry one. In order to make the center of impact of two shotgun barrels correspond to 40 yards, or the two barrels of a double rifle shoot at the same point at a hundred yards, the individual barrels must literally be bent as, and after, they are soldered or brazed together. The makers of fine double guns do not advertise the fact that their close shooting guns have bent barrels, but they do, and this is what makes them shoot to the same point—trial-and-error barrel bending.

A splendid idea which eliminated all of this by guess-and-by-God gunsmithing, was the development of the Wender, or turn-over double gun. The Wender, with its two pivoted barrels, did not present the same problem to the gun assembler. As long as the barrels looked reasonably parallel the Wender was a success, as the barrel on top was the one that was being sighted and shot. Where the under barrel pointed at that moment, and its relative position to the upper barrel was of no importance. First appearing in the pattern book of Francois Marcou in 1657, and, in the metal, in an example in the Livrustkammaren collection in Stockholm, the Wender type seems to have been first built by the French gunsmith Thuraine of the partnership of Thuraine and Le Hollandois, and by Jean Berain and Le Conte, both of whom were working in Paris after 1660. Thuraine's design survives in the pattern book of Jacquinet (1650-1660), and in a single example which was auctioned at Sotheby's in 1960. Le Conte's Wender, which is decorated with engraving and signed by Jean Berain, was a present from Louis XIV of France to Charles XI of Sweden. This is the famous piece in the Livrustkammaren, resplendent with gold damascening on the blued barrels, with silver inlay work covering virtually every inch of the stock.[1]

These Wender guns, with their single locks and double pans and frizzens, had barrels which rotated on a pin fixed between the barrels and attached to the center of the frame. The upper barrel was fired first. Then both barrels were rotated to bring the under barrel up into top position. The barrels were usually locked in firing position with a sliding catch in front of the trigger guard.

While Henry VIII had to be satisfied with a single double-barreled pistol with fixed barrels: "Itm one dagge with two peces in one stock,"[2] Louis XIII's inventory—the Cabinet d'Armes—lists a number of double guns, fixed barrel wheel locks and Wender flintlocks, three of which are known to survive. One Wender, now back in the Musée de l'Armée in Paris, was described in the original list as "Un mousquet de 4 pieds 2 pouces, a deux canons séparez par leurs deux baguettes qui se tournent sur la culasse, liées d'un cercle et d'un grande plaque sous le canon, gravez en taille d'espargne,

[1] *Pollard says that the first person to describe a Wender was Guilino Bossi, Captain, of Rome, who apparently built Wenders and wrote about them in 1625. The original does not exist, but in 1679, in Paris, his book appeared under the title* Breve tratato d'alcune inventione che sone state futte per rinforzare e raddoppiare el tiri degli arciubugi a ruota.

[2] *List of Arms of Henry VIII at the Greenwich Armory in 1547.*

ILLUSTRISSIMI GENEROSISSIMIQUE PRI. HENRICI
MAGNÆ BRITANNIÆ ET HYBERNIÆ PRINCIPIS,
Vera Effigies.

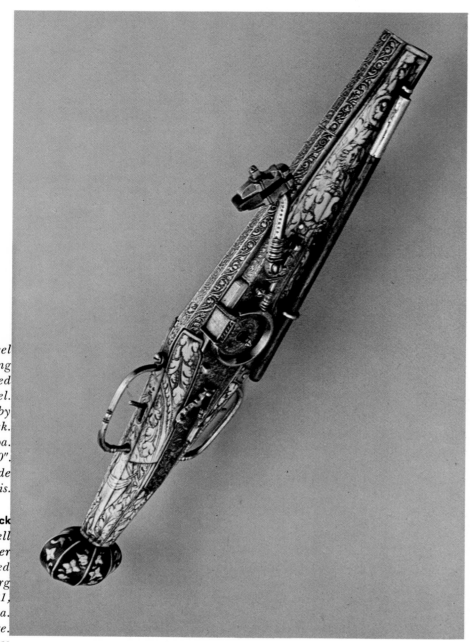

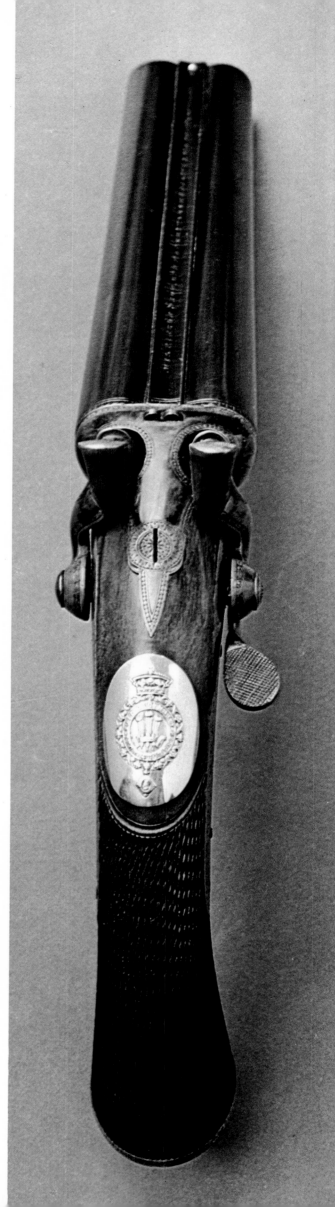

Double over and under *wheel lock pistol with converging barrels. Pistol was turned over to fire second barrel. Initials "B.H.", divided by an arrow, on the lock. German, 16th century. loa. 16¾", bbls 8⅝", cal. .40". No.# M/1618, Musée de l'Armée, Paris.*

Double-barrel flintlock shotgun. *Tortoise-shell veneered stock with silver inlays. Bolt action, enclosed locks. Made in Regensburg or Prague c, 1715-21, possibly by Paczelt. loa. 54½", bbls 31½", 22 gauge. No.# 13/589, Bayerisches Nationalmuseum, Munich.*

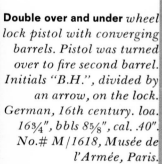

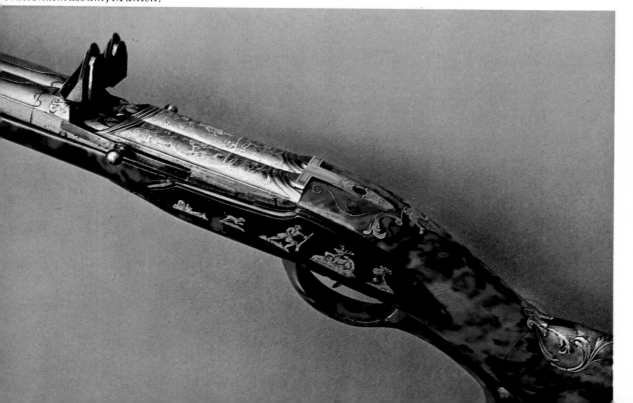

DOUBLE-BARRELED

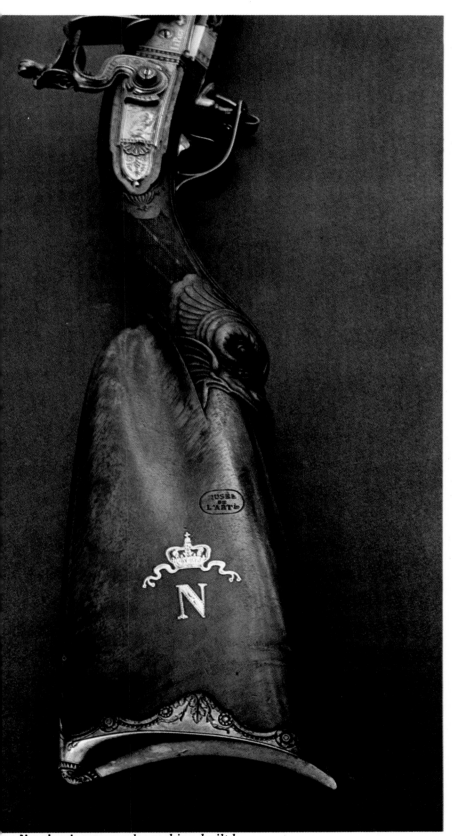

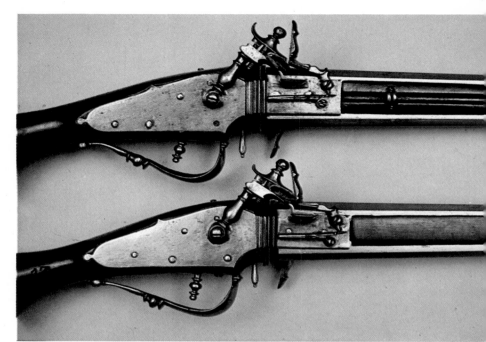

"Lazarino Cominazzi" *wender pistols with straight stocks, made before 1637. loa. 22¼", bbls. 14" cal. .52". Nos.# 3777 — 3778, Museo Storico Nazionale d'Artiglieria, Turin.*

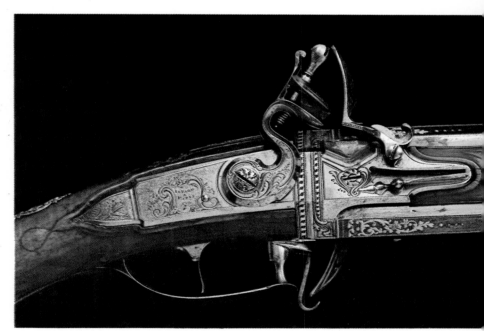

Louis XV LePage *wender dated 1767, from the Versailles collection. One of the guns which escaped Napoleon's cartouche. Russell Aitken Collection.*

Napoleon's own *wender carbine, built by LePage for the Emperor. loa. 35", bbls 19½", bore .60", multigroove rifling. No.# M 639, Musée de l'Armée, Paris.*

Left: **Edward VII** *as Prince of Wales owned this Howdah pistol made by Williamson. Illustration shows the royal crest (the 3 feathers of the Prince of Wales) and the Star of India. Cal. .577". Russell Aitken Collection.*

Double-barrel wheel lock pistol. *Silver wire wound pistol-grip, container in the butt for extra pyrites. Vermeersch Collection, loa. 30½", bbl. 22⅛", cal. .29", prob. Augsburg, c. 1560. No.# IX/94 A (2233) Museé de la Porte de Hal, Brussels.*

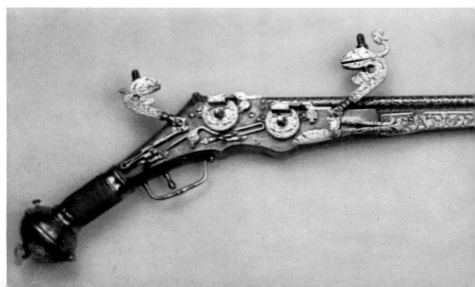

DOUBLE-BARRELED

un seul chien pour tous les deux coups, sur un bois rouge, dont la crosse se termine en console ouverte par le dessus et pientre sur le dessus d'ornements couleur d'or sur un fonds noir, la plaque de ladite crosse gravée."[3]

The Wender guns became popular in Germany and Holland as well as France, and many fine examples survive which were made between 1650 and the early nineteenth century. The gun illustrated here was one of the few that escaped the "N" stamp of Napoleon with which he improved all the royal weapons when he liberated them from the collections of the latter Louises. This Wender, which is dated 1767 on the butt, was made by the first of the famous LePage family of gunmakers, Jean. Now in the Aitken collection in New York, it was originally in Versailles, having been made for Louis XV.

There are lots of theoretical explanations of how, when, and why, side-by-side double guns came into their own. Powder undoubtedly had something to do with it. Quicker burning gunpowder permitted shorter barrels. Shorter barrels made for less weight, and less weight permitted two barrels to be put together with a rib and two locks without building to a staggering amount of weight which the shooter could neither support nor aim. The ability to make light barrels was another factor, and it would therefore be logical to look for an early example of a double-barreled shotgun from the workshop of the Cominazzos. Sure enough, in the museum in Munich there is a wheel lock shotgun with interchangeable barrels, one a set of doubles, the other four-barreled, which is signed "Lazari Cominaz" (1563-1646). Another early side-by-side double signed and dated. "Ind à Tann 1966" is in the Tøjhus Museet. The gunsmith who made this gun has avoided the ticklish problem of soldering the long thin shotgun tubes, by the simple device of inletting the side-by-side barrels into a wooden stock and securing the barrels with the conventional pins of the period.

Shotguns and rifles were not clearly differentiated in the old days, except for the German guns, which were truly rifled.

Most guns, whether pistol, carbine or rifle length were smoothbore muskets, which functioned as shotguns or rifles depending on whether they were loaded with shot or ball.

Early bird shooting was done at birds sitting on the ground, in trees, or on the water. It was considered unsporting to shoot a bird on the wing. Besides that, with the equipment that was generally being used, you couldn't hit a bird on the wing. An interest in wing shooting and the guns to go with it started in the early part of the eighteenth century. Typical side-by-side doubles of the first quarter of the century had visible lumps of lead used as spacers between the barrels, instead of a continuous bridge or rib. The first continuous ribs made of soft solder were produced at St. Etienne around 1730. Soft solder was first used as it required less heat, which meant less chance of damaging or distorting the relatively thin barrels of a shotgun. Jean Le Clerc brought the idea to Paris some time before his death in 1739, and his son Nicolas collaborated wth Chasteau in producing a side-by-side double that is now in the Livrustkammaren in Stockholm. The La Roche family, also in Paris, produced double-barreled guns with solid hard-soldered ribs, but the sole surviving example of their work, also in a Swedish collection, is a pistol. By the middle years of the century the best Paris gunsmiths were making fine double guns: Puiforcat in 1756-7, and LePage in the '60's.

Books began to be written about the art of wing shooting. In England, a 1686 rewrite of Gervase Markham's book, *The Whole Arte of Fowling by Water and Land,* published first in 1621, was revised to include a section on leading a flying bird. By 1727, Markland's *Pteryplegia, Or the Art of Shooting-Flying,* a poetic guide book to wing shooting, appeared and was reprinted many times. Before 1700 Guiseppe Mitelli did a series of engravings on hunting, including illustrations of wing shooting. These illustrations were pirated by many English, French and German printers in the eighteenth century. Later in the century (in 1788) Magne de Marolles wrote his book *La Chasse au Fusil,* which appeared within a

[3] *Item 176 from the "Cabinet d'Armes" of Louis XIII first compiled in 1663.*

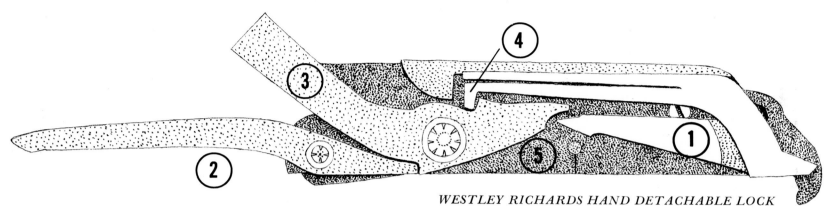

year in a pirated English edition under the title *An Essay on Shooting*. In the meantime, Thomas Page had written a book which appeared in London in 1766-67. It is a dialogue on shotgun shooting which borrows the name *The Art of Shooting-Flying* and sometimes the exact words of Markland's earlier poem.

From the beginning of the eighteenth century, single-barreled "birding guns" had barrels of four and a half feet in length. Pollard[4] calls them "little more than refined large barrelled musket." Even the shorter double guns, whether over-and-under, Wender, or side-by-side, had barrels that usually measured 42 inches. By the '50's in France and by the '60's in England, side-by-side guns had shrunk to a mere 36 inches and the modern shape of the shotgun was emerging. LePage and Boutet in France built some of the most beautiful double guns ever, including the gun with extra barrels illustrated here. This gun, now in the Metropolitan Museum, is such a work of art that it was spared the damage of being converted to percussion from flint. Instead, a whole new set of barrels, and a replacement set of percussion locks, were made to supplement the original flintlock mechanism.

The eighteenth century saw improvements such as half-stocks, still shorter barrels, and flintlocks with funnel- or sugar loaf-shaped cavities connecting the touchhole with the powder chamber for faster and more even ignition. The false breech was introduced by Henry Nock of London in 1775. Anti-friction rollers on the frizzen spring tip, gold- and plati-

num-lined touchholes and flashpans—all contributed to the effectiveness of the side-by-side double gun. Stanislaus Placzelt of Prague evidently invented the shotgun choke in the 1730's.

In England, bird shooting became a cult, a mania, almost a religion. Even with today's bad manners one's behavior at a shoot is of greater importance than hitting the bird. Estates were stocked with birds, and gamekeepers kept jealous watch over their charges. The bird population, which had been on the decline ever since Cromwell's soldiers had shot off the natural game on the big estates, began to increase, and in such number that the phenomenal shoots of Colonels Thomas Thornton and Peter Hawker were possible. Hawker's grand total of game birds shot during his lifetime included 7,035 partridges and 575 pheasants, not to mention innumerable wild chickens, swans, ducks, and geese. His biographer "Thormanby" apologizes for this wretched record: "It must be remembered that Colonel Hawker was limited in the

[4] *Major H. B. C. Pollard,* History Of Firearms, *(Butler & Tanier, London, 1933).*

DOUBLE-BARRELED

extent of ground he had to shoot over, and, suffering constantly from ill-health, was severely handicapped."

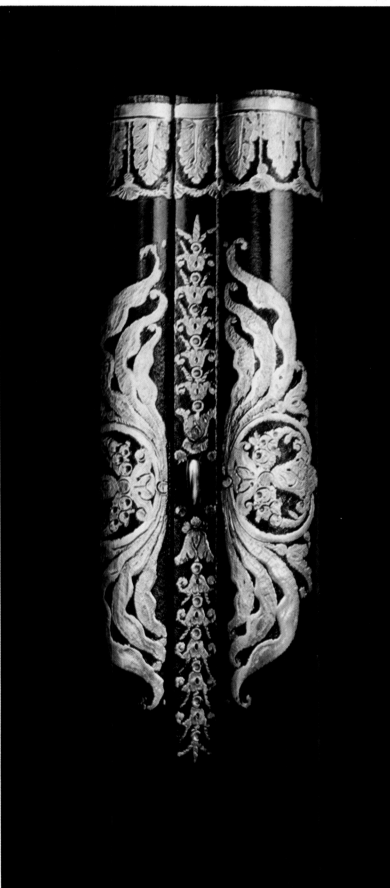

This national mania of the British found a ready response from the London gun trade, which produced more and better guns, overshadowing the fine work of LePage and Boutet. Durs and Joseph Egg, Henry and Samuel Nock, Joseph and Joe Manton, William Parker, and Twigg and Wogdon turned out their browned beauties before and after 1800. Around 1780 the top rib appeared, and in 1805 Joe Manton's guns were built with the same drop and lessened curve of stock as today's best double guns.

With the arrival of percussion, the London and Paris trade concentrated on different types of ignition systems, which resulted in the fixed cartridge and breech-loading doubles. Pauly had contributed the cartridge and Lefaucheux introduced the drop-down action with a lever under the fore end. Invention followed invention in true nineteenth-century style, but the most important developments affecting the double gun can be summarized as follows: Charles Lancaster introduced his center-fire under-lever gun with extractor in 1852; Westley Richards, the doll's-head top lever lock in 1862 (after that William Greener developed the cross-bolt lock); Murcott, the first true hammerless in 1871-2; and Anson and Deely in 1876 brought out their simple four-piece action with a solid frame that is used today in both double rifles and shotguns. With controlled burning of smokeless powders after 1900, Robert Churchill was able (without loss of efficiency) to reduce the length of shotgun barrels again. His favorite length was 25 inches.

The affection with which the British had taken up the side-by-side double-barreled shotgun carried over to rifles, and the finest double rifles came out of England, as they still do. The first double rifle designed to shoot a rifled bullet was built, believe it or not, with the intention of having it used as a military weapon. Major John Jacob, Commander of the Scinde Irregular Horse, submitted his idea and sample guns which had been made in London by John Manton and

Napoleon's Boutet flintlock *with extra percussion barrels and locks made for Prince Osten-Sachen (military governor of Paris in 1814). The Boutet barrels are signed "Manufacture de Versailles" c. 1815. The percussion barrels are signed "Leopold Bernardo, Canonnier de Paris". The percussion locks are signed "Zaoué". No.# 42.50.7, Metropolitan Museum of Art, New York, Dick Fund, 1942.*

DOUBLE-BARRELED

others, to the Military Board of the East India Company in Bombay. This was in 1856, and the Military Board of the East Indian Company *was* the British Army in India. Of course, the double rifle was rejected, but before his death Jacob had succeeded in equipping a regiment with his guns. The rifles shot very well and he proved the value of them to his own satisfaction by blowing up ammunition wagons at long distance using explosive shells. Jacob published the specifications for his army rifle: "double 24in. barrels of 32 bore (.56 caliber, 1747 grain bullet) the four grooves making four-fifths of a turn, with four points to be inserted inside the barrel near the breech for tearing open a blank cartridge when rammed down whole". The gun was equipped with folding leaf sights for ranges up to 300 yards and a vertical sight with a sliding bar which folded away when not in use for ranges up to 2,000 yards.

This gun was percussion, of course, and a muzzle loader. Other percussion sporting rifles were made by Purdey and Lancaster in the 1850's. They were designed to shoot 32 bore, two- and four-groove belted balls at large game. These guns were used to shoot tiger in India and Burma, elephant, rhino and lion in Africa. There was no place, not even the plains of Kansas, secure from the peripatetic Englishman with his trusty double rifle, as we discover in Parkman's *Oregon Trail,* written in 1846. "Our transatlantic companions were well equipped for the journey. They had a wagon drawn by six mules, and crammed with provisions for six months, besides ammunition enough for a regiment; spare rifles and fowling pieces, ropes and harness, personal luggage and a miscellaneous assortment of articles, which produced infinite embarassment. They had also decorated their persons with telescopes and portable compasses and carried English double-barrelled rifles of sixteen to the pound calibre slung to their saddles in dragoon fashion."

In 1840, the sportswriter Sir Samuel Baker found that a four-ounce projectile was sufficient while shooting in India, but preferred a half-pound bullet for his percussion rifle when he went down the Nile. He admitted that it spun him "like a weathercock in a hurricane" when it went off.[5]

These monsters, many with Jacob's design of four-groove bullets, sometimes copper jacketed and sometimes loaded with explosive heads, were the forerunners of the enormous four- six- and eight-bore black-powder cartridge loads that were still in use when Teddy Roosevelt first went to Africa to hunt. The story told about the famous man is that he was offered one of the big bore rifles at a ceremony in honor of his arrival on a hunting trip. He accepted the rifle graciously, but returned it after the show was over, saying that he would rather be trampled by an elephant. The English had to take some kidding about being too weak to carry their own rifles in the bush, but no man who has carried a sixteen- to twenty-pound rifle around all day can shoot it with enthusiasm or accuracy when the need arises.

Even the resolute Sir Samuel had had enough spinning around by the black powder cannons. In 1864, when Jacob Snider sold the British Army its first breechloader, Baker had Holland & Holland build him a black powder double rifle shooting the service caliber cartridge—a mere .577. This cartridge became the prototype for the heavy smokeless loads; the .600, the .577 and the .500 nitro express loads—all straight taper cartridges (no shoulder), and all loaded with the old string-like cordite gunpowder. They were guns designed to stop elephant and were also effectively used to shoot buffalo, rhino, lions and tigers. These guns still weighed as much as sixteen pounds. The weight and the caliber were an improvement but still a heritage from their black powder predecessors.

Modern double rifles are built for medium- and small-bore cartridges as well as in the elephant killer sizes. The smallest double gun built by Westley Richards on custom order is chambered for the high velocity .22 caliber—the .22/3000 Lovell; and in the medium calibers, from .30/06 to .470 nitro express, the weight of the double rifles compares well with bolt-action magazine guns; 8½ to 10½ pounds.

The continued popularity of the double rifle is explained by John Taylor, a white hunter from Portuguese East Africa, who has shot doubles out of choice all his life. He points out that at close distances in thick bush, wounded game will hear the clickety-click of a bolt action being worked and will either charge, or run away from the direction of the noise.

[5] *Sir Samuel Baker,* The Albert N'yanza, The Great Basin Of The Nile And Exploration Of The Nile Sources.

Shooting sitting ducks. *Illustration of bird shooting from* Venationes Ferarum *of* Tempesta.

Taylor's other point in favor of doubles is that with the more powerful cartridges, you are always sure of two shots. Whereas, with a magazine rifle shooting extremely heavy loads there is always the possibility of a jam-up, especially in African game country, where the guns get so hot that the barrels cannot be touched. He gives the example in his book *African Rifles And Cartridges* of a .35 caliber Newton which delivered an accurate and effective first shot, but was then *hors de combat* because the recoil of the gun had ejected the clip magazine. Anyway, Taylor prefers doubles and is a Mohammedan to boot.

While no double rifles are being built in America, and their construction in England has always been on a custom order basis, the U.S. does produce one fine double-barreled shotgun. It won't compare in finish or in smoothness of action with the finest English doubles, but it has one shining virtue: the barrels, for all practical purposes, cannot be shot out. This gun is the Model 21 Winchester, which has been manufactured since 1931. While it was the first double gun that Winchester had manufactured in its own plant (they had previously imported some cheap English double guns), it did not have the reputation of good American guns such as the Parker. However, in 1930 Winchester had set up its own specifications for "Winchester proof steel." This called for a special alloy of chrome molybdenum electric furnace steel. For the first time in history a gun company had a special heat of steel made to its own specifications.[6] The barrels of the

[6] *A special heat of electric furnace steel having finer grain and closer alloy control—lower in sulphur and phosphorous. Modified A.I.S.I. 4137-chrome molybdenum.*

English breech-loading shotgun *c. 1820. Barrels move forward. loa. 38", bbls 21½", 16 gauge. No.# M/61, Armeria Reale, Turin.*

DOUBLE-BARRELED

double-barreled Model 21[7] were made of this electric furnace steel. Samples were then sent to the Winchester Ballistic Laboratory Range to be test shot and so were samples of every fine English shotgun. The test was a strenuous one. Each gun was hand loaded and fired until it actually wore out, broke down or blew up. Day after day, week after week, the guns were shot continuously from dawn 'til dusk. One after another the fine English guns refused to continue functioning under this brutal treatment. Where the guns did not develop mechanical troubles, the barrels were literally shot out, to the point where they had no accuracy and were so thin that they were dangerously apt to explode—and some of them did. That is—all except the Winchester 21 with the electric furnace steel barrels. When the last English double gun had quit—it was distressing to the author, who witnessed the test, to watch so many burned out and broken—the Model 21 was still shooting. Another 10,000 rounds were pushed through the gun for good measure and then the gun was shot for pattern and accuracy and the internal diameters of the barrels were measured. There was no appreciable wear, and the barrels patterned as well as if they were new. Winchester now sells Model 21 starting at $1,000. At these prices undoubtedly the finish and hand fitting will be improved so that that it will compare favorably with good English guns.

Double guns, rifles or shotguns, have a grace and elegance about them that is hard to put a finger on. Automatic shooters, however, have no use for them, and few are found in competition on trap or skeet ranges in the United States. Nevertheless, with the shortage of game and the game law quotas, there is very little need for much more firepower than a double provides. The proof of this is that five-shot pump guns and automatics are required to have a wooden plug in the magazine limiting them to three shots. Fine doubles are hard to build and are therefore expensive—a good reason why they are not more popular—but fine doubles will continue to be built for a long time and the gentle art of barrel bending will continue to be practiced. In the meantime, let us consider some of the recoil and gas-operated automatics and their beginnings.

[7] *The only double shotgun that is manufactured to shoot with a 4" center of impact at 40 yards.*

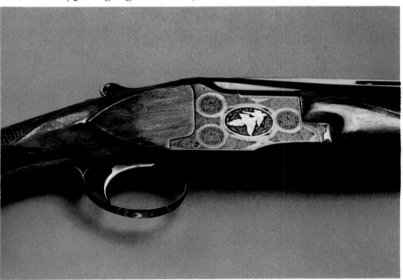

Browning over-and-under *engraved and inlaid by Fugger. 12 gauge. Russell Aitken Collection.*

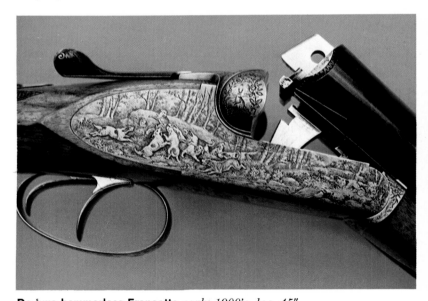

De luxe hammerless Francotte *early 1900's. loa. 45", bbls 28", 12 gauge. No.# Ao 56, #5445, Musée d'Armes, Liège.*

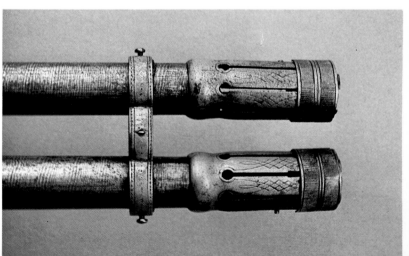

First polychoke shotgun *1881 Système Roland, 12 gauge. No.# Am 9, Musée d'Armes, Liège.*

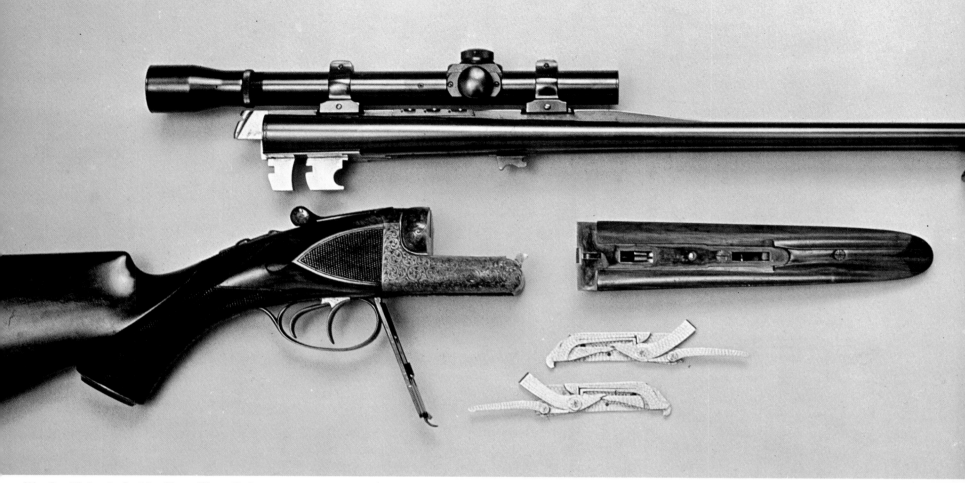

Westley Richards double rifle *calibre .375" magnum, with hand removable locks. George Rowbottom Collection.*

Cased double rifle *with two sets of barrels, .300" rook, George Rowbottom Collection.*

CHAPTER XVIII

SELF-LOADERS: FULL AND SEMI-AUTOMATICS

THE EMPEROR MAXIMILIAN was ahead of his time when he fearfully signed an edict outlawing pistols in 1517. It is noticeable that he is often depicted wearing parade armor, and he may have slept in it. At any event, although he died a mere two years later, he was not felled by an assassin's bullet. One of his descendents was not so lucky. Franz Ferdinand of Austria was only wearing a cloth military tunic when Gavarillo Princip shot him above the heart with a semi-automatic pistol on June 28, 1914. The weapon was a .32 caliber pocket model Browning made by the Fabrique Nationale in Liège. Alexander of Yugoslavia and several innocent bystanders were shot by an assassin clutching and still shooting a pair of twenty-shot magazine full-automatic Mauser pistols, as the Marseilles police clubbed his brains out. Carlos I of Portugal and his son were both victims of an assassin. This time the murder weapon was a little Winchester .22 semi-automatic, model of 1903.

Self-loaders make good assassins' weapons because of the speed with which they can be fired. Oswald's use of a bolt action rifle was a throwback which might have foiled the success of his attempt had not he been shooting from a concealed position in a darkened window out of the immediate reach of the presidential police escort. Oswald was able to take several leisurely, well-aimed shots with a military antique that he had bought from a mail-order sporting goods store. It was a 6.5mm clip-loading bolt action Mannlicher-Carcano carbine—the official arm of the Italian infantry when was was declared in 1914. The Mannlicher-Carcano is designated Model '91 for its date of issue. The gun is 40 inches long, weighs seven pounds, and has a thumb safety on the rear of the bolt. Oswald's gun had a four power "sharpshooter's telescope." The gun, with the telescope mounted, cost him $19.95. The ammunition was extra.

The term "automatic" as it is popularly used, needs a word of definition. Most of the so-called automatics are actually auto-loading or semi-automatic. The trigger mechanism includes a disconnector, thus requiring a pull on the trigger to fire each shot. A full automatic, such as the burp gun, shoots as many times as there are cartridges in the magazine, as long as the trigger is held back. Some guns are designed so that they can be fired either full or semi-automatic. In this category is the Thompson sub-machine gun and some models of the Mauser military .763 and 9mm pistol. These models, with the magazine ahead of the trigger guard, were used primarily in the First World War. They have a button on the side of the action which will make the weapon semi- or full automatic depending on the selection.

The full automatic or machine gun has, of course, no legitimate sporting use. However, from its inception, it was never conceived of as a sporting weapon. In the kindly words of advice to Hiram Maxim, inventor of the Maxim-Vickers machine gun in 1889 from a disgruntled friend: "invent something that will make it easier and quicker for these Europeans to cut each others' throats."

In any event, the full automatic—the machine gun—has no place in this volume except, as in its infancy, it served as a prototype for semi-automatic weapons.

The development of the self-loader was a slow process, starting in the mid-nineteenth century with the invention of a gas-operated under-barrel piston which unlocked and raised the breech of a percussion breechloader. This principle was the invention of Edward Lindner of New York, who got a U.S. patent for it in 1854. While the gas-operated piston ejected the spent cartridge and loaded a new one in the chamber, the gun still had to be primed with a conventional percussion primer and cocked by hand before each shot. The Lindner is of interest only because it was the first to use the gas from the gunpowder to operate the mechanism. The gun itself was not a success. Neither were the experiments of other Americans between 1866 and 1874. The names of Curtis, Lutze and Plessner are not even listed in Gardner's compendium of *Small Arms Makers,* although they were still remembered by Pollard who was writing his book in the 'teens and twenties.

Imperator Caelar Diuus Maximilianus Pius Felix Augustus

SELF-LOADERS

The early successful automatic actions were heavy, and were designed for large caliber machine guns or light cannon. They were not hand-held as their weight demanded legs or a carriage of some kind. The first, the Maxim, filled a military need for a greater concentrated fire power. Prior to the Maxim, several ingenious solutions had been brought to actual production but as none were in any sense automatic, they are merely noted for their historical interest.

The Billinghurst-Requa, a curiosity to compete with Puckle, was a throwback to the earliest multibarrel guns of the fourteeneth century. A row of twenty-four barrels stretched between two cannon wheels. The barrels rested on the axle. When the gun was fired the cartridges were designed to ignite one another. Once the miserable thing was started, you could not turn it off. The Billinghurst-Requa "Platoon Battery Gun" was patented in 1862 as a Civil War weapon, but despite a demonstration in front of the New York Stock Exchange it was neither a financial nor a military success.

In France, or really in the gun capital of the world, Liège, designers Montigny and Fusnot designed the Mitrailleuse, a hand-cranked job that shot 37 rounds from a loading plate through as many barrels clustered together in a hexagon-shaped clump inside a round sleeve. The shots could be fired individually, and the action stopped by stopping cranking. With a crack crew it would discharge 370 shots a minute and would keep on without jamming for some time, as the number of barrels kept each individual one from getting too hot. The Mitrailleuse, which was shown for the first time at the Crystal Palace International Exhibition in London in 1851,[1] attracted the attention of the French, who adopted it and used it during the Franco-Prussian War twenty years later. The Montigny Mitrailleuse looked like a big bore cannon with its round barrel sleeve and big wheels and gun carriage. For this or other wrong reasons the French supplied these weapons to their artillery, where they lacked sufficient range, instead of to the infantry where they would have served admirably as a short-range anti-personnel weapon. As

[1] *The same industrial exhibition where Colt first showed his revolvers to a European audience.*

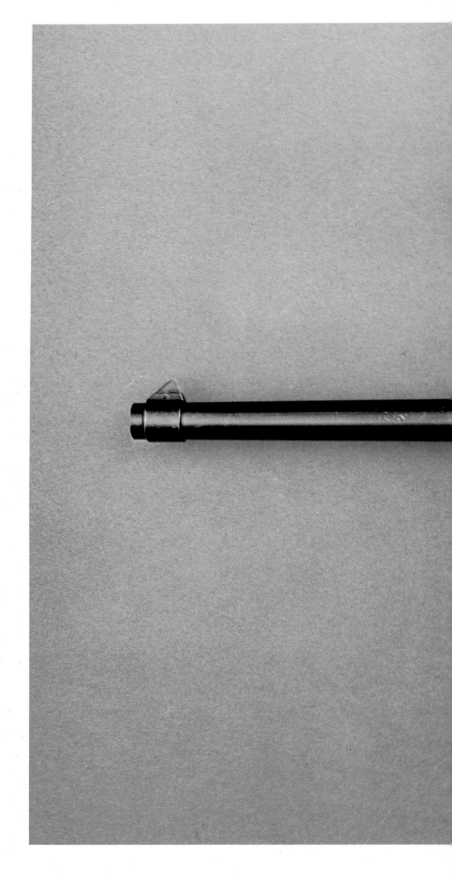

Pre-1914 boar gun *Luger carbine
with detachable stock
cal. 7.65 Luger 10-shot.*

Bergman automatic *model 1894
5-shot, calibre 7.65. Borchardt
8-shot automatic 7.65 calibre,
patent 1893, made by Loewe,
Berlin. Nos. 5294 and 5268,
Musée d'Armes, Liège.*

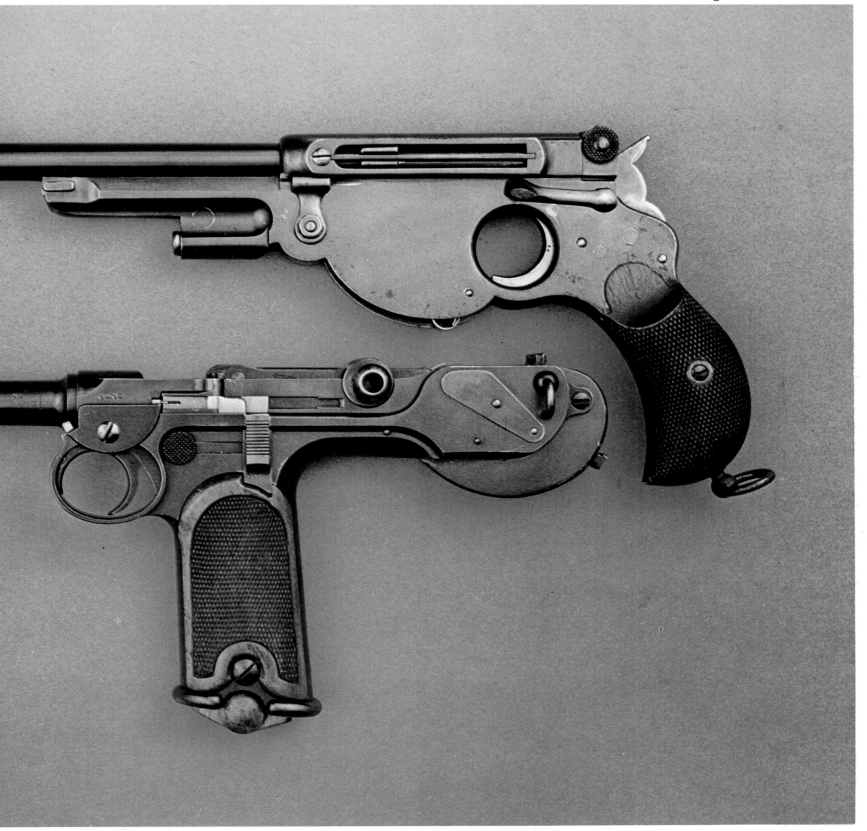

SELF-LOADERS

a result, the Mitrailleuse fell into disrepute, and, according to some authorities, the misuse of the weapon led to the French losing the war.

At the same time—1862—that the Billinghurst-Requa was setting gun design back by 500 years, Dr. Richard Gatling, appropriately from Chicago, patented his "battery or machine" gun. According to Johnson and Haven [2] "This was probably the first real 'machine gun' in that the charges were fed into the chambers, fired, and extracted by the actual operation of machinery."

The Gatling, while it can certainly be classed as a machine gun, was no automatic The faster you cranked it, the faster it shot. Later on, a motor was attached to it to increase the cyclic rate.

The Maxim, however, was automatic. The single barrel of the Maxim, locked to the breech block, recoiled a short distance. Then a toggle unlocked the barrel from the breech, which continued its travel. The moving breech extracted the fired case, reloaded a new cartridge on its spring-propelled return, and the cycle was repeated as long as the ammunition held out and the trigger was held back. The Maxim single barrel was kept cool by a jacket of water around it. The gun was fed ammunition from a canvas belt. It was built in a number of calibers including 37mm, which saw action in the Boer War. The noise it made in the rapid discharge of its twenty-five-shot belts gave rise to the alliterative Pom-Pom.

Unfortunately, Maxim's gun was invented in the days when the British Army was still using black powder, and besides individual idiosyncrasies, these black powder weapons had one fault in common; they jammed interminably because of the great amount of black powder fouling. It was easy to identify the Maxim in action—an impenetrable cloud of acrid smoke protecting the onlooker from a veritable perfection of cussing, the pearls of Anglo-Saxon expletives preserved and cherished by British Foot since the Battle of Hastings.

The Maxim machine gun is classed as a short recoil action. The next important invention in automatic weaponry was the Browning gas-operated, air-cooled, heavy machine gun, and this brings up a problem in semantics. While automatics and semi-automatics are variously classed as short and long recoil-operated, blowback, gas-operated, and short stroke gas-operation, they all in fact could be called gas-operated. When the recoil pushes back the shell case, breech and barrel in a unit, the operating force is the expanding gas. This is not, however, the conventional definition. The breakdown of the various types of self-loaders is as follows:

1) Short recoil, which action has been described and includes not only the Maxim and its descendents, but the Borchardt pistol, the Luger, the Mauser pistol and the Walther P-38.

2) Locked breech, long recoil (where the barrel and breech are locked together for the full length of the recoiling stroke). The Remington Model 81 rifle and the Browning auto-loading shotguns are typical of this system.

3) Original gas-operated: These include the Browning gas-operated machine gun of 1881, the Potato Digger of W.W. I, and the Hotchkiss machine gun.

4) Short-stroke piston principle of gas operation developed by David M. Williams and used in the famed U.S. M-1 .30 caliber carbine, where the slide is given a substantial belt for a short distance and subsequently travels on to unlock the breech and complete the rearward stroke.

5) Finally, one of the earliest and simplest systems, the blowback action developed by John Browning in 1898 and marketed by Fabrique Nationale in Liège since 1900. Examples of the blowback action range from the low-powered European and American pocket pistols to the later versions of the .45 caliber Thompson. Also included are the .351 and .401 Winchester self-loading rifles and .22 rimfire semi-automatic rifles and pistols.

Historically, the first of the semi-automatics was the work of Hugo Borchardt whose gun designing career stretched from the Sharps-Borchardt "Old Reliable" single-shot rifles to the Borchardt automatic pistol, which design he had to take from Bridgeport, Connecticut, to Berlin, Germany, to

---

[2] *Johnson and Haven,* Automatic Arms, Their History, Development and Use, *(William Morrow, New York, 1941) p. 14.*

find a manufacturer. In point of time, his patents were issued between 1876, for the Sharps-Borchardt single-shot, to 1893 for the automatic pistol. The Borchardt was an ugly-looking brute with very poor balance, as both the clip and a bulbous housing for the toggle and mainspring were to the rear of the trigger. The gun fired a .30 caliber bottle-necked cartridge. The German designers, not wanting to be left behind by an American upstart, came up with two new automatics in the next two years. They were in too much of a hurry to be successful and neither the Bergmann in 1894 nor the Schwarzlose in 1895 made much of a lasting impression.

In 1900 Georg Luger brought out his improved version of the Borchardt, called the Parabellum. The Luger, chambered either for the necked-down .30 caliber (.765mm) or the popular 9mm European cartridge, had a better fitting grip and a mainspring housing more in proportion to the shape and size of the gun. The Luger has remained a sporting as well as a military weapon in a variety of barrel lengths, from a 3½-inch German Army model to the twelve-inch sporting carbine made before W.W. I. Before the Luger

Vegetius, De Re Militari

refinements had been applied to the Borchardt, Paul Mauser got his patent for an automatic in 1897 and commenced manufacturing in 1898. The Mauser was manufactured until W.W. II. Both the military Mauser and the Luger had been replaced in the German Army by the double action P-38 Walther. This double action gun has the advantage of a cartridge in the chamber with the hammer down, firing the first shot double action as in a revolver.

The first automatic pistol made in the United States was the Browning .38 caliber rimless produced by Colt in 1900. Smaller caliber blowback and locked breech recoil-operated automatics had been produced a few years earlier under Browing patents by the Fabrique Nationale in Liege. The .38 Colt was discovered to be not quite enough of a man-stopper when fired at cloth armored Moros in the Philippines during the Spanish-American War. In 1905 Colt introduced Browning's first .45 caliber automatic. With minor improvements in the spur, the grip angle and the shaped backstrap safety, it is used today by all branches of the U.S. services though the importance of automatic pistols has diminished with the growing use of the carbine and submachine gun.

In the smaller calibers of police and defense weapons, the Colt blowbacks became the models which were copied extensively by every country in Europe. Forty-three brand names have been recorded from Spain alone. While Savage, Smith & Wesson, Harrington & Richardson, and Remington all brought out creditable automatic pistols during the early 1900's, Colt and John Browning had the cream of the United States market, which they reinforced by introducing the first .22 caliber target automatic, the Woodsman type, in 1915.

While some of Gene Stoner's military designs, such as the AR 15 or the AR 10 may turn up with custom stocks as sporters in the next generation, and the M-1 carbine is considered an ideal deer rifle in some circles, the trend of gun design for hunting and target weapons is following a new direction. According to Harry Sefried, who should know, having designed guns for Winchester, Hi-Standard and Sturm Ruger, gun designers are primarily concerned with the development of methods which utilize new materials and

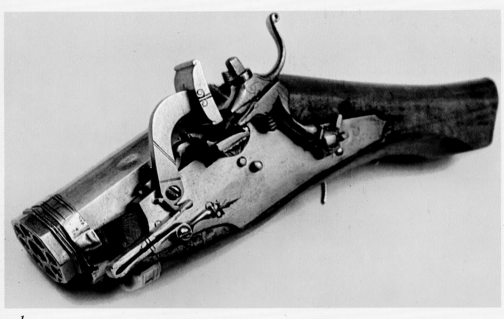

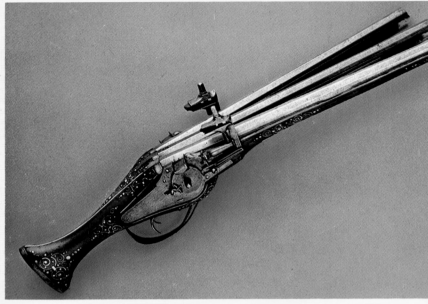

1   **Small 9-barreled snaphaunce,** *c. 1600. No.# 285, Tøjhus Museet, Copenhagen.*

2   **Cabinet of Louis XIII,** *No. 240. Right and center barrel fired together. No.# 10315, Musée de l'Armée, Paris.*

3   **Heinrich Himmler's** *present to Gen. Karl Wolff. 7.65 Walther. No. 2400, West Point Museum.*

4   **Duck foot flintlock** *with sliding safety and belt hook. Goodwin and Co. c. 1790, Winchester Gun Museum, New Haven, Conn.*

5   **13-barrel flintlock,** *calibres range from .45" to 60", c. 1690-1720. No.# 3797 N36, Museo Storico Nazionale d'Artiglieria, Turin.*

6   **Dardic pistol** *which shoots round bullets from triangular cases. Harry Sefried Collection.*

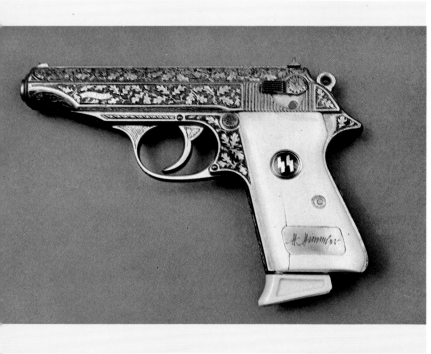

processes. Nobody needs a new way to detonate powder or an earth-shattering patent to add to the heap, but good guns are being made better by the use of, for example, investment castings instead of forgings. Take the Ruger single action revolver. Its frame is an investment casting in comparison with the original Colt single action with a frame which was first forged and then machined. The Colt frame was much more expensive to manufacture in terms of labor, but even if that were unimportant, the investment casting can be stronger and have a more uniform grain structure because of the absence of stress raising machining marks in critical areas.

Perhaps even a better example, and one that Harry contributed to, was the practical application of button rifling. Button rifling had been thought of in 1921 by James Hatcher and he had patented a button rifling machine. However, nothing came of it until the development of cemented carbides and extreme pressure lubricants, which when applied with imagination made the process a success. Harry started button rifling barrels at Hi-Standard in 1951 on a production basis, and today, Hart barrels are winning all the bench rest trophies for accuracy.

Before button rifling, forged barrels were scrape rifled, and the best barrels were scrape rifled by perfectionists like Harry Pope and Eric Johnson. Between the eighteen-nineties and the nineteen-thirties, first Harry Pope and then Eric Johnson scraped out the rifling grooves of match barrels a few hundred thousandths of an inch at a time. That this method made superb barrels is attested to by Mann in his ballistic classic, *The Bullets' Flight,* but today's bench rest groups (¼ inch at 100 yards) would make an old timer snort with disbelief—or cry.

As we leave the scene of automatics and automatic machines to produce them, some with data processed computer guidance, we can look forward to owning a gun whose barrel was not made with horseshoe nails, but was swaged in a single operation over a mandrel. Winchester is already making them and they may show up next at the Bench Rest Matches.

CHAPTER XIX

ROCKETS AND BLUE SKY

THIS FIRE THEY made by the following arts. From the pine and certain such evergreen trees inflammable resin is collected. This is rubbed with sulphur and put into tubes of reed, and is blown by men using it with violent and continuous breath. Then in this manner it meets the fire on the tip and catches light and falls like a fiery whirlwind on the face of the enemy."[1]

The girl, Anna Comnena, who wrote this description of Greek fire in the year ten hundred and something was the daughter of the emperor of the Roman Empire, then headquartered in Constantinople. One of the secret strengths that kept her father and his dynasty on the throne of the Eastern Empire was the formula for brewing Greek fire. It is a certainty that papa did not spill the entire recipe to his daughter. Greek fire remained the secret weapon with which the Greeks—pardon me, Romans—fought off the Muslim hordes for another 300 years, and it is still a secret today.

This blowing fire through tubes would seem to be the earliest form of rocketry, if one can call it that. It was not until the fourteenth century that we find Arabic and French illustrations of men holding sticks with tubes attached to them. These objects, thought to be guns, may well have been primitive rockets or horse scarers not unlike the skyrockets used in pyrotechnic displays today. It is a matter of conjecture just when the saltpeter was added to the sulphur and charcoal to make real explosive gunpowder. Without the saltpeter, sulphur and charcoal or sulphur and resin, or sulphur and crude oil would burn, of course, with a fierce enough flame to scare off horses and simple peasant soldiers.

By the seventeenth century, pyrotechnics had become a highly developed art both at the French and Chinese courts, and the lavish displays of fireworks at the court galas of Louis XIV have been the subject of a number of paintings and illustrations. By this time, the idea of a self-propelling missile, for that is what a rocket is, had been reapplied to weaponry, and we have the example here of a flintlock rocket launcher. These rocket launchers, along with grenade launchers, do not seem to have contributed much to the pleasures of civilized warfare and few were manufactured and fewer still survive.

Reference to the effect of rockets used in actual combat does not appear until the beginning of the nineteenth century, and it was the action between the British and the Americans in the War of 1812 that inspired the line: "by the rocket's red glare."

Turning festival skyrockets to serious military use was the work of the Englishman William Congreve, prior to 1806. The Indians were supposed to have used rockets in warfare and he is supposed to have seen them there.[2] Anyway, the experiments that he performed, leading to their use by the British in a naval attack on Boulogne, won him a knighthood. Congreve's rocket was simply a larger metal-cased version of a common skyrocket, including the stick. Of course, it had an explosive head. Later improvements by the British, especially Hale, eliminated the stick, but with or without sticks, fired from trough or tube, they were never accurate enough to hit the broad side of a barn. However, they were used with fair to middling success as a military weapon or as a signalling device until late in the nineteenth century, when they again became obsolescent military hardware.

Experiments with rockets were again commenced by an American, Robert H. Goddard, during World War I and continued by the Germans in the late 1920's. Crow, an Englishman, fiddled with them in the '30's, but it was the Russians who made practical employment of rocket barrages in war. With better controlled burning rate of the propellant, the accuracy of the rocket was improved; and with explosive heads, the Russians were able to penetrate the armor of German tanks. Trucks mounted with from 12 to 16 rocket launchers were a deterrent to German armor at Stalingrad.

What makes the bazooka a fearsomely effective weapon is not controlled acceleration of the projectile speed on its way to the target, but the effect of the shaped charge which is detonated on impact. Launched from its open-ended tube, the bazooka missile, like the recoilless rifle projectile, lobs

---

[1] *Anna Comnena,* Alexias *(circa 1100); translated in Partington's* Greek Fire and Gunpowder *(Heffer, Cambridge, 1960).*

[2] *"Iron rockets have been used as military weapons, or machines in the East Indies, as far back as can be remembered, and are still in great fashion and estimation." Francis Grose,* A History of the English Army, *(London, 1789).*

An invention that never was, *from Vegetius'* De Re Militari, *page 125, Paris, 1553.*

Military Antiquities *by Francis Grose, 1786.*

through the air until impact. The impact energy will detonate a shaped charge, and it in turn will penetrate through ten to twelve inches of tempered, proof steel armor. It will push the now-molten plate-steel ahead of it to become a terrible grenade in the vitals of the tank. This led the tankers to revert to body armor. The late Leonard Heinrich, armorer of the Metropolitan Museum, was called away from a job of restoring Maximilian parade armor, to design modern helmets and cuirasses for tankers to wear in World War II.

The hand-held recoilless rifle used by the U.S. Army is made in three calibers—76mm, 105mm and 155mm. Thus even the smallest of the bazookas[3], requiring only a two-man crew—one man to hold and aim, the other to load the rocket from the open rear end of the tube—is larger in bore and many times as deadly as the French "75" field piece of World War I fame.

Unlike rockets, which have had an on-again, off-again military career, the hand grenade has been a military staple for a long time, as this wheel lock grenade launcher demonstrates. Of course, grenades can be thrown by hand or launched from a catapult or gun. Hand throwing takes both guts and skill and it takes more than a good baseball player's arm to pick up and return a five-second fused grenade. For this reason, the French, in 1667, organized elite companies of grenadiers equipped with grenade launching flintlocks. These guns were either made with a cup at the end of the barrel to hold the grenade in place until it received the propelling charge from gunpowder in the barrel, or were reversible weapons, shooting conventional ball from one end and launching grenades from a tube where the gunstock would normally be.

The career of the modern hand grenade began with the Japanese at the siege of Port Arthur in 1904 during the Russo-Japanese War. With little change in shape or principle it has been a staple of the infantry in the two world wars. The contemporary grenade comes in two basic shapes, the pineapple and the potato masher. Both contain charges of explosives housed in an iron box which fragments into shrapnel when the charge explodes. These grenades are fused, usually for five seconds, to allow for travel time. The grenade is armed by pulling a pin, and the fuse ignited when the thumb piece is released as it is thrown. These latest descendants of fire arrows and fire bombs of the late Middle Ages make a nasty anti-personnel weapon.

Flame throwers employing Greek fire kept the Arabs out of Constantinople for 400 years, and descriptions, other than Anna Comnena's, have come down to us of the tubes lashed to bows of galleys of the Eastern Empire. One learns of tubes (aimed over the city walls of Constantinople) through which the Greek fire was fed, being ignited at the muzzle. While the ingredients of Greek fire were such a well-kept secret for so long, the effect of its use must have been similar to that of napalm, an intensely hot burning mixture with a petroleum base,[4] used to rout or roast out the Imperial Japanese Army from their nearly impregnable emplacements in the South Pacific islands in World War II.

Brand-new weapons, the anathema of the well-ordered military mind the world over, have usually had to find civilian acceptance first. This was as true of the revolver as it was of the hand cannon. But today, in an effort to change a stultifying tradition, the United States Army Ordnance Corps has established Project Blue Sky which actually invites inventors to submit new inventions and has issued development contracts to those who have seemingly good ideas.

Ideas for weapons which have been submitted or will be submitted to the Blue Sky Project are only a little more conservative than the cartoonist's favorite weapon, the death-ray pistol. Drawing board and pilot model examples include the still wildly inaccurate rocket pistol (that old, controlled burning problem all over again) developed by a California inventor, guns that shoot lethally impregnated needles, and guns that shoot "icicle" bullets which dissolve leaving no trace. While these James Bondish weapons, if they have any merit at all, would find greatest application in the hands of espionage agents, there are other innovations which come nearer to having military utility.

---

[3] *The bazooka's dimensions—2.36 inches in diameter and 21.6 inches long. The "gun" weighs only 3½ pounds.*

[4] *Aluminum naphthenate is used as a thickening agent with gasoline to produce an incendiary jelly.*

SHAPED CHARGE (MONROE EFFECT) USED IN BAZOOKA SHELLS, RECOILLESS RIFLE SHELLS, ETC.

1) *Aerodynamic fairing (shell casing)*
2) *Explosive—Composition B (improved dynamite) shaped charges*
3) *Propellant*

Gunner's quadrant *built in the shoulder stock of the flintlock grenade launcher illustrated next page, lower right.*

ROCKETS

One invention, still in the testing stage, is the baby of George Rowbottom, President of Kodiak, a sporting arms manufacturer, and a veteran of jungle warfare in Malaysian rain forests. He has apparently solved the age-old problem of how to fight back when you can't see who's shooting at you.

This was the problem that confronted the early settlers of the American colonies who couldn't see the Indian behind the tree. It bothered the British in turn, who couldn't see the Kentucky rifleman sniping at them from wooded cover. Even today, poisoned darts and blowguns hold their own in tropical Amazonian vegetation, and the Viet Cong infantry, with their rusty little carbines, are accounting for an uncomfortable number of U.S. soldiers disembarking from their helicopters. The middle of a clearing or a rice paddy is nowhere to be when the shooting starts, and by the time the survivors reach the jungle edge, naturally there's nobody there. Rowbottom's gadget is a light, air-cooled machine gun with a specially chambered smoothbore barrel shooting a case with the base diameter of a present .50 caliber shell. But his shell case is not necked-down. The case is filled to the brim with a variation of No. 4 shot, which hurtle out by the hundreds with a muzzle velocity of 2200 f.p.s. at a cyclic rate close to a thousand rounds per minute. The number of individual pellets thus fired is astronomical. The effect is to denude every leaf from every tree for a depth of 20 yards—farther into the jungle than a sniper could see out to shoot. Naked as jay birds, the sniper group either has had it from the pellets or are in line of fire from the serious stuff.

New materials, such as fiberglass spun on a mandrel to make the Hartley-inspired Winchester shotgun barrels, should be a must for the military rifleman. The barrels won't rust, of course, and in addition they virtually cannot be broken. Run over by a tank, they flex and bound back into shape and the bugaboo of every shooter, the obstruction in the barrel, instead of making the shooter a candidate for the Headless Horseman Club, is spewed out by the barrel, which enlarges like a python swallowing a pig.

This spun fiberglass uses the principle of autofrettage, as the glass fibers are woven over a thin tube of stainless steel —a new version of the principle which has been employed since iron hoops were sweated on over iron staves to make fourteenth-century bombards. More recently it was employed by the Philippine Moros—no engineering school graduates among them—who wrapped string made from hemp fibers around stolen U.S. Engineer Corps one-inch water pipe, thus making their Spanish-American War version of the zip gun.

Another gun of tomorrow, with both military and sporting possibilities, is the invention of Fred Stevens. Superficially it looks like a king-sized, stainless steel Allen and Thurber pepperpot. It shoots a cartridge of .38 caliber which is as long as the cylinder. The gun is designed for underwater shooting, and by keeping the water out of the barrels with the full length cartridges, Stevens has been able to produce a gun that shoots an impressive distance with remarkable penetration and delivers a wallop at both ends.

Nobody much, as was stated at the end of the last chapter, is trying to patent an invention which will make a radical change in sporting guns. Perhaps no one ever did. From the first hand cannons 'till now, the prototypes of most sporting weapons have been military.

Several years ago, the talented industrial designer of Trylon and Perisphere fame, Norman Bel Geddes, was invited by the Remington Arms Company to try his luck at streamlining their line of shotguns and rifles. A study of the market was in order. An honest man and a freshman in economics, Bel Geddes refused the job after making the study. Sure, he could streamline away the traditional lines of a Remington or any other gun, but nobody but nobody would buy the things after they were made.

Today, the entire output of the sporting gun business for a year—both guns and ammunition—is worth less in dollars and cents than the costume jewelry manufactured during the same period in Providence, Rhode Island. The information that so-and-so is a gun designer, is often greeted with the amazed response: "Does anyone *design* guns?" The answer, of course, is "yes", yet the pious desire of Hans Zwicka,[5] the crossbow maker of 1628, is more deeply felt and with more reason today than ever. Perhaps this is why target shooters and hunters both have been looking over their shoulders nostalgically at the "shooters" of the recent past. These "shooters" and "decorators" will be the subject of the last chapter.

[5] —

Mit Bogen schiessen zur Wand,
Bedeutet Fride im Land,
Mid nu schoeden aber Krige,
Dafur uns Gott Behide.

Shooting bows against the walls,
Means peace throughout the land,
But God protect us from the call,
To war, where havoc takes command.
Translation: Lynn Mertke

Fred Steven's *stainless steel underwater 6-shot .38" cal. dart-shooting pepperpot.*

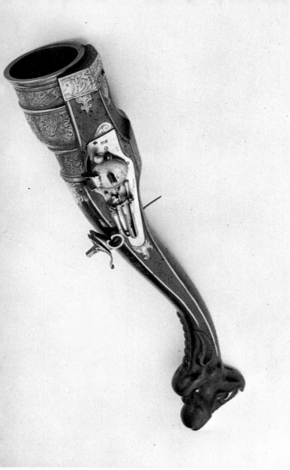

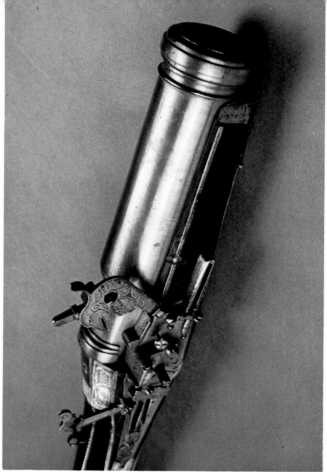

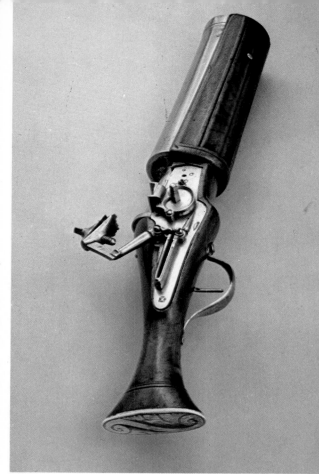

The term grenadier comes from the special French troops (c. 1750) who shot these wheel lock grenade launchers. loa. 24½", bbl 5½", bore 3". No.# M 439, Musée de l'Armée, Paris.

"Grafenstein a Gotha", "1731". Match-and wheel lock grenade launcher. The lock plate is stamped with crossed axes and an "S" and the butt plate is engraved with a cavalier in short pants and a pumpkin hat. loa. 26", bbl 10½", bore 1¹³⁄₁₆". No.# WR 1450, Bayerisches Nationalmuseum, Munich.

Wheel lock "mortar" of the 17th century. Barrel insulated with a wood sheath. loa. 22½", bbl 9½", cal. 2¼". No.# IX/101, Musée de la Porte de Hal, Brussels.

Bronze barrel grenade launcher signed "Gebauer Rensburg" "1744". loa. 24", bore 2¹³⁄₃₂". No.# B 1479, Tøjhus Museet, Copenhagen.

'1731" "Grafenstein a Gotha" "T.A.N.D.E.M." "Vigilantia vincet" inscribed on this flintlock. A bronze gilt dog forms the rear sight. loa. 32½", bbl 17¼", bore at muzzle 2⅞". No.# 13/725 Bayerisches Armeemuseum, Munich.

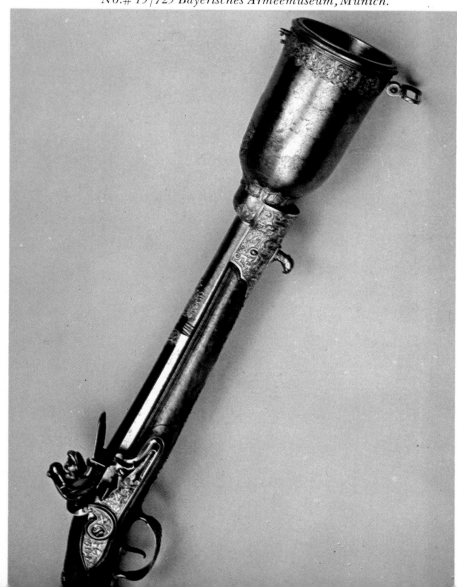

CHAPTER XX

"SHOOTERS" AND "DECORATORS"

AT THIS POINT we have perhaps reached the moment when we can look objectively at the whole picture of personal firearms. That this is so is due to the lessening military significance of such weapons. We can look back now and evaluate which hand arms were most influential, and by studying these arms gain first-hand knowledge of history. What we learn won't always correspond with textbooks or political history. It's a case of geology versus the Book of Genesis.

Did the invention of gunpowder liberate the little people? Probably not. Maximilian I, foreseeing the possibility of heading Europe's greatest political bloc since Charlemagne, encouraged the construction of hand weapons and cannons (magnificent specimens still exist) and increased the pay of Masters of Arms,[1] despite his fear of being shot by an assassin. Maximilian could afford foundries to make gun barrels and cast cannon, and could subsidize an elite corps of Master Gunners. In contrast, it was the little fellows, the Italian condottiere who couldn't afford gun factories, who took such affront to the new weapons which threatened their strong-arm tactics. It was Gian Paolo Vitelli who threatened hysterically to cut off the hands of any paysan who dared to shoot a gun at his men.

Did the coonskin-capped boys from old Kaintuck drive the redcoats into the water at Jones Beach and back to Blighty with their accurate, rifled Pennsylvania squirrel guns? I don't think so. The crude home-made product of the Pennsylvania blacksmiths with their borrowed English pistol locks were more often than not *smoothbored* and no more accurate than you might suspect, considering the primitive boring machinery. Four out of five of the best Kentuckys in the best Kentucky collection in the world, Joe Kindig's in York, Pennsylvania, are smoothbored as a Cadillac cylinder. The accurate rifled Kentuckys which took after the German *Jaegers* were not built in quantities enough to have any military significance until after the War of 1812.

Did the superb strategy of Field Marshal Montgomery and the heroic courage of Winston Churchill lick the Germans in World War II? Well, maybe! But in addition, if you will look at a German Military Mauser made in Spandau or Oberndorf of Brno, Czechoslovakia, and dated 1942—three years before the Reich said "uncle"—you will find that the finish is shoddy. The Germans had run out of their own skilled labor, they had run out of slave labor, and they were running out of economic and industrial capacity to build basic weapons for their infantry.

However, if history lessons were the only thing that old guns are good for, it would be sufficient to keep a few of them available for scholars in the study collections in museums, and the rest could be burned up and forgotten. This is not what's happening. There is more interest in antique guns today than ever before. As the older guns no longer have a dread connotation, they are being looked at from a fresh viewpoint. Some of them, many illustrated in this volume, constitute not only a secondary art in themselves, but are also a compendium of the best of the arts and skills of the jeweller, the engraver, the sculptor, wood carver and armorer.

Others, such as the Kentuckys illustrated here, recall an era of personal bravery and the practice of life-and-death skills. This is why there are more guys shooting more Kentucky rifles today than there were when Morgan took his little band of backwoodsmen to drink tea in Boston. Muzzle-loader clubs are springing up all over the U.S.A. Zouave Remingtons and percussion revolvers are being fired with greater accuracy than grandaddy ever boasted of. The black powder boys are having a field day. In England, Dr. Christopher Roads, the Deputy Director of the Imperial War Museum, is away weekends with an ever-growing group of enthusiasts to see how far and how accurately the black powder long-range single-shot rifles will shoot. In Germany, Austria and Switzerland the leisurely sport of the *Scheutzen Platz* has been revived. In Italy, France and Spain there are the most avid *tireurs* of rabbits and small game in the world. These sportsmen undoubtedly have in mind a rabbit stew, but they are giving the rabbit a more than sporting chance when they prefer to hunt with black powder sporters made by Gastinne Renette.

---

[1] *Letter from Maximilian to his governor of Crain, translated by Ludwik Krzyzanowski:*

Maximilian I, by God's Grace, Roman Emperor, etc.

Noble, dear, faithful governor! Since, in our opinion, our fellow countrymen, charges, and subjects in our princedom of Crain do not have at their service, as is necessary these days, Masters of Arms (gunmakers) and such men as can operate a gun for them, it is our gracious intention to provide for them and that in such manner that, provided those who are willing to employ one of several Masters of Arms according to our proposal, pay a minimum salary and board-expenses to them. We shall decree to pay over and above, an annual gratifica-tion and contribution to each of these Masters of Arms in order that they may thus stay in their office. We recommend to you earnestly to make this, our gracious intention, known to our fellow countrymen, charges, and subjects in our princedom of Crain, and then to write us which of them are willing to accept our proposal. Then, according to your statement and as explained above, we are going to provide for Masters of Arms and to decree that an annual gratification and contribution be paid to them over and above their annual minimum subsistence. And if you act on this promptly, be sure of our appreciation.

Given the last day of August, 1518, in the 33rd year of our reign.

Duck decoy, *from Antonio Tempesta, 1556-1630.*

The gunmaker *(making barrels)—see below.*

The gun stocker *(left) and the hunter (right) from* Abbildung der Gemeinnützlichen Hauptständ *by Christoff Weigel.*

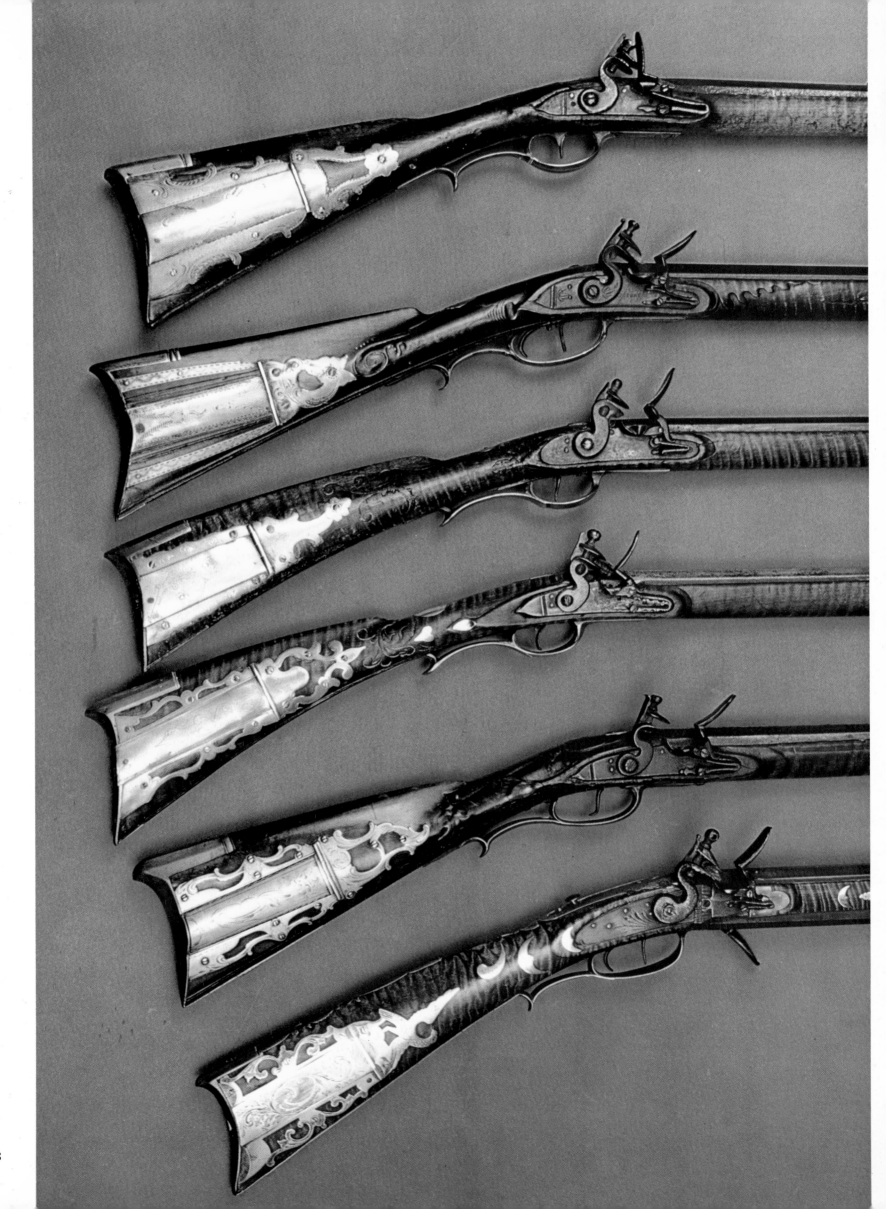

"SHOOTERS" AND "DECORATORS"

LEFT: **(1)** *c. 1770 Lancaster or York, Pa. Kentucky by an unknown maker. ill. no. 17 in Joe Kindig's* Thoughts on the Kentucky Rifle. *loa. 58¾", bbl 43½", cal. .59", smooth bore.* **(2)** *Horse head patch box, signed M. Fordnay, probably a Dreppard lock. Lancaster, c. 1820. Kindig ill. no. 42. loa. 69¼", bbl 44", cal. .51" smooth bore.* **(3)** *Signed "M. Aldenderfer 1809" Berks County. 4 silver inlays. Kindig ill. no. 48. loa. 59", bbl 43¾", cal. .47" smooth bore.* **(4)** *"Samuel Pannabecker", Lancaster, c. 1815. 16 silver inlays. Kindig ill. no. 69. loa. 60", bbl 44¾", cal. .50" smooth bore.* **(5)** *"G. (George) Eister", York, Pa. c. 1795. "A superb Kentucky". Kindig ill. no. 127. loa. 61", bbl 45½", cal. .42" smooth bore.* **(6)** *"P. Smith" wender or swivel breech. Franklin County, Pa. c. 1825. 33 silver and brass inlays. Ship engraved on side plate. Kindig ill. no. 250. loa. 53½", bbls 38", cal. .52" rifled. Joe Kindig Jr. Collection.*

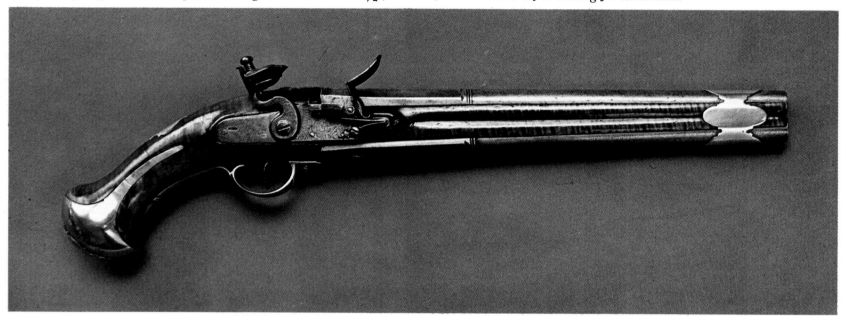

Over and under Kentucky *pistol with Golcher lock and sheet silver decoration. Two-storey flash pan with sliding cover. Russell Aitken Collection.*

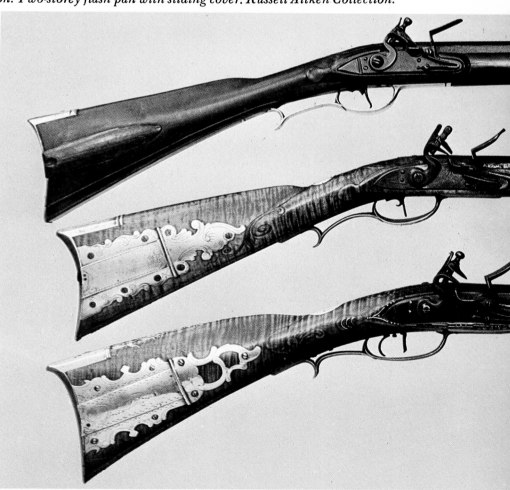

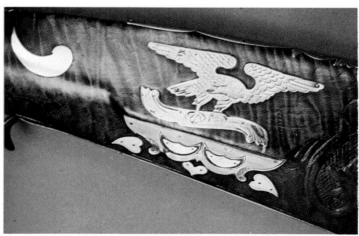

Lock and stock details *of P. Smith wender on* **lower left.** *No. (6), Joe Kindig, Jr. Collection.*

TOP: **Wooden sliding patch box** *indicates pre-revolutionary dating. Cherry stocked. .50" calibre smooth bore.*

MIDDLE: **Made by John Bonewitz,** *Berks County, Pa. c. 1780-1800. .50" calibre, octagon cut smooth bore.*

BOTTOM: **"J. Alb."** *Jacob Albright, Northumberland County, Pa. 1800. Silver inlays, cal. .45", rifled, 7 groove. Three Kentuckys from Dr. Harman Leonard Collection, Cheshire, Conn.*

"SHOOTERS" AND "DECORATORS"

There is obviously a romance and a mystique about old guns. I hope that some of the words and some of the pictures in this book will serve to whet the appetite of both the shooter and the collector. While some of the oldest guns in this book are still "shooters," they are much too fragile and valuable to take out in the woods. Others, guns that were "shooters" to the author as a child, the .41 Swiss and the single-shot Springfield, the rolling block Remington, and the percussion '51 Colt Navy, still shoot as well as they ever did, but if they are in particularly fine condition, it seems like tempting fate not to wax them and hang them up for a couple of more generations to admire. Besides that, who wants to destroy an investment?

In the late 1920's, Pollard compiled a *List of Easy Pieces To Acquire For a Representative Collection*. He probably had in mind an investment of a hundred pounds ($500.00 at that time) at the outside. Just for the fun of it, I asked Bob Abels, one of New York's major arms dealers, to put today's prices on the guns that Pollard then suggested for the beginner. Here it is:

One pair military flint carriage or holster pistols	$	285.00
One pair 1750 pistols	$	850.00
One pair "Queen Anne" ball butt pistols	$	850.00
One pair semi-side lock cannon barrels	$	900.00
One "Charles I" wheel lock pistol	$	3,000.00
One Scotch pistol	$	850.00
One snaphaunce	$	775.00
One 16th-century wheel lock pistol	$	2,500.00
		$13,825.00
One pair flint box lock pistols (late)	$	175.00
One pair flint carriage pistols (late)	$	350.00
One pair percussion military or holster pistols	$	275.00
One pair percussion duelling pistols	$	700.00
One pair percussion saw-handled duelling pistols	$	850.00
One pair percussion pocket pistols	$	65.00
One pair flint duelling pistols	$	950.00
One pair flint carriage or holster pistols	$	450.00

With skill and some luck, your modest collection may be worth in the next thirty years, ten times what you invested in it. And this is more than an outside chance. Most of the guns illustrated here from private collections are already headed for some museum, which makes the guns that remain in private collections all the more valuable. The '51 Navy Colt that I used to shoot, which cost $15 at Bannermans, is now hard to find in mint condition for $400.00.

There is a lot more than money in the collecting of guns, although investment makes a good justification. There is a one-of-a-kind craftsmanship to the pre-nineteenth century pieces, and there has been a personal relationship between gun and man which has existed for these past six hundred years. No one but an incurable romantic misses the passing of the six-gun era, anymore than they do the demise of the hand cannon days, but there is something about a fine gun over the fireplace. It may be a greater or lesser work of art, but it is one thing for certain: it is a reminder of a day nearly gone when individuality and *the* individual man were pretty important.

Hungarian artilleryman *with linstock. c. 1550.*

Ivory-stocked flintlock (*one of a pair*) *with silver helmet is signed: "Aquisgrani Leonardus Graef" "1725" "Aachen". This ivory wheel lock* (*one of a pair*) *with a carved knight's head was carved 30 miles away and 30 years earlier in Maastricht Nos.# 14.25.1408A and 14.25.1432B, Metropolitan Museum of Art, New York. Gift of William H. Riggs, 1913.*

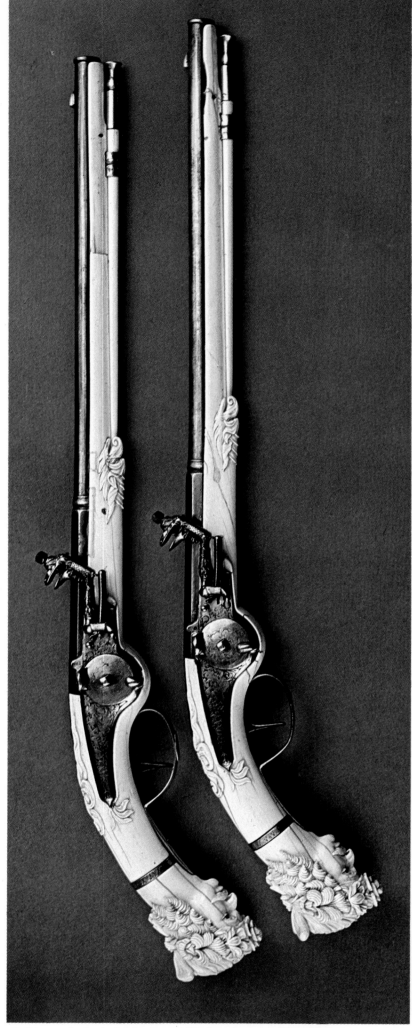

Full ivory stocked pistols *signed "Johan Louroux" (c. 1660-1700) on the locks and "Maastrict" behind the dogs. Russell Aitken Collection.*

"SHOOTERS" AND "DECORATORS"

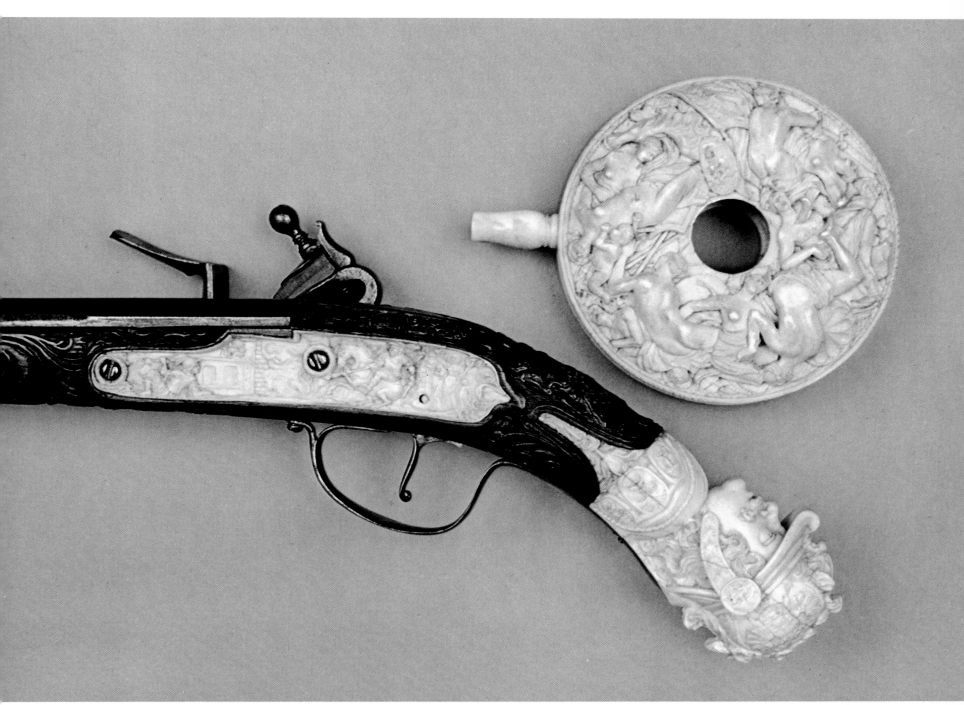

Michael Maucher *of Schwäbisch Gmund carved these pistols for Graf von Arco-Valley around 1680. loa. 20½", blued barrels 15", cal. .54". No.# 51/124, Bayerisches Armeemusem, Munich. Carved ivory powder flask has a naked lady holding up a flag on which is lettered "AMAZON". No.# 4961, also Munich.*

THE GUN NUT

I'm an upright citizen,
Can't stand the smell of powder even,
Yet I own all kinds of weapons,
Bringing me but few laudations,
Since I know not how to use them,
Just see that rust do not suffuse them.

From the *Narrenspiegel* of Christoff Weigel, tr. Lynn Mertke.

PROOF and CONTROL MARKS

When gunpowder was invented and guns were first made, gunmakers did not sign their work. There are several reasons for this. In the first place, the guns were so rough in comparison with the swords and armor of the period, that the barrel maker had no desire to advertise the crudity of his work. In the second place, guns were looked on with disflavor by the knights and professional military class. The gun founder had little desire to attract the attention of sword-wielding heroes who publicly offered to chop off the hands of any soldier caught with one of the "infernal weapons." Well-finished hunting guns, in which the maker could take pride, did not evolve until long after guns were used in warfare. Hunting was done with the crossbow, the boar spear and the hunting sword. The first illustrations of hunters using guns does not occur until the time of Maximilian —in the early 1500's. It was about this time that regular proof or control marks began to be used. Before 1500, one will occasionally find a crude mark of the maker stamped in the barrel. The mark might be an animal, an arrow, or a simplified coat of arms, but no name and seldom initials. Even today these crude, half obliterated marks are the exception, not the rule.

The earliest marks are called "control" marks, not "proof" marks, because there is little evidence that there was any attempt to "prove" the weapons. Probably the marks were used to indicate the place of origin and to support the tight control of the guild which jealously guarded the secrets of gunmaking.

Proving of swords and body armor had been a practice before guns came down the pike. Crossbow quarrels were shot at armor, and the resulting dents were the earliest proof marks. Later on, the man who made the armor put his stamp under the dent. There were qualifying marks as well. These indicated the distance from which the quarrel was shot and the strength of the bow used for proving. The French broke down the proof marks by a system of grading. TOTAL PROOF, or ALL PROOF, and HALF PROOF were the marks which correspond to our grading of olives as Colossal, Huge, and Large.

Swords were proved by testing their cutting strength against armor, bone, and meat. The Japanese proved their samurai swords on jailbirds who were going to be killed anyway. Western sword cutlers started putting their marks on the blades of weapons which had been proved in the early 1400's. The wolf mark of Passau and a variety of stamps from Solingen are the first examples that survive.

The earliest city guild stamps that survive on guns are from Nuremberg and Augsberg. Both cities were already well known for their armor and had strong metal-working guilds with reputations to defend. Madrid, London, Liège, and St. Etienne all seemed to have a reputation to maintain or a tight union shop and early began to mark their guns.

In both Spain and Italy there was a degree of independence which led to individual maker's proof marks rather than city guild marks. The same thing happened in the United States. Guns made before the Revolution in the U.S. were seldom marked because of fear of the British, who sought to control all manufactured goods. After the Revolution, individual gunmakers proudly signed their own work with their initials and later on, when they learned to spell, with their full names. Even today there is no such thing as a government proof on sporting weapons made in the U.S. The name of Winchester or Remington on a weapon means that the *maker* has proofed the gun with an extra heavy overload and guarantees his steel and workmanship.

Control marks were often combined with makers' marks in the 1500's. Little by little these were superseded by initials or combined with them. In Germany, everybody got into the act. Stockmakers put their initials on the stock behind the tang. Barrel makers put their mark alongside of the town control marks, and the locksmiths—most modest of all —started putting their identifying marks alongside of the Augsburg or Nuremberg controls.

The Italian were the most egocentric of the group. They signed their names on the barrels of the guns and on the insides or faces of the locks which they made. The only problem, as Engelhardt has pointed out, was that none of the gunmakers could have won a spelling bee. The Cominazzo family had so many different spellings of their name that it prompted Stephen V. Grancsay, the Curator of Arms and Armor of the Metropolitan Museum of Art, to write an article on the twenty-odd variations.

Among the old English marks to be found are the various London proof marks. These seem to have been applied with the idea of both protecting the customer and supporting the monopoly of the Worshipful Company of Gunmakers. These marks—initiated in 1672—indicate with a "V" that the rough piece has been "viewed" and with a "GP" that the barrel has been shot with an overload and is approved with the "Gunmakers Proof."

For a period of over 500 years a bewildering number of control marks and proof marks came to be used. By the 19th century, governments instead of cities established standards and insisted on the marking of approved weapons. By this time the ability to read and write had become widespread among the gunmaking and gun shooting fraternity and it had long been the fashion to spell out the name of the maker, his address, and sometimes even the date of manufacture. Even little advertisements were incorporated into the stampings. "Gunmaker to His Majesty the King," and "Arquebusier à l'Empereur" were among the stronger "sell" lines. A pair of duellers belonging to the author are marked on the barrels, "Reynolds from Jos. Manton, London," which means that Thomas Reynolds learned his trade in Joe Manton's gun shop, the most famous in England, and the most expensive place to buy a gun in London in 1820.

The proof and control marks shown here, as well as individual early maker's marks will serve as a beginning guide to the identification of a firearms by country, area, city or the time of manufacture. Marks on old guns are apt to be partially or totally obliterated by rust or polishing. Sometimes copies of old marks are stamped on heretofore unmarked old locks and barrels to make them more important. It is vital, therefore, to study the gun as a whole and to be able to recognize characteristics of periods and places of manufacture. Gunmakers by the nature of their trade have

been logical if not always literate and there is almost always a reason for the style, the shape and the size of a particular weapon. Gunmakers also have tended to conservatism. Styles did not change overnight, but evolution moved slowly out from the larger centers of manufacture. Styles of construction started in London or Paris in one century may still be found employed by country gunsmiths in the next. Motifs for decoration of guns have been known to be retained for over a century by the same workshop. A study of these habits and trends will be most rewarding. Next best to studying firsthand the known and documented guns in museums, try to gain a familiarity with the shape, color and patina of the firearms illustrated here. It will pay off in the collecting game.

The best and most complete guides to the identification of marks on firearms will be found in Støckel's two volumes, *Haandskydevaabens Bedømmelse* (Handweapons' Analysis), published in 1938 and reprinted in 1964 by the Tøjhus Museum in Copenhagen. The Danish text is supplemented by German translations, and English, French and German glossaries are appended to the two volumes.

The other important work on this subject is to be found in the *Gun Digest Treasury,* published in 1961, or in individual issues of the *Gun Digest* from prior years (1952-1961). This is A. Baron Engelhardt's *The Story of European Proof Marks.* Both of these works add the results of original research to prior published material on individual makers and individual gunmaking communities.

Since the publication of Støckel and Engelhardt, further investigations have been made of the old archives and the records of the gunmakers' guilds. An important example is the study of the gunmakers of Brescia by General Agostino Gaibi. Similar studies are being made or need to be made wherever ancient city archives still survive. A compilation of the work done in the last ten years plus an updating of Støckel and Engelhardt would be a boon both to collectors, scholars and museum curators. I hope that the summary list provided here will make someone mad enough to undertake the job.

BIBLIOGRAPHY
PROOF and CONTROL MARKS

ANONYMOUS
A Short Account of the Worshipful Company of
Gunmakers. . . . London, 1937

"BOEHEIM, WENDELIN
Ueber den Wert der Meistermarken"
Z.H.W.K., Vol. II, p. 161
Dresden, Leipzig, Munich, 1900-1902

CLAUDELIN, B.
Catalogue of Arms & Armour at Hallwylska Museet,
Stockholm
Stockholm, 1926

DE CORDOBA, J. F.
Catalógo de la Real Amería
Madrid, 1854

DUBESSY, RAYMOND
Historique de la manufacture d'armes de guerre
de St. Etienne
1900

EHRENTHAL, MAX VON
Die Waffensammlung des Fürsten Salm-Reifferscheidt
zu Schloss Dyck
Karl W. Hiersemann, Leipzig, 1906

ENGELHARDT, BARON ARMIN
ALEXANDER CONSTANTIN
"The Story of European Proof Marks"
The Gun Digest. . . . *Chicago, 1952-1961*

THE GUN DIGEST TREASURY
(the best from the first 15 years) . . . . *Chicago, 1961*

FFOULKES, C. J.
European Arms and Armour in the University of Oxford
Oxford, 1912

GRANCSAY, STEPHEN V.
American Rifleman
"Napoleon's Gunmaker"
Page 35 . . . . July, 1948

HARRIS, CLIVE
A History of the Birmingham Gun-Barrel Proof House
Birmingham, 1946

HAW TREY-GYNGELL, D.S.
Armourers Marks
(Second edition). . . . 1966

LAVIN, JAMES D.
A History of Spanish Firearms
Arco, New York, 1965

MANN, SIR JAMES G.
Wallace Collection Catalogues—European Arms
and Armour
2 volumes, including bibliography
Clowes, London, 1962

MUJICA, GREGORIO DE
  Monografía Histórica de la Villa de Eibar
    Eibar, 1910

POLAIN, A.
  Recherches Historiques sur l'épreuve des armes
    à feu au pays de Liège *(2nd edit.)*
    Liège, 1891

SCHEDELMANN, HANS

  *Die Wiener Büchsenmacher und Büchsenschäfter
    a book published by Z.H.W.K. . . . . Berlin, 1944*

SMITH, O.
  Der kongelige Partikulaere Rustkammer, 1775
    Copenhagen, 1938

SOUHAIT, R.
  Bibliographie Général des Ouvrages sur la Chasse,
  La Venerie et la Fauconnerie
    Rougette, Paris, 1886

STØCKEL, JOHAN F.
  Haandskydevaabens Bedømmelse *(Gunmakers marks)*
    Copenhagen, 1938-1943

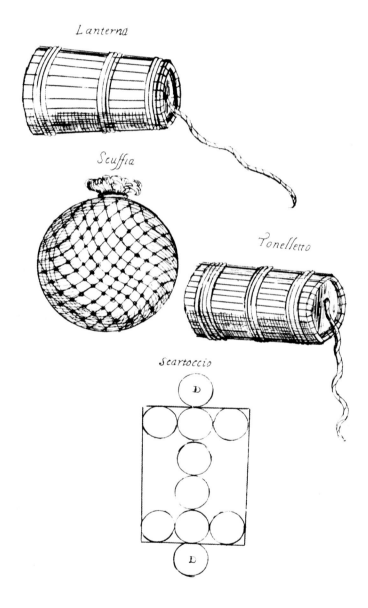

CONTROL MARKS
CITY

CITY CONTROL AND PROOF MARKS

AMSTERDAM

These city control marks are found most usually on military weapons, sometimes on hunting arms. The marks are always on the barrels of guns, never on the locks.

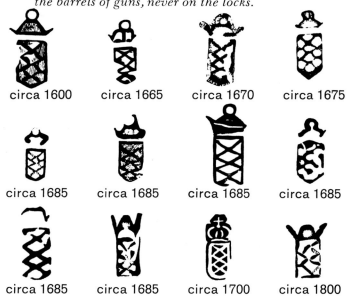

circa 1600	circa 1665	circa 1670	circa 1675
circa 1685	circa 1685	circa 1685	circa 1685
circa 1685	circa 1685	circa 1700	circa 1800

AUGSBURG

The Augsburg control marks are the earliest known marks to be used on guns. The oldest survivor is on the barrel of a bronze gun. Støckel places the date of this piece at 1480. Other marks are found on crossbows. Augsburg had for a long time been a center for the manufacture of armor and had used identifying marks.

Barrel Marks

circa 1480	circa 1550	circa 1550	circa 1600

circa 1600 circa 1600 circa 1625

Military Muskets

circa 1590 circa 1600 circa 1614 circa 1620

circa 1620

Hunting Weapons

circa 1580 circa 1580 circa 1585 circa 1585

circa 1600 circa 1600 circa 1620

Wheel Lock Pistols

circa 1575 circa 1580 circa 1580 circa 1585

circa 1590 circa 1595 circa 1600 circa 1600

circa 1600

CONTROL MARKS
CITY

Mark on Gun Lock

circa 1580

BARCELONA
This mark appears on the barrels of hunting and presentation arms.

On Barrels

circa 1720

circa 1746

On Pistols

circa 1735

circa 1735

circa 1735

circa 1740

BIRMINGHAM
These proof marks were made by the "Guardians of the Proof House" from 1813 until 1904. Birmingham proof marks often appear on guns marked "London." Both "viewed" and "proofed" marks were used as illustrated.

Barrel Markings

 1747

 circa 1790

Marks on Flintlock Pistols

circa 1780

circa 1790

circa 1810

CHARLEVILLE

This mark is of interest to American collectors as many Charleville muskets and some pistols were brought to America by French troops before and during the Revolution, and the Charleville was the model for the first U.S. military muskets.

circa 1690   circa 1755   1717-1728   1717-1728

1717-1728   1717-1728   1717-1728

1717-1728   1690   1690

COPENHAGEN (DENMARK)

The Danish marks are also those of the Danish Royal family. The "C" which is often incorporated in the design is the royal cipher for the dynasty of kings whose names were "Christian."

On the Barrel
Christian IV

1611-1619   1611-1620   1611-1622

Christian V

1661   circa 1685   circa 1685   circa 1685   circa 1685

CONTROL MARKS
CITY

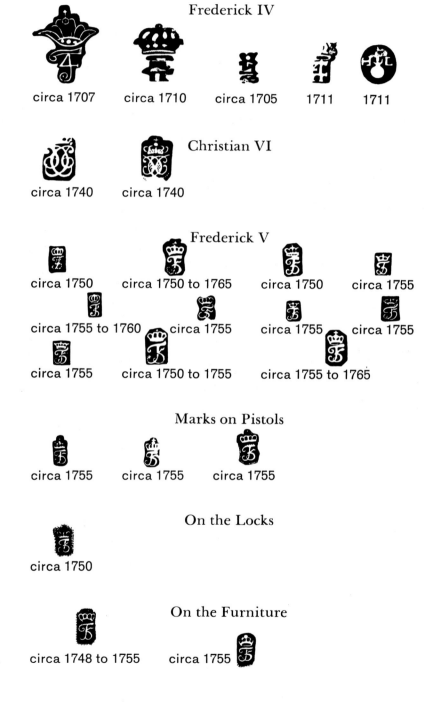

Frederick IV

circa 1707   circa 1710   circa 1705   1711   1711

Christian VI

circa 1740   circa 1740

Frederick V

circa 1750   circa 1750 to 1765   circa 1750   circa 1755

circa 1755 to 1760   circa 1755   circa 1755   circa 1755

circa 1755   circa 1750 to 1755   circa 1755 to 1765

Marks on Pistols

circa 1755   circa 1755   circa 1755

On the Locks

circa 1750

On the Furniture

circa 1748 to 1755   circa 1755

ST. ETIENNE

Proving of guns at St. Etienne was ordered by Louis XIV's Minister, Colbert, in 1665 and the first surviving example that we have dates from the 1730's; it is a crown with an "L" for Louis XV.

On the Barrels of Military Weapons

circa 1740 to 1760   circa 1740-1770   circa 1763 to 1770

circa 1770   circa 1820   circa 1800

Hunting and De luxe (Presentation) Weapons

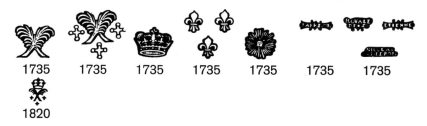

1735   1735   1735   1735   1735   1735   1735

1820

Pistol Proof Marks

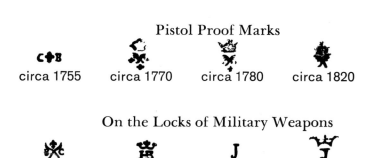

circa 1755   circa 1770   circa 1780   circa 1820

On the Locks of Military Weapons

circa 1690   circa 1770   1807-1814   circa 1800   1801

circa 1750   circa 1700

CONTROL MARKS
CITY

GRAZ (AUSTRIA)

There is plenty of opportunity to study the marks of Graz as the military arsenal in Graz still stands unchanged, filled with thousands of military matchlocks, wheel locks and wheel lock pistols among the body armor, pikes, drums, helmets and other accoutrements of war.

On the Barrels of Military Weapons

circa 1670   circa 1670   circa 1670

Wheel Lock Pistols

circa 1640   circa 1640

JONKOPING (SWEDEN)

The Swedish mark, which has now become a national emblem flying at the mast of Swedish ships was the royal mark of the kings of Sweden.

On the Barrels of Guns

1713   1716   1711   circa 1625   1713

1716   1775   1799

1600—1700

On Pistols

1714 and 1716   1746   circa 1700

On Locks

circa 1625

LIEGE (BELGIUM)

Liège was one of the early European towns to mine iron and make guns. Their earliest datable control stamp is a simplified representation of a monument or tower which stands in the middle of Liège over a fountain. The mark, which is also used in the coat of arms of the city, was used as a gun proof mark from 1672 until 1810 and again after 1853. Public proofing and stamping was required in 1672.

circa 1675   circa 1685   circa 1715   from 1811

circa 1875   circa 1875   circa 1875

LONDON (ENGLAND)

London used the system of viewing and proofing, and each test had its mark. There are Tower marks and private Tower Marks. The Broad Arrow denotes a government-owned weapon, which was not required to have other proof marks but usually did. The special marks of the East India Company were a heart or a lion. The proving of guns was initiated by Charles I in 1631, but the earliest authorized use of proof marks dates from 1672.

CONTROL MARKS
CITY

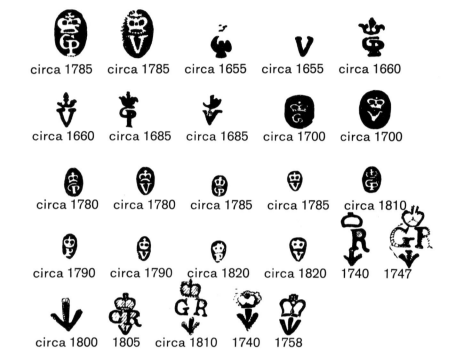

circa 1785	circa 1785	circa 1655	circa 1655	circa 1660
circa 1660	circa 1685	circa 1685	circa 1700	circa 1700
circa 1780	circa 1780	circa 1785	circa 1785	circa 1810
circa 1790	circa 1790	circa 1820	circa 1820	1740 1747
circa 1800	1805	circa 1810	1740	1758

MAASTRICHT (BELGIUM)

Now in Belgium, but as a gun-producing town a part of Holland, Maastricht, with its neighbor Aachen, produced many presentation pistols with carved ivory stocks. Both Maastricht, Aachen, and Liège are in the same neighborhood. The cities form a triangle not over forty miles on its longest side. The mark is usually found on the barrel of the pistol or hunting weapon.

circa 1660	circa 1720	circa 1700	circa 1730

circa 1730	circa 1730

MUNICH (Germany)

The little figure of the priest or bishop giving his blessing is found on the furniture of some early Munich-made guns. The famous Munich iron carvers and stock makers preferred and usually used barrels from Nuremberg.

circa 1600

circa 1780

circa 1585

NUREMBERG

The most famous of all gun marks are the "N", the split eagle in a shield and the serpent of Nuremberg. Any museum having a weapons collection can show you an original Nuremberg mark. The mark is a control mark of the Nuremberg guild. It appears often on both barrels and locks. While there is no record of early proofing of Nuremberg guns, the barrels and locks were held in high repute and the guild must have exercised some quality control. After 1655 the barrels were proved with either one or two shots with proof loads.

Marks on Barrels

1592

1595

circa 1600

circa 1625

circa 1650

Marks on Locks

circa 1585

1592

circa 1580

circa 1600

circa 1625

circa 1690

CONTROL MARKS
CITY

Marks on Pistols

circa 1580   circa 1580   circa 1585   circa 1600

More Barrel Marks

circa 1500   circa 1500   circa 1690   circa 1520   1599

N   N   N   N
R

1599   1595   circa 1680   circa 1595

SCHWABISCH GMUND
Schwäbisch Gmünd was a gun-making community which achieved its fame as the home of the Maucher family of gunsmiths.

Barrel Stamps

circa 1675   circa 1660   circa 1645 to 1663   1663

circa 1665   1656   circa 1640   circa 1590?

SUHL

Just as Solingen was famous at an early date for its cutlery and especially for its swords, steel from Suhl went into the barrels and locks of guns, rifles, pistols and rampart guns.

On the Barrels of Military Weapons

circa 1590   circa 1600   1601   circa 1620   circa 1660

1661   circa 1650 to 1695   circa 1710   circa 1735

circa 1750

Under the Barrels of Military Muskets

J U L
circa 1790   1799 S U L

Marks on Rampart Guns

1602   1613   1618   circa 1640

On Sporting Guns

circa 1585   1602   circa 1625   circa 1625   circa 1750

On Pistols

circa 1610   circa 1625   circa 1650   circa 1660

CONTROL MARKS
CITY

Under the Barrels of Pistols

circa 1610   circa 1715   circa 1725   circa 1755

On the Locks of Military Weapons

circa 1600   circa 1600   1601   circa 1620

Rampart Guns

circa 1620

Hunting Weapons

circa 1590   1595

Suhl proof marks with the Henneberg county marks (Suhl is in Henneberg).

Barrel Marks

circa 1600   circa 1600   circa 1650   circa 1660   1661

Rampart Gun Marks

circa 1600   circa 1600

Hunting Gun Marks

circa 1635

Pistol Marks

circa 1610   circa 1660

Military Arms

circa 1570   circa 1570   circa 1590   circa 1600

circa 1620   circa 1660

Rampart Guns

circa 1600   1602   circa 1610   1613   1615   1618

1618   circa 1650

Hunting Guns

circa 1595   1602   circa 1625   circa 1690   circa 1750

CONTROL MARKS
CITY

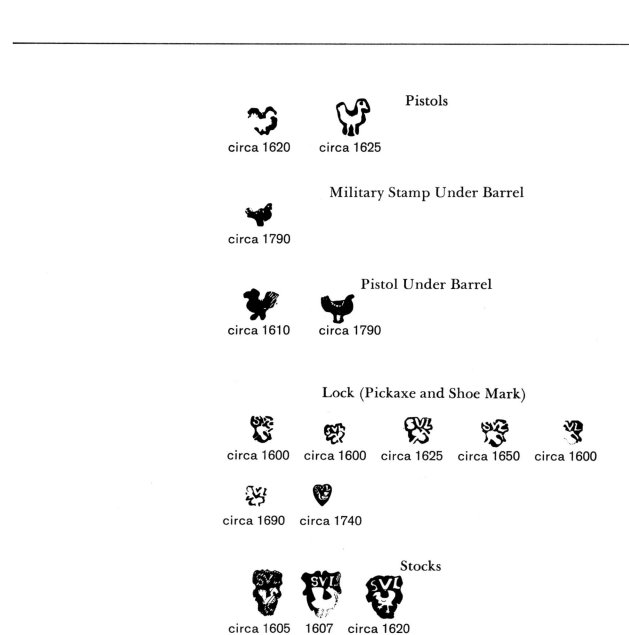

Pistols

circa 1620   circa 1625

Military Stamp Under Barrel

circa 1790

Pistol Under Barrel

circa 1610   circa 1790

Lock (Pickaxe and Shoe Mark)

circa 1600   circa 1600   circa 1625   circa 1650   circa 1600

circa 1690   circa 1740

Stocks

circa 1605   1607   circa 1620

UTRECHT

circa 1665   circa 1710   circa 1725   circa 1730

circa 1665   circa 1680   circa 1720   circa 1660

circa 1655   circa 1660   circa 1670   circa 1660

circa 1685

VIENNA (AUSTRIA)

Vienna used a city control mark which Støckel has found on the barrels of wheel locks, matchlocks and combination wheel-matchlock guns. The datable guns were all marked in 1661.

      Barrel Marks

1661   1661

NATIONAL PROOF MARKS

National proof marks coming later than city marks often incorporated the city marks or continued their use with supervision by the state. The old pickaxe and crossed shoe sole of Nuremberg, used in the 1600's, was revived in modern Germany in 1950. In England, the national government passed a law in 1813 requiring London or Birmingham proof stamps on the barrels of all guns offered for sale in England. France, while observing an international convention on the proving of guns, still retains the individual stamps indicating the city where the gun was made, Paris or St. Etienne. In Russia, as in the United States, there has never been a national proof mark required on sporting weapons. Individual gunmakers did their own proving. Baron Engelhardt says that Russian gunsmiths under the czars used two proof loads, firing a reduced load on the second shot.

AUSTRIA-HUNGARY

Austria-Hungary set up standards for proving firearms in 1882, but they were optional until 1891. City marks were used, and in addition the marks of first and second proving. Marks for smokeless proof were added later.

Ferlack	Prague	Weipert	Vienna	Budapest

Ferlack   Prague   Weipert   Vienna   Budapest

First Proof

Second Proof

Third Proof or visual examination					
Smokeless powder proof					

BELGIUM

Belgium, which had the first national proof marks, was instrumental in establishing international standards of proof which were adopted by the major countries after a conference in Brussels in 1914. The country was under French rule during the reign of Louis XIV, and again during the French Revolution and Napoleon. Then it was under Dutch rule until it became an independent monarchy in 1830. During the years of French rule, Napoleon and later the Dutch, inflicted the ELG mark. The "E" stood for the French word "éprouvé" and the "L G" for Liège.

 Inspection mark from 1672 to 1810 and again from 1853 to the present.

 Black powder proof mark in use from 1810 to the present.

 Provisional black powder proof mark used from 1852.

 Inspectors' marks with crown (could be any letter) 1853-1877.

 Smokeless powder proof (optional) 1891 standard after 1898.

 Definitive proof mark 1893 to present.

CZECHOSLOVAKIA

Czechoslovakia was part of the Austro-Hungarian Empire and had the same proof laws. The Czech marks were those of Prague and Weipert. Although made independent in 1918, Czechoslovakia used two old marks until 1931. Since then, both as an independent country and under German and Russian rule, the same marks have been used. If the mark has a star over it, it was made in Weipert (Vyprty) before 1945, in Brno after 1945, when the Weipert proof house was closed.

PROOF AFTER 1931

 First provisional proof of rough bored but not rifled barrel (optional).

 Second black powder proof for machined barrels and barrels to be soldered together for shotguns and combinations.

 Third proof for rifled arms and pistols using black powder.

 Fourth proof, smokeless, for shotguns.

 Fifth proof, smokeless, for pistols and rifles.

DENMARK

Denmark has been a small country in modern times. The proof marks for Danish guns, whether made in Copenhagen, Elsinore, or at the Royal Arsenal at Kronberg (after 1766) have been either a "C" or an "F" depending on whether the king was a Christian or a Frederick. The initial of the king is surmounted by a crown and sometimes incorporates a numeral—"F-4" standing for Frederick IV and "C-7" for Christian VII. When the letter "R" is used (not shown in Støckel) it stands for the Latin word rex. *Danish marks are shown under city marks.*

ENGLAND

British proof marks and the marks of the Worshipful Company of Gunmakers were one and the same thing until the Birmingham gunmakers proved their worth to the crown by supplying vast quantities of arms for the wars against Napoleon. The Birmingham makers were rewarded with their own authorized proof mark in 1813. From that time on, until 1904, it was the Worshipful Company versus the Guardians (of Birmingham). Smokeless proof was introduced in 1904. Exceptions are the private proof marks of the Tower, Irish (Dublin . . . Dublin Castle), imported guns, and guns belonging to the government or the Honorable East India Company.

  1637 London mark, "V" for viewed, "GP" for Gunmakers' proof.

  1672 Tower of London proofs in oval versus earlier lozenge shape.

  1702 London mark with simplified crown.

  Pre 1813 Birmingham marks (derived from the Private Tower Marks).

  Marks used on foreign guns.

 Provisional proof mark of the Tower.

 Private Tower proof (double)

CONTROL MARKS
NATIONAL

ENGLAND

 Definitive Tower mark.

 Definitive Birmingham mark.

   East India Company.

 NP Smokeless powder marks ("N" is for nitro powder).

 BV 1904 Birmingham marks.

 Broad arrow denoting government property.

 O×S Broad arrow plus "O" or "O S" former government property ("O" equals obsolete).

Other marks and combinations of marks indicated the bore of shotguns, extra proving of express rifles, etc.

FRANCE

Historians of French arms and armor claim that armor and crossbows were required to be proved in Paris as early as 1350, and guns were supposed to have been proved in St. Étienne in 1450. This is all rather tenuous; however, documentary proof of the testing of guns by having the soldiers shoot them is mentioned in a letter from Dalliez de la Tour, director of the Companie du Levant to Colbert (see St. Etienne). Proof on commercial firearms was required in 1700, but it is not until the 18th century that we find actual examples of guns with proof marks on them. From 1776 on, military weapons were required to have both proof and date stamps. In 1810 Napoleon required proofing of all firearms made in France although allowing the proof houses of Paris and St. Etienne to keep their identifying marks combined with the "E" standing for "éprouvé."

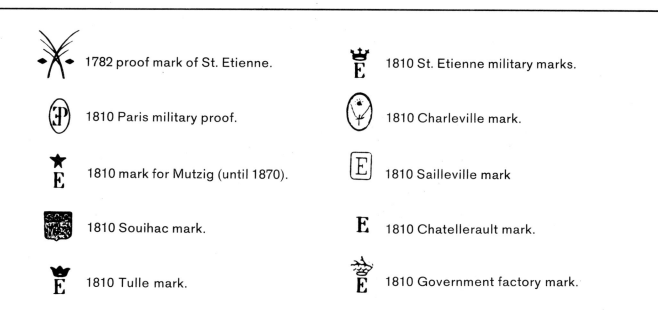

1782 proof mark of St. Etienne.

1810 St. Etienne military marks.

1810 Paris military proof.

1810 Charleville mark.

1810 mark for Mutzig (until 1870).

1810 Sailleville mark

1810 Souihac mark.

1810 Chatellerault mark.

1810 Tulle mark.

1810 Government factory mark.

PARIS	ST. ETIENNE	PROOF AFTER 1897
		Proof marks for rough barrels.
		Proof marks for finished barrels.
		Special proof for finished barrels assembled to the gun.
		Proof marks for finished guns.
		Special proof for finished guns.
		Pistol proof mark.
P.J.	P.J.	1896 proof for smokeless powders.
P.M.	P.M	1898 proof for smokeless powders. (different types of powders)
P.T.	P.T.	1900 proof for smokeless powders.

CONTROL MARKS
NATIONAL

GERMANY

Germans and Swiss proved their cannon as early as 1375. The many individual city-states used their own proof or control marks from 1500 on, the earliest surviving mark being on a bronze hand cannon from Augsburg dating from around 1480. The nearest thing to a national German proof mark was established by the Prussians at the Royal Proof House in Solingen in 1867. In 1891 Germany established standard proof marks for the entire country.

 Provisional proof mark stamped on the lower round of the barrel ahead of the flat.

 Second proof or viewing ("U" for **Untersuchung**—inspection).

 "V" was stamped on guns made prior to the proof laws in 1891.

 Stamp on guns which had to be reproved after repairs.

 The "U" and crown used separately was the single proof mark required on pistols and revolvers.

 Nitro (smokeless) proof mark used since 1891.

 *The spread wing eagle proof mark was introduced in 1939 with a variety of letters: "M" and "SP" for black powder, "N" for smokeless, "FB" for voluntary proof (Freiwilliger Beschuss).*

Proof Marks used by East and West Germany after 1945

Acceptance mark   Second (Nitro) Proof

ITALY

Proof marks in Italy have been under discussion since 1910, and have been employed on a quasi-legal basis since 1924. Laws have been written but never ratified. The legal confusion is extraordinary. Nevertheless, proofing has been done on an internationally acceptable basis, first by a private proof house in Brescia, and since 1930 by a national proof house in Gardone's Val Trompia. The national proof house uses both the marks of Brescia and Gardone. In 1951 the crown on top of the proof was replaced by the republican device, a star in a wheel.

BRESCIA	Proof in use between 1930 and 1951	GARDONE
	All proofed arms carry this mark.	
	First black powder proof mark.	
	Final black powder proof mark on finished guns.	
	First proof of guns with smokeless powder.	
	Final proof of guns with smokeless powder.	
	Proof mark for guns tested with 30% overloads and punt guns.	

Provisional proof mark for barrels in the **white**.

243

CONTROL MARKS
NATIONAL

ITALY	BRESCIA			GARDONE	
		Proof in use after 1951			
		All proofed arms carry this mark.			
	PN	First black powder proof mark.		PN	
	PN FINITO	Final black powder proof mark on finished guns.		PN FINITO	
	PSF	First proof of guns with smokeless powder.		PSF	
	PSF FINITO	Final proof of guns with smokeless powder.		PSF FINITO	
	PN or PSF	Proof mark for guns tested with 30% overloads and punt guns.		PN or PSF	
		Provisional proof mark for barrels in the **white.**			

PRIVATE PROOF MARKS

RUSSIA

While there was never a national proof mark employed in Czarist Russia, the military, sporting and deluxe presentation guns made in Tula at the Royal Armory and the guns made at the Kremlin Armory were clearly marked both as to place of origin, maker and the date. The dates on older Russian guns, according to Engelhardt, were old calendar (pre-Gregorian) or sometimes dated from the day the world was created (according to the Russian Orthodox Church). Modern Russian military weapons, and there are few others in the West, are stamped with the same five-pointed star which is the U.S.S.R. national emblem.

PRIVATE PROOF MARKS

SPAIN

Guns made in Eibar on the Atlantic and northern coast of Spain were proved by the Royal Arms Factory at nearby Placencia as early as 1521. This is the information supplied by de Mujica in his book on Eibar which was published in 1910. In any event, Spanish barrels became world famous without benefit of state inspection or proofing for hundreds of years. In 1844 the Spanish government ordered the Eibar gunsmiths to build their own proof house and to prove their barrels there. However, the state did not put up any money for the proof house and the proving of guns was on a voluntary basis. This was the period when so many pot metal guns were made, giving Spanish guns a bad reputation, after they had enjoyed such a good one for generations. In 1923, Spain decided to do something about a bad situation and adopted the rules concerning proof which had been recommended by the Brussels Convention of 1914. Changes in markings were made in 1929 and again in 1931. Then there were government proof houses in both Eibar and Barcelona. Spanish guns are gaining in reputation today both because of the decorative skills of Spanish craftsmen and because of the influx of German gunsmiths who were unable to practice their trade in Germany after World War II.

1929 proof used on automatic pistols and revolvers.

1910 Eibar provisional proof used on black powder smoothbore guns.

1910 final proof on muzzle loaders and second proof for breech-loading black powder breech loaders

1910 provisional mark for shotguns.

1910 proof for single shot and nonautomatic pistols.

1929-1931 admission proof at Eibar.

1929-1931 admission proof at Barcelona.

CONTROL MARKS
NATIONAL

SPAIN

    1929-1931 proof marks on rifled guns fired with a 30% overload.

    1929-1931 proof on revolvers fired with 30% overload.

    1929-1931 proof on automatic pistols fired with a 30% overload.

Proofs Used After 1931

    Eibar admission proof.

    Barcelona admission proof (until 1925).

    Single shot and non auto-pistol proof.

    Proof on all guns that met manufacturers' own standards.

    Voluntary smokeless powder proof on shotguns.

    Final (3rd) black powder proof.

SWEDEN

The Swedish Royal mark has been used on guns made at the government gun factory at Jönköping since 1713. Cannon have been proved in Sweden since 1766. After discontinuing the use of the Swedish king's initials in the 19th century, various letter stamps have been used at the arms plant at Husqvarna. A crown was still in use in 1825 according to Støckel. Since then, two letter stamps have been used in addition to the spelled out Husqvarna name. Sweden has not been a major factor in the manufacture or export of firearms since the days of her more warlike kings, who commissioned the manufacture and purchase of the arms that were used against the Russians, the Poles and the Prussians. Surviving military and sporting arms of this area are displayed in the once royal arsenal, now the Livrustkammaren Museum, and in the collection which was once the arsenal of Baron Wrangel at the castle of Skokloster.

PROOF
PRIVATE
MARK

   Swedish proof mark on a lock   1625   Norrtälje

   circa 1680 to 1690   Söderhamns

   Jönköping, from 1600—1700   Proof mark of 1799

   Jönköping control mark   1713   Proof mark on a flintlock pistol of 1825

   Orebro, 1700   Husqvarna barrel proof marks from 1837   GL

GUNMAKERS and THEIR MARKS

ACQUA FRESCA
See: CECCHI

ADAMS, Robert
Inventor of a double action revolver in 1851, later of the firm of Deane, Adams and
Deane, London

ALBRECHT, Johann Heinrich
Darmstadt and Wetzlar. Worked circa 1667-1711. Gunmaker to the Landgrave of
Hesse-Darmstadt

ALBRIGHT, J.
Pennsylvania flintlock maker, circa 1800

ALDENDERFER, M.
Pennsylvania, flintlock maker, circa 1790-1810

ALLEN, Ethan (1806-1871); ALLEN, THURBER & COMPANY (1842-1856);
ALLEN AND WHEELLOCK (1856-1871)
Invented a pepperbox in 1837.

ALLIN, Erskine S. (1809-1879)
Springfield Armory. Patented a system for converting muzzle loaders to breech loaders
in 1865

ALMAIN, John The
Circa 1580. Cannon founder for Henry VIII. German armourer who worked in Greenwich

ALSOP, Charles R., and Joseph W.
w. 1859-1868, Middletown, Conn. Produced 5-shot percussion revolvers in .36 and .44 caliber

ALTENSTETTER, David (1547-1617)
Augsburg goldsmith and engraver

ANNALY
London, circa 1660-1682. Built pistols with superimposed loading

ANSELL
London, England. Gunsmith, foreman for Joe Manton, circa 1820

ANSIAUX, J. L. and DEWALLE
Liège, 1842-1850   *See:* DEWALLE

ANSON, William
Anson and Deely. Birmingham, England. Worked 1874-1886

APPIANO, Paolo
Circa 1662-1671. Milan. Designer, gunmaker

AQUISTI, Gio. Maria
Italian locksmith, circa 1700

ARAULT
Versailles, circa 1780. Gun in Bayerisches Armeemuseum in Munich

ARNOLD, David
Liège, circa 1634. Revolving snaphaunce at Porte de Hal c. 1660

ARROWSMITH
Promoter, receiver of patent assignment for "Volcanic" from Walter Hunt, 1849

ASTON, Henry (1803-1852)
Middletown, Conn. Worked for Simeon North, organized H. Aston and Co. in 1843 to manufacture government contract pistols

AUBUSSON, Pierre
Circa 1480. Cannon founder

BAERTMANS, Hendrick
The Hague, circa 1641. Patented repeating wheel lock

BAKER, Ezekiel
Whitechapel, London, circa 1800-1838. Designed and built muzzle-loading military rifles used in the Napoleonic Wars

BALL, (BALL & LAMSON)
Worcester, Mass. Albert Ball patented a self-loader in 1861

GUNMAKERS

BALLARD, Charles H.
Worcester, Mass. Patented a breech loader in 1861. Many of the Ballard single shots were made by Marlin

BAR, H. (Bähr) (C. Bär)
Perhaps from Dresden, though one marked "C. B." with a bear rampant in the Metropolitan Museum of Art has Nuremberg control marks on both barrel and lock. Circa 1585-1627

BARBAR (Barber), Louis (Lewis)
Gunmaker. London. Worked 1695-1730

BARDINO, Giovanni
Florence, circa 1620. Built lemon-butted miquelet pistols which fired superimposed loads. (Capodimonte and Dresden)

BARNE (Barnes, Barnee), Harman
Dutch. Worked in London 1635-1660. Died 1661. Gunmaker to Prince Rupert and Charles I

BARTON AND WOGDON, *see* WOGDON AND BARTON

BATTISTA (Baptista), Michele (1716-1788)
Naples. Gunmaker to King Ferdinand

BAUDUIN (Baudouin, Beaudouin), Charles
Liège, 1750-1790. "Charles Badouin et frère"

BAUER (Gebauer Andreas), G. F.
Rensburg and Copenhagen, circa 1744

BAZZONE, Bernardi
Italian, circa 1650. Gun and barrel maker

BEALS, Fordyce
Springfield, circa 1854-1866. New Haven rolling block revolvers, Beals revolver, Remington revolvers and Eli Whitney revolvers

BECKER, Elias I & II
Augsburg, circa 1633-1674. Stockmakers

BECKWITH, WILLIAM
London, circa 1838. Gunmaker

BEHR (Beer, Bähr, Beehr, Beehrt, Bher, Böhr, Phär), Johann Jacob (Jean Jacques)
Most often found signature, J. J. Behr, on wheel lock and flintlock rifles and pistols.
Würzburg in Bavaria, 1700, Maastricht, Belgium, 1724. Worked also in Wallerstein, Weimar,
Darmstadt, and Liège between 1690 and 1750. Used "I.I." initials also (Munich gun)

BELEN, Juan (1673-1691)
Madrid. Spanish barrel maker and gunsmith to Carlos II

BELLO, Pietro
Brescia, circa 1650. Lockmaker

BELTON, Joseph
Philadelphia, 1777-1784. Invented an 8-shot controlled fire repeater. London, 1784-?
Jover and Belton, built seven-shot muskets for the East India Co. *See:* JOVER

BENNETT, C. H.
American, circa 1850. Chain rifle

BENNETT, T. G.
1876-1906. Oliver Winchester's son-in-law and successor. Separated Browning from Winchester

BENSON, J.
London, circa 1760. Two-shot flintlock in Kindig collection

BERAIN, Jean Baptiste (1639-1711)
French—author of DIVERSES PIECES TRES UTILES POUR LES ARQUEBUZIERS.
Goldsmith, engraver and artist. Family were engravers and gunsmiths since 1591

BERDAN, Colonel Hiram
Worked 1865-1892, invented the Berdan primer. Commanding officer of own company of
Berdan's sharpshooters in American Civil War

GUNMAKERS

BERETTA, Claudio
1580-1640

BERGAMINI, Giorgio
Brescian, circa 1592

BERGAMINI, Giovanni Maria
Brescian, circa 1622. Made matchlock revolver wall gun in Palazzo Ducale, Venice

BERGIER (Berger, Bevier), Pierre
Grenoble, France, circa 1634-1635. Clock and gunmaker. Built waterproof wheel lock pistols with clock springs and superimposed loads for Louis XIII, now in the Musée de l'Armée

BERGMANN, T.
Gaggenau, Bavaria. Automatic pistol. Worked 1894-1903

BERSELLI, Giacomo
Circa 1666-1720. Bolognese gunmaker. Built "Lorenzoni" system breech-loading flintlock. May have built Cookson guns

BERTE (Barte), Marc Antonio
Brescia, circa 1670

BIDET
French gunmaker in London, circa 1715. Built guns on La Chaumette principle

BILLINGHURST, William (1807-1880)
Rochester, New York. Built target guns and the Billinghurst Requa platoon battery gun

BIS, Nicolas (The Elder)
Madrid, worked 1692-1730. Apprenticed to Belén 1684-1691. Gunmaker to Carlos II. Stamp found on the barrels and locks of miquelet guns and pistols. Made barrels from horseshoes

BISSELL, Isaac
Birmingham, circa 1780. All-metal Scotch regimental pistols. Usually engraved "R.H.R."
—Royal Highland Regiment

BLAIR, David
Birmingham, worked 1796-1817. Gun- and pistol maker with various partners

BLAND, John
Philadelphia, circa 1815—"black and white smith"—five-shot superimposed (Roman candle) gun

BOND, P. (1780) and E. (1810-1850)
London. E. Bond was gunmaker to the East India Company. The Bonds made both flint and percussion pistols and blunderbusses signed on both barrel and lock

 BOND, T.
Signed E. and T. Bond, circa 1850

BOND, W.
Lombard Street, London

BONEWITZ, John
Kentucky flintlock maker, Pennsylvania, circa 1779-1809

BONGARDE (Bongard), Hermann (Armand)
Düsseldorf, 1678-1727. Bongarde's father and his son were both gunmakers. He made beautifully decorated flintlocks with gold and silver lock inlays. His best known work is a garniture made for the Elector Johann Wilhelm of Pfalz consisting of a shotgun, two pistols, a sword and a powder flask. They are now in the Bavarian Army Museum in Munich

BORCHARDT, Hugo
Bridgeport, Conn. Worked 1876-1893. Invented Sharps' Borchardt rifle and Borchardt pistol

BORSTORFFER, Hieronymus
Munich gun stock maker and decorator for Rudolf II and Maximilian I, Elector of Bavaria. Worked 1598-1637

BOSS, Thomas (BOSS & CO., LTD)
Piccadilly, London. Company started in 1832. Boss retired in 1859. The business of making fine shotguns was continued

GUNMAKERS

BOSSI, Capt. Guiliano (1606-1679)
Captain of Rome and inventor of over-and-under and 2-shot superimposed wheel lock carbines. Author—BREVE TRATATO D'ALCUNE INVENTIONE CHE SONE STATE FUTTE PER RINFORZARE E RADDOPPIARE LI TIRI DEGLI ARCIUBUGI—A RUOTA. Worked in Holland

BOSSLER (Bosler), J. Phillipp
Darmstadt, 1731-1793. Invented magazine flintlock now in Tøjhus Museum

BOTTI, Giovanni
Brescia, circa 1688-1730. Lockmaker

BOURGEOIS, Marin le
See: LE BOURGEOYS

BOUTET, Nicolas Noël
Versailles, 1761-1833. Gunmaker to both Louis XVI and Napoleon. He headed a large workshop which produced lavishly decorated presentation pieces for Napoleon as well as military weapons of all kinds and styles

BOXER, Colonel Edwin M.
Center fire cartridge, 1866. Superintendent of the laboratory of the British Army's Woolwich Arsenal, improved Snider cartridge, circa 1860

BROWNING, John Moses (1855-1926)
Ogden, Utah. Prolific gun inventor. 68 patents

BRUNEEL
Lyon, circa 1840. Built percussion guns

BURGESS, Andrew
Buffalo, N.Y. 1837-1908. Patented magazine firearms and automatic weapons

BURNSIDE, General Ambrose E. (1824-1881)
American Civil War general. Inventor of Burnside patent breech loader. Bristol, Rhode Island

BURTON, Bethel
See: WARD BURTON

BUSTINDUI, Agostino (1740-1802)
Worked in Eibar and Madrid; in Madrid he worked in the gunshop with Zelaya. A
presentation pair of pistols to Ferdinand VII of Spain are now in the Real Armeria in Madrid

BUSTINDUI, Juan Esteban
Worked 1800-1827. Son of Agostino

CADDELL, Thomas
Circa 1646-1678. Doun, Scotland

CADDELL, Thomas II
Circa 1764-1785. Doun, Scotland

CALIN (Callin), Gio. Pietro
Genoese gunmaker to Carlo Emmanuel II. Worked circa 1658-1685. Repeating flintlock maker

CALTRANI, Bartolomeo
Tuscany, circa 1750

CAMPBELL, Alexander
Doun, Scotland, 1735-1750

CAMPBELL, John
Doun, Scotland, circa 1700. Pupil of Thomas Caddell I

CAMPELL, John, Jr.
Doun, Scotland, 1785-1790

GUNMAKERS

CANO, Jose (Josef) (1730-1751)
Madrid. Made a breech-loading gun for Phillip V of Spain in 1736
See: FERNANDEZ, Juan

CAPO BIANCO, Giovanni, Giorgio of Schio
First half of sixteenth century. Goldsmith, designer, mathematician. Made an alarm clock gun
for Consul General Andrea Alciati and Cardinal Matteo Schnier (1511) which also lit a candle

CARCANO
Turin, 1868. Mannlicher-Carcano. Bolt action Italian military rifle

CARON
Paris, circa 1868. Built de luxe sporters including cased gun stocked entirely in translucent horn.
W. Keith Neal Collection

CASLON, William
Circa 1719, London. Type founder and gun engraver

CATANE (Gatane, Catine), Giovanni
Brescia, circa 1690-1730

CECCHI, (Family)
Snaphaunce and flintlock gunmakers and decorators of Bargi
Sebastiano—1619-1692
Luigi—1680-1709
Matteo—circa 1651-1738
Pietro Antonio (?-1809)

CECCHI, Sebastiano (1619-1692)

CHAFFEE, Reuben S.
Springfield, Mass. active 1875-1887. Chaffee-Reece patents on magazine firearms
manufactured by Winchester

CHAMLEMBRON (Chelambron)
French flintlock magazine gun maker, circa 1785. Pondicherry, India

CHAMBERS, Benjamin
Washington, D.C. 10-shot flintlock made by S. North

CHAMBERS, Joseph C.
American, circa 1815. Seven-barrel, 224-shot swivel gun. West Middletown, Washington County, Penn. Patent issue 1812. Built 200 swivel guns for the Navy in 1812 and 100 pistols

CHASSEPOT, Antoine (1833-1905)
Paris. Patented military rifle in 1866

Barrel Stamp

CHASTEAU, C.
Paris, circa 1643-1715. Made flintlock guns for Louis XIV, an example of which survives in the Tøjhus Museum with an amusing representation of Louis as Hercules

CHAUMETTE
See: LA CHAUMETTE

CHINELLI AND ROSSI (Company)
18th century

CHINELLI (Del Chino, Chinei)
Family, 1487-1810
Geronimo del Chino, circa 1533
Giobatta del Chino, circa 1542
Venturino del Chino, circa 1546
Apollonio Chinelli, circa 1595-1635

Paolo Chinelli, circa 1615-1645

Tomaso Chinelli, circa 1620-1640
Ercole Chinelli, circa 1630
Francesco Chinelli, circa 1630
Bartolomeo Chinelli, circa 1630
Guilio Cesare, circa 1700
Gabriello Chinelli, circa 1720
Alberto Chinelli, circa 1725
Paolo Chinelli II, circa 1725
Antonio Chinelli, circa 1730

GUNMAKERS

CHRISTENSEN, Georg H. (1819-1883)
Copenhagen

CHRISTIE, James
Circa 1810. Perth, Scotland. Scotch pistol maker

CHRISTIE, John
Doun and Stirling, Scotland. Worked circa 1750-1765

CHURCHILL, Robert
Contemporary author—THE SHOTGUN. London gun manufacturer

CLARKSON, Joseph
London, 1720's and 1730's. Invented automatic priming magazine

CLAUDIN, F.P.
Paris, circa 1855-1870

CLEMMES
Shug Lane, London. Worked 1750-1780; successor to Barbar

CLOETER
See: CLOTER

CLOS
See: DU CLOS

CLOTER (Cloeter), Christian
Mannheim, circa 1680. Iron-stocked guns

CLOTER
Family, 1643-1740

CLOTER, Jan
Grevenebroch, circa 1643-1700

COCHRAN, John Wester (1814-1872)
"Turret" revolver and cannon inventor

COLAS, Ezechias
Sedan, France, circa 1640. Superimposed flintlock pistols

COLLIER, Elisha H.
Flintlock revolver inventor. Worked 1817-1850. Boston, London

COLLIN, J.
London, circa 1850-1854. Pepperbox manufacturer and percussion pistol maker

COLLOMBE
See: LA COLLOMBE

COLOMBO, G. (1575-1650)
Gardone, Val Trompia, Italy

COLT, Samuel (1814-1862)
Inventor and manufacturer of revolvers. Paterson, N.J., Whitneyville, Conn., Hartford, Conn.

COMA (Comas) (Family?)
Ripoll, Spain, circa 1675-1700, circa 1720-1740. Locksmiths

COMBLAIN—COMBLAIN AND MANGEOT
Brussels, circa 1855-1877. Made breech-loading conversions and breech loaders

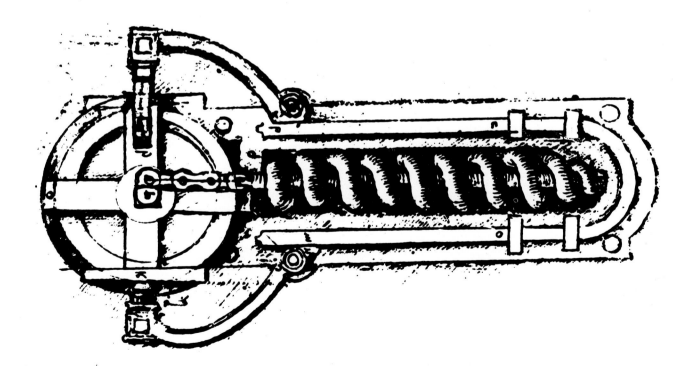

GUNMAKERS

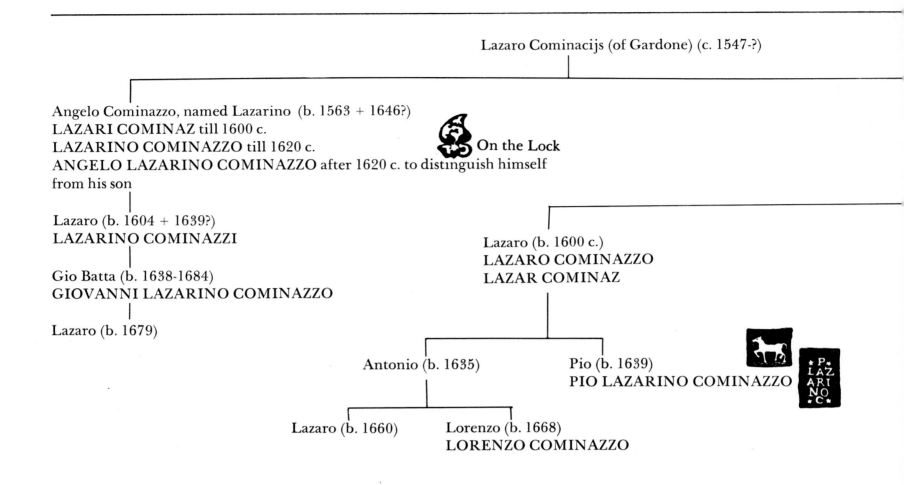

Lazaro Cominacijs (of Gardone) (c. 1547-?)

Angelo Cominazzo, named Lazarino (b. 1563 + 1646?)
LAZARI COMINAZ till 1600 c.
LAZARINO COMINAZZO till 1620 c.
ANGELO LAZARINO COMINAZZO after 1620 c. to distinguish himself
from his son · On the Lock

Lazaro (b. 1604 + 1639?)
LAZARINO COMINAZZI

Gio Batta (b. 1638-1684)
GIOVANNI LAZARINO COMINAZZO

Lazaro (b. 1679)

Lazaro (b. 1600 c.)
LAZARO COMINAZZO
LAZAR COMINAZ

Antonio (b. 1635)

Pio (b. 1639)
PIO LAZARINO COMINAZZO

Lazaro (b. 1660)

Lorenzo (b. 1668)
LORENZO COMINAZZO

Gio Marco (c. 1688 + 1700 c.)

We are not sure of the family relationship of

Bartolomeo (1760c.-1810c.)
BORTOLO COMINAZI

*The names in capital letters are the known signatures engraved on guns
General Agostino Gaibi who provided the basic information for this geneological tree says:
"The history of the Cominazzi is far from complete".

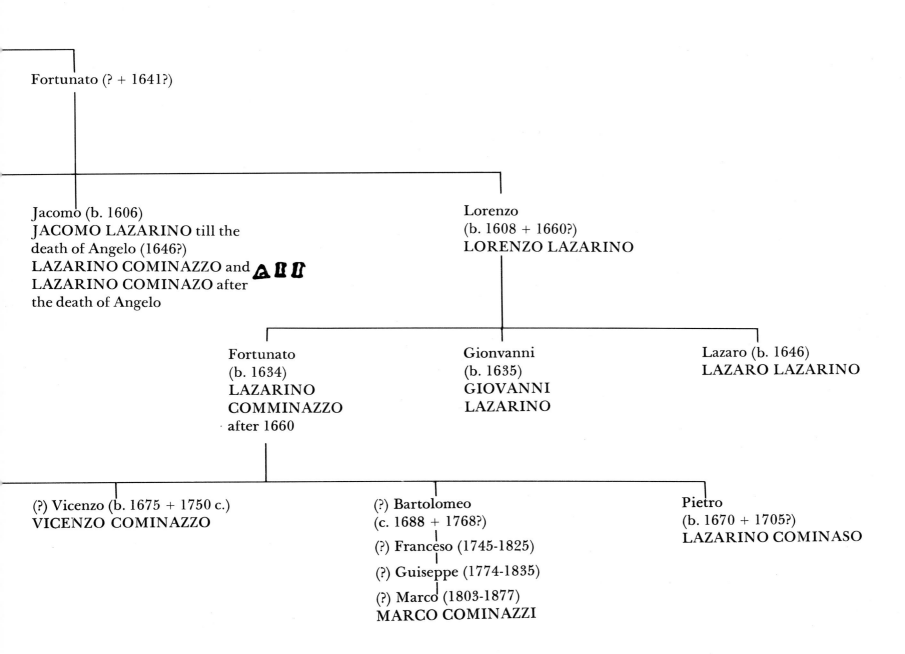

Fortunato (? + 1641?)

Jacomo (b. 1606)
JACOMO LAZARINO till the
death of Angelo (1646?)
LAZARINO COMINAZZO and
LAZARINO COMINAZO after
the death of Angelo

Lorenzo
(b. 1608 + 1660?)
LORENZO LAZARINO

Fortunato
(b. 1634)
LAZARINO
COMMINAZZO
· after 1660

Gionvanni
(b. 1635)
GIOVANNI
LAZARINO

Lazaro (b. 1646)
LAZARO LAZARINO

(?) Vicenzo (b. 1675 + 1750 c.)
VICENZO COMINAZZO

(?) Bartolomeo
(c. 1688 + 1768?)

(?) Franceso (1745-1825)

(?) Guiseppe (1774-1835)

(?) Marco (1803-1877)
MARCO COMINAZZI

Pietro
(b. 1670 + 1705?)
LAZARINO COMINASO

COMINAZZO
Brescia. While the Cominazzo family in Brescia and Gardone worked between 1547 and 1887,
their most famous guns date before 1750. Most of their guns have their names spelled out on the
barrels; sometimes, but rarely, on the locks as they were primarily barrel makers. The
signatures most commonly found (and imitated) are Lazari Cominaz, Lazarino Comminazzo,
and Lazaro Lazarino (circa 1680). The marks shown here are unusual. The spelling
combinations and the fake signatures are numerous

GUNMAKERS

CONSTABLE, Richard
Philadelphia, Pa. 1817-1851. Gun- and pistol maker.

CONTRINER, Joseph
Viennese gunsmith, circa 1800-1850. Military guns and fine percussion sporters
See: GIRADONI

COOKSON, John, Sr.
London. Worked 1686-1700. Built or sold Berselli repeater, ten-shot flintlock gun

COOKSON, John, Jr.
Circa 1701-1762. Boston

COOLIDGE, Cornelius
Boston. Patentee and agent for Collier in France in 1819

COOPER, Joseph Rock (1838-1886)
Worked in Birmingham, England, 1843-1853. Patented six-and 12-shot revolvers

CORDIER, Isaac
Gunsmith, wheel lock pistol maker. Fontenay, Paris. Worked 1628-1632

COSTER, Cornelius
Utrecht, Holland, circa 1650. Made repeating loose powder weapons

COTEL, Bartolomeo
Circa 1670-1740. Italian. Built Lorenzoni system breech-loading flintlock, circa 1690.
Example in the Tower of London

CRAUSE, Carl Philipp
Kassel, circa 1803-1823

CRESPI, Guiseppi
Milan, circa 1760-1780. Designed breech-loading carbines with tip-up chambers used by
Austrian Cavalry in 1770's

CURTISS
American Civil War small-arms maker. Saugus Center, Mass.

DAFTE, John
London gunmaker. Worked 1656-1685. In 1680 made snaphaunce revolver

DAFINO, Giovanni Battista
Brescia, circa 1690-1720

DAMM, Peter
Nuremberg, circa 1590. Seven-barrel wheel lock pistols

DAUBIGNY, Phillip (Cordier d'Aubigny)
France, circa 1635-1640. Carved pistol stocks in the form of animal heads

DAUER (Daner, Danner), Peter
Nuremberg, circa 1580-1595. Peter Dauer made fine all-metal dags. There are examples of his right angle ball-butt pistols in the Metropolitan Museum of Art and in the Aitken collection among others. His initials are usually found on the barrel separated by the Nuremberg snake mark

DAUER (Danner), Hans
Nuremberg, circa 1585. 2-shot petronel in Metropolitan Museum of Art. Stock decorated with hunting scenes, arabesques, castles. Gun has "L.S." Strauss lock

DAVID
See: ARNOLD, David

DAX, Johann Georg
Munich, circa 1715-1743

DEANE
See: ADAMS

DEELY, ANSON (and Company)
English gunmakers. Worked 1873-1898

DELCOMYN (Family)
Copenhagen, circa 1790-1850

GUNMAKERS

DELLA PORTA, Giovanni Batista
Naples, circa 1658. Multishot superimposed brass guns. Described Roman candle loading in "Natural Magick", translated into English in 1658

DEL MORO, Natale
Roman gunmaker, built airguns. Worked 1750-1790

DELVIGNE, August (1799-1876)
France. Delvigne breech (sleeve in barrel on which ball was seated by hammering with ramrod)

DEMRAHT (Demrath)
Berlin, circa 1700-1720

DERINGER, Henry, Jr. (1806-1869)
Philadelphia gunmaker

DESELIER, Gilles
Paris, circa 1700-1735

DES GRANGES
Paris, circa 1660-1675

DE VALDEHON, Leboeuf
Designer of straw-contained primer, 1831

DEVILLERS (Villers, Des Willers, Devilliers) G. and I. and J.
Liège, circa 1750-1829

DEVISME, F.P.
Paris, circa 1840-1870

DEWALLE FRERES
Liège, circa 1845

DICKSON, John, AND SON
Edinburgh. 1820 to date

DOLEP, Andrew
Circa 1680-1715. Flemish Huguenot who built fowling pieces and pistols in London after 1681

DOLNE
"In Vur". Dolne patents, circa 1870. Apache guns

DOUGLAS, Sir Howard
London, 1817. Invented flintlock cock with double reversible jaws

DREPPARD
Pennsylvania lockmaker, circa 1838-1869. Lancaster. Gunmaker and locksmith

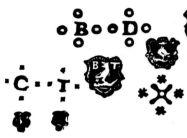

DRESSLER (Dreschsler, Dreshler, Drexler, Tresseler, Treschel, Drechsel),
Abraham, Anton, Balthasar, Christof, David and Lorentz
A large family of Dresden gunsmiths who worked between 1549 and 1624. Balthasar I was
gunmaker to the Elector of Saxony. Balthasar III was born in Vienna in 1625 and died in 1683

DREYSE, Franz Carl Rudolf (1822-1894)
Sommerda. Son of Johann Nikolaus (below)

DREYSE, Johann Nikolaus von (1787-1867)
Sommerda, Germany. Invented needle gun

DU CLOS, François
French, circa 1635. Match, wheel, and flintlock maker and gun stocker. Some of his guns
were decorated by Lisieux artist Thomas Picquot who published his pattern book in 1638. (In
Metropolitan Museum of Art and Paris.) Musée de l'Armée gun is superimposed load
dual lock gun

 DUPE AND COMPANY
Birmingham, circa 1793. Built 14-barrel gun for Col. Thornton now in Liege

EGG, Durs
Circa 1777-1834. London gunsmith. Built the Ferguson rifle. Sporting guns and brass-barreled
Dragoon pistols

EGG, Joseph
Circa 1785-1815. Made a flintlock in 1816 with an airtight slide protecting the touchhole
which was fired on test after repeated dunking in water

GUNMAKERS

EICH (Family)
Oberstedten, Friedberg and Hamburg. 1688-1775

EISTER, George
Kentucky flintlock maker, York, Penn., circa 1741-1810

ELLIS, Henry (C. 1695-1700)
Doncaster, England. Longfowlers and Simonon pattern silver furniture

ELLIS, Reuben
New York, circa 1828. Gunmaker who built the Ellis-Jennings sliding lock rifles
See: JENNINGS

ENDORFER, Georg
Circa 1404. Innsbruck cannon founder

ERHARDT, Jacob
Basel, Switzerland, circa 1650. Master of the Gun Makers' Guild in 1614 in Basel.
Three-shot flintlock rifle

On the Barrel ERTTEL (Ertel, Oerttel) (Family)
Dresden, 1660-1791

ERTTEL, Johann Georg (1700-1763)
Dresden

ESCHER (Family)
Leipzig and Weimar, 1653-1679

ESPINAR, Alonzo Martinez del
Miquelet maker and gunsmith. Author—ARTE DE BALLESTERIA y MONTERIA (1644)

ESQUIBEL (Esquivel), Diego and son F. or J.
Diego, circa 1690-1732; son F. or J. circa 1734-1768. One of the great Spanish barrel and
gun making families whose work and marks were copied almost as extensively as Cominnazo

ESTEVA, Pedro
Barcelona, circa 1680-1740

FARMER, James
Birmingham, 1747. Wall and swivel guns

FARQUHARSON, John
Circa 1872, Edinburgh, Scotland

FASCHANG, Hanns
Vienna, circa 1625-1650. Vienna gunmaker, worked with stockmaker "Meister der Tierkopfranken"

FECHT, von der (Family)
Berlin, 1675-1827

FERGUSON, Patrick
1744-1780. Aberdeen, Scotland. Designed gun on La Chaumette principle. Killed at King's Mountain, Georgia

FERNANDEZ, Juan
Madrid, circa 1726. Teacher of Manuel Sutil, Josef Cano, Joaquin Zelaya and Josef López. Fernández being such a common Spanish name, there were gunmakers by that name in Cordoba, Salamanca, and Toledo and still others in Madrid. Juan was *the* Fernández whose work is in the Palace of the Kings of the Two Sicilies now the Palace of Capodimonte near Naples. His barrels brought fantastic prices in Paris as late as the 1780's and 1790's.

FILIPINO, Vicenzo
Brescia, circa 1645. Locksmith

FISCHER
See: VISCHER

GUNMAKERS

FITSHOLSKY, Daniel
Breslau, circa 1730. Built silver inlaid wheel lock with a rifled barrel fitted into a larger rifled barrel

FLEISCHER, Hans
Dresden stockmaker, circa 1585-1600. Worked with Dressler, stocked pistols for the bodyguards of the Electors of Saxony

FLOBERT, Louis
Paris. Saloon gun, rimfire originator, circa 1846. Company was in business in 1900

FLOCK, Jan
Amsterdam. Maker of Kalthoff-type repeating breech loader. Worked 1680-1709

FLOTNER (Flattner), Peter
1485-1546. Painter, Nuremberg wheel lock decorator, and ivory carver. Worked 1523-1546

FORDNAY, Melchior
Kentucky flintlock maker. Pennsylvania, worked 1811-1840

FORDNEY, Jacob
Lancaster, Pa. 1808-1878. Indian contract rifles

FORSYTH, Reverend Alexander John
1768-1843. Born at Belhelvie, Aberdeenshire, Scotland. Invented scent bottle lock mechanism to use detonating powders in 1806

A. H. FOX GUN CO.
Philadelphia, Pa. (founded 1902) now owned by SAVAGE ARMS CO. (*q.v.*)

FRANCINO (Franci, Francini), Antonio
Brescia, circa 1630-1660. Built de luxe pistols and fowlers. Family 1600-1750

FRANCINO, Gio. Batt.
Brescia, circa 1630-1670

BORTOLO
1570 − 1620

FRANCOTTE, Auguste
Liège, circa 1845-1885. The Francotte family has been making sporting weapons for well over a hundred years. Some of their early pieces included tap action miniature flintlock pistols, but they are most famous today for their fine inlaid and engraved shotguns which are prized all over the world. In the U.S. they are imported by Abercrombie and Fitch.

FRAPPIER
Paris, prior to 1664. Huguenot gunmaker who worked with Pierre Monlong 1664-1684.
Built breech-loading, turn off barrel pistols

FRASER, Daniel
Edinburgh. Built Farquharson action rifle, circa 1875-1881

FRASER, Thomas.
Aberdeen, Scotland, circa 1705

FREEMAN, James Paul
London, circa 1710-1732. Made fine silver mounted mask-butt pistols at the very beginning
of the London trade's golden age. Examples of his work are in museums and great collections

FRESCA, Acqua
See: CECCHI

FREUND, Frank William, 1837-1893
From Heidelberg, Germany. Designed and built guns in Denver, Salt Lake City, and Cheyenne

FREUND, Karl
Fürstenau and Würzburg, circa 1730-1790

FUCHS, Felix
Danish cannon maker to Christian IV, circa 1633

FUSNOT, Charles
Brussels. Worked 1851-1879. Designed the Mitrailleuse with Montigny

GANS, Andreas
Augsburg, circa 1715-1760

GARAND, John C.
b. 1887. Springfield Armory. Developed military rifle bearing his name which was used by the
U.S. Army in World War II

GARCIA, Francisco Antonio
Spanish barrel maker. Gunmaker to Charles IV of Spain. Worked 1762-1792 in Madrid

GASSER, Johan (1847-1871)
Vienna

GUNMAKERS

GASSER, Leopold (1836-1871)

GATLING, Richard Jordan, Dr.
1818-1903. American inventor of Gatling gun

 GAVACCIOLO, Giovanni Antonio
Brescia, circa 1635-1650. One of the few Brescian makers to stamp his locks with a mark.
"G.A.G." is also his stamp found on the inside of lock plate of guns with Cominazzo barrels

GEBAUER
See: BAUER

GERHARDT, Adam Anton
Born 1705. Darmstadt and Stockholm 1732

GEIGER, Leonard
Invented breech loader with rolling block, often mistakenly attributed to Beals.
Patents—1863-1866

GESSLER, Georg
Dresden, circa 1607-1629

GIBBS, George
Bristol, England. Circa 1850. Gibbs-Farquharson

GIBSON, T. (GIBSON AND WILLMORE)
London, circa 1760. Two-shot tap action side lock pistols with silver wire inlays in the
stocks and silver butt plates

GIRARDONI
Ampezzo, Italy. Circa 1765. Built breech-loading flintlocks; invented the tank-in-stock military
air rifles which were built by Contriner in Vienna

GOLCHER
Philadelphia, circa 1800-1820. Kentucky lock maker and importer of English locks

GOLCHER, John
Easton, Pa., circa 1780-1795

GOLCHER, James
Circa 1805

GOLCHER, Joseph
Circa 1820
See: RUGGLES

GOMEZ, Antonio
Madrid, circa 1760-1762. Pupil of Zelaya. Gunmaker to Carlos III

GOODWIN G. AND COMPANY
Birmingham, 1790. Duck foot pistols, brass barrel coaching blunderbuss

HAYWARD AND GOODWIN
(Same Goodwin as above), Birmingham, circa 1805-1807

GORGO, Jacques (James)
London. Worked 1660-1700. Screwbarrel breech-loading flintlock rifle maker. Also made three-barrel pistols and two-shot funnel breech

GOTTORP, The Master of
See: HABRECHT, Heinrich

GOULCHER, *See* GOLCHER

GRAFF (Graf, Graff, Grafe), Joseph
Aachen. Ivory stock flintlock maker, circa 1725

GRAFENSTEIN (Graefenstein, Gräfenstien, Grävenstein), Tobias
Gotha, circa 1729-1750. Wheel lock grenade launchers

GRAS
1874. French artillery officer who developed needlefire military breech-loader used in the Franco-Prussian War

GREENER, William W. (1827-1869)
Newcastle, Birmingham, England. Hay Market, London. Gunmaker

GUNMAKERS

GREENER
Company. London. 1907 to date

GRICE, William
Birmingham, England, circa 1760-1770. Built commercial and service flintlocks

GRIFFIN AND HOWE
American. 20th century gunmakers, New York

GRIFFIN, I. or J. (1730-1779)
London gunmaker

GRIFFIN AND TOW (1779-1796)

GRUNTOF, Matvei
St. Petersburg, circa 1810. Gunmaker—signed Boutet pistols

GULL (Güll), Michael
Vienna, circa 1650-1668. One of the greatest of the Viennese gunmakers and one of the most ingenious. He built at least two completely different breech-loading mechanisms. Examples of his work are naturally in the Kunsthistorisches Museum in Vienna. Other examples in the W. Keith Neal collection

GUMMI, Martin
Culmbach, Germany, circa 1620-1650. Locksmith who stamped initials in a crest over a rampant lion

GUTIRREZ, Joseph
Seville, Spain. Manufactured percussion lock miquelets—1818-1822

HABRECHT, Heinrich (The Master of Gottorp)
Schleswig-Holstein. Made Kalthoff system repeating breech loader with floating barrels. Circa 1650

HACKHA (Häckhl, Häckl, Höckhl), **F.**
Miespach, Germany, circa 1616

HAHN, Gottfried
Dresden, circa 1695-1707

HALL, John H.
Worked 1811-1840. Harpers' Ferry Arsenal 1816-1840. Inventor of flintlock breech
loader with removable chamber, 1811

HARKOM, Joseph
Edinburgh, circa 1850

HARRINGTON AND RICHARDSON
Worcester. Manufacturers of revolvers and shotguns. 1888 to date

HARTLEY, James
Contemporary. Developed lightweight spun fibreglass barrels used on Winchester shotguns

HATCHER, James
Contemporary gun designer. Invented button rifling

HAWKEN, Henry and sons Jacob and Samuel T.
Produced plains rifles in St. Louis, Mo. between 1820 and 1884

HELBIG (Helwig), Peter
Dresden (1618-1683)

HELWIG (Helbig), Johann David
Reval

HELWIG (Helbig), Simon
Father of Peter. Dresden, circa 1609-1639

HENEQUIN, Jean (of Metz)
Early French flintlock maker, engraver. Made guns for Louis XIII, circa 1620.
Pattern book designer

HENRY, Alexander (1824-1894)
Edinburgh, Scotland. Barrel maker, inventor of rifling system (Martini-Henry)

HENRY, B. Tyler (1821-1898)
Patented magazine rifle in 1860. Worked at Henry Arms Co., New Haven Arms Co.,
Winchester Arms Co. Henry rifle prototype of Winchester

GUNMAKERS

HENRY, François Antoine
Paris. Designed magazine breech loader with tubular magazine for powder and ball on top of gun barrel in 1837

HENRY, J. Joseph (1786-1836)
Philadelphia, circa 1814. Contracted with Tryon to build swivel guns and repeating muskets for U.S. Navy

HEROLD, Zacharias
Dresden, circa 1586-1628

HESS, C.
Zweibrücken, circa 1720-1780

HESS, J. D.
Zweibrücken, circa 1795

HEURTELOUP, Baron Charles Louis Stanislaus
1793-1864. Urologist. Patented tube primer "koptipteur"—1836-1839

HIGH STANDARD MANUFACTURING CO.
New Haven, Conn. 1926 to date.
See: SWEBILIUS

HILL, Abraham
London. Patents for breech loader, multi-shot weapon in 1664

HILLIARD, D. H.
Cornish, New Hampshire. Under hammer percussion carbine, circa 1850

HIRST, John
London, circa 1740-1773. Manufactured 298,700 muskets for the British Army during the Seven Years War.

HOLLAND AND HOLLAND
London gun factory. Famous for double rifles. 1834 to date

HOLLENBECK
See: THREE-BARREL GUN COMPANY

HOLLIS, I.
London (1854-1900)

HOLLOWAY, Jonadab
London, 1667. Silver, gilt and damascened pistols

HOLNER
Prag (Prague), circa 1700. Alarm clock flintlock

HOPKINS AND ALLEN
Norwich, Conn. U.S. cartridge revolver manufacturers. 1868-1917

HOTCHKISS, Benjamin Berkely (1826-1885)
New York-Paris. Invented Winchester-Hotchkiss rifle and Hotchkiss cannon

HOWARD, Charles (HOWARD BROS.)
Invented single shot underloader built by Whitney Arms Co. 1865-1869

HUNT, Walter
New York (?-1859). Invented rocket ball cartridge bullet in 1848; the volition repeater in 1849.
Also invented the safety pin and the sewing machine

ITHACA GUN COMPANY
Ithaca, New York, 1873 to date. Manufacture shotguns

JACKSON
London, circa 1780. Two-shot tap action flintlock pistol

JACOB, Major John
Commander of the Scinde Irregular Horse. Developed double barrel, four-groove military
rifle in 1858

JARRE ET CIE
Harmonica guns. Paris. 1858-1880

JEFFERYS
Double rifle manufacturers. London, 1888 to date

JEIADTEL
See: JERADTEL

GUNMAKERS

JENKS, Alfred, and son Barton H.
Manufactured 5,000 Springfield rifled muskets each month during the American Civil War.
Bridesburg, Penn.

JENKS, William
Springfield, Mass. Circa 1838-1841. Breech-loading carbines

JENNINGS, Isiah
New York, 1821. Patented superimposed loading gun with sliding lock, Middletown, Conn.
Simeon North, maker, 1825-1828

JENNINGS, Lewis
Inventor of a tubular magazine breech-loading rifle. Windsor, Vermont. Worked 1849-1851

JERADTEL, Franz
Vienna, circa 1650. Breech loader inventor (Tøjhus Museum)

JESSEN, Neils Stall
Danish inventor of the Tige or pillar breech and the oval bored rifle, circa 1850. Copenhagen.
In charge of the Danish Navy's small arms workshop, 1829-1862

JOHN THE ALMAIN
See: ALMAIN

JOHNSON, Eric
Contemporary gunmaker and barrel maker. Connecticut

JOHNSON, Iver
Gunmaking factory in Massachusetts from circa 1900

JOSLYN, Benjamin F.
Worcester, Mass., Stonington, Conn. Worked 1855-1879. U.S. cartridge revolver manufacturer.
Produced military breech loading carbines and rifles during the Civil War

JOVER, William
London, circa 1775. Gold and silver decorated pistols, also built contract guns for the
East India Company

KALESNIKOW, B.
Circa 1740-1780. Tula, Russia. Flintlock revolver and gunmaker. Royal Russian gunmaker

KALTHOFF, Caspar
London. Worked 1625-1664. Gunsmith. Built breech loader for Earl of Worcester

KALTHOFF, Caspar (II)
Russia, circa 1675

KALTHOFF, Mathias
Copenhagen. Worked 1646-1672. Repeating military long gun

KALTHOFF, Peter
Born in Solingen, Germany. Worked in Flensburg and Copenhagen. Repeating breech-loading long guns. Worked 1641-1672. Earliest dated Danish flintlock, 1646

KALTHOFF, William
Gunsmith in Paris in 1660's. Repeating breech loader

KANT, Cornelius
Amsterdam, 1670's. Made repeaters

KAPPEL, Heinrich
Denmark, circa 1676-1723. Built breech-loading guns

KEISER (Kaiser, Kayser), Georg
Vienna, 1647-1736. Probably the son of Caspar or Hans Keiser. Royal gunmaker to the Dresden and Viennese courts. His son Georg was also a gunmaker in Vienna. Georg, the father, lived to be at least 93 and used to put his age as well as his name on guns that he made in later life

KEISER, Kaspar
Eger, circa 1665

GUNMAKERS

KENDALL, Nicanor
1807-1861. Kendall, Hubbard & Smith in Windsor, Vermont. Kendall & Lawrence.
Lawrence & Robbins. Harmonica rifle.

KETLAND, Thomas
Birmingham, circa 1765. Ketland and Walker, 1805—died 1815

KETLAND AND COMPANY
William Ketland, son, 1800-1820

KHAN, Aba Muslem
Daghestan, circa 1825. Snaphaunce maker

KIEFUSS, Johann
Reputed inventor of wheel lock. Nuremberg in 1517 per Moritz Thierbach

KLETT, Valentin (Johann Paul, Sigmund, Cornelius)
Suhl, circa 1575-1692. A famous member of an outstanding gunmaking family that worked
in Suhl and Salzburg for nearly 200 years, between 1550 and 1750. Cornelius and his brothers
made guns for the Emperor of Austria and the Bishop of Salzburg. Sigmund built an
improvement on the Kalthoff magazine breech loader. The Kletts were also known for their
Wender and their superimposed load guns. Cornelius Klett—Salzburg, circa 1653-1680
Valentine Klett—1590-1610
Hans Klett, 1600-1604—Stockholm; 1618 Suhl
Johann Paul Klett, 1634-1650 and 3 sons, moved from Suhl to Salzburg in 1636. They were:
Cornelius, circa 1653-1680, four-barrel, eight-shot revolver in Kindig Collection; Johann
Paul II, 1660-1692; Sigmund, 1650-1661 and son-in-law Johann Krack; Johann Paul III,
1663-1692, also signed his name Jean Paul Cleff

KNOD (Knot, Knodt) Johann Adam
Carlsbad, 1690-1750. Built three-barrel revolver as well as breech-loading pistols on the
Chaumette system

KNOOP, Jan
Utrecht, circa 1650-1670

KOENIG, C. G.
Coburg and Mehlis, circa 1800-1886

KOLBE
London, circa 1750. Gunmaker to George II. Built air gun now in Victoria and Albert Museum

KOTTER, Augustinus (August)
Augsburg and Nuremberg, circa 1616-1635. Triangle and square bore guns—1627

KRAG, Ole H.
Norwegian inventor (1837-1912). Krag Jørgensen bolt action magazine rifle

KRAUS, Hans (?)
Initials "H.K." with a pair of spectacles, probably a father and son, Nuremberg, circa 1565-1590.
Revolving wall gun in Cluny Museum, eight-shot revolving wheel lock carbine in the
Tower of London

KROPATSCHEK, Alfred von
Worked 1870-1885. Developed the military tubular magazine bolt action rifle used by
Austria, France, and Portugal

KRUG
Family of gunmakers. Augsburg, circa 1585. Guns marked with "jug" stamp

KRUPP, Alfred
1810-1887. German manufacturer of steel cannon

KRUTZCH, W.
English pump gun—1866

KUCHENREUTER, Johann Andreas I (1716-1795); Johann Christoph I and II;
Johann Jacob (1709-1783); Joseph I and II and Joseph Anton
Regensburg, between 1626 and 1898. Johann Andreas I was gunmaker to the Princes of
Thurn and Taxis. Nearly a hundred of his guns and pistols survive. His sons succeeded him as
court gunmakers. Most of their output was pistols, many with rifled barrels

GUNMAKERS

KUNZE, Peter
Philadelphia, 1776

KYHL, Johann Christian
Copenhagen (1762-1827)

LA CHAUMETTE, Isaac de
Paris gunmaker who developed a new system of breech loading in 1704. Emigrated to England.
Circa 1704-1732

LACOLLOMBE, de
Circa 1705. French royal gunmaker and pattern book designer

LA FONTEYNE
Paris, circa 1642. Waterproof wheel lock pistols

LAGATZ, Daniel
Danzig, circa 1685-1740. Used a vertical screw breech plug

LAMSON, E. G. AND COMPANY
Windsor, Vermont. Gunmakers, 1850-1867

LANCASTER, Charles
Built pillar-breech sporting and military rifles in 1848; developed center fire under-lever gun
with extractors, circa 1852 and eliptical (oval) bored carbines for the Royal Sappers and
Miners in 1855
See: THOUVENIN

LANG, Joseph
English revolver maker. Worked 1821-1875

LANGUEDOC
See: LE LANGUEDOC

LA ROCHE (Jean Baptiste, father and son)
"Aux Galeries du Louvre." French gunmakers with *logement* from Louis XV. Circa 1715-1774

LASONDER, Gerret
Utrecht, circa 1710-1750

LAWRENCE
See: ROBBINS AND LAWRENCE

LAZARINO, Lazaro
See: COMINAZZO

LEAVITT, Daniel
Chicopee, Mass. Worked 1837-1859. Patented a revolver with a slide-off cylinder in 1837

LEBEDA, Antonin Vincene
1795-1857. Apprenticed with Contriner in Vienna. Prague; circa 1850. Made de luxe sporting arms, invented the "Kastenschloss" or back action lock in 1829, made guns for Czar of Russia, King of Sweden, Franz Joseph of Austria, etc.

LEBEL, Nicolas
French soldier and inventor (1835-1891). 8mm military tubular magazine bolt action rifle in 1886

LE BOURGEOYS, Jean
French flintlock maker and jeweller. Circa 1610. Brother of Marin

LE BOURGEOYS, Marin
Lisieux (1550-1634). French flintlock inventor; painter, watchmaker, jeweller and goldsmith. Worked circa 1575-1634. Gunmaker by appointment to Henri IV and Louis XIII

LE CLERC, Jean
St. Etienne, Paris (?-1739). Gunmaker

LE CLERC, Nicolas
Circa 1780-1830. Son of Jean. Side-by-side double. Worked with Chasteau after his father died. In 1782 he was appointed gunmaker to Louis XVI

LE CONTE, L.
Circa 1683. Paris gunmaker to Louis XIV

LEE, James
Short Beach, Conn. (1831-1904). Straight-pull magazine rifles

GUNMAKERS

LEFAUCHEUX, Eugene
Paris, France (1820-1871). Pinfire inventor and manufacturer. Drop-down action with lever under fore-end

LEFEVER, Charles F.
Syracuse, N.Y. U.S. shotgun manufacturer—1892-1920

LE HOLLANDOIS (Adrian Reynier)
Thuraine et le Hollandois, Paris, circa 1650-1660

LE LANGUEDOC, J. Laurent
French flintlock maker. Paris, circa 1685

LE MAT, Dr. (Colonel) Alexander
Worked 1855-1865. New Orleans, La. Designed nine-shot revolvers for the Confederate Army, which were built in France and England

LEONTOFF, A.
Tula, Russia, circa 1740-1760

LEPAGE
Family of gunmakers

LEPAGE, H. Fauré
c. 1840-1920

LEPAGE, H. Fauré, Jr.
c. 1900-1920

LEPAGE, Henri
Paris gunmaker. Worked 1822-1842

LEPAGE, Jean (1746-1834)
Paris gunmaker. Worked 1779-1822. Built guns for Louis XVI and Napoleon

LEPAGE, Michele
Circa 1800-1805. Gunmaker to Napoleon as First Consul and then as the Emperor

LEPAGE MOUTIER and FAURE
Paris gunmaking company, circa 1840-1865

LEPAGE, Perrin L.
Circa 1860. Percussion breech loader in Liège. Paris gunmaker. Mother's maiden name Perrin

LEPAGE, Pierre
Paris gunmaker. Worked circa 1743-1749

LES LAROUCHEUX, Jean-Baptiste Laroche
Jeweller and gunmaker, circa 1743-1769

LILLYCRAP, J.
London, 1837. Revolving percussion musket and 15 barrel pistol belt

LINDNER, Edward
New York City. Worked 1854-1863. Inventor of gas-operated under-barrel piston which unlocked and raised the breech of a percussion breech loader in 1854

LINDSAY, John Parker
Springfield Armory Naugatuck and New Haven, Conn. Worked 1859-1869. Single barrel two shot pistol musket and double-loaded percussion revolver

LØBNITZ, Nicolaj Johann
Danish gunmaker (1798-1867). Worked 1833-1850. Breech-loading gun, airguns, under hammer percussion guns. Became court gunmaker in 1842

LOEWE, L. & COMPANY (LUDIVE, LOEWE & COMPANY)
Berlin, circa 1890

LOPEZ, Juan
Madrid, circa 1767-1795. Joseph, Madrid 1742; Francisco, Madrid, circa 1749-1766. Juan learned his trade from Antonio Gómez, Francisco was gunmaker to Carlos III of Spain in 1761. A gold and silver mounted pair of Francisco's pistols are in the Wallace Collection in London. A flintlock of Joseph's is in the Tower, dated 1820
See: GOMEZ, Antonio

LORENZONUS, Michael (Lorenzoni, Michele)
Worked 1684-1733. Breech-loading flintlock magazine guns and revolvers. Florence, Italy

Barrel Markings

LOUROUX, Johan
Maastricht, circa 1660-1700. Ivory pistols at Metropolitan Museum of Art

GUNMAKERS

LOVELL, George
Worked circa 1805-1854. Woolwich and London, England. Lovell back-action percussion locks in 1805. Inspector of small arms of British Army, 1840

LUGER, Georg
Charlottenburg, Germany. Improved Borchardt. Worked 1889-1907. Parabellum pistol—1900

LUTZE
American small arms maker, circa 1866-1874

LYMAN, William
Founded the Lyman Gun Sight Co. 1878 to date, Middlefield, Conn. Manufacturers of iron and telescopic sights. William Lyman worked 1878-1898

MACKENZIE, David
Circa 1707-1728. Dundee, Scotland

MACKENZIE, James
Circa 1728-1735. Dundee, Scotland

MACNAB, Patrick
Dalmally, Scotland, circa 1735

MALHERBE, P. J.
Liège, circa 1836-1865

 MAMBACH, Francisco
Germany, circa 1660. Invented and built a four-barrel flintlock carbine which was capable of firing 29 shots on a superimposed load basis with a single pull on the trigger. The carbine is in the Tower of London.

MANGEOT, H.
See: COMBLAIN

MANHATTAN FIREARMS MANUFACTURING COMPANY
New York, 1864-1869. U.S. cartridge revolver manufacturers

MANNLICHER, Ferdinand, Ritter von (1848-1904)
Mainz, Germany. Invented clip feed, 1885

MANTON, John
Gunsmith in London, England. Percussion pistols and shotguns, 1825. Worked 1818-1834. Brother of Joseph.

MANTON, Joseph (1766-1835)
English gunmaker, London. One of the finest gunmakers of his period

MANTON, Thomas
London, circa 1816

MARBLE ARMS & MFG. CO. (Walter L. and Webster L.)
Gladstone, Mich. 1898 to present

MARCKWARDT (Marquart, Marcuarte), Peter (Pedro), Simon I and II, Bartholomeus
Augsburg and Madrid, circa 1530-1621. Peter was brought to Madrid from Augsburg by Charles V, then Carlos I of Spain. The family built the first wheel locks in Spain. Simon II, circa 1580-1620, is credited with the invention of the miquelet lock. The family were gunmakers to both Philip I and II of Spain

MARCOU, François
1595-1660. 17th century gun designer, decorator and author of PLUSIEURS PIECES D'ARQUEBUZERIE

MARLIN, John Mahlon
U.S. cartridge revolver and magazine rifle manufacturer. Worked 1870-1915. Patents 1892

MARR, Valentin
1696-1786. One of a large family of Danish gunsmiths. He became the Master Armorer at the Tøjhus Arsenal in 1759

MARTINEZ, Alonzo
Madrid, Lisbon, Barcelona and Palma, 1619-1750. Worked with Nicolas Bís, Luis Santos and Juan Belén in Madrid. First to make a gun barrel of horseshoe nails. Later, official gunmaker to King John V of Portugal

GUNMAKERS

MARTINI, Friedrich von
Frauenfeld, Switzerland. Co-inventor of Martini-Henry breech-loading rifle in 1869

MASON, William
American gun designer, inventor and manufacturer. Tauton, Mass., New Haven, Conn.
Worked 1860-1907

MASSACHUSETTS ARMS COMPANY
Chicopee Falls, Mass., 1849-1876

MAUCHER, Johann Michael
Schwäbisch Gmünd, 1645-1680; Würzburg, 1680-1700. Did fine ivory and wood carving. Noted
for his pistol butts carved out of ivory in the form of classical heads, and for his inlaid ivory
panels in pearwood stocks. He called himself "sculptor and gunmaker" and the popularity of
his baroque carving then and today seems to substantiate his claim

MAUSER, Paul
Oberndorf, Germany (1838-1914). Gun designer. Worked 1868-1908

MAXIM, Sir Hiram Stevens
1840-1916. American inventor of the Maxim-Vickers machine gun in 1889

MAYNARD, Dr. Edward
Washington, D.C. Dentist and gun inventor. Maynard tape primer. Worked 1845-1886

MCKENZIE, I. A. (John)
Brechin, Scotland, circa 1750

MEIDINGER, Johan Franz
Stockholm, circa 1720-1769

MEISTER DER TIERKOPFRANKEN
See: TIERKOPFRANKEN

MERIDEN MANUFACTURING COMPANY
See: TRIPLETT AND SCOTT

MERRILL, LATROBE AND THOMAS—James H. Merrill
Baltimore, circa 1855-1860. Breech-loading percussion carbine

MERWIN, Joseph (Merwin and Bray) (Merwin Hulbert & Co.)
1862-1891. Worcester, Mass. and New York

METZGER (Family)
Stockholm, circa 1697-1790

MILLS, William
Holburn, London, circa 1825. Fine sliding-lock percussion sporting rifles

MINIE, Claude Etienne
Vincennes, France (1814-1879). French army officer and gun inventor. Minié rifle. Hollow soft
lead cylindrical bullets with anvils at base to force the lead into rifling. Anvils later found
unnecessary and discarded by Minié

MITELLI, Guiseppe
Bolognese engraver (1634-1718)

MOLL, John (1772-1794), John Jr. (b. 1773 married 1795), John III (b. 1796-d. 1883)
All built Kentucky rifles in Allentown, Pa.

MONDRAGON, Manuel
Mexico City. Worked 1896-1907, invented a gas operated, semi-automatic bolt action
breech loader

MONEY (Money and Walker)
19th century. English

MONLONG, Pierre
"Frappier and Monlong." Angiers and Paris, circa 1664-1684. London, 1684-1690

MONS, Joseph
German. Built sporting rifle in 1750's with cloverleaf-shaped bore

MONTAIGU, D. A.
Metz, circa 1640's. Superimposed pistols

MONTIGNY
French designer of mitrailleuse, circa 1850 with Fusnot

GUNMAKERS

MONT-STORM, Willam
London, 1865-1871. Percussion breech loader—military

MOON, William and Jessie
Clark Township, Ohio, 1809-1826. Built rifles

MOORE, Charles
English. Built pellet lock pistols in 1820. London 1815-1835

MOORE, D., AND COMPANY
Makers of single action revolvers. Brooklyn, New York, 1862-1863

MOORE, William
London, 1827

MORETTI (Moreta, Moreto, etc.)
Brescian gunmaking family—1665-1740
Antonio—worked circa 1720-1725
Pietro—worked circa 1665-1680
Pietro (Moretto) worked circa 1725-1740
Filippo, circa 1730

MORITZ, I. D. and son
Family of gunmakers from Kassel since 1642. Leipzig, circa 1890. De luxe sporting gun manufacturers

MORO
See: DEL MORO

MORTIMER, Harvey Westlake
English. Worked 1783-1802. Gun and pistol maker. Gunmaker to George III

MORTIMER, Harvey Westlake, Jr.
Maker of flintlock magazine pistols. Worked circa 1800-1820. A Thomas Jackson Mortimer (same family) received an order from the U.S. Government for presentation guns for the Bey of Tunis in 1801

MORTIMER, Thomas (?) J.
London. Shotgun and pistol maker. Worked 1825-1832

MOSSBERG, Oscar F.
(O.F. MOSSBERG, New Haven, Conn. 1818 to date) Active 1892-1937. Patented gun designs and manufactured fire arms.

MOUTIER-LEPAGE
French gunmakers. Active in 1842-1865

MULLER, Georg
Munich, circa 1590. Made a two-shot superimposed lead rifle which was stocked by Borstorffer

MURCOTT, William
Gunmaker. Inventor of first true hammerless. London gunsmith, navy model pistols. Worked on hammerless in 1871-1872

MURDOCH, John (Io.)
Doun, Scotland, circa 1775-1800

MURDOCH, H.
Doun, Scotland, circa 1646-1675

MURDOCH, Thomas
Doun, Scotland, circa 1784-1790. Leith, 1800

MUTTI, Gei (su)
Gardone, circa 1720

NAGANT, L.
Liège. Worked 1875-1896. Patented revolver in 1884, designed Russian rifle used in World War I

NAVARRO, Antonio
Madrid, circa 1796. Gunmaker to Don Carlos IV

NEAL, Daniel
Mt. Gilead, Ohio, circa 1855. Patented two-shot percussion rifle

NEAVE, Thompson, (and Son)
Percussion gunlock markers, 1836-1860 Cincinnati, Ohio,

GUNMAKERS

NEEDHAM, Joseph and William
Soft lead cylindrical bullet—1843-1852. Needham breech-loading conversion and Needham needle-fire musket

 NEIDHARDT, Andreas
Helsingfors (Elsinore) from 1631, Copenhagen, 1653—Built wheel lock sporting guns with unusual cookie-cutter shapes for multi-ball loads for King Christian IV of Denmark

NEIDHART, Peter
Pennsylvania, circa 1786. Kentucky rifle manufacturer

NEWTON, Charles (Newton Arms Co.)
Buffalo, N.Y. 1914-1930

 NICHOLSON, E. D. and William
Worked circa 1760-1808 in London. Flintlock pistols including tap action and seven-barrel pepperboxes

NIEMEYER, J.
Pennsylvania, plains rifles, circa 1840's

NIMSCHKE, L. D.
New York gun engraver. 1832-1904

NOCK, Henry
London lockmaker and gunmaker (1741-1804). Built screwless locks, muskets for the East India Co., reloadable cartridge guns, brass cannon locks, etc.

NOCK AND JOVER
Circa 1775. Made contract pistols for East India Company

NOCK, Samuel (1812-1862)
"Gunmaker to his Majesty". Related to Henry and J. Nock. London

NORMAND, Paul Nielsen
Copenhagen, circa 1661-1691

NORTH, Simeon (1765-1852)
Manufacturer of contract pistols for U.S. Government. Middletown, Conn.

NORWICH LOCK MANUFACTURING COMPANY
U.S. cartridge revolver manufacturers. 1873-1878

NOWOTNY, J.
Prague, circa 1860-1900

NUSBAUM, Albrecht Heinrich
Breslau, circa 1663-1733

NUSBAUM, Jakob
Stockholm, circa 1756-1802

PACZELT, Stanislaus
Prague, Bohemia. Hammerless flintlock sporting guns. Worked 1730-1738. (Supposed to have invented the choke in shotguns)

PANNABACKER, PANNABECKER
See: PENNABEKER

PARAUBE (Piraube), Bertrand (Bernard)
Paris (Louvre). Gunmaker to Louis XIV. Circa 1685-1717

PARKER BROTHERS
Meriden, Conn (1868-1934). Founded by Charles Parker. One of the best American double-gun makers. Bought out by Remington in 1934.

PARKER, William
Holborn, London. Gunmaker to George III. Worked 1800-1840

PARKER
Bury St. Edmunds, circa 1780-1800. Crossbow maker

PAULY, Samuel Johannes
Swiss inventor. Worked in Paris and London, 1808-1821. In 1812 made the first breech loader which fired obturating center fire cartridges

PEABODY, Henry O.
Patented his breech-loading rifle in 1862. Manufactured by The Providence Tool Company 1862-1880. This gun became the Peabody-Martini and then Martini-Henry

GUNMAKERS

PECK, Peter
1503-1596. Munich, circa 1540-1560. Matchlock and wheel lock maker to Philip II of Spain when he was a prince; and also to Charles V after he became Holy Roman Emperor. A double barrel over-and-under wheel lock pistol with a dagger shaped grip is in the Metropolitan Museum of Art and a *breech-loading* matchlock is in the Bayerisches Armeemuseum in Munich. (1553) Both are finely decorated and inlaid with bone ivory.

PEDERSON, Elias
Odense, Denmark, circa 1665. Gunmaker. Built segment lock

PENNABECKER (PANNABECKER), Samuel, Jeff, Jesse, John
Kentucky flintlock maker. Lancaster, Pennsylvania, circa 1783-1850

PERREAUX A VERRUE
Turin (1670-1730). Repeating flintlock maker

PERVUSHKIN (Pervusha), Isay (Issayev)
Russian gunmaker (Kremlin Armory), circa 1620

PETRINI, Antonio
Brescia, circa 1640
Guiseppi, Brescia, circa 1650

PICKFATT, Capt. Charles
London, circa 1720's. Military and civilian arms

PICKFATT, Humphrey
London, circa 1680's

PICQUOT, Thomas
Lisieux, France, pupil of Marin le Bourgeoys. Goldsmith, came to Paris in 1636. Decorated DuClos gun in Musée de l'Armée, #151

PIM, John
Boston, circa 1722. Demonstrated an eleven-shot repeater

PIN, Warner
London, circa 1640

PIRAUBE
See: PARAUBE

PISTOR (Family)
Schmalkalden, Germany
Bernhard I—1760-1780
Bernhard II—1810-1840
Bernhard III—circa 1860
Ernst Wilhelm—1820-1840
Matheus Conrad (Kassel)—1728-1743; 1743-1761—Schmalkalden

PIZZI, Andreas
Brescia, circa 1660-1700

PIZZI, Pietro (Piero)
Brescia, circa 1655

PLANT MFG. CO.
New Haven and Southington, Conn. 1859-1868 manufactured the Plant revolver and the Eagle revolver.

PLESSNER
American, circa 1860. Inventor of repeating arms

PLOMDEUR
Paris, 1850-1870. Gunmaker to Louis Napoleon—1851-1870. (Haaken-Plomdeur, 1850); (Vivaro-Plomdeur, 1870)

POPE, Harry M. (1861-1950)
Jersey City, N.J. Famous American barrel maker

PORTA
See: DELLA PORTA

PORTER, E. W.
New York. Invented a vertical cylinder breech loader, 1851

PORTLOCK, John
Circa 1815-1820. Birmingham, England, barrel maker

GUNMAKERS

PORTLOCK, Thomas
Circa 1800-1811. Birmingham, England, barrel maker

POTTET, Clement
Invented a paper and metal cartridge with a percussion cap in the base in 1829, and modern center fire cartridge in 1855. Worked in Paris from 1812. Patented a two-shot flintlock gun in 1818. Apprenticed to Pauly

POTTET, Henri (probably a brother of Clement)
Paris, patented breech loader in 1824

PRELAT, François
Paris. Patented Forsyth detonating lock in 1810. Percussion lock in 1820 in France

PRESCOTT, Edwin A.
U.S. cartridge revolver inventor and manufacturer. Worked 1853-1875

IP PROBIN, John
Birmingham, circa 1780. Four-bore carbines fitted for bayonets. Gunmaker to the Prince of Wales (later George IV)

PUCKLE, James
London, circa 1720. Gunsmith and promoter. Invented revolving breech-loading cannon.

PUIFORCAT, L.
Parisian gunsmith, circa 1750-1785—"seul arquebusier du Roy"

PURDY, James
1825-1879. London gunmaker. Founded Purdy Gun Co., makers to date of best quality shot guns.

PUSHKIN (Puschkin), Ivan
Moscow, circa 1775

RASMUSSEN, Peder
Denmark. Invented eight-shot military revolving rifle in 1845. Worked 1827-1845

RASO, Nicola
Italian lockmaker, circa 1700

REMINGTON, (E. Remington and Sons)
Eliphalet, Sr.—?-1828
Samuel and Eliphalet III failed in 1886. Remington Arms continued by Hartley and Graham.
Now owned by DuPont

 RENETTE, Gastine
Paris. Famous maker of percussion arms and duellers. Worked 1838-1880's. Gunmaker to the
king of Spain

REQUA, J.
With Billinghurst—*q.v.*   Rochester, New York. Inventor of platoon battery, circa 1860

REWER (Röwer, Röber), Valentine
Dresden, circa 1703-1737. Royal gunmaker to the Saxon Court

REYNIER, Adrian (Le Hollandois)
Paris. "Arquebusiers du Roi". Circa 1660. Adrian II, circa 1723-1743. *Logement* in galleries
of the Louvre.

RICHARDS, John
Circa 1780-1800. London. Tap action superimposed load flintlock pistols. J. and
W. Richards—1800-1812

RICHARDS, Westley
Worked 1812-1873. Birmingham and London. Gunmaker, perfected the doll's head top lever
lock in 1862. Company continued to date as Westley Richards Co.

RIDER, Joseph
Newark, Ohio. Worked 1858-1895. Inventor of Remington rolling block breech loader

RIGBY, William and John
Gunmakers, Dublin, circa 1820's to date

ROANTREE
Durham, England. Gunsmith, worked circa 1820. (May have built first percussion gun for
Joshua Shaw)

ROBBINS AND LAWRENCE
Windsor, Vermont. Built Jennings and Sharps rifles. 1844-1852

GUNMAKERS

ROBBINS, W. E.
Roaring Spring and Elk Run, Pennslvania, circa 1860. Mule ear, side hammer percussion rifles

ROBERT, J.A. (possibly the same as A.J. Roberts of Rheims)
"Robert à Paris." Inventor of hinged block pinfire system. Worked 1824-1834

ROBERT, S.
Naples, circa 1873. Cannon founder

ROLAND
Liège, circa 1881. Invented polychoke

RONGE, Antoine.
Liège, circa 1785-1845. J.B. 1745-1883

ROOP, J.
Circa 1815. Pennsylvania, Kentucky flintlock maker using superimposed system.

ROOT, E. K.
Worked 1853-1867, Hartford, Conn. Designed the Root patent sidehammer rovolver which was manufactured by Colt.

ROSSI DI PARMI, Andreas (1620-1680)
Italian snaphaunce maker

ROVIRA (Ruira)
Ripoll and Barcelona, circa 1675-1702. Nothing is known of this maker except that two fine examples of his work come down to us. Both are in England. One is a four-barrel flintlock revolver dated 1702, in the Tower of London. It is signed and inscribed "Rovira. Pera Carbunell en Barcelona." The other piece is a miquelet carbine with a Ripoll stock and decoration signed and dated "Rovira-1694" in W. Keith Neal's collection. An Antonio Rovira (Ruira), possibly a son, was court gunmaker to Ferdinand VI of Spain in 1758

ROWLAND, R.
London, circa 1720

ROWBOTTOM, George
Contemporary inventor. President of Kodiak Gun Co., North Haven, Conn.

RUGER, William (STURM RUGER COMPANY)
Southport, Conn. Gunmaker. Automatic pistols, single six, Black Hawk revolver and single shot rifles

RUGGLES, A.
Stafford Hollow, Conn., circa 1820-1830. Underhammer percussion pistols; rifles with Joseph Golchers locks and doubleset triggers. *See:* GOLCHER

RUHR, Hans
Coburg, 1620-1654

RUPERTUS PAT'D PISTOL MFG. Co.
Philadelphia, Pa. (1858-1900) Jacob Rupertus

SADELER, Daniel
Prague and Munich. Worked 1620-1632. Barrel and lock maker, made guns for Maximilian I, Elector of Bavaria

SADELER, Emanuel
Sword cutler and iron gun part maker and decorator. Older brother of Daniel. Worked for Duke Wilhelm V of Bavaria. Worked in Munich. b. 1514-d. 1610

SADELER, Johannes
Iron worker and engraver. Cousin of Emanuel. Worked with Adam Vischer. Worked circa 1600-1625

SANCHES DE MIRUENA, Juan
Spanish (circa 1600). Sixteenth century innovator of barrels forged with six or seven pieces of steel. Gunmaker to Phillip III

SANDE, van den
Zutphen, Netherlands, circa 1650-1660

SANDER, Jan
Hanoverian breech loader flintlock maker (1670-1715)

GUNMAKERS

SANTOS, Luis
Madrid, circa 1700-1720; Juan (son), Madrid 1714-1750; Sebastian, Madrid, circa 1760. A pair of elegant barrels made by Juan Santos turned up in the Tøjhus Museum mounted to a pair of guns made by the Danish gunmaker Valentin Marr for King Christian VI and his queen. Sebastian Santos was a barrel maker whose work survives in the Palace of Capodimonte, Naples. Sebastian was gunmaker to the Spanish king, Ferdinand VI

SAUER, J. P.
Suhl, circa 1790-1820

SAUER & SOHN (Company)
1790 to date

SAVAGE ARMS CO.
Utica, New York, 1893 to date. Founded by Arthur W. Savage (1857-1938) the company bought out Stevens, The Springfield Arms Co., and A. H. Fox Co.

SCHERTIGER, Jonas I
Stockholm, circa 1666-1715. Jonas II—1696-1748, Stockholm

SCHIAZZANO (Schiazzono)
Italian locksmith, circa 1700

SCHLUTER, Dietrich
Gottorp, circa 1658. Holland, circa 1675, and possibly Suhl

SCHOFIELD, George W.
U.S. Army. Gun and revolver inventor. Patents: 1870-1880. Smith and Wesson produced his revolvers

SCHREIBER, John, Sr.
Circa 1775. Pennsylvania, Kentucky rifles

SCHREIBER, John, Jr.
Circa 1801. Pennsylvania, Kentucky rifles

SCHROEDER, SALEWSKI AND SCHMIDT (Smith), H. Schroeder, L. Salewski, William Schmidt
U.S. gun inventor and manufacturer. 1856—Needham needlefire carbine.
U.S. Army contracted for 10 needle fire guns from Schmidt

SCHWIND (Schwend), G. E.
Germany, circa 1715

SCOTT
Patented magazine self-loader in 1864 with Louis Triplett in Meriden, Conn.

SEFRIED, Harry H.
Contemporary American gun designer. Miracle trigger (Winchester) and Sentinel revolver (High Standard)

SEGALAS (Segallas, Segalles) Israel, Sr. and Jr.
London gunmakers, whose name was used on Liège all-metal fakes—1750-1800. Israel, Sr. worked 1715-1720. Israel, Jr. Worked ?-1772, becoming proofmaster of the Honorable Company of Gunmakers

SELIER, Phillipe de
Paris, 1690-1740

SEMPERT-KRIEGHOFF
Schuetzen rifle manufacturers. Suhl, Germany, circa 1922-1940

SIMONIN, Claude
Paris, circa 1684-1693. Gun designer and engraver

SHARPS, Christian
American gun designer and builder (1811-1874). Worked with Hall at Harpers Ferry. Designed the Sharps breech-loading rifle, built Sharps naval carbine and four shot pistol in Philadelphia

SHATTUCK, C. S.
Hatfield, Mass. Revolver manufacturer. Worked 1880-1908

SHAW, Joshua
1777-1860. Patented percussion cap in Philadelphia in 1822. Inventor and artist.

SMITH, Horace
Gun inventor and manufacturer. (1808-1865?). Springfield, Mass.

SMITH, P.
Kentucky Wender flintlock maker. Washington, Penn., and after 1810, Lancaster, Penn.

GUNMAKERS

SMITH AND WESSON
Revolvers and metallic cartridge manufacturers. 1857 to date

SMITH (Smyth), **William** (Guilielmus)
Castle Grant, Scotland, 1629-1686

SMOOT, William S.
Washington, D.C. and Ilion, New York gunmaker and inventor. Worked 1868-1880.
Guns produced by Remington

SNIDER, Jacob
Baltimore, Maryland. Patent for breech conversion of percussion musket in 1859
adopted by the British Army

SOLER, Isidro
Madrid, circa 1780-1785. Isidro was not only gunmaker for Carlos IV, but wrote an
important contribution to gunmaking history: COMPENDIO HISTORICO DE LOS
ARCABUCEROS DE MADRID

SOLER, Manuel
Son of Isidro, Madrid c. 1795

SOLIS, Virgil
German engraver (?-1562), designs used for ornamentation and decoration for guns and stocks

SPANGENBERG (Family)
Suhl—1605-1842. Støckel lists 35 members

SPAT, Caspar
Munich engraver and iron carver. Worked 1635-1691

SPENCER, Christopher M.
b. 1841. Patented a tubular magazine cartridge gun in 1860 and piloted airplanes in the 1920's

SPIES, H.
New York gun importer, circa 1860

STARBUS (Stahrbus)
Peter—Amsterdam—1684-1718
Peter II—Stockholm and Amsterdam—1687-1724
Peter III—Ørebro and Stockholm—1711-1745

STARR, Eben T.
Yonkers, N.Y. (Worked 1856-1882). Starr Arms Co., New York City (1858-1867)

STENGL, Johann Christoph
Munich, circa 1690-1740. Iron carver and engraver

J. STEVENS ARMS AND TOOL CO.
Chicopee Falls, Mass., 1864 to date. Founded by Joshua Stevens (1814-1879) it is now a part of
Savage Arms Corp.

STEVENS, Fred
Contemporary American. Gun and .38 caliber cartridge for underwater shooting

STOCKMANN, Hans
Signature: "H.S." Dresden, circa 1600-1620. Wheel lock pistols in Aitken collection, breech
loader at Victoria and Albert Museum

On the Barrel  STOCKMAR
Johann Christof, Johann Georg, Johann Nikolaus, Johann Wolf Heinrich. All worked at
Suhl between 1731-1750

STONER, Gene
Contemporary American. Military gun designer

STRACHAN, Andrew
Edzell, Scotland, circa 1701-1725

STRAUSS, L.
"L.S." with an ostrich in a shield. Lockmaker, Nuremberg, circa 1585
See: DAUER, Hans

STUART, John
Doun, Scotland, circa 1700-1750

GUNMAKERS

SUTIL, Manuel
Madrid and Astorga, circa 1734-1741
See: FERNANDEZ, Juan

SWEBILIUS, Carl Gustave
1879-1948. Gun designer; founded HIGH STANDARD MANUFACTURING CO. *(q.v.)*

TEZENAS, F.
St. Etienne, circa 1690-1720

THOMAS (Tomas, Thoma), P.
Parisian gunsmith, circa 1640. Made guns for Swedish royal family

THOMERAT (Thomerot)
Circa 1675. Made guns for Louis XIV

THORNTON, William
Flintlock breech loader with removable chamber, 1811. Co-inventor with John H. Hall

THOUVENIN, Colonel Louis Etienne de
French. Inventor of the Tige or pillar breech system for spreading the soft lead ball into the grooves of a gun barrel. Patent date: 1843. A fixed rod or pillar at the breech served as an anvil to spread the soft lead bullet into the grooves of the barrel

THREE-BARREL GUN COMPANY
Moundsville, West Virginia. 1906-1908 owned by Frank A Hollenbeck (1881-1911), gun designer and inventor

THUER, F. Alexander
Hartford, Conn. 1868-1870. Revolver patents assigned to Colt

TIESING, Frank W.
New Haven, Conn. Worked 1869-1881. Prolific gun inventor whose patents were assigned to Eli Whitney

THURAINE and THURAINE, Jr.
No first names are known. Paris, 1630-1720. The older Thuraine originally worked alone, then in partnership with Le Hollandois (Adrian Reynier) and finally with his son who became gunmaker to Louis XV in 1723. This was the year that Louis was declared of age and married (Louis was 13). Many of Thuraine's guns survive in Copenhagen, either in the Tøjhus or Rosenborg. Thuraine's name appears with Le Hollandois' on the title page of Jacquinet's pattern book of gunmakers' designs PLUSIEURS MODELS DES PLUS NOVELLES MANIERES QUI SON EN UAGE EN L'ART D'ARQUEBUZIERIE published in Paris in 1660

THURBER, Charles T. (ALLEN AND THURBER CO.)
Maker of pepperboxes. Worked 1842-1855. Worcester, Mass, patent date: 1837

TIERKOPFRANKEN, MEISTER DER
Name unknown. Similar work initialed "H.N." and "A.S." on examples.
Worked circa 1628-1659. Vienna? Stock carver whose crisp style of carving tiny animals in borders as well as monkeys, camels, etc. won him the name. Stocked guns built by Viennese master Hanns Faschang.

TINKER, John
London 1681. "Tinkers invention" butt firing grenade launders.

TINLOT, J.N.
Liège, circa 1850-1860. Shotgun, rifle, and pistol manufacturer, engraver and wood carver. Preferred working in ebony.

TORNIER (Tournier), Jean Conrad
Masseveux (Marevaicx), France. Gun designer and decorator, circa 1646

TOW
London, 1780-1810
See: GRIFFIN AND TOW

TRANTER, William
Birmingham, England. Double action revolvers. Worked 1846-1863

TREXLER
See: DRESSLER

GUNMAKERS

TRIPLETT AND SCOTT (Meriden Arms Co.)
Built patented magazine breech loader, 1864

TRUELOCK (Trulocke, Trulock, Truelocke), William
London, circa 1655-1685. Truelock was a gunmaker in London at the time of the restoration
of Charles II. He, with Harman Barnes of London and Des Granges in Paris, made
breech-loading rifled pistols. Nobody knows who made which parts. One signed "Trulock"
is in the Tøjhus Museum. Truelock also made conventional pistols and brass blunderbusses.
J. N. George illustrates one and Støckel knew of two

TRYON, George
Philadelphia. 1791 till after 1829, contracted and built Chambers guns for the
U.S. Navy with J. J. Henry in 1814

TURVEY, William
London, circa 1727

TWIGG, I.
Built flintlock fowlers and pistols. Worked 1764-1801

ULRICH, Conrad
Steel engraver. Niensbach, Germany to Hartford, Conn. in 1852 where he worked at
Colt's until 1870. Sons John and Herman worked at Winchester's from 1868 to about 1920.
Conrad Junior worked at Marlin's from 1881 to 1907.

ULRICH, George
Son of Conrad Junior. Marlin 1905-1913; Winchester 1913 to circa 1950

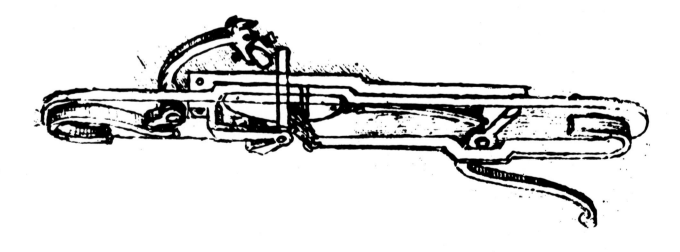

VARENA, Giovanni
Brescia, circa 1690. Locksmith who built two-shot fowler (in the Artiglieria in Turin)

VAUBAN, Sebastian le Pretre de
Circa 1632-1707. Paris. Fortification expert and artillery chief for Louis XIV. Invented fusil-musket—a combination lock with both match and flint lock

VENTURA (Bentura), Diego
Madrid, circa 1720-1762. Learned his barrel making trade from Alonzo Martínez and became gunmaker to Carlos III of Spain. A flintlock with the stock completely veneered with tortoise shell and inlaid with gold and cameos belonging to Charles VI, Holy Roman Emperor (1711-1740), dated 1722, is in the Kunsthistorisches Museum in Vienna

VETTERLI, Frederich
1822-1882. Swiss inventor of magazine rifle

VISCHER, Adam
Munich stockmaker and engraver, circa 1600-1610. Signature:

VOLCANIC REPEATING ARMS COMPANY
Norwich, Conn. 1855-1857. Prototype of Winchester made under Smith and Wesson regime

WAGNER, C. Christian
Dresden and Warsaw—1676-1720

WAGNER, Michael
Cronach—1686-1718

WALCH, John
Worked in New York City, 1859-1862; designed a 10 to 12 shot superimposed load revolver which was made for him by LINDSAY.

GUNMAKERS

WALKER, J.J.
Pennsylvania? Circa 1830. Mules ear percussion superimposed loads.

WALLER, James
1755

WALLER, Richard
1740-1777

WALLIS, S.
Circa 1800, London. Military rifles

WALLIS, T.
Scots gunsmith in London, circa 1680

WATERS, John
Birmingham, England, 1767-1780—London after 1789. Pocket pistols,
blunderbusses and army muskets

WALTHER
German, circa 1917-1945. Automatic pistols. Saxe-Coburg, Gotha. Zella-Mehlis

WARD-BURTON
American gun manufacturers, circa 1855-1885. Bolt action breech-loading sporters.
General William G. Ward, Bethel Burton—Springfield Armory, circa 1871

WATSON, William
England, circa 1650. Manufactured doglocks. Master of the Gun Makers Company in 1645

WEBLEY, James
Birmingham gunmaker. Worked 1857-1864

WEBLEY AND SCOTT, LTD.
Birmingham gunmakers. 1898 to date

WEBSTER AND COMPANY
Gunsmiths, London, 1825-1832

WERDER, Felix
Zurich, circa 1630-1650. Built, decorated and gold inlaid wheel locks. One in the
Metropolitan Museum of Art may have belonged to Charles II of England

WESSON, Daniel B.
Springfield (1825-1906). Founded Smith and Wesson

WESSON, Frank
Springfield. Gunmaker. Worked 1854-1877

WESTLEY RICHARDS
See: RICHARDS, Westley

WETSCHGI, Emanuel (Augustus)
Augsburg, circa 1700-1725

WETSCHLI, August (Probably same as above)
Vienna 1676-1690

WHEELER, Captain Artemus
Concord, Mass. Patented repeating flintlock in 1818

WHITE, Rollin
1817-1892. Hartford, Conn. and Lowell, Mass., Davenport, Iowa. Gun designer

WHITNEY, Eli, Eli Jr., and Eli III (Whitney Arms Company)
Whitney Armory. New Haven, 1798-1888

WHITNEY ARMORY
New Haven, Conn., 1798-1888

WHITWORTH
English, circa 1850. Precision rifle

WILKINSON, James and Son
Gunmaker to Edward VII as Prince of Wales, London, 1812-1889. Built military carbines.
Wrote ENGINES OF WAR, 1841

GUNMAKERS

WILLIAMS, David (Marsh)
Contemporary. Godwin, North Carolina. Gun designer and developer of
short stroke piston principle of gas operation

WILSON, William
London, 1718. Made muskets which were prototypes of the Brown Bess

WINCHESTER, Oliver Fisher
1810-1880. Volcanic, New Haven Arms Co., Winchester Repeating Arms Co. Shirt
manufacturer, financier and gunmaker

WINCHESTER REPEATING ARMS COMPANY
New Haven, Conn. 1866 to date. (Since 1933 a division of Olin—now Olin Mathison Co.)

WOGDON (WOGDON AND BARTON)
London, circa 1760-1820. Manufacturers of duelling pistols

WOODWARD GUN COMPANY
Thomas Woodward. Birmingham, England, circa 1890

WOOLDRIDGE (Wolldridge) Richard
Worked circa 1704-1743. Was Master Furbisher of the Gunmakers Company in 1718
in London. Musket in the Tower of London

WURFFLEIN, Andrew, John and William
Gunmaking family in Philadelphia that worked between 1835 and 1875. Particularly
noted for their Derringers, double guns and parlor guns.

ZAOUE
Marseilles, circa 1820

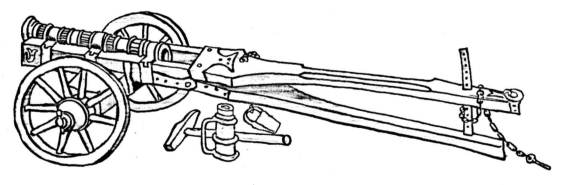

ZEGARRA (Cegarra, Zegara), Miguel de
Madrid, circa 1735-1781. Gunmaker to Carlos III. A miquelet long gun or fowling piece obviously intended for the use of royalty is in the collection of W. Keith Neal.
The barrel is inlaid with gold lettering and stamping in the form of sickles and thistles.
Six examples of his work were known to Støckel

ZELAYA, Joaquin
Madrid, circa 1753-1760. Gunmaker to Ferdinand VI
See: FERNANDEZ, Juan

ZELLNER (Zelner, Zollner, Zoller), Caspar
Salzburg and Vienna, circa 1680-1725. Caspar had two sons, Caspar II, Vienna 1700-1740 and Johann George who worked in Salzburg between 1733-1750. Other Zellners include Christian, Kilian I and II, Lorentz and Marcus. Caspar II was the most famous and prolific with examples of his work including a flintlock in the Kunsthistorisches Museum in Vienna and a pair of silver and gold mounted wheel lock rifles in the von Kienbusch collection in New York. Caspar's brother, Johann George, made many fine guns for the Archbishop of Salzburg, Cardinal von Schrattenbach

ZISCHANG, August O.
1846-1925. Made fine target rifles in Syracuse, N.Y. from 1879

ZWICKA, Hans
German crossbow maker, circa 1628

BIBLIOGRAPHY

This bibliography is a selective one covering only those books and articles in periodicals and manuscripts which have a bearing on the text of this volume. Bibliographies on hunting, "how-to" books, etc. are listed below.

A substantial portion of the constructive research and writing about guns has appeared in periodical form. The highlights of this material have been covered for the first time in this bibliography.

The arms journals which are referred to in the bibliography are:

THE AMERICAN ARMS COLLECTOR, quarterly, Towson, Md., 1957-1958
THE AMERICAN RIFLEMAN, Washington, D.C.
ARMES ANCIENNES, Geneva, Switzerland, 1953-59
ARMI ANTICHE, Turin, Italy
LES ARQUEBUSIERS DE FRANCE, Paris, France
BULLETIN DE L'ASSOCIATION BELGE D'AMATEURS D'ARMES ET
   D'ARMURES, Brussels, Belgium
BULLETIN OF THE METROPOLITAN MUSEUM OF ART,
   New York, New York
GUNS AND AMMO, Hollywood, California
GUNS AND HUNTING, New York, New York
THE GUN COLLECTOR'S LETTER, Madison, Wisconsin, 1946-1947
THE GUN COLLECTOR, Madison, Wisconsin, 1947-1953
THE GUN DIGEST, Chicago, Illinois
GUNS MAGAZINE, Skokie, Illinois
THE GUN REPORT, Aledo, Illinois
GUNS REVIEW, London, England
GUN WORLD, Covina, California
JAHRBUCH DER KUNSTHISTORISCHEN SAMMLUNGEN . . . , Vienna, Austria
JOURNAL OF THE ARMS AND ARMOUR SOCIETY, London, England
LIVRUSTKAMMAREN JOURNAL OF THE ROYAL ARMOURY,
   Stockholm, Sweden
SVENSKA VAPENHISTORISKA SALLSKAPETS SKRIFTER, Stockholm, Sweden
TRUE MAGAZINE GUN ANNUAL, New York, New York
VAABENHISTORISKE AARBØGER, Copenhagen, Denmark
VESNIK, BULLETIN DU MUSEE MILITAIRE DE L'ARMEE POPULAIRE
   YUGOSLAVE, Belgrade, Yugoslavia
ZEITSCHRIFT FUR HISTORISCHE WAFFEN-UND KOSTUMKUNDE,
   Munich, Germany

In addition, specific articles are referred to which have appeared in outdoor and general magazines. Many fine short articles have appeared in the *American Rifleman*. In addition to those listed here, a directory of them up until 1962 may be found in the volume, *American Rifleman Magazine Author and Subject Index*, published by Burrell in Galesburg, Michigan.

The serious student is advised to consult five other bibliographies in English which are listed. Cockle's *Bibliography of Military Books up to 1642*, Wirt Gerrare's *A Bibliography of Guns and Shooting*, the bibliography in the back of Mann's *Wallace Collection Catalogues*, Ray Riling's *Guns and Shooting, A Bibliography*, and Schwerdt's *Hunting, Hawking, Shooting—A Bibliography*.

Three publications have been referred to so frequently in the bibliography that initials have been used instead of spelling out the full names. The *Zeitschrift* has had variations in its name during its many years of publication. We have used the one by which it is most commonly known. Town names are spelled in English except for older books and manuscripts of historical interest.

Jahrbuch der Kunsthistorischen Sammlungen des Allerhöchsten Kaiserhauses   J.D.K.S.
Journal of the Arms and Armour Society   J.A.A.S.
Zeitschrift für Historische Waffen-und Kostümkunde   Z.H.W.K.

ABRIDGEMENT OF THE PATENT SPECIFICATIONS RELATING TO FIRE-ARMS, *etc.*
1558-1858....Holland Press, London, 1960

AGRICOLA, GEORGIUS (GEORG BAUER)
De Re Metallica
> *Translated English by Herbert Clark and*
> *Lou Henry Hoover....(Discusses the method of*
> *obtaining iron pyrites, sulphur, iron)*
> *First Edition....(Latin) Froben, Basel, 1556*
> *The Mining Magazine, London, 1912*
> *Latest Edition....(English) Dover, New York,*
> *1950*

ALBERTUS MAGNUS
De Mirabilibus Mundi
> *Manuscript at St. Marks, Venice, Vol. XIV,*
> *page 40, circa 1300 (earliest reference to guns)*

ALM, JOSEPH
Arméns Eldhandvapen förr och nu
> *(old handguns and origins of wheel locks)*
> *Stockholm, 1933*

AMBER, JOHN T.
The Gun Digest (annual)....*Chicago, 1944 to date*
The Gun Digest Treasury II
> *(The best from the first fifteen years of the*
> *Gun Digest....Chicago, 1956)*
> *"This Gun Collecting Game"*
> *The Gun Digest Treasury, p. 252-264....*
> *Chicago, 1961*
Gun Digest Treasury III....*Chicago, 1966*

BIBLIOGRAPHY

AMERICAN ARMS COLLECTOR, THE *(quarterly, 8 issues)*
The Collectors Press, Towson, Md., 1957-1958

AMERICAN GUN, THE
Herb Glass, Larry Sheeren, Larry Koller, Patricia Graves (3 issues) Madison Books, New York, 1961

AMERICAN RIFLEMAN, THE *(monthly periodical)*
Washington, D.C., since 1885

AMERICAN RIFLEMAN MAGAZINE
(Author and Subject Index *compiled by Burrell)*
Burrell, Galesburg, Mich., 1962

AMMAN, JOST
Kunstbüchlein
(Illustrations of barrel makers, stock makers, etc.)
Nürnberg, 1591 (pub. 1599)
Stände und handwerker—mit Versen von Hans Sachs
Francfort, 1568
(reprint) Geo. Hirth, Munich, 1884
Venatus et aucupium
(Woodcut designs used by stockmakers)
Francfort, 1582
(German edition: Neuw Jag unnd Weydwerck Buch)

ANGELUCCI, ANGELO
Catalogo dell' Armeria Reale
(Catalog of the Royal Armory of Turin)
Turin, 1890

Della artigleria da fuocco
(A compilation of articles).... Turin, 1862
Documenti inediti per la storia della armi da fuocco Italiane
(Ferrara Archives—1522 edict forbidding the carrying of guns including wheel locks)
Turin, 1869
Gli schioppettieri milanesi del XV secolo
(A compilation).... Milan, 1865

ANONYMOUS
A Short Account of the Worshipful Company of Gunmakers.... *London, 1937*

ARANTEQUI y SANZ, DR. JOSE
Artilleria Española en los siglos XIV y XV *(Vol. I)*
en la primera mitad del siglo XVI *(Vol. II)*
(Early artillery and handcannon) Fortanent, Madrid, 1887 (Vol. I) Cuerpo de Artilleria, Madrid, 1891 (Vol. II)

ARMES ANCIENNES *(periodical, semi-annual)*
Geneva, Switzerland, 1953-1959

ARMI ANTICHE *(annual).... Turin, Italy, since 1955*

ARQUEBUSIERS DE FRANCE, LES *(bulletin, bi-mestriel)*
Directeur de la Publications, M. Moy, Paris, 1966 and preceeding

L'ART ANCIEN A l'EXPOSITION NATIONALE BELGE *(illustrated catalog)*

(*Van Zuylen and Van der Meersch collections illustrated*). . . . *Rozez, Brussels, 1882*

ARSENAL
Kwartalnik Kola Milosników Dawny Broni i Barwy przy Museum Narodowym w Krakowie
Cracow, Poland, 1957

AUGSBURG, STADTARCHIV (MSS)
"Stadtarchiv zu Augsburg"
Edited by Adolf Buff
(Statement of accounts, payment for armor of the city of Augsburg)
J.D.K.S., Vol. I, pp, 94 & 195 and pp. I through XXV . . . . Leipzig, Prague, Vienna, 1892

AYALON, DAVID
Gunpowder and Firearms in the Mamluk Kingdom
Valentine Mitchell, London, 1956

BAARMANN, VON HAUPTMANN z. D.
"Die Faule Magd der Königlichen Arsenalsammlung zu Dresden"
Z.H.W.K., Vol. IV, p. 229
Berlin, 1906-1908

BACON, ROGER
De Mirabilis Potestate Artis et Naturae *(circa 1267)*
(Invention of gunpowder). . . . Simon Colinaem, Paris, 1542
Fratris Rogeri Bacon, *Samuel Jebb, London, 1733*
Also see: *HIME, H.W.K.*

BADALUCCI, W.
The Mausoleum of Hadrian and Castel Sant' Angelo in Rome—National Military and Art Museum
Itinerary—Guide
(In English, French, German, Italian)
Rome, 1956

BAILLIE-GROHMAN, WILLIAM A.
Sport in Art
Simpkin, Marshall, Hamilton, Kent, London, 1919

BAKER, EZEKIEL
Remarks on Rifle Guns
(11th edition). . . . London, 1835

BAKER, SIR SAMUEL WHITE
The Albert N'Yanza and the Great Basin of the Nile
London, 1864
Ismailia, a Narrative of the Expedition to Central Africa
London, 1874
Wild Beasts and Their Ways
Macmillan & Co., London and New York, 1890

BARBOUR, JOHN, Archdeacon of Aberdeen
Metrical Life of King Robert Bruce
Manuscript, circa 1375 (Mentions use of guns)
Carmichael & Miller, Glasgow, 1737

BARNES, JOSHUA
The History of that Most Victorious Monarch Edward III
(Guns at Crecy and Agincourt)
John Hayes, Cambridge, 1688

BIBLIOGRAPHY

BAXTER, D. R.
Superimposed Load Firearms—1360-1860
Baxter, Hong Kong, 1966
"Early Lever-Action Repeating Rifles"
Guns Review, *Vol. V, No. 1 . . . . London, January, 1965*
*"English All Metal Flintlock Pistols of the Eighteenth
and Early Nineteenth Century"*
Armi Antiche . . . . *Turin, 1966*

BEATSON, ALEXANDER
A View of the Origin and Conduct of the War with
Tippoo Sultrun
W. Bulmer, London, 1800

BEAUFOY, COL. H.B.H.
Scloppetaria—Consideration of the Nature and Use of
Rifled Barrel Guns
C. Roworth for T. Egerton, London, 1808

BEDFORD, PETER A.
"Gold, Platinum and Touch-holes"
J.A.A.S., Vol. V, No. I, p. 27 . . . . March, 1965

BENDEL, MAX
Woodcut Engravings
*(Hunting scenes used by gun engravers and
stockmakers) . . . . Alsace-Lorraine, 1570-1580*

BENNETT, G. E.
"The Mechanism of the Wheel-lock"
J.A.A.S., Vol. I, No. II, p. 14 . . . . London, 1940

BERAIN, JEAN I.

Diverses pièces très utiles pour les arquebuziers
Paris, 1659-1667
(See: GRANCSAY, Stephen—Master French
Gunsmiths Designs)

BERTHELOT, M.
Sur la Force de Matières Explosives
Gauthiers Villars, 1883, Paris

BIRINGUCCIO, VANUCCIO
De la pirotechnia
Roffinello, Venice, 1540
Biringuccios Pirotechnia
*(German edition—translated and commented on by
Dr. Otto Johannsen) . . . . Verlag von Friedrich
Vieweg & Sohn, Braunschweig, 1925*
De la Pirotechnia, libri X
*(English edition translated by C. S. Smith and
Martha T. Gnudi) . . . . American Institute of
Mining and Metallurgical Engineers,
New York, 1943*

BIRMINGHAM
See: HARRIS, Clive

BLACKMORE, HOWARD L.
British Military Firearms
Herbert Jenkins, London, 1961
Firearms
Dutton, London and New York, 1964
Guns and Rifles of the World
Clowes, London & Viking, New York, 1965
"The Experimental Firearms of Henry Nock"
J.A.A.S., Vol. II, No. IV, p. 69

London, December, 1956
"The Seven-Barrel Guns"
J.A.A.S., Vol. I, No. X, p. 165
London, June, 1955
"Chambers Repeating Flintlock"
The American Rifleman, *pp. 21-23*
September, 1958

BLAIR, CLAUDE
European and American Arms
Batsford, London and Crown, New York, 1962
"A Note on the Early History of the Wheel-lock"
J.A.A.S., Vol. III, No. IX, p. 221 ff
London, March, 1961
"A Further Note on the Early History of the
Wheel-lock"
J.A.A.S., Vol. IV, No. IX, p. 187 ff
London, March, 1964

BLANCH, H. J.
A Century of Guns
John Blanch, London, 1909

BOCKLER, ANDREAS
Theatrum Machinorum Novum
(Early Weapons)....Nuremberg, 1688

BODENSTEIN, GUSTAV
"Urkunden und Regesten aus dem k.u.k
Reichfinanz-Archiv in Wien—1626-1629"
J.D.K.S., Vol. 33, p. 1....1906

BOEHEIM, WENDELIN
"Die Ambraser Sammlung"
J.D.K.S., Vol. XIX....Vienna 1898
Kunsthistorische Sammlungen des Allerhöchsten
Kaiserhauses. ALBUM hervorragender Gegёnstande
aus der Waffensammlung.
(2 volumes)....Vienna, 1898
Handbuch der Waffenkunde
Seemann, Leipzig, 1890
"Stadtarchiv zu Augsburg"

BIBLIOGRAPHY

J.D.K.S., *Vol. I, pp. 94-195 . . . . Vienna, 1882*
"Studie über die Entwicklung des Geschützwesens
in Deutschland"
Z.H.W.K., *Vol. I, p. 57 . . . . Berlin, 1897-1899*
"Uber den Wert der Meistermarken"
Z.H.W.K., *Vol. II, p. 161*
Dresden, Leipzig, Munich, 1900-1902
"Uber einige Jagdwaffen und Jagdgeräthe"
(Crossbows, quarrels, ivory and enamelled
wheel locks)
J.D.K.S., *Vol. IV, p. 52 . . . . Vienna, 1886*
J.D.K.S., *Vol. V, p. 97 . . . . Vienna, 1887*
"Zeugbücher des Kaisers Maximilian I"
(Important report on 16th century weapons,
cannon and handguns)
J.D.K.S. *Vol. XIII, p. 94 . . . . Vienna, 1892*
J.D.K.S., *Vol. XV, pp. 295-391 . . . . Vienna, 1894*
(See: KOLDERER, Jörg)

BOHLMANN, ROBERT
"Die Braunschweigischen Waffen auf Schloss
Blankenburg"
Z.H.W.K., *Vol. IV . . . . Berlin, 1912-1914*
"Johann Sebastian Hauschka, Braunschweigischer
Hofbüchsenmacher"
Z.H.W.K., *Vol. III (new), p. 187*
Berlin, 1929-1931
"Waffenkundliches aus einer Denkschrift des
Herzogs Julius von Braunschweig von 1573"
Z.H.W.K., *Vol. IV (new), p. 229*
Berlin, 1932-1934

BOHNE, CLEMENS
"Uber Kanonenrohre"
Z.H.W.K., *Vol. I, p. 67 . . . . Vienna, 1964*

BOILLOT
Modelles artifices de Feu
Chaumont, Paris, 1598

BOL, HANS
Venationis, Piscationis, et Aucupii Typi
(Hunting scenes)
Etched by Philipp Galle . . . . Antwerp, 1582

BONFADINI, CAPT. VITA
La Caccia dell'archobugio
(Hunting with guns) mentions the Cominazzis
as well-known Brescian barrel makers
Bologna, 1648

BOOTHROYD, GEOFFREY
Gun Collecting
Arco Publications, London, 1961

BOSSI, CAPT. GUILIANO
Breve Tratato d'Alcune Inventione Che Sone State
Futte per Rinforzare e Raddoppiare li Tiri
Degli Arcibugi—a Ruota
(Early wheel locks) . . . . Parigi, 1679

BOSSON, CLEMENT
Les Pistolets à Rouets du Musée d'Art et d'Histoire
(Wheel locks) . . . . Geneva, 1953
"Quelques Armes du Musée d'Art et d'Histoire
de Genève"
Armes Anciennes, *Vol. I 1953*

BOSTON, NOEL

Old Guns and Pistols
Ernest Benn, London, 1958

BOTTET, M.
La Manufacture d'Armes de Versailles—Boutet,
Directeur-Artiste
Paris, 1903
Monographie de l'arme à feu portative des armées
francaises de terre et de mer de 1718 à nos jours
Paris

BOUDRIOT, JEAN
Armes à Feu Françaises Modèles Reglementaries
(General issue French guns—1700-1800)
Boudriot, Paris, 1963

BOULENGER, JACQUES
The Seventeenth Century
(Translated from the French)
(Description of French military equipment)
Heinemann, London, 1920

BOUTELL, CHARLES
Arms and Armour in Antiquity and the Middle Ages
Scribner & Armstrong & Co., New York, 1874

BOWMAN, H. W.
Antique Guns
Fawcett, Greenwich, Conn., 1953
Famous Guns from Famous Collections
Fawcett, Greenwich, Conn., 1957
Famous Guns from the Winchester Collection
Arco, New York, 1958

BRADFORD, WILLIAM
History of Plymouth Plantation—1606-1646
(Collection of the Mass. Historical Society, 1898),
Charles Scribner & Sons, New York, 1908
(See: PETERSON, H.L., Arms and Armor of the
Pilgrims 1620-1692)

BRAUN, HUGH
The English Castle
B. T. Batsford, London, 1936

BRENNAN, W. A.
(Translator of On Wounds and Fractures
by Guy de Chauliac, 1363)
Chicago, 1923

BREVETS DE LOGEMENTS SOUS LA GRANDE
GALERIE DU LOUVRE
(Gunmakers of the Kings of France)
Archives de l'Art Francais, T.I., pp. 193-258
Paris, 1851-1852

BRODIE, BERNARD and FAWN
From Crossbow to H-Bomb
Dell, New York, 1962

BROWNING and GENTRY
John M. Browning, American Gunmaker
Doubleday, New York, 1964

BRUSSELS—PORTE DE HAL
See: MACOIR
MALDERGHEM

BIBLIOGRAPHY

PRELLE
VINKELROY
SQUILBECK, JEAN

BRY, JOHANN THEODORE DE
  Künstbuchlein von Geschütz und Fewerwerck
  Paul Jacobi, Franckfurt am Mayn, 1619

BUCANAN, GEORGE
  Rerum Scoticarum Historia
  Alex Arbuthnot, Edinburgh, 1582

BULLETIN DES ARQUEBUSIERS DE FRANCE
  (publication)
  Les Arquebusiers de France, Paris

BULLETIN DE L'ASSOCIATION BELGE
D'AMATEURS D'ARMES ET D'ARMURES
  Brussels, Belgium

BUFF, ADOLF
  See: Augsburg

BULLETIN OF THE METROPOLITAN MUSEUM
OF ART
  New York

BURGKMAIR, HANS
  "The Triumph of the Emperor Maximilian"
  (1473-1531)

Adam Bartsch, Vienna, 1796
J.D.K.S. (reprint). . . . Vienna, 1883-1884
Dover, New York, 1964

BURRARD, MAJOR SIR GERALD
In the Gunroom
Herbert Jenkins, London, 1951

BUTTIN, CHARLES
"Pistolets de Louis XIII par Pierre Bergier de
Grenoble et P. Chabrioux de Montelimar"
Armes Anciennes, Vol. II, No. X, p. 3
Geneva, Switzerland

CAMDEN, WILLIAM
Remaines Concerning Britanie: But Especially England
and the Inhabitants Thereof: Artillarie (page 238)
John Legall, London, 1614

CANBY, COURTLANDT
A History of Weaponry
(Also published in French and German)
Hawthorne, New York, 1963

CAPO BIANCO, CAPT. ALLESANDRO VICENTINO
Corona e palma militare di artiglieria
(Early cannon)
Francesco Bariletti, Venetia, 1516

CAREY, A. MERVIN
English, Irish and Scottish Firearms Makers
New York, 1954

CARMAN, W. Y.
A History of Firearms
London, 1955

CARPEGNA, NOLFO DI
"Armi da Fuoco dell'Italia Centrale"
Z.H.W.K., Vol. II, p. 120. . . .1962
"La Collezione d'Armi Odescalchi in Roma"
Z.H.W.K. 1961

CARPENTER, A. C.
"A Fifteen Shot Wheellock Repeating Pistol of
Circa 1650"
J.A.A.S., Vol. IV, Nos. V & VI, p. 93
London, March/June, 1963

CASSANI, JOSEPH
Escuela Militar
Antonio Gonçales de Reyes, Madrid, 1705

CEDERSTROM, RUDOLF OCH GOSTA MALMBORG
Den äldre Livrustkammaren, 1654
(Swedish Royal Armory collection)
Nordiska, Stockholm, 1930
"Danska och Svenska Drag Hos Jen Forna
Gränsbygdens Bösser" (Gönge guns)
Vaabenhistoriske Aarbøger, Vol. III
Copenhagen, 1960
"Ha Gevässlåsen Uppstått ur Elddon?"
Livrustkammaren Bd 1, H4, pp. 66-76
(Wheel lock from Da Vinci)
Stockholm, 1937-1939

CELLINI, BENVENUTO

BIBLIOGRAPHY

Memoirs
(Written 1536, refers to "Sciopetto" which Duke
Alessandro Medici received from Germany)

CHANLER, WILLIAM ASTOR
Through Jungle and Desert
(Using small bore bolt actions for big game)
Macmillan, New York, 1896

CHAPEL, CHARLES EDWARD
The Gun Collector's Handbook of Values
Coward-McCann, New York, 1940 and following

CHAPMAN, BENJAMIN
The History of Gustave Adolphus
(Leather cannon)
Longman, Brown, Green and Longmans,
London, 1856

CHARLES, ROBERT-JEAN
"La Collection Georges Pauilhac au Musée
de l'Armée"
La Revue Française, *No. 182*
Paris, November, 1965

CHESMAN
Observations on the Past and Present State of Fire-Arms
London, 1852

CHIDSEY, DONALD BARR
Goodbye to Gunpowder—An Informal History of
Gunpowder from its Introduction in the Fourteenth
Century to the Atom Bomb
Alvin Redman, London, 1964

CHURCHILL, ROBERT
Churchill's Shotgun Book
Alfred Knopf, New York, 1955

CLAUDELIN, B.
Catalogue of Arms & Armour at Hallwylska Museet,
Stockholm
Stockholm, 1926

CLEPHAN, ROBERT COLTMAN
Early Ordnance in Europe
Andrew Reid & Co., London, 1903
The Ordnance of the Fourteenth and
Fifteenth Centuries
Hunt Barnard, London, 1911
An Outline of the History and Development of Hand
Firearms from the Earliest Period to About the
End of the Fifteenth Century
Walter Scott, London, 1906
(Facsimile edition . . . . Standard Pubs.,
Huntington, West Virginia, n.d.)

CLEVELAND, H. W. S.
Hints to Riflemen
D. Appleton, New York, 1864

COCKLE, MAURICE J.D.
A Bibliography of Military Books up to 1642
Holland Press, London, 1957

COLLADO, LUIGI
Practica Manvale di Arteglieria
Presso Pietro Dusinelli, Venice, 1586

COMMINES, PHILIP DE
The Historie of Philip of Commines
Ar. Hatfield for I. Norton, London, 1601

COMNENA, ANNA (1083-1148)
Alexias
*(Selection translated in Partington's
Greek Fire and Gunpowder)
Heffer, Cambridge, 1960
(Greek Edition)....Schoepen, Bonn, 1878*

CONGREVE, WILLIAM
A Concise Account of the Origin and Progress
of the Rocket Systems
J. Whiting, London, 1810

COPENHAGEN
*See: HOFF, Arne
Museum Catalogs
Tøjhus*

CORNAZZANO, ANTONIO
De Re Militari
Magio, Pesaro, 1507

CORTES, JAVIER
Guia Illustrada de la Real Armeria de Madrid
Editorial Patrimonio National, Madrid, 1956

COSSON, BARON C. A. DE
*"The Crossbow of Ulrich V, Count of
Wurtemburg, 1460"*
Archaeologia, LIII
1893

CROUCH, NATHANIEL
The History of Oliver Cromwel
Printed for Nath. Crouch, London, 1715

CRUSO, JOHN
Military Instructions for the Cavallrie
Roger Daniel, Cambridge, 1644

DANIEL, R. P. G. (Père)
Historie de la Milice Françoise
*Vol. I, page 427
(Early history of firearms)....Amsterdam, 1724*

DATIG, FRED A.
The Luger Pistol
Beverly Hills, California, 1955

DA VINCI, LEONARDO
Il Codice Atlantico di Leonardo da Vinci nella
Biblioteca Ambrosiana di Milano
*(First drawings of prototype wheel lock mechanism
plus other guns, cannon and siege crossbow)
Hoepli, Milan, 1894-1904*
Leonardo Da Vinci *including parts of* Codex Atlanticus
Reynal & Co., New York, 1956

DEAN, BASHFORD
Catalogue of European Arms and Armour
Metropolitan Museum of Art, 1911
"A Seventeenth Century Wheellock Pistol"
Metropolitan Museum of Art Bulletin,
*Vol. V, pp. 16 & 17
New York, 1910*

BIBLIOGRAPHY

DEANE, J.
    Deane's Manual of the History and Science of Firearms
        Longman, London, 1858; Standard, Huntington,
        W. Va., 1946

DE BRY
    See: BRY

DE CHAULIAC, GUY
    Ars Chirurgica *(1363)*
        Lyon, 1478, Venice, 1546, Brennan, Chicago, 1923

DE CORDOBA, J. F.
    Catalógo de la Real Amería
        Madrid, 1854

DE GHEYN, JACOB
    The Exercise of Armes for Calivres, Muskettes, and
    Pikes after the Order of His Excellence Maurits Prince
    of Orange . . . Sett Forthe in Figures by Jacob de Gheyn.
    With Written Instructions for the Service of all
    Captaines and Comaundours. For to Shewe Hereout
    the Better Unto Their Yong or Untrayned Soldier the
    Playne and Perfett Maner to Handle These Armes.
    They are toe Bye at Amsterdam bye Robert de Boudous,
    Amsterdam, 1607
        Robert de Boudous, Amsterdam, 1607

DEL FUCAR, PABLO
    Ballestas Mosauetas y Arcabuces
        Naples, 1535

DE LUCIA, G.
    "La Sala d'Armi nel Museo dell'Arsenale di Venezia"
    Revista Marittima, *Rome, 1908*

DE MILIMETE, WALTER
    De Officiis Regum
        (Earliest pictures of vase cannon). Two
        manuscripts. 1336 manuscript at Christ Church,
        Oxford; and Roxburgh Club, Oxford. Facsimile
        reprint—Oxford—1913

DEMMIN, AUGUST
    Arms and Armour
        George Bell, London, 1877
    Die Kriegswaffen in ihrer historischen Entwickelung
        Leipzig, 1886, Repr. Hildesheim, Germany, 1964
    Guide des Amateurs d'Armes
        Paris, 1869

DENISOV, I. DENISOVA, M. M. and PORTNOV, M. E.
    Russian Arms from the XI to the XIX Centuries
        (In Russian). . . . Moscow, 1953

DENISOVA, M. M. and PORTNOV, M. E.
    Fine 18th and 19th Century Arms from Tula in the
    Collection of the State Historical Museum
        (In Russian). . . . Moscow, 1952

DE ROSNAY, DU METZ
    Cabinet d'Armes *(de Louis XIII)*
        ("Intendent et controleur général du mobilier
        de la couronne" to the kings of France until 1673)
        (manuscript). . . . Archives Nationales 0'3330
        3333, Paris, 1673
    See: LENK, Torsten
            The Flintlock
        GUIFFREY, Jules
            Inventire Général du Mobilier de la
            Couronne Sur Louis XIV

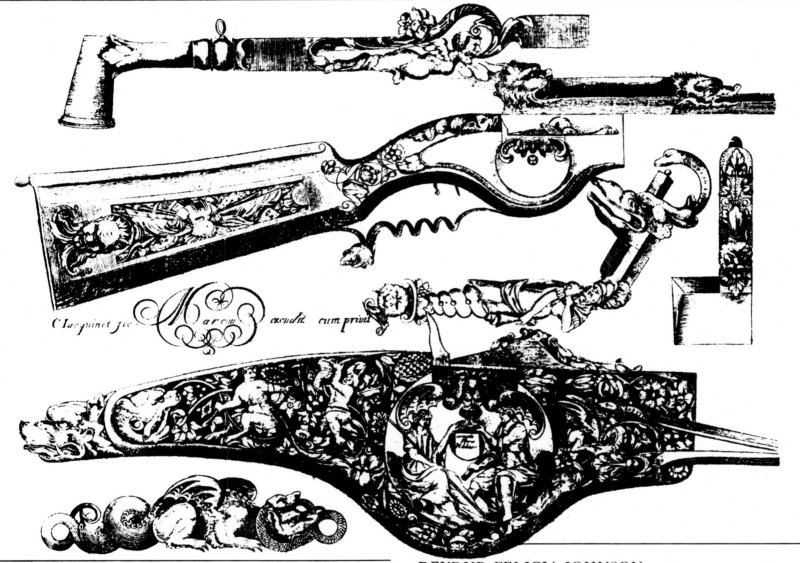

DE RUYTERS, ADMIRAL
Auction Catalog of Weapons in 1680
Leyden, 1750

DEXTER, F. THEODORE
Thirty-Five Years Scrapbook of Antique Arms
2 volumes . . . . Topeka, Kansas, 1947

DEYRUP, FELICIA JOHNSON
Arms Makers of the Connecticut Valley *(1798-1870)*
Smith College, Northampton, Massachusetts, 1948

DIDEROT and **D'ALEMBERT**
Encyclopédie
(Illustrations of guns and gunmaking machinery)
Lebreton, Paris, 1751

BIBLIOGRAPHY

DILLON, H. A., VISCOUNT
Arms and Armour at Westminster, the Tower
and Greenwich, 1547
Manuscript as reprinted by Gustave Brander, 1775
"Arms and Armour at Westminster, the Tower
and Greenwich, 1547"
Archaelogia, *LI, pp. 219-80 . . . . 1888*
Illustrated Guide to the Armouries, Tower of London
London, 1910

DOLLECZEK, A.
Monographie der k.u.k. osterr.-ung. Blank-und
Handfeuerwaffen
Vienna, 1896

DOMANIG, KARL
"Peter Flötner als Plastiker und Medailleur"
J.D.K.S., Vol. XVI, p. 1 . . . . Vienna, 1895

DRESDEN, HISTORISCHES MUSEUM
Pistolen
Bildheft, Dresden, 1962

DU BELLAY, GUILLAUME
Instructions for the Warres . . . *translated by Paul Ive*
Printed for Thomas Man, and Tobie Cook,
London, 1589

DUBESSY, RAYMOND
Historique de la manufacture d'armes de guerre
de St. Etienne
1900

DUCHARTRE, PIERRE LOUIS
Histoire des Armes de Chasse et de leurs emplois
Crepin, Leblond et Cie, Paris, 1955

DU FOUILLOUX, JACQUES
New Jägerbuch
(German edition of La Venerie with illustrations
by Tobias Stimmer) . . . . Strassburg, 1590

DUNLAP, JACK
American, British and Continental Pepperbox Firearms
Dunlap, Los Altos, California, 1964

ECKHARDT, WERNER and MORAWIETZ, OTTO
Die Handwaffen des brandenburgisch-preussisch-
deutschen Heeres, 1640-1945
Helmut Gerhard Schulz, Hamburg, 1957

EDWARDS, HENRY
A Volunteer's Narrative of the Hythe Course of
Instruction in Musketry
Simpkin, Marshall & Co., London, 1860

EGG, E.
Der Tiroler Geschutzguss, 1400-1600
Innsbruck, 1961

EHRENTHAL, MAX von
Die Waffensammlung des Fürsten Salm-Reifferscheidt
zu Schloss Dyck
Karl W. Hiersemann, Leipzig, 1906
Führer durch die königliche Gewehr-Galerie
zu Dresden
Druck von Wilhelm Baensch, Dresden, 1900

EMERSON, EDWIN, JR.
A History of the 19th Century
Page 1217 . . . . Collier, New York, 1901

ENCYCLOPEDIA OF FIREARMS
Edited by Harold L. Peterson
Dutton, New York, 1964

ENGELHARDT, BARON ARMIN
ALEXANDER CONSTANTIN
"The Story of European Proof Marks"
The Gun Digest. . . . *Chicago, 1952-1961*

THE GUN DIGEST TREASURY
(the best from the first 15 years). . . . Chicago, 1961

ERBEN, WILHELM
Beiträge zur Geschichte der Landsknechte
Artillery Museum Pub., Vienna, 1905
"Beiträge zur Geschichte der Geschützwesen
im Mittelalter"
Z.H.W.K., Vol. VII, p. 118 . . . . Berlin, 1915-1917

ESPINAR, ALONZO MARTINEZ del
Arte de Ballesteria y Monteria
(mentions Simon Marqarte, Jr.). . . . Madrid, 1644

ESSENWEIN, A.
Quellen zur Geschichte der Feuerwaffen
(Encyclopedic history of firearms with pictures)
Leipzig, 1877, Repr. by Akademische
Druck-Verlagsanstalt, Graz, 1967

EVELYN, J.
Diary
(Account of buying a gun from the Cominazzos)
Edited by W. Bray (first publication)
London, 1818, London, 1879, E.S. de Beer,
London, 1955

FALKE, JACOB von
Römisch Kaiserlicher Majestät Kriegsvölker im
Zeitalter der Landsknechte
August Johann Graf Breunner
Enkevoërth, Vienna, 1883

FARROW, EDWARD SAMUEL
Farrow's Military Encyclopedia
N.Y. Military-Naval Pub. Co., New York, 1885

FARROW, W. MILTON
How I Became a Crack Shot
(By a Creedmoor shooter)
Davis & Pitman, Newport, R.I., 1882

FELDHAUS, F. M.
"Geschützkonstruktionen von Leonardo da Vinci"
Z.H.W.K., Vol. VI, p. 128 . . . . Berlin, 1912-1914
"Handfeuerwaffen bei Leonardo da Vinci"
Z.H.W.K., Vol. VI, pp. 30-31 1912-1914
"Eine Nürnberger Bilderhandschrift"
Mitteilungen des Vereins für Geschichte der
Stadt Nürnberg
Vol. 31, p. 222 . . . . Nuremburg, 1933
"Das Radschloss bei Leonardo da Vinci"
Z.H.W.K., Vol. IV, p. 153-154 1906-1908
"Waffentechnisches aus der Nürnberger
Löffelholz-Handschrift von 1505"

BIBLIOGRAPHY

Z.H.W.K., *Vol. XV, p. 123 . . . . 1937-1939*
"Was wissen wir von Berthold Schwarz?"
See: PLOT, R.
Z.H.W.K., *Vol. IV, pp. 65, 113*
Berlin, 1906-1908
Die Technik
Leipzig & Berlin, 1914

FERGUSON, JAMES
Two Scottish Soldiers
(Including Patrick Ferguson's biography)
D. Wyllie & Sons, Aberdeen, 1888

FERGUSON, JOHN
"Letters of John Ferguson"
Kansas Historical Quarterly, *Vol. XII 1943*

FEUERWERKEBUCH
See: FURWERCKBUCH

FFOULKES, C. J.
Armour and Weapons . . . . *Clarendon, Oxford, 1909*
European Arms and Armour in the University of Oxford
Oxford, 1912
The Gun Founders of England *(XIV-XIX Centuries)*
University Press, Cambridge, 1937
Inventory and Survey of the Armories of the Tower
of London
London, 1915

FIAMMELLI, GIOVANI FRANCESCO
The Fields of Mars
Printed for J. MacGowan, London, 1781

FIRTH, C. H.
Cromwell's Army
(Fourth edition) . . . . Methuen & Co., London, 1962

FITZGERALD, J. HENRY
Shooting
G. F. Book Co., Hartford, 1930

FLEETWOOD, GEORG
"Die Waffensammlung des Vatikans in Rom"
Z.H.W.K., *Vol. III (new), p. 283 . . . . Berlin, 1931*

FORRER, DR. R. VON
*"Die ältesten gotischen ein-und mehrläufigen
Faustrohrstreitkolben"*
Z.H.W.K., *Vol. IV, p. 55 . . . . Berlin, 1906-1908*
*"Geschützminiaturen aus den Mss. 'Christan de Pisan'
und 'Histoire de Charles Martel' 1470"*
Z.H.W.K., *Vol. VI, p. 277 . . . . Berlin, 1912-1914*
*"Gotische und exotische Stangenbüchsen
in Drehgabeln"*

*Marcou ex cum pri-
Q'ec.*

Z.H.W.K., *Vol. VII, p. 334 . . . .Berlin, 1915-1917*
"Ein Kalendar fur Konig Matthias Corvinus mit
Darstellungen gotischer Büchsenschützen"
Z.H.W.K., *Vol. VIII, pp. 221-240*
Berlin, 1918-1920
"Uber kombinierte Waffen"
Z.H.W.K., *Vol. V, p. 97 . . . . Berlin, 1909-1911*

FRANK, GEORG
Waffen und Munition
Georg Frank, Hamburg, circa 1930

FREMANTLE, T. F.
The Book of the Rifle
Longmans, Green, London, 1901

FRIDOLIN, STEPHAN
Schatzbehalter oder Schrein der wahren Reichtiemer
des Heils und ewiger Seligheit
(Woodcuts by Michael Wolgemut)
Anton Koberger, Nuremberg, 1491

FROISSART, JOHN (JOHANN)
Chronicles, *Vol. I, p. 129*
(Guns used by the French and English in the
14th century) Translated by Sir John Bourchier,
Lord Berners. . . . Stratford-on-Avon, 1927

FROUDE, JAMES ANTHONY
English Seamen in the 16th Century, *p. 60*
Longmans, Green, London, 1932

FUCAR, PABLO DEL

Ballestas Mosauetas y Arcabuces
Naples, 1535

FULLER, CLAUD C.
The Breech-Loader in the Service
Arms Reference Club, Topeka, 1933
The Whitney Firearms
Standard, Huntington, W. Va., 1946

FURTENBACH, JOSEPH
Buchsenmeisterey-Schul . . . und Feuerwerken
Johann Schutes, Augspurg, 1643

FURWERCKBUCH *(Feuerwerkbuch)*
Mss. Vienna Nationalbibliothek #3062—circa 1437
Mss. Germanische Museum, #1481a, Nurnberg
Das Feuerwerksbuch von 1420—*Wilhelm Hassenstein*
Verlag der Deutschen Technik, GmbH,
Munich, 1941
Rust und feuerwerck buych, *15 cent, mss.*
Town Library, Frankfort (See:
GUTTMAN)
Munich Mss. Codex Germanicus #600

GAIBI, GENERAL AGOSTINO
"Appunti sull'origine e sulla evoluzione meccanica degli
apparecchi di accensione delle armi da fuoco portatili"
(Evolution of the wheel lock from Da Vinci
(part I)—evolution of other locks (part II))
Armi Antiche, pp. 81-210 . . . . Turin, 1956
Armi Antiche, pp. 37 to end . . . . Turin, 1957
"Le Armi da Fuoco"
Storia di Brescia, Parte XV, Vol. III
Treccani, Brescia, 1952
Le Armi da Fuoco Portatili Italiane
Bramante Editrice, s.p.a., Milan, 1962

BIBLIOGRAPHY

"Biografiske Undersøgelser om Familien Cominazzi"
Vaabenhistoriske Aarbøger, *XIa*
Copenhagen, 1962
"Un Codice Manoscritto della Fine del '500"
Armi Antiche....*1959*
"Un manoscritto del '600 l'Arte Fabrile di
Antonio Petrini" (Petrini was a gunsmith)
Armi Antiche....*Accademia di S. Marciano,*
Turin, 1962, 1963, 1964
"Un raro cimelio piemontese del trecento"
(Early mortars)
Armi Antiche....*Accademia di S. Marciano,*
Turin, 1965

GAIER, CLAUDE
Contribution à l'étude de l'armement au XVe siècle
Paris, 1960
See: TOURNAI

GARDNER, COLONEL ROBERT E.
Small Arms Makers, a Directory of Fabricators of
Firearms, *etc.*
Crown, New York, 1963

GAUBIL, PERE ANTOINE
(Translator of the Annals of the Moguls *about the*
Chinese invention of gunpowder)
Paris, 1723

GAY, GENERAL PAOLO
"Della nomenclatura delle bocche da fuoco antiche"
"Gli esemplari custoditi nel Museo Nazionale
d'Artiglieria di Torino"
Armi Antiche, *pp. 64-80....Turin, 1965*

GAY, VICTOR
Glossaire Archéologique du Moyen Age et de la
Renaissance
Gay (A. G. 1882), Paris, 1887
Text revised and completed by Henri Stein (H-Z),
Picard, Paris, 1928

GAYA, LOUIS DE
Traité des armes, des machines de guerre, etc.
Cramoisy, Paris, 1678
Reprint edited by Charles ffoulkes with preface by
Viscount Dillon
London, 1911

GEORGE, J. N.
English Guns and Rifles
Stackpole, Harrisburg, Pa., 1947
English Pistols and Revolvers
Samworth, Harrisburg, Pa., 1947

GERRARE, WIRT (William Oliver Greener)
A Bibliography of Guns and Shooting
Roxburghe Press, London, 1895

GESSLER, E. A. and MEYER-SCHNYDER, J.
"Beträge zum altschweizerischen Geschützwesen"
Z.H.W.K., *Vol. VI, pp. 3-50*
Berlin, 1912-1914
Katalog der historischen Sammlungen im Rathaus
in Luzern
Lucern, 1914 (?)

GHEYN, JACOB DE
Manual of Arms

Title in English (1607) in Dutch (1608)
(Matchlock muskets and calivers)
Badous, Amsterdam, 1608

GIBBON, EDWARD
The Decline and Fall of the Roman Empire
(First edition) London, 1776-1788
(Recent edition) Heritage Press, New York, 1946

GILCHRIST, HELEN IVES
A Catalogue of the Collections of Arms and Armour
Presented to the Cleveland Museum of Art by
Mr. and Mrs. John Long Severance
Cleveland, 1924

GILLE, FLORENT and ROCKSTUHL, A.
Musée de Tsarskoé-Sélo, au Collection d'Armes
de sa Majesté l'Empereur de Toutes les Russies
3 volumes
St. Petersburg & Karlsruhe, 1835-1853

GLUCKMAN, ARCADI and SATTERLEE, L. D.
American Gun Makers
Ulbrich, Buffalo, N.Y., 1945

GOHLKE, W.
"Das Geschützwesen des Altertums und des
Mittelalters"
Z.H.W.K., Vol. V, pp. 281, 354, 379
Berlin, 1909-1911
Z.H.W.K., Vol. VI, p. 12 . . . . Berlin, 1912-1914

GOODRICH, CARRINGTON, FENG CHIA SHENG
"The Early Development of Firearms in China"
Isis, *XXXVI, p. 114-23, 1946*

GORDEEV, H. R.
The State Arms Collection of the Moscow-Kremlin
(In Russian). . . . Moscow, 1954

GRAECUS, MARCUS
Liber Ignium
(Gunpowder, Greek fire—a later interpolation)
Biblioteque National—mss—
Nos. 7156 and 7158—Paris—circa 1350
Munich mss—197 and 367—circa 1438
See: HIME, H. W. L.
PARTINGTON, J. R.

GRAEVENITZ, G. von
"Das Arsenal zu Venedig und seine Sammlungen"
(Palazzo Ducale, Venice)
Z.H.W.K., Vol. V, p. 65 . . . . Berlin, 1909-1911

GRANCSAY, STEPHEN V.
American Engraved Powder Horns
The Metropolitan Museum of Art, New York, 1946
(new edition). . . . Ray Riling, Philadelphia, 1965
Arms and Armor—Allentown Art Museum Loan
Exhibition—1964
Allentown, Pa., 1964
The Bashford Dean Collection of Arms and Armour
in the Metropolitan Museum of Art
Southworth, Portland, Maine, 1933
"Carved Gunstocks by Johann Michael Maucher"
(21 figures) Journal, Walters Art Gallery,
Vol. 2, p. 43-53 1939

BIBLIOGRAPHY

"Early Firearms in the George F. Harding Museum,
Chicago" The Gun Digest . . . Chicago, 1952
Master French Gunsmiths' Designs
    Ray Riling, Philadelphia, 1950
Metropolitan Museum of Art: Loan Exhibition of
European Arms and Armour . . . . New York, 1931
American Rifleman
"Firearms of the Mediterranean"
    Page 21 . . . . February, 1949
    Page 31 . . . . March, 1949
"Ivory on Firearms"
    Page 44 . . . . March, 1951
"Miniature Firearms"
    Page 28 . . . . July, 1949
"Napoleon's Gunmaker"
    Page 35 . . . . July, 1948
"Powder Horns and American History"
    Page 17 . . . . December, 1950
"Scottish Pistols in the Metropolitan Museum of Art"
    Pages 18-20, 9 figures . . . . November, 1947
Metropolitan Museum of Art Bulletin
"The Charles Noé Daly bequest of firearms"
    (Includes a pistol of Lord Nelson (1758-1805)
    by H. W. Mortimer and a pair of flintlock pistols
    made by Durs Egg that belonged to George IV
    as Price of Wales (1762-1830).
    Vol. 30, pp. 189-192, 4 figures 1935
"A chased pistol lock"
    (Snaphaunce pistol lock, date 1679 "Acqua
    Fresca A Bargi")
    Vol. 29, pages 43-44 1934
"The Craft of the Early American Gunsmith"
    Vol. 6, pages 54-61, 16 figures . . . . October, 1947
"A Gun from the Caucasus"
    (Made in Daghestan; barrel damascened in gold;
    stock decorated in niello. Kubatchi?)
    Vol. 30, pages 174-174, 2 figures 1935

"A Hapsburg gun"
    (Archduke Ferdinand of Tyrol; matchlock/
    wheel lock; mark "KP" over frog)
    Vol. 29, pages 173-175, 3 figures 1934
"A Saxon wheel lock pistol"
    (Made entirely of steel, dated 1596)
    Vol. 32, pages 248-251, 2 figures 1937
"A Sculptured pistol by Daniel Sadeler"
    (Wheel lock pistol; arms of Elector Maximilian I)
    Vol. 27, pages 16-18, 2 figures 1932
"A Set of English percussion pistols"
    (About 1830; locks "I. Purdey, No. 314½ Oxford
    Street, London")
    Vol. 30, pages 252-254, 2 figures 1935
"A Versailles gun by Boutet, Directeur-artiste"
    Vol. 31, pages 163-166, 5 figures 1936
Art Bulletin of New York (College Art Association)
"A Pair of Seventeenth century Brescian Pistols"
    (Walters Art Gallery. Locks engraved "Piero Alsa
    in Brescia"; stocks stamped "Gio Marno in Brescia
    fece"; barrels stamped "Gio. Batt. Francino")
    Vol. 18, pages 240-247, 6 figures 1936

GRANT, JAMES J.
  Single-Shot Rifles
    William Morrow, New York, 1947
  More Single-Shot Rifles
    William Morrow, New York, 1959

GRAY, JOHN
  A Treatise on Gunnery
    Printed for William Jennys, London, 1734

GREENER, W. W.
  The Gun and its Development
    Longman, Rees, Orme, Brown, Green and

Longman, London, 1835 (and numerous
succeeding editions)

GROSE, FRANCIS
Military Antiquities Respecting a History of the
English Army and a Treatise on Ancient Armour
S. Hooper, London, 1786-1789

GROSZ, AUGUST and THOMAS, BRUNO
Katalog der Waffensammlung in der Neuen Burg
*Schausammlung, Kunsthistorisches Museum,
Vienna, 1936*

GUERARD, NICHOLAS
Diverses Pieces d'Arquebuzerie
(Decorations of Guns)
N. Guerard, Paris, 1710-1730

GUIFFREY, JULES
Inventaire Général du Mobilier de la Couronne
Sur Louis XIV
(Louis XIII Cabinet d'Armes). . . . Paris, 1886

GUNS AND AMMO
*Peterson Pub. Co., Hollywood, California,
since 1958*

GUN ANNUAL
(True Magazine)
Fawcett Publications, New York, since 1961

GUN COLLECTOR, THE
Madison, Wisconsin, 1947-1953

Clacq. fec.   Mareou ex Cum priul reg.

BIBLIOGRAPHY

GUN COLLECTOR'S LETTER, THE
Madison, Wisconsin, 1946-1947

GUN COLLECTOR'S HANDBOOK
Nat'l Rifle Association, Washington, D.C., 1959

GUN DIGEST, THE
John Amber, Chicago, since 1944

GUN DIGEST TREASURY
(The best from the first 15 years of the Gun Digest)
Chicago, 1956

GUNS AND HUNTING (monthly magazine)
Maco, New York, since 1957

GUNS MAGAZINE
*Publishers Development Corp., Skokie, Illinois,
since 1955*

GUN REPORT, THE
Aledo, Illinois, June 1955 to date

GUNS REVIEW
London

GUN WORLD
Gallant Pub. Co., Covina, California, since 1953

GUTTMAN, OSCAR
Monumenta Pulveris Pyrii
*(Early guns and gunpowder, manuscript
illustrations). . . . Artists Press, London, 1906*

HAENEL, ERICH
*"Zur ältesten Geschichte der Dresdner Rüstkammer"
Z. H.W.K., Part I, Vol. VII, p. 311,
Part II, Vol. VIII, p. 181 . . . . 1918-1920*
Kostbare Waffen der Dresdner Rüstkammer
Karl W. Hiersemann, Leipzig, 1923

HAILLES, D. D.
Annals of Scotland
Vol. II, p. 236 . . . . London, 1909

HALL, THOMAS E.
"Forerunners of the First Winchester"
Gun Digest Treasury, *pp. 96-113*
Chicago, 1961

HALSALL, EDWARD
A Journal of the Siege of Lathom House
Harding, Mavoc and Lepard, London, 1823

HAMPE, DR. THEODOR
*"Archivalische Forschungen zur Waffenkunde"
Z.H.W.K., Vol. V, pp. 364-399
Berlin, 1909-1911*

HANSJAKOB and HEINRICH
Der Schwarze Berthold, der Erfinder des Schiesspluvers
und der Feuerwaffen. *Freiburg im Breisgau, 1891*
See: PLOT, R.

HANSON, CHARLES E., JR.
The Plains Rifle
Bramhall, New York, 1960

HANZELET, JEAN APPIER
Pyrotechnie of Hanzelet
Paris, 1630

HASSENSTEIN, WILHELM
Das Feuerwerksbuch von 1420
*Verlag der Deutschen Technik, GmbH,
Munich, 1941*
"Uber die Feuerwaffen in der Seeschlacht von Lepanto"
(Battle of Lepanto, October, 1571)
Z.H.W.K., Vol. VII (new), p. 1 . . . . Berlin, 1940

HARRIS, CLIVE
A History of the Birmingham Gun-Barrel Proof House
Birmingham, 1946

HATCH, A.
Remington Arms in American History
Reinhart & Co., New York, 1956

HAVEN, C. T. and BELDEN, F. A.
A History of the Colt Revolver
William Morrow, New York, 1940

HAW TREY-GYNGELL, D.S.
Armourers Marks
(Second edition) 1966

HAWKER, COLONEL PETER
Instructions to Young Sportsmen
*J. Johnson & Co., London, 1814, Philadelphia,
1846, Herbert Jenkins, London, 1922*

HAYWARD, JOHN F.
"Armourers and Gunmakers of the French Crown"
J.A.A.S., Vol. I, No. XII, p. 215
London, December, 1955
The Art of the Gunmaker, *Volumes I and II*
Barrie & Rockliff, London, 1962 and 1963
(Second revised edition) 1965
"Les Collections du Palais de Capodimonte, Naples"
Armes Anciennes, Vol. I, No. VI, p. 121
Geneva, Switzerland, 1956
"Designs for Ornaments on Gunstocks"
Livrustkammaren, Vol. V, pp. 109-138 1950
"The Earliest Forms of the Flint-Lock in England"
Livrustkammaren, Vol. IV, pp. 185-202 1947
"English Firearms of the 16th Century"
J.A.A.S., Vol. III, No. V, p. 177
London, March, 1960
"English Pistols of the 17th Century"
Apollo, XLVI, pp. 94-96
Apollo, XLVII, pp. 5-8, 51-53, 84-86
"English Pistols of the 18th Century"
Apollo, XL, pp. 56-59, 114-117, 154-157
London, 1944-1945
Apollo, XLI, pp. 70-74
Apollo, XLII, pp. 166-170, 231-234
Apollo, XLIII, pp. 15-16, 44-46
European Firearms
H. M. Stationery Office, London, 1958
*"Fine Arms Made for the Dukes of Bavaria in
London Museums"*
Apollo, XLIV, pp. 67-70, 119-122
"The Huguenot Gunmakers of London"
Proceedings of the Huguenot Society of London,
Vol. XX, pp. 649-663 1966
*"The Firearms Collection of the Armeria Reale
at Turin"*
*Apollo, III, p. 50-53, 126-128 . . . . London,
May, 1951*

BIBLIOGRAPHY

Iacquinet fe. Marcou ex Cum Priuil · reg

"A German Design for a Pair of Wheel-Lock Pistols"
    Connoisseur, Vol. 123, pp. 16-18 1949
"A Gun from a Grand-Ducal Armoury"
    Connoisseur, Vol. 129, p. 109
"The Imperial Russian Arms Factory of Tula"
    Apollo, Vol. L, pp. 43-45, 69-71 . . . . London, 1950
"Pierre Monlong, Bøssemager hos to Könger"
    (English translation)
    Vaabenhistoriske Aarbøger, Vol. VIII, pp. 104-121
    Copenhagen, 1956
"The Musket Rest from the Emanuel Sadeler
Garniture in the Armeria Reale, Turin"
    Bolletino—Societa Piemontese d'Archeologia,
    pp. 87-94 . . . . Turin, 1949
"The Sources of Ornament on a German
Wheel-Lock Arquebus"
    Connoisseur, Vol. 120, pp. 102-104 1947

HELD, ROBERT
    The Age of Firearms / A Pictorial History
    Harper, New York, 1957

HENDERSON, JAMES
    Firearms Collecting for Amateurs
    Frederick Muller, London, 1966

HEURTELOUP, M.
    Memoire sur le Fusil de Guerre
    (French manual 1836

HEWITT, JOHN
    Ancient Armour and Weapons in Europe
    (3 volumes) . . . . John Henry & James Parker,
    Oxford, 1855-1860. Reprinted by Akademische
    Druck-und Verlagsanstalt, Graz, Austria, 1967
    "Notice of the Combined Use of the Match-lock
    and the Flintlock"
    Archaelogical Journal 1860

HEXHAM, HENRY
    The First Part of the Principles of the Art Military
    Delf, Holland, 1642

HIME, LT. COL. H.W.K.
    Gunpowder and Ammunition: Their Origin
    and Progress
    Longmans, Green & Co., London, 1904
    The Origin of Artillery
    Longmans, Green & Co., London, 1915

HOFF, DR. ARNE
    Aeldre Dansk Bøssemageri

(Oldest Danish gunsmiths) . . . . *Copenhagen, 1951*
"Danske Perkussionsbøsser"
    Vaabenhistoriske Aarbøger, *Vol. VIII, p. 150-165*
    Copenhagen, 1955-1956
"Late Firearms with Snap Matchlock"
    Four Studies on the History of Arms, *p. 30*
    Copenhagen, 1964
"Gottorpmesterene"
    Svenska Vapenhistoriska Sällskapets Skrifter,
    Vol. V (new). . . . *Stockholm, 1957*
"Hjullaase med Seglformet Hanefjer"
    (Wheel lock with the cock spring placed around
    the wheel)
    Vaanbenhistoriske Aarbøger, *Vol. III, p. 68-89*
    Copenhagen, 1940-1942
"Luftbøsser fra 1600-Arene"
    English summary—17th century air guns
    Svenska Vapenhistoriska Sällskapets Skrifter,
    Vol. IV (new), p. 35-56. . . . *Stockholm, 1955*
"Noch eine Schnellfeuerpistole aus dem 17.
Jahrhundert"
    (17th century German 9 barrel snaphaunce pistol)
    Z.H.W.K., *Vol. VI (new), p. 247*. . . . *Berlin, 1939*
"Quelques inventions de la famille Klett à Salzburg"
    Armes Anciennes, *Vol. II, No. 6, pp. 133-139*
    Geneva, 1959
    Royal Arms at Rosenborg
    (with SCHEPELERNS & BOESEN)
    Copenhagen, 1956
"Scottish Pistols in Scandinavian Collections"
    J.A.A.S., *Vol. I, No. XII, p. 199-214*
    London, December, 1955
"Gunmakers' Marks in The Spanish Manner"
    Vaabenhistoriske Aarbøger, *Vol. I, pp. 143-149*
    Copenhagen, 1935-1942

HOGG, OLIVER F. G.

English Artillery—1326-1716
    Royal Artillery Institution, London, 1963

HONDIUS, HENRIK
    Description et breve declaration des Regles Generales
    de la Fortification, de l'Artillerie, des Amunition
    et viures; des officiers et de leurs commissions
    Hagae Comit., 1625

HOOPES, THOMAS T.
"Ein Beitrag zum französischen Radschloss"
    Z.H.W.K., *Vol. V (3), pp. 50-53*
    Berlin, 1935-1936
"Drei Beiträge zum Radschloss"
    Z.H.W.K., *(new) Vol. IV, (old XIII), No. X, p. 224*
    Berlin, 1934
"Das Früheste datierbare Radschloss im
Nationalmuseum in München" (part of above)
    Z.H.W.K., *(new) Vol. IV, (old XIII), pp. 224-225*
    (part of above). . . . *Berlin, 1932-1934*
"Radschlösser nach Leonardo da Vinci?"
    Z.H.W.K., *(new) Vol. IV, (old XIII), pp. 225-227*
    (part of above). . . . *Berlin, 1931-1933*
"Ripollsche Radschlosspistolen"
    Z.H.W.K., *(new) Vol. IV, (old XIII), pp. 227-229*
    (part of above). . . . *Berlin, 1931-1933*
"Notes on the Development of the Baltic Flintlock"
    A Miscellany of Arms and Armor, *pp. 45-51*
    Rudge, New York, 1927
    The American Rifleman. . . . *November, 1946*
"The Double Set Trigger"
    A Miscellany of Arms and Armor, *pp. 36-38*
    Rudge, New York, 1927
"A Decimal Classification of the Discharge Mechanism
of Hand Firearms"
    (With William G. Renwick)

BIBLIOGRAPHY

A Miscellany of Arms and Armor (pp. 64-103)
Rudge, New York, 1927
"Pistolen oder kurze Karabiner?"
Z.H.W.K.....Munich, 1950
Armor and Arms
St. Louis City Art Museum, 1954
"The German Back-striking Lock"
The Gun Collectors' Letter, *No. 8*
February 28, 1947
"Loan Exhibition: Firearms of Princes"
Bulletin of the City Art Museum, *XXV, No. 1*
St. Louis, Mo., Jan., 1940
"A Matchlock Gun"
Bulletin of the City Art Museum, *XXXVI, No. 4*
St. Louis, Mo., 1951
"A Semi-Automatic Matchlock"
J.A.A.S., Vol. XXX, No. XII, p. 293-294
London
"Three XVIII Century Pistols"
Bulletin of the City Art Museum, *XXXVIII, No. 1*
St. Louis, Mo., 1953
"Two Early Revolvers"
The American Rifleman, *Vol. XCV, No. 2*
February, 1947

HOUDETOT, ADOLPHE D'
Le Tir au Pistolet
Paris, 1850

HUMMELBERGER, WALTER and SCHARPER, LEO
"Die osterreichesche Militar-Repetierwindbüchse
und ihr Erfinder Bartholomäus Girandoni"
(Military repeating airguns)
Z.H.W.K., Vol. I, p. 24 1964
Z.H.W.K., Vol. II, p. 81 1965

HUNTER
"Itemized Expenses of Robert de Mildenhale for
Guns and Powder and Saltpeter for Edward III"
Archaeologia, *XXXII, 385 .... 1847*

ILGNER, EMIL
"Maastrichter Elfenbeinpistolen"
Z.H.W.K., XII (Vol. III, new), pp. 210-214
Z.H.W.K., XIII, pp. 19, 68-69, 288 1929-1931

JACKSON, HERBERT J. and
WHITELAW, CHARLES F.
European Hand Firearms of the Sixteenth, Seventeenth
and Eighteenth Centuries with a Treatise on
Scottish Hand Firearms
Holland Press, London, 1959

JACOBI, VON WALLHAUSEN JOHANN
Archiley Kriegskunst
Hanaw, 1617
Kriegs-Kunst zu Fuss
Oppenheim, 1615
Kriegs-Kunst zu Pferd
Wolffgang Hofmann, Franckfurt am Mayn, 1633
Manuale Militare, oder Kriegs Manual
Uldrick Balck, Franckfurt, 1616

JACOBS, DR. JOHANNES
"Die Königliche Gewehrkammer in München"
Z.H.W.K., Vol. VI, p. 164 1912-1914

JACQUINET, C.
Plusieurs Modeles des Plus Nouvelles Manieres

qui Sont en Usage en l'Art d'Arquebuzerie
Drawn from Thuraine and Le Hollandois
Paris, 1660 . . . . Reprinted by Quaritch, Paris, 1888

JAHNS, MAX
Entwicklungsgeschichte der alten Trutzwaffen
Berlin, 1899
Geschichte der Kriegswissenschaft in Deutschland
Munich, 1889-1891

JAHRBUCH DER KUNSTHISTORISCHEN
SAMMLUNGEN DES ALLERHOCHSTEN
KAISERHAUSES IN WIEN *(A Periodical)*
Prague, Wien, Leipzig, 1883 to 1936
Adolf Holzhausen, Vienna, 1952 to date

JALOFSKY
De Inventore Pulveris et Bombarde
Jena, 1702

JESSEN, N. S.
Description de quelques nouveaux armes pour
les militaires . . . . *Copenhagen, 1862*

JOHNSON, MELVIN M. JR., and HAVEN, CHARLES T.
Automatic Arms, Their History, Development
and Use . . . *Morrow, New York, 1941*

JOINVILLE (1224-1319)
"Histoire de Saint Loys"
Edited by Petiton
Collection complète des mémoires relatifs à
l'histoire de France . . . . *Paris, 1824*
English translation Joinville, *Everyman,*
London, 1915

JOINVILLE, JOHN LORD DE
Memoirs of . . .
At the Hafod Press by James Henderson, 1807

JOURNAL OF THE ARMS AND ARMOUR SOCIETY,
THE *(periodical)*
London, since 1953

JOURNAL OF THE ONTARIO ARMS COLLECTORS
ASSOCIATION *(semi-annual)*
Highland Creek, Ontario, since 1957

JUET, ROBERT
The Third Voyage of Master Henry Hudson
Charles Scribner & Sons, New York, 1908

KAEMMERER, G. L. C.
Une visite au Musée Impérial de Tsarskó Sélo
St. Petersburg, 1881

KALMAR, JOHANNES von
"Beiträge zur Geschichte der Kriegsrakete"
(Rockets in Nedschm Eddin, 1275-1295)
Z.H.W.K., Vol. VII (new), p. 18 1940
"Ein dreiläufiger Lunten-Drehling im
Zeughausmuseum zur Kopenhagen"
Z.H.W.K., Vol. VI (new), p. 85 1937

BIBLIOGRAPHY

KARGER, VIKTOR
    "Neue Teschner Beiträge zur Herkunftsfrage der
    Teschinken"
        Z.H.W.K., Vol. I, pp. 29, 42 1964

KARPENSKI, LOUIS C.
    See: SPAULDING, THOMAS M.

KARR, CHARLES & CARROLL
    Remington Handguns
        Military Publishing Co., U.S.A., 1947

KAUFFMAN, HENRY J.
    Early American Gunsmiths—1650-1850
        Bramhall House, New York, 1952
    The Pennsylvania-Kentucky Rifle
        Harrisburg, 1960

KEITH NEAL, W. and BACK, D. H.
    The Mantons: Gunmakers
        Walker & Co., New York, 1967

KEITH, NEAL W.
    Spanish Guns and Pistols
        Benn, London, 1955

KENNARD, A. NORRIS
    "Jean Conrad Tornier"
        Burlington Magazine, *LXXVII, pp. 127-128*
        October, 1940
    "A Pair of Seventeenth Century English Pistols"
        J.A.A.S., Vol. II, No. 6, pp. 131-135
        London, 1957

KIENBUSCH, C. O. von
    Kretzschmar von Kienbusch Collection of
    Armor and Arms
        Princeton University, Princeton, 1963

KIENBUSCH, C. O. von   and
GRANCSAY, STEPHEN V.
    The Bashford Dean Collection of Arms and Armour
    in the Metropolitan Museum of Art
        Portland, Maine, 1933

KINDIG, JOE, JR.
    Thoughts on the Kentucky Rifle in its Golden Age
        Hyatt, Wilmington, Del., 1960

KIRK, JOHN and YOUNG, ROBERT
    Great Weapons of World War II
        Walker & Co., New York, 1964

KOLDERER, JORG
    Manuscript for Maximilian I (Munich Codex #222)
        Innsbruch, 1504
    Jörg Kölderers Miniaturen zum Triumphzug Kaiser
    Maximilians—*WAETZOLDT, Wilhelm*
        Velhagen & Klasings, Berlin, 1939
    "Die Zeugbücher des Kaisers Maximilian I"
        J.D.K.S., Vol. XIII, p. 94 (see BOEHEIM)
        Vol. XV, p. 295 . . . . Vienna, 1892-1894

KOLLER, LARRY, PETERSON, H. L. and
GLASS, HERB
    The Fireside Book of Guns
        Simon & Schuster, New York, 1959

The Gun
> *Pocket Books, New York, 1964*

KONIGER, ERNST
> *Ein unbekanntes Bildnis des Regensburger
> Hofbüchsenmachers Johann Jacob Kuchenreuter"
> Z.H.W.K., Vol. I, p. 43 . . . . 1964*

KREMLIN ARMORY
> *See: GORDEEV
> TARASSUK*

KRETSCHMAR, OBERST von
> *"Eine Mittelalterliche Handgranate"
> Z.H.W.K., Vol. VI, p. 288 . . . .1912-1914*

KROPATSCHEK, ALFRED
> Die Umgestaltung der . . . Osterreichischen Gewehre
> in Hinterlader
>> *(Breech loading)
>> L. W. Seidel & Sohn, Vienna, 1867*

KUGELMAN
> Histoire des Arms offensive et defensives en Italie
> *Paris, 1860*

KUHLHOFF, PETER and KOLLER, LARRY
> Guns—the Complete Book—All Guns—All Ammunition
> *Maco, 1953*

KULHOFF, PETER, HALL, THOMAS and
WATROUS, GEORGE
> The History of Winchester Firearms—1866-1966
> *North Haven, 1966*

KUHLHOFF, PETER
> *"Beautiful Brownings"
> The Gun Digest, page 29 . . . .1966*

KUJAWSKI, MARIAN
> *"The Battles of Kircholm; a Masterpiece of Early XVII
> Century Military Tactics"*
>> *(The German reiters and their dags)
>> The Polish Review, Vol. XI, No. 1
>> New York, Winter, 1966*

KUNSTHISTORISCHES MUSEUM
> *See: BOEHEIM, WENDELIN
> THOMAS, BRUNO*

KYESER, CONRAD OF EYSTADT (1366-1405)
> Bellifortis
>> *Manuscript in the Fürstenberg Library of
>> Donaueschingen, circa 1470
>> Gottingen, circa 1400*

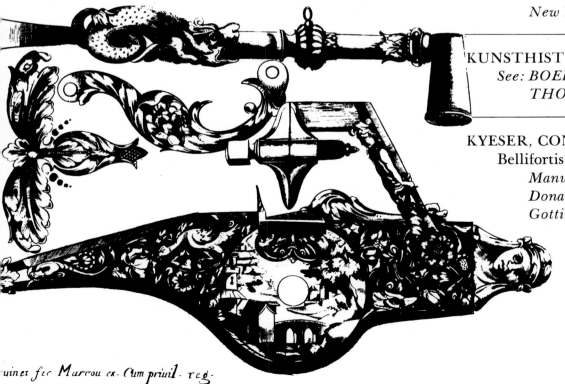

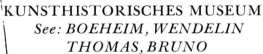

uin et fec Marcou ex. Cum privil. reg.

BIBLIOGRAPHY

LA BRUNE, JEAN DE
    The Life of ... Charles V ...
        Printed by Edward Jones for Randal Taylor,
        London, 1691

LACOLLOMBE, DE
    Nouveaux Dessins d'Arquebuseries
        Paris, 1730

LACOMBE, M. P.
    Les Armes et les Armures
        (Ordonnances de Chasse of Francis I)
        L. Hachette et Cie, Paris, 1868

LACROIX, PAUL
    L'Ancienne France ...
        Librarie de Firmin-Didot, Paris, 1886
    Vie Militaire et Religieuse au Moyen Age
        Librairie de Firmin-Didot, Paris, 1873

LAKE, STUART
    Wyatt Earp
        Houghton Mifflin Co., New York, 1931

LAKING, SIR GUY FRANCIS
    The Armoury of Windsor Castle, European Section
        Bradbury, Agnew, London, 1904
    Catalogue of the European Armour and Arms in the
    Wallace Collection at the Hertford House, *Revised by*
    Sir James G. Mann
        Darling & Son, London, 1900
    A Record of European Armour and Arms Through
    Seven Centuries *(1000-1700)*
        5 volumes....G. Bell & Sons, London, 1920-1922

LAMMERT, FRIEDRICH
    "Von den Deutschen Pistolenreitern und ihrem
    Führer Graf Günther von Schwartzburg"
    (1556 portrait)
    Z.H.W.K., Vol. III, p. 226....April, 1931

LANGUEDOC, LAURENT LE
    Plusieurs Pièces de Armements d'Arquebuziere
        Paris, 1685

LARCHENKO, M. N.
    West European Arms and Armour of the 15th-17th
    Centuries in The Hermitage
        (In Russian)....Leningrad, 1963

LASSON, T.
    "Hand Cannons to Flintlock"
    (Performance of early handguns)
    The Gun Digest *(10th edition)....Chicago, 1955*

LAVIN, JAMES D.
    "An Examination of Some Early Documents Regarding
    the Use of Gunpowder in Spain"
    J.A.A.S., Vol. IV, No. IX, p. 163....March, 1964
    A History of Spanish Firearms
        Arco, New York, 1965
    "Miquelet Accessories"
        The American Rifleman, *p. 34*
        Washington, D.C., July, 1966

LAVOISIER, ANTOINE
    Sur la Combustion en General
        Paris, 1777

LE BLOND, GUILLAUME
A Treatise on Artillery
Printed by E. Cave, London, 1746

LEITNER, QUIRIN von
Artillerie-Arsenal-Museum in Wien
Vienna, 1866

LENK, TORSTEN
Flintlåset: des uppkomst och utveckling
(*Swedish edition*). . .*Stockholm, 1939*
The Flintlock, Its Origin and Development
(*English edition*) *Edited by J. F. Hayward*
Holland Press, London, 1964
"History of the Pistols of the 16th Century" (Vienna)
Livrustkammaren Journal, *Vol. IV, Nos. 11-12,*
pp. 349, 358. . . . Stockholm
"Ett Internationellt Hjullaskriterium"
Livrustkammaren Journal, *Vol. IV, parts I & II*
Stockholm, 1946
Thomas Picquot peintre 1638 (*reprint*)
Imprimerie Nordisk Rotogravyr, Stockholm, 1950
"Zwei Büchsen von Thuraine und le Hollandois"
Vaabenhistoriske Aarbøger, *Vol. I, p. 13*
Copenhagen, 1935

LENSI, ALFREDO
Il Museo Stibbert
Florence, 1917

LENZ, EDWARD von
Collection d'Armes de l'Ermitage Impérial
Petrograd, 1908
"Die Waffensammlungen Russlands"
Z.H.W.K., *Vol. I, p. 57. . . . 1897-1899*

Die Waffensammlung des Grafen S.D. Scheremetew
Verlag von Carl W. Heirsemann, Leipzig, 1897

LENZ, ELLIS CHRISTIAN
Muzzle Flashes
Standard, Huntington, W. Va., 1944

LENZ, P. A.
"Nouvelles Archives, Philosophiques et Littéraires"
Revue Trimestrielle, *II, 589-609. . . .1840*
BritishMuseum Periodical Publications, 4475

LEPIACZZYK, J.
"Arsenal Wladyslawa IV w Krakowie"
("Das Köngliche Zeughaus zu Krakau")
Arsenal. . .Krakowie, *Vol. I, No. II*
Crakow, 1958

LEY, WILLIE
Rockets, Missiles and Space Travel
New York, 1961

LIEGE, MUSEE D'ARMES
See: PURAYE, JEAN
TECHY, D.

LINARES, HENRI DI
Catalogue . . . Musée International de la Chasse à
Tir et de la Fauconnerie
Imp. Jeanne d'Arc, Gien, 1960's

LINDSAY, MERRILL K.
"Beauty But No Bang"
True Magazine. . . .*New York, September, 1966*

BIBLIOGRAPHY

"Gunpowder, or How It All Didn't Start"
    Armi Antiche . . . . *Accademia di S. Marciano,*
    Turin, 1967
"Guns, the Collector's Viewpoint"
    Status Magazine . . . . *New York, January, 1967*
"A History of Breech-Loading"
    Gun Digest . . . . *Chicago, 1968*

**LIVRUSTKAMMAREN, JOURNAL OF THE
ROYAL ARMOURY**
    Stockholm, Sweden

LOGAN, HERSCHEL C.
    "All-Metal Pistols"
        The American Rifleman
        Washington, D.C., November, 1958
    Cartridges
        Standard, Huntington, W. Va., 1948
    Hand Cannon to Automatics
        Standard, Huntington, W. Va., 1944
    "J. M. Marlin's Handguns"
        The American Rifleman
        Washington, D.C., October, 1958

LONDON—A Short Account of the Worshipful Company
of Gunmakers *(Anon)*
        London, 1937

LONDON—**TOWER OF LONDON**
    See: DILLON, VISCOUNT
        FFOULKES, C. J.
        HEWITT, JOHN

LONDON—**VICTORIA AND ALBERT MUSEUM**
    See: HAYWARD, JOHN

LONDON—**WALLACE COLLECTION**
    See: MANN, SIR JAMES G.

LONDON SPORTING GAZETTE
    London, 1873

LORD, BEMAN
    Look at Guns
        Henry Z. Walck, Inc., New York, 1963

LOSSNITZER, J. von
    "Studien aus der Waffensammlung der Veste Coburg"
        Z.H.W.K., Vol. III (new) 1918-1920

LOT, FERDINAND

Jac. Marcou Excudit cum privil. regis

L'Art Militaire et Les Armies du Moyen Age
2 volumes....Paris, 1946

LUCIA, G. DE
La Sale d'Armi nel Museo dell'Arsenale di Venezia
Revista Marittima, Rome, 1908

LUGS, JAROSLAV
"Antonin Vincene Lebeda 1795-1857"
Guns Review....London, June, 1964
Handfeuerwaffen
Rucni Palné Zbrané
2 volumes....Prague, 1956

LYDGATE, JOHN
The Fall of Princes
Englished Boccaccio's De Casibus Virorum
Richard Pynson, London, 1494

MACHIAVELLI, NICCOLO
The Arte of Warre...
Thomas East for John Wright, London, 1588

MACKAY-SCOBIE, I. H.
"The Regimental Highland Pistol"
Journal of the Society for Army Historical
Research, Vol. VII, p. 52....London

MACLENNAN, BRIGADIER A.
"The Needle Gun and the Chassepot"
Guns Review, No. VI....London, June, 1966

MACOIR, GEORGE
La Salle des Armures du Musée de la Porte de Hal
Vandamme et Rossignol, Brussels, 1910

MADIS, GEORGE
The Winchester Book
Madis, Dallas, 1961

MADRID
See: VALENCIA, DON JUAN DE
"Armeria Nacional Bilderinventar der Waffen"
J.D.K.S., 90 - Bd 10 p. CCCLIII
J.D.K.S., Bd 11 - 2 Theil, p. CCXLII....1889

MAGLIOLI, VITTORIO
Armeria Reale di Torino, Guida Breve
Turin, 1959

MAGNE DE MAROLLES
See: MAROLLES

MAHRHOLDT, RICHARD
Waffen-Lexikon für Jäger und Schützen
(first edition)....Innsbruck, 1931
(third edition)....F. C. Mayer, Munich, 1952

MAINDRON, MAURICE
Les Armes
Paris, 1890

MAIZEROY, JOLY DE
Translator of Valterius' De Re Militari....Paris, 1555

MALDERGHEM, JEAN VAN
Catalogue des armes et armures du musée de la
Porte de Hal
Brussels, 1902

BIBLIOGRAPHY

MALLET, ALLAIN MANESSON
Les Travaux de Mars ou l'Art de la Guerre
Henault, Paris, 1684
(*Trs.*) On the Physical Conditions . . . Artillery
London, 1856

MANGEOT, H.
Traité du Fusil de Chasse et des Armes de Précision
Paris, 1858

MANN, F. W.
The Bullets' Flight *(1909)*
Ray Riling, Philadelphia, 1965

MANN, SIR JAMES G.
"*Brescia. Luigi Marzoli, Italian arms and armour*"
Great Private Collections,
Edited by Douglas Cooper, pp. 50-59
Weidenfeld and Nicolson, London, 1963
"*The Influence of Art on Instruments of War*"
Journal of the Royal Society of Arts, *p. 740*
London, 1941
"*Italian Arms and Armour*"
Archaeologia, *Vol. 87, p. 311 . . . .London, 1938*
"*The Royal Armoury at Windsor*"
The Connoisseur, *pp. 258-267*
London, May, 1935
Wallace Collection Catalogues—European Arms
and Armour
2 volumes, including bibliography
Clowes, London, 1962

MARCHESI, JOSE MARIA
Catalogo de la Real Armería
Aguado, Madrid, 1849

MARCOU, FRANCOIS
Plusieurs Pièces d'Arquebuzerie
Paris, 1967

MARKHAM, FRANCIS
Five Decades of Epistoles of Warre
Augustine Matthewes, London, 1622
Soulders Accidence
London, 1625

MARKHAM, GERVASE (JERVIS)
The Whole Arte of Fowling by Water and Land
(printed) 1621 . . . .(revised) 1686

MARKLAND, ABRAHAM (GEORGE)
Pteryplegia, or the Art of Shooting-Flying,
A poem, 1727 . . . .J. Lever, London, 1767

MAROLLES, G. F. MAGNE DE
La Chasse au Fusil
(first edition) T. Barrois, Paris, 1788
An Essay on Shooting
(John Acton). . .(English edition) T. Cadell,
London, 1791
(new edition) Paris, 1836

MARQUETTE, PERE JACQUES
Mississippi Voyage of Jolliet and Marquette *(1673)*
Charles Scribner & Sons, New York, 1908

MASSENA MUSEE
Catalogue de la Collection Joubert, Ville de Nice
L'Elaiseur, Nice, France, 1926

MAXIMILIAN I
Freydal
Woodcuts by Dürer and others
Edited by Quirin von Leitner
Vienna, 1880-1882
Teurdanck—Theuerdank
(PFINTZING, MELCHIOR)
Woodcuts by Hans Schäufelein and
Hans Burgkmair—1517
Tewrdannckh
Holbein Society, London, 1884
"Theuerdank"
J.D.K.S., Vol. VIII, p. 15 . . . . Vienna, 1888
Zeugbücher des Kaisers Maximilian I
(See: KOLDERER)
The Triumph . . . . Adam Bartsch, Vienna, 1796
Der Weisskünig
By Marx Treitzsaurwein von Ehrentreitz—original
plates by BURGKMAIR, Hans and BECK,
Leonard, Edited by Alwin Schultz
Vienna, 1775
J.D.K.S., Vol. V, p. 97 . . . . Vienna, 1887
J.D.K.S., Vol. VI, p. 1 . . . . Vienna, 1888

MAYR, ADLWANG, M.
"Urkunden und Regesten aus dem k.k. Statthalterei-
Archiv in Innsbruck" (1364-1490)
J.K.D.S., Vol. XX, p. CXXV
J.D.K.S., Vol. XXI to end . . . . Vienna, 1900

MCKEE, THOMAS HERON
The Gun Book
Henry Holt, New York, 1918

MECKENEM, ISRAHEL VAN
Judith and Holofernes

Print in the late XV century
[Illustrations of breech-loading cannon with
chambers (field pieces)]

METROPOLITAN MUSEUM OF ART
See: METROPOLITAN MUSEUM OF ART
BULLETIN
DEAN, Bashford
GRANCSAY, Stephen V.

METROPOLITAN MUSEUM OF ART BULLETIN
Volumes to 37—November, 1905 to June, 1942
New York
New Series—Vol. 1—Summer, 1942 to date
New York

MEYERSON, AKE
Stockholms Bössmakare
Stockholm, 1936

MEYRICK, SAMUEL RUSH and SKELTON, JOSEPH
A Critical Inquiry into Antient Armour
3 volumes . . . . Robert Jennings, London, 1824

MEZERAY, FRANCOIS EUDES DE
A General Chronological History of France
Printed by T. N. for Thomas Basset, Samuel
Lowndes, Christopher Wilkinson, William
Cademan and Jacob Tonson . . . . London, 1683
Histoire de France depuis Faramond jusqu'a
Louis Le Juste
3 volumes . . . . Paris, 1643-1651

MILIMETE, WALTER DE

BIBLIOGRAPHY

De Nobilitatibus, Sapientiis, et Prudentiis Regum
and a translation of Aristotle's De Secretis Secretorum
Pictures of cannon in decorative border
Manuscript at Christ Church, Oxford, 1326 and
Library of Earl of Leicester, Roxburgh Club
Facsimile—Oxford—1913
See: POST, PAUL

MILLER, JURI A.
Sammlung der Staatlichen Eremitage
Berlin, 1890 (?)

MODENA, CITY OF
Archives—Archivo di stato, Modena, 1507
(Prohibition of concealed weapons)
Flippo Valenti, Rome, 1953
"A Modenai Hippolit codexek" by NYARY, ALBERT
Szazadok, p. 679 . . . . Budapest, 1870

MOORE, WARREN
Guns, the Development of Firearms, Airguns
and Cartridges
Grosset & Dunlap, New York, 1963

MORA, DOMENICO
Il Soldato
Gabriel Giolito di Ferrari, Venetia, 1570

MORDECAI, CAPT. ALFRED
The Ordnance Manual for the Use of Officers of the
United States Army
Gideon & Co., Washington, D.C., 1850

MORDEN, ROBERT

Fortification and Military Discipline . . .
(Improved designed by Capt. T.S.)
Robert Morden, London, 1688

MUJICA, GREGORIO DE
Monografía Histórica de la Villa de Eibar
Eibar, 1910

MULLER, JOHN
A Treatise of Artillery
(third edition) . . . . John Millan, London, 1780
Reprinted with a preface by H. L. Peterson by
Museum Restoration Service, Ottowa,
Ontario, Canada, 1965

MUNICH
See: STOCKLEIN

MUNICH MANUSCRIPT
Codex Germanicus
#222 (circa 1400)—Staatsbibliotek, Munich
(Early gun pictures) . . . . (See: KOLDERER)
Codex Germanicus
#600 (circa 1390)—Staatsbibliotek, Munich
(Early gun pictures; making and testing saltpeter)
(See: GUTTMANN)

NAGANT, EM. & L.
Le fusil Nagant
Liège, 1880

NAUDI, SYEDALIU ZAFAR
"The Use of Cannon in Muslim India"
The Hyderabad Quarterly Review, *XII, p. 405-18*
1938

NAPOLEON (NAPOLEON BONAPARTE III) and
FAVE, ILDEFONSE
    Etudes sur le Passé et l'Avenir de l'Artillerie
        6 volumes. . . . J. Dumaine, Paris, 1846
        Libraire Militaire, Paris, 1862

NATTA-SOLERI, RAFFAELE
    "En Visite a l'Armeria Reale de Turin et le but
    de l'Accademia di San Marciano"
    Armi Antiche, *pp. 5-133 . . . . Turin, 1958*

NEAL, ROBERT J. and JINKS, ROY J.
    Smith and Wesson—1857-1945
        A. S. Barnes, New York, 1966

NIENHOLDT, EVA
    "Eine Musketierfigur in einem gemalten Trachtenbuch
    vom Ende des 16. Jahrhunderts"
        Z.H.W.K., Vol. VI, p. 1 (Mitteilungen)
        January, 1958

NEW YORK
    See: METROPOLITAN MUSEUM OF ART

NICHOLS, HAROLD E.
    "The Schuetzen Rifle"
    The American Rifleman, *p. 38*
    Washington, D.C., March, 1965

NIDA, C. A. von

Cfec Marcou ex cum priuil reg.

BIBLIOGRAPHY

"Die Steinbüchsen"
      Z.H.W.K., p. 118 . . . . Berlin, November, 1924

NORMAN, VESEY
      Arms and Armour
            Weidenfeld & Nicholson, London, 1964

NORTH, F.
      "The Fabulous Farquharson"
            Guns and Hunting . . . . New York, January, 1966

NORTH, SIMEON N. D. and RALPH H.
      Simeon North, First Official Pistol Maker
      of the United States
            Rumford Press, Concord, N. H., 1913

NORTON, ROBERT
      The Gunner
            London, 1628

NUNEZ, ALVAR CABEZA DE VACA
      Relacion *(History of exploration in America)*
            Charles Scribner & Sons, New York, 1907-1915

NURNBERG
      See: RODER, ERNST; and FURWERCKBUCH

NUTTER, WALDO E.
      Manhattan Firearms
            Stackpole Co., Harrisburg, Pa., 1958

OMAN, CHARLES W. C.
      A History of the Art of War in the Middle Ages
            Oxford, 1885, Houghton Mifflin, Boston, 1905
            and 1924, Great Seal, Cornell University, 1960

PAGE, THOMAS
      The Art of Shooting Flying
            Crouse, Norwich, 1766-1767

PARIS, MUSEE DE L'ARMEE
      See: ROBERT, COL. L.

PARKMAN, FRANCIS
      The Oregon Trail
            1846, Little, Brown, Boston, 1872

PARSONS, JOHN E.
      Henry Deringer's Pocket Pistol
            Morrow, New York, 1952
      The Peacemaker and Its Rivals
            Morrow, New York, 1950
      Smith and Wesson Revolvers
            Morrow, New York, 1957

PARTINGTON, J. R.
      Greek Fire and Gunpowder
            Heffer, Cambridge, 1960

PATTERSON, C. MEADE
      "A Breech-Loading, Self-Spanning Wheel Lock"
            The American Arms Collector, *Vol. II, No. II*
            Towson, Md., April, 1958

PAUILHAC
      See: CHARLES

PAYNE-GALLWEY, SIR RALPH
      The Crossbow
            (first edition) 1903
            (second edition) . . . . Holland Press, 1964

PELADEAU, MARIUS B.
"The Leonard Pepperbox"
The American Rifleman, p. 42
December, 1964
"The Palmer Carbine"
The American Rifleman, p. 42....August, 1964
"Underhammer Firearms"
The American Rifleman, p. 23....April, 1966

PEPYS, SAMUEL
Diary
November 11, 1663
Tr. Grenville....London, 1825

PERRIN, NOEL
"Onward and Upward with Technology—
Giving up the Gun" (History of Japanese firearms)
New Yorker Magazine, p. 211
November 20, 1965

PETERSON, HAROLD L.
Arms and Armor of the Pilgrims, 1620-1692
Plimoth Plantation, Inc., Plymouth, 1957
Arms and Armor in Colonial America, 1526-1783
Bramhall House, New York, 1956
Encyclopedia of Firearms
Dutton, New York, 1964
"Famous Firearms"
Series of short illustrated articles running
currently (1967) in
The American Rifleman....Washington, D.C.
"The Kentucky Rifle"
The American Rifleman, Vol. 112, No. 11, p. 28
Washington, D.C., November, 1964
(See: MULLER, JOHN)
"A Man to Remember. A. A. Chassepot"
American Rifleman, Vol. 106, No. 11

Washington, D.C., November, 1958
"A Man to Remember. Dr. R. J. Gatling"
The American Rifleman, Vol. 105, No. 10
Washington, D.C., October, 1957
"A Man to Remember. John Mahlon Marlin"
The American Rifleman, Vol. 108, No. 6
Washington, D.C., June 1960
"The Rifle in the American Revolution"
The American Rifleman, Vol. 106, No. 7
Washington, D.C., August, 1958
"The Schuetzen Rifle"
The American Rifleman, Vol. 112, No. 11
Washington, D.C., November, 1964
The Treasury of the Gun
Golden Press, 1962
A History of Firearms
Scribner's, New York, 1961
The Pageant of the Gun
Doubleday, New York, 1967
The Remington Historical Treasury of American Guns
Thomas Nelson, New York, 1966
Plus numerous articles in: American Rifleman,
Gun Collector, Guns and Hunting and
Muzzle Blasts

PETRASCH, ERNST
"Uber einige Jagdwaffen mit Elfenbeinschnitzerei
im Badischem Landesmuseum"
(Ivory sporters)
Z.H.W.K., Vol. I, pp. 11-26....1960

PETRINI, ANTONIO
L'Arte Focile (1642) (Guns and gunsmithing)
Manuscripts at the Tower of London,
Metropolitan Museum of Art, etc.
Reprint see: GAIBI, Armi Antiche, 1962, 1963,
1964

BIBLIOGRAPHY

PETROVIC, D.
   "Collection d'arbalètes au Museé Militaire de
   l'Armée Yougoslave"
      Vesnik, Vol. IV 1957

PFINTZING, MELCHIOR
   Theuerdannckh of Maximilian I
      Nuremberg, 1517
      See: MAXIMILIAN

PHILIPPOVICH, EUGEN von
   "Pulverflaschen mit eingebauter Uhr"
      Z.H.W.K., Vol. II, p. 128 1962
   "Elfenbeinpistolen"
   (Ivory pistols)
      Z.H.W.K., Vol. II, p. 97 1963

PICQUOT, THOMAS
   Livre de Diverses Ordonnances de Feuillages,
   Moresques, etc. (1638)
      Reprinted by LENK, Torsten
      See: LENK, TORSTEN

PISAN, CHRISTINE DE
   Histoire de Charles Martel
      Attributed to Jean de Meung
      (Mss illustration of hand cannon and cannon)
      Manuscript, Paris, 1470
      Reprint: GHEYN, Jan der—Christine de Pisan,
      Histoire de Charles Martel
      Bibliothèque Royale, Brussels, 1910(?)
      See: FORRER, Dr. R. von, "Geschützminiaturen
      aus den Mss. 'Christan de Pisan' und
      'Histoire de Charles Martel' "—
      Z.H.W.K., Vol. VI, p. 277

PLOT, R.
   Natural History of Oxfordshire
      Page 256 (Bertholdus Schwartz) . . . . Oxford, 1705

POLAIN, A.
   Recherches Historiques sur l'épreuve des armes
   à feu au pays de Liège (2nd edit.)
      Liège, 1891

POLLARD, MAJOR H. B. C.
   A History of Firearms
      Butler & Tanner, London, 1926

POLO, MARCO (1254-1323)
   Travels
      Le Livre de Marco Polo 2 volumes
      Pauthier, Paris, 1865
      Sir Henry Yule, Everyman, London, 1926

POPE, DUDLEY
   Guns
      Weidenfeld & Nicholson, London, 1965

PORTE DE HAL — BRUSSELS
   La Salle d'Armes de la Porte de Hal by Georges Macoir
   See also: PRELLE, VINKELROY, MACOIR and
   MALDERGHEM
      Brussel, 1910

POST, PAUL
   "Die früheste Geschützdarstellung von etwa 1330"
   (Milimete mss. vase cannon)
      Z.H.W.K., Vol. VI (new), p. 137 1938
   "Eine Mittelalterliche Geschützkammer mit Ladung

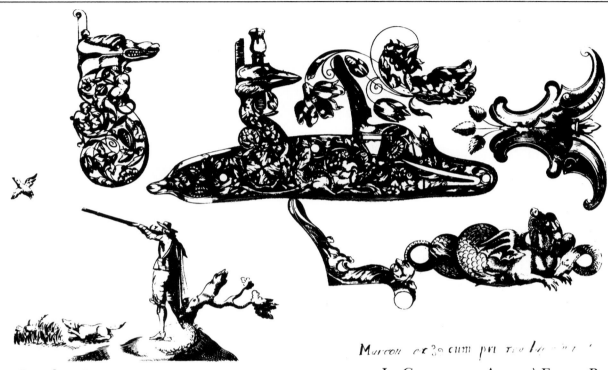

Marcon ct39 cum pri ro ba ti

im Berliner Zeughaus"
   Z.H.W.K., *Vol. IX, p. 117 . . . . May, 1922*
*"Ein Paar Französischer Radschlosspistolen von
Isaak Cordier Daubigny"*
   Z.H.W.K., *Vol. IV (new), p. 255 . . . . 1932-1934*
   Z.H.W.K., *Vol. V (new), p. 54 . . . . 1935-1936*
   Das Zeughaus, Die Waffensammlung
   (First part) . . . . Berlin, 1929

PRELLE DE LA NIEPPE, EDGAR DE
   Catalogue des Armes et Armures du Musée de la
   Porte de Hal à Bruxelles
      Emile Bruylant, Brussels, 1902

PURAYE, JEAN
   Le Damas
      Liège, 1966

La Gravure sur Armes à Feu au Pays de Liège
      Liège, 1964

PURDON, CHARLES J.
   "The Snider Rifle"
      The American Rifleman, *Vol. 106, No. XII*
      Washington, D.C., December, 1958

RADISAVLJEVIC, S.
   "Une contribution à l'étude de l'origine des Pistolet"
      Vesnik, *Vol. IV . . . . Belgrade, 1957*
   "L'evolution de la fusil à mèche"
      Vesnik, *Vol. I . . . . Belgrade, 1954*
   "Quelques renseignements sur les arquebuses à rouet"
      Vesnik, *Vol. III . . . . Belgrade, 1956*

BIBLIOGRAPHY

RANDALL, RICHARD H.
"The Master A.S."
(School of the Meister der Tierkopfranken)
The American Arms Collector, Vol. I, No. I, p. 17
1957

RATHGEN, B., and SCHAFER, DR. K. H.
"Feuer-und Fernwaffen beim Päpstlichen Heere
im 14. Jahrhundert"
"Feuer-und Fernwaffen beim Päpstlichen Heere
im 14. Jahrhundert in Flandern"
Z.H.W.K., Vol. VII, p. 1
Bainsch-Stiftung, Dresden, 1915
Z.H.W.K., Vol. VII, p. 276-306
Bainsch-Stiftung, Dresden, 1915

RATHGEN, BERNARD
Das Geschütz im Mittelalter
V.D.I. Verlag GmbH, Berlin, 1928
Die Pulverwaffen und des Antwerk
V.D.K. Verlag GmbH, Berlin, 1922

REID, SIR ALEXANDER JOHN FORSYTH
Alexander John Forsyth
University Press, Aberdeen, Scotland, 1909

REID, WILLIAM
"The Fire-Arms of Baron Heurteloup"
J.A.A.S., Vol. III, p. 59, pls. XVIII-XXII
London, September, 1959
"The Present of Spain"
The Connoisseur, CXLVI, pp. 21-6
London, August, 1960
"The Heart-Butt Pistols of East Scotland"
Scottish Weapons, Vol. 9, No. 1 . . . . Scottish Art
Review Special Number, Glasgow Art Gallery and
Museums Association, Glasgow 1963

"Lady Seafield's Scottish Guns"
The Connoisseur, p. 258 . . . . London, May, 1961
"Lady Seafield's Scottish Pistols"
The Connoisseur, p. 155 . . . . London, July, 1962
"Pauly, Gun Designer"
J.A.A.S., Vol. II, p. 181-210, pls. LV-LVIII
London, 1958
"Pauly, A Postscript"
J.A.A.S., Vol. II, p. 254-258, pl. LXX
London, 1958
"Scottish Firearms 1600-1700"
The American Rifleman, Vol. 109, No. 9
Washington, D.C., September, 1961
"Tortoise-Shell Veneered Pisols in the Scott Collection"
The Scottish Art Review, Vol. VI, No. I
Glasgow, 1956

REIMER, PAUL
'Die älteren Hinterladungsgeschütze"
Z.H.W.K., Vol. II, pp. 2-9, 39-44 1900-1902
"Nochmals; Die älteren Hinterladungsgeschütze"
Z.H.W.K., Vol. IX, p. 194 1922

REITZENSTEIN, ALEXANDER FREIHERR von
Der Waffenschmied
Prestel, Munich, 1964
"Zwei Steinschlosspistolen des Bayerischen
Nationalmuseums"
Z.H.W.K., Heft 1-2, p. 110 1959

RICKETTS, HOWARD
Firearms
Weidenfeld, London, 1962

RILING, RAY
Guns and Shooting, a Bibliography
Riling, Greenberg, New York, 1951

RITTER, KARL
Aufbau und Herstellung der Schmiedeeisernen
Steinbüchsen des Mittelalters
Technische Mitteilungen, Krupp, Essen, 1938

ROADS, C. H.
The British Soldier's Firearm, 1850-1864
Herbert Jenkins, London, 1964
"The Introduction of the Brunswick Rifle"
J.A.A.S., Vol. II, No. IV, p. 85
London, December, 1959

ROBERT, COL. L.
Catalogue des Collections Composant le Musée
d'Artillerie en 1889
Imp. Nationale, Paris, 1893

ROBBINS, BENJAMIN
New Principles of Gunnery
London, 1742

ROD AND GUN (weekly)
American Sportsman
Rod and Gun Association, New York, 1871 and after

RODAKIEWICZ, ERLA
The Edito Princeps of Robert Valturio's De Re Militari
in Relation to the Dresden and Munich Manuscripts
Maso Finigverra, Milan, 1940

RODER, ERNST
"Auf der Waffensammlung des Germanischen
Nationalmuseums" (Nurnberg)
(Including the Tannenberg gun)
Z.H.W.K., Vol. III, pp. 97-103-5

ROLT, RICHARD
Memoirs of the Life of the Late Right Honourable
John Lindesay...
Printed for Henry Kopp, London, 1753

ROMOCKI, S. J. von
Geschichte der Explosivstoffe
2 volumes....Berlin, 1895

ROUX, HENRI
Fusils de Chasse
(Pauly's gun)....Delaunay, Paris, 1822

RYBAKOW, B. A.
Der Moskauer Kreml—Die Rüstkammer
Artia Verlag, Prague, 1962

SAINT AUGUSTINE
Les Manuscrits de la Cité de Dieu de St. Augustin
by A. de Laborde (Mss. illumination of firearms)
Paris, 1909

ST. DENIS
Les Grandes Chroniques de France
Chroniques de Saint Denis
(Pictures of early siege weapons)
British Museum manuscript, Sloane, 2433
Text published....M. Paulin, Paris, 1837

SAINT JULIEN, ANTOINE DE
La Forge de Vulcain
Guillaume de Voys, The Hague, 1606

SAINT-REMY, PIERRE SURIREZ DE
Memoires d'Artillerie
3 volumes....Jean Neaulme, The Hague, 1741

BIBLIOGRAPHY

SALZLE, KARL
   "Das Deutsche Jagdmuseum in München"
   Z.H.W.K., Vol. II, p. 128 1961

SANCTA CLARA, ABRAHAM à
   Centifolium Stultorum (Der Narranspiegel)
   Basel, 1709, Karl Bertsche, Munich, 1925
   (reprint)

SATTERLEE, L. D. and GLUCKMAN, ARCADI
   American Gun Makers
   Ulbrich, Buffalo, 1945

SAWYER, CHARLES WINTHROP
   Firearms in American History
   Plimpton Press, Norwood, Mass., 1910

SCHALKHAUSSER, E.
   "Die Handfeuerwaffen des Bayerischen
   Nationalmuseums"
   "I. Handfeuerwaffen mit Luntenschloss"
   Z.H.W.K., Vol. I, pp. 1-12 . . . . Munich, 1966

SCHEDELMANN, HANS
   "Jean Conrad Tornier, an Alsatian Gunstock-Maker"
   J.A.A.S., Vol. II, No. XII, p. 261
   London, December, 1958
   "Der Meister der Tierkopfranke"
   Z.H.W.K., Vol. I, p. 1 . . . . Munich, 1962
   Die Wiener Büchsenmacher und Büchsenschäfter
   a book published by Z.H.W.K. . . . . Berlin, 1944

SCHMIDT, RUDOLF
   Die Handfeuerwaffen, ihre Entstehung und
   technisch-historische Entwicklung bis zur Gegenwart
   B. Schaube, Basel, 1875
   Repr. by Akademische Druck-und Verlagsandalt,
   Graz, Austria, 1966

SCHNEIDER, RUDOLF
   "Die Geschütze des Mittelalters"
   Z.H.W.K., Vol. V, p. 232 1909-1911
   Schutzwaffen aus sieben Jahrhunderten aus dem
   Schweizerischen Landesmuseum I
   Bern, 1953

SCHON, CAPTAIN J.
   Geschichte der Handfeuerwaffen
   Rudolf Kuntze, Dresden, 1858
   Modern System of Small Arms
   Translator—J. Gorgas, U.S.A.)
   Meuse, Yorktown, Va., 1965

Fec Marcou ex ·cum pri· reg.

SCHRAMM, ERWIN
"Das Geschütz des Altertums"
Z.H.W.K., Vol. VIII, p. 41 1918-1920

SCHWARZ, OTTO
Das Steiermarkische Landeszeughaus in Graz
Graz, Austria, 1953

SCHWERDT, C. F. G. R.
Hunting, Hawking, Shooting—A Bibliography
(Illustrated—3 volumes)
Waterlow & Son, London, 1928

SCHWERTFEGER, BERHARD and
VOLKMANN, ERICH OTTO
Die deutsche Soldatenkunde
2 volumes . . . . Leipzig, 1937

SCOTT, J. G.
"Scottish Arms"
Armi Antiche, pp. 51-8 . . . . Turin, 1963

SCURFIELD, R.
"British Military Smoothbore Firearms"
Journal of the Society for Army Historical
Research, *Vol. XXXIII, No. 134, p. 63*
Summer, 1955
Journal of the Society for Army Historical
Research, *Vol. XXXIII, No. 135, p. 110*
Journal of the Society for Army Historical
Research, *Vol. XXXIII, No. 136 and 147*

SELOUS, FREDERICK COURTENAY
A Hunter's Wanderings in Africa
R. Bentley & Son, London, 1881

SERVEN, JAMES E. (author and editor)
Americans and Their Guns
Stackpole, Harrisburg, 1967
The Collecting of Guns
Stackpole, Harrisburg, 1964
Colt Firearms from 1836
Santa Ana, California, 1964
"Colt's New Lightning Rifle"
The American Rifleman . . . . *Page 38*
Washington, D.C., August, 1966
"Guns of Yesterday"
Page 28 . . . . Washington, D.C., March, 1965
"What Makes an Old Gun Valuable"
Page 27 . . . . Washington, D.C., January, 1964
Plus more than 100 articles in The American
Rifleman, The American West, Guns, Guns and
Hunting *and* The Gun Digest

SEVERANCE COLLECTION CATALOGUE
Cleveland Museum of Art

SHARPE, PHILIP B.
The Rifle in America
Morrow, New York, 1938

SHAW, JOSHUA
A Sketch or History of the Copper Cap
Bordentown, N.J., 1847

SIEMIENOWICZ, KAZIMIERZ
Vollkommene Geschütz-Feuerwerck und
Buchsenmeisterey-Kunst . . .
(Text on military fireworks and cannon)
Friessen, Franckfurt Am Mayn, 1676
English edition . . . . J. Tonson, London, 1729

BIBLIOGRAPHY

SIMONIN, CLAUDE and JACQUES
> Plusieur Pieces et autres Armament par le Arquebuzers
> *(Designs for gunstockers and lockmakers)*
> *Paris, 1685 . . . . Paris, 1693*

SIXL, MAJOR P. von
> "Entwickelung und Gebrauch der Handfeuerwaffen"
> *Z.H.W.K., Vols. I-IV 1897-1908*
> "Zur Geschichte des Schiesswesens der Infanterie"
> *Z.H.W.K., Vol. II, pp. 327 and 374 . . . . 1900-1902*

SKELTON, JOHN
> *MEYERICK, engraved illustrations of Ancient Arms
> and Armour from the Collection at Goodrich Court . . .*
> *Bohn, London, 1854*

SKRIVANIC, G.
> "Quelques donnés pour l'étude de l'évolution des
> armes à feu"
> *Vesnik, Vol. II 1955*

SMISCHECK, JOHAN
> Neues Groteschgen Büchlein
> *Munich, 1604-1627*

SMITH, CAPTAIN GEORGE
> An Universal Military Dictionary . . .
> *Printed for J. Millan, London, 1779*

SMITH, CAPTAIN JOHN (1580-1631)
> Generall History of the Virginia Colony
> Original Narratives of Early American History
> *Charles Scribner & Sons, New York, 1906*

SMITH, SAMUEL E.
> The American Arms Collector
> "Evolution of the Plant Revolvers", Vol. I, No. 2
> *April, 1957*
> "Henry Flintlock Pistols," Vol. I, No. 3
> *July, 1957*

The American Rifleman
> "South Carolina Ante-Bellum Pistols"
> *November, 1955*

The American Society of Arms Collectors Bulletin
> "Lindsay Pistol Exhibit," No. 1
> *September, 1955*
> "The North & Cheney Pistols," No. 2
> *November, 1956*

The Gun Collector
> "The American London Pistol Company," No. 5
> *December 25, 1946*
> "Are These The Missing Chamber Guns?," No. 40
> *May, 1952*
> "Box-Lock Rarity," No. 43 . . . . *January, 1953*
> "A French Flintlock and its American Cousins,"
> *No. 23 . . . . July, 1948*
> "The Newbury Arms Company," No. 18
> *December, 1947*
> "James Reid's Knuckledusters," No. 42
> *November, 1952*
> "The Survival Rate of Sharps Pistols," No. 15
> *August 21, 1947*
> "Walch and Lindsay," No. 32 . . . . *May, 1950*

The Gun Report
> "Alsop Revolvers" . . . . *June-July, 1960*
> "The Darling Pepperbox," Vol. III, No. 3
> *January, 1942*
> "The Gold Rush Colt Dragoon" . . . . *June, 1964*
> "The Lindsay Pistols," Monograph #12, Vol. 1,
> *No. 4 . . . . October, 1940*
> "Rare Allen & Wheellock Rifle" . . . . *June, 1959*

Hobbies
> "The Arms of Stephen Badlam"
> *(Halbach & Sons flint pistol) . . . . January, 1947*

"A Revolutionary War Powder Horn, With An Early American Flag" . . . . *May, 1951*
The Collecting of Guns ·
(*Edited by James E. Serven*)
"The Single Shot Martial Pistols of the U.S."
Chapter 9
"The Rare and the Valuable," Chapter 24
The Stackpole Publishing Co., Harrisburg, Pa., 1964
Forty-Two Years' Scrapbook of Rare Ancient Firearms
Compiled by F. Theodore Dexter
"A Group of United States Martial Pistols and Other American Arms Rarities," Section III
Warren F. Lewis, Los Angeles, 1954

SMITH, W. H. B.
Gas, Air, and Spring Guns of the World
Military Service Publishing Co., Harrisburg, Pa., U.S.A., 1957
Pistols and Revolvers
Military Service Publishing Co., Harrisburg, Pa., U.S.A., 1946

SMITH, W. H. B. and JOSEPH E.
Small Arms of the World
Stackpole, Harrisburg, Pa., 1962
(New Edition) Stackpole, Harrisburg, Pa., 1966
The Book of Rifles . . . .(*third edition*)
Stackpole, Harrisburg, Pa., 1963

SMITH, O.
Der kongelige Partikulaere Rustkammer, 1775
Copenhagen, 1938

SMITH, WINSTON O.
The Sharps Rifle
Morrow, New York, 1943

SMYTHE, SIR JOHN
Certain Discourses, Concerning the Formes and Effects of Divers Sorts of Weapons
Richard Johnes, London, 1590

SOBRERO, CARLO
Teoria Chimica della Composizione delle Polvere a Fuoco
Turin, 1852

SOLER, ISIDORO
Compendio Histórico de los Arcabuceros de Madrid
Pantaleon Mellizo, Madrid, 1795

SOUHAIT, R.
Bibliographie Général des Ouvrages sur la Chasse, La Venerie et la Fauconnerie
Rougette, Paris, 1886

SPADONI, NICOLA
Caccia del Schioppo
Bologna, 1673

SPAULDING, THOMAS M. and KARPENSKI, LOUIS C.
Early Military Books in the University of Michigan Libraries
University of Michigan Press, 1941

SPITZER, FREDERICK
La Collection Spitzer

BIBLIOGRAPHY

Catalog books by J. B. Giraud and Emile Molinier
Maison Quantin, Paris, 1892

SQUILBECK, JEAN
Un Visite au Musée Royale d'Armes et d'Armures, 1957
Porte de Hal Museum, Brussels, 1957

STERN, WALTER M.
"Gunmaking in Seventeenth-Century London"
J.A.A.S., *Vol. I, No. V, p. 58*
London, March 1954

STERNE, LAWRENCE
Tristram Shandy. . . . *London, 1769*
London, 1780 (collected)

ST. ETIENNE
Manufacture Française d'Armes de St.-Etienne
Manufacture Française, Paris, 1899
See: DUBESSEY, R.

STIMMER, TOBIAS
Künstliche Wolgerissene Figuren und Abbildungen . . .
(Album of illustrations for the first German edition
of Jacques du Fouilloux' La Venerie q.v.)
Johann Carola, Strassburg, 1605

STOCKBRIDGE, V. D.
Digest of Patents Relating to Breech-Loading and
Magazine Small Arms *(1863-1873)*
Washington, 1874
(reprint). . . . Norman Flayderman, 1963

STØCKEL, JOHAN F.

Haandskydevaabens Bedømmelse *(Gunmakers marks)*
Copenhagen, 1938-1943

STOCKLEIN, HANS
Das Bayerische Armee Museum in München *1879-1929*
Paul Neff Verlag, Munich, 1930
Meister der Eisenschnittes
(Sadelers and Caspar Spät of Munich)
Esslingen, 1922

STONE, GEORGE CAMERON
Glossary of the Construction, Decoration and
Use of Arms and Armor
Southport, Portland, Maine, 1934
(reprint). . . . New York, 1961

STRADANUS (JAN VAN DER STRAET) (1530-1605)
Venationes
Engraved and published by Philipp Galle
(Source illustration for gun decorators)
Philipp Galle circa 1580

SWIFT, COL. EBEN
The Pistol, the Mellay: and the fight at Devil's River
Leavenworth, Kansas, 1914

SUTTON, RICHARD L.
An African Holiday
C. V. Mosby, St. Louis, 1924
The Long Trek
C. V. Mosby, St. Louis, 1930

SVENSKA VAPENHISTORISKA SALLSKAPETS SKRIFTER

Stockholm, Sweden

SZENDREI, JOHANN
Ungarische Kriegsgeschichtliche Denkmaler
Budapest, 1896

TARASSUK, Leonid
"The Collection of Arms and Armour in the State Hermitage, Leningrad"
Part II: "The Collection of Russian Arms and Armour"
J.A.A.S., Vol. V, Nos. 4-5, pp. 205-216
London, March, 1966
European and American Firearms in the State Hermitage Museum....*(With English translation)*
P.H. "Arts", Leningrad, 1968
"To The History of Russian Hand-Firearms in the 16th and 17th Centuries"

(In Russian)
Sovietskaya Arkheologia (Soviet Archaeology),
No. 2, pp. 104-120 1965
"Introduction de la platine à silex à la française dans les armes à feu russes"
Armi Antiche, *pp. 3-14 . . . . Turin, 1964*
"The Meaning of the Term Samopal" (self-shooters)
(In Russian)
Vestnik Leningradskogo Universiteta (Bulletin of the Leningrad University), *No. 14, pp. 152-156 1965*

TARTAGLIA, NICOLO
Nova Scientia Inventa *(Treatise on artillery)*
Tartalea B., Vinegia, 1537
Questi e Invenzioni Diversi
Venturino Ruffinelli, Venice, 1546

TAYLERSON, A. W. F.
Revolving Arms
Walker, New York, 1967
"The London Armoury Company"
J.A.A.S., Vol. II, p. 45 . . . . London

TAYLOR, JOHN
African Rifles and Cartridges
Samworth, U.S.A., 1948

TECHY, D.
Guide Somaire du Musée d'Armes de Liège
(second edition) . . . . Liège, 1961

TEMPESTA, ANTONIO DE
Venationes Ferarum
(Woodcuts of hunting with wheel lock guns)
1555-1630

BIBLIOGRAPHY

TERENZI, MARCELLO
> L'Arte de Michele Battista, Armaiolo Napoletano
> *Edizioni Marte, Rome, 1964*

THEUERDANK
> *(Reproduction of mss—entire issue)*
> *(Cannon: pp. 180-229, 364; Handgunners: pp. 342, 360)*
> J.D.K.S., Vol. VIII, p. 15 . . . . Vienna, 1888
> *(See: MAXIMILIAN)*

THIEBAUD, J.
> Bibliographie des ouvrages français sur la Chasse
> *Paris, 1934*

THIERBACH, MORITZ
> *"Die ältesten Radschlösser deutcher Sammlungen"*
> Z.H.W.K., Vol. II, p. 138 1900-1902
> Beiträge zur Geschichte der Handfeuerwaffen.
> Festschrift für M. Thierbach *by various authors*
> *Verlag und Druck von W. Baeensch, Dresden, 1905*
> Die Geschichtliche Entwicklung der Handfeuerwaffen
> *Carl Hockner, Dresden, 1886*
> *(reprinted)) . . . . Akademische Druck-und*
> *Verlagsanstalt, Graz, Austria, 1965*
> *"Die Handfeuerwaffen der sächsischen Armee"*
> Z.H.W.K., Vol. III, pp. 89, 126, 160 & 190
> 1903-1905
> *"Ueber die erste Entwicklung der Handfeuerwaffen"*
> Z.H.W.K., Vol. I, p. 129 1897-1899
> *"Ueber das Radschloss"*
> Z.H.W.K., Vol. I, p. 245 1897-1899
> *"Uber die Entwicklung des Steinschlosses"*
> Z.H.W.K., Vol. III, p. 305 1903-1905

THOMAS, BRUNO
> *"Armes"*
> Lorraine-Autriche *(exhibition catalogue)* p. 57-71

> *Lunéville, 1966*
> *"Die Artillerie in Triumphzug Kaiser Maximilians I"*
> Z.H.W.K., Vol. VI (new), p. 229 1939
> *"Eine deutsche Radschlossbüchse von 1593 mit*
> *Beineinlagen nach Adrian Collaert"*
> Die graphischen Künste N.S., Vol. 3, pp. 72-77
> *Vienna, 1938*
> *"Des Fürsten Nikolaus Christoph Radziwill*
> *Geschützrohre aus Niéswiez"*
> Svenska Vapenhistoriska Sällskapets Skrifter,
> N.S., Vol. 6, pp. 5-37 . . . . Stockholm, 1959
> *"Modell eines Geschützrohres von Oswald Baldner"*
> Festschrift fur Erich Meyer zum 60. Geburtstag
> 1957, pp. 175-180 . . . . Hamburg, 1959
> *"Eine Radschlossbüchse Sigmunds III. in Wien"*
> Livrustkammaren, Vol. I, pp. 93-100
> *Stockholm, 1938*

THOMAS, BRUNO, GAMBER, ORTWIN and
SCHEDELMANN, HANS
> Die schönsten Waffen und Rustüngen, *etc.*
> *Keysersche Verlagsbuchhandlung, Heidelberg*
> *und Munchen, 1953*
> Arms and Armour of the Western World
> *McGraw Hill, New York, 1964*
> Armi e armature europee
> *(51 pp., 196 plates, 30 in color)*
> *Bramante Editrice, Milan, 1965*

THOMAS, BRUNO and GRIMSCHITZ, BRUNO
> *"A.E.I.O.V."*
> Ars Venandi in Austria
> *Osterreichische Staatsdruckerei, Vienna, 1959*

THOMAS and GOUCH
> *"The John Browning Legacy—Blessing or Blight"*
> The Gun Digest, *p. 79, 21st edition* 1967

"THORMANBY" (DIXON, WILMONT)
Kings of the Rod, Rifle and Gun
Hutchinson, London, 1901

THORNTON, COLONEL THOMAS
A Sporting Tour Through Various Parts of France
in the Year 1802
Longman, Hurst, Rees, & Orme, London, 1802

TØJHUS MUSEUM
The Armoury Hall, The Cannon Hall, *(Both in
English), CHRISTENSEN, Lt. Col. Erik (tr.)
Royal Danish Arsenal Museum, Copenhagen,
1948 and 1953*

TONTY, HENRY DE
Editor of Memoir on La Salle's Discoveries *and explorer
and lieutenant to La Salle, assisted in the founding of
the Colony of Louisiana—1674-1704*
Original Narratives of Early American History
*Charles Scribner & Sons, New York,
1904 and following*

TOURNAI
Book of Hours for the Use of Tournai, *1440-1460.
Ms. 421, (See: GAIER)*

TOUT, T. F.
"Firearms in England in the 14th Century"
English Historical Review, *XXVI, No. 104, pp. 66,
702, (669-688). . . . October, 1911*

TRAPP, GRAF OSWALD & MANN, J. G.
Die Churburger Rüstkammer
*(The Armoury of the Castle of Churburg)
Prefaced (English edition) by James G. Mann*

Metheun & Co., London, 1929

TREITZSAUERWEIN, MARX VON EHRENTREITZ
"Der Weisskunig"
J.D.K.S., *Vol. V, p. 97 . . . . 1887*
J.D.K.S., *Vol. VI, p. 1 . . . . Vienna, 1888
(Early cannon illustrations—hand cannon,
folio 278b and opposite 290)
See: MAXIMILIAN*

TRUE MAGAZINE, GUN ANNUAL
New York

TUNIS, EDWARD
Weapons
World Publishing, New York, 1954

TURGENIEFF, IVAN
Memoirs of a Sportsman
Lamley, London, 1895

TURIN; *Armeria Reale, Museo Storico d'Artiglieria
See: ANGELUCCI, ANGELO
GAY, PAOLO
HAYWARD, JOHN
NATTA-SOLERI, RAFFAELE*

20 BORE (Basil Tozar)
Practical Hints on Shooting
Kegan, Paul, Trench, London, 1887

UFANO, DIEGO
Artillerie
David du Petit Val, Rouen, 1628
Tratado de la Artilleria y uso de practicado
Antwerp, 1613

BIBLIOGRAPHY

UHL, ROBERT
"The Great International Shooting Matches"
The American Rifleman, *Vol. 102, No. VIII*
August and September, 1954

ULIMAN, KONRAD
Schmuck alter Büchsen und Gewehre
(Decoration of old guns). . . . Verlag Paul Paray,
Hamburg and Berlin, 1964

UPMAN, J.
Das Schiesspulver
Vieweg und Sohn, Braunschweig, 1874

U.S. INFANTRY MANUAL, 1841
"Manual of Arms for the Musket"

U.S. INFANTRY TACTICS
"Manual of Arms for the Musket"
J. B. Lippincott, Philadelphia, 1863

VAABENHISTORISKE AARBØGER
(Journal of the Danish Arms and Armour Society)
Copenhagen

VALENCIA, DON JUAN de, EL CONDE Vdo
"Bilderinventar der Waffen, Rüstungen, Gewänder
und Standarten Karl V. in der Armeria Real zu Madrid"
J.D.K.S., Vol. II, p. CCXLII & ff (see plate 54)
Vienna, 1890
Catalogo historico—descriptivo de la Real Armeria
de Madrid
Phototipias de Hauser y Menet, Madrid, 1898

VALTURIUS (VALTURIO, ROBERTO)
De l'Arte Militari *(illustrations of ballistae and*
early cannon). . . . Verona, 1483
The Edito Princeps of Robert Valturio's De Re Militari
in relation to the Dresden and Munich manuscripts
by RODAKIEWICZ, Erla
Maso Finiguerra, Milan, 1940

VANDER HAEGEN, G.
Armes et Munitions
H. Desoer, Liège, 1919
Les Pistolets automatiques
Poncelet, Liège (n.d.)

VAN DER STRAET (STRADANUS) JAN (1530-1605)
Venationes
Etched by Philipp Galle . . . . Antwerp, circa 1580

Iacquinet fecit Marcou ex cum privile re

VAN RENNSELAER, STEPHEN
     American Firearms
       New York, 1947

VAUBAN, SEBASTIAN LE PRESTRE DE
     Science Militaire
       Paris, 1689

VEGETIUS (FLAVIUS VEGETIUS RENATUS)
(375-392 A.D.)
     De Re Militari
       Mss French translation by de Meung, 1284
       (Pictures of guns added)....(printed)
       Utrect, 1475, Carol Perier, Paris, 1553

VENICE
     "La Sala d'Armi nel Museo dell'Arsenale di Venezia"
     by G. de Lucia
       Revista Marittima, Rome, 1908

VENN, CAPT. THOMAS
     Military and Maritime Discipline
     Militarie Observations
       E. Tyler and R. Holt for Robert Pawlet,
       London, 1672

VERGIL, POLYDORE (born Urbino)
     (Archdeacon of Wells, lived in England, 1501 to 1550)
     De Inventoribus Rerum....*Pancirollius, London, 1715*

VESNIK (Bulletin du Musée Militaire de l'Armée
Populaire Yugoslave)
       Belgrade, Yugoslavia

VIENNA—*Arms Collection of the Kunsthistorisches
Museum*
       See: BOEHEIM, WENDELIN
         THOMAS, BRUNO

VIENNA, *Manuscripts in the Nationalbibliothek:*
Nos. 3060, 3062, 3069, 10824
       (10824 is an inventory of weapons in southern Austria
       in 1500-1507)....Kunst. Sammlungen Nos. 34, 55

VINKELROY, E. VAN
     Armes et Armures *(Port de Hal catalogue)*
       Lelong, Brussels, 1885

VILLANI, GIOVANNI, MATTEO and PHILIPO
     Chroniche di Giovanni Villani *(mss - 1348-1364)*
     Bibliotheca Classica Italiana, Secola XIV
       No. XXI, pp. 483-484....Trieste, 1857

VIOLLET-LE-DUC, E.
     Dictionaire Raisonné du Mobilier Français
       Armes de Guerre, *Vol. V & VI....Paris, 1868-1875*

VOGEL, HEINRICH
     Kurzer Unterricht in der Artillerie-Wissenschaft
       Zurich, 1739

VOLTAIRE, FRANCOIS MARIE (1694-1778)
     Candide
       English translation by Charles S. Merrill, Jr., 1929
       Random House, London, 1929

BIBLIOGRAPHY

WAFFEN-UND KOSTUMKUNDE
See: ZEITSCHRIFT FUR HISTORISCHE
WAFFEN-UND KOSTUMKUNDE

WAHL, PAUL and TOPPEL, DON
The Gatling Gun
Herbert Jenkins, London, 1966

WALLACE COLLECTION
See: MANN, SIR JAMES G.

WALLHAUSEN, JOHANN JACOB von
Kriegskunst zu Fuss
Frankfurt am Mayn, 1615
Kriegskunst zu Pferd
Frankfurt am Mayn, 1616

WARD, ROBERT
Anima-adversions of Warre...
John Dawson, London, 1639

WARSAW—MUSEUM WAJSKA POLSKIEGO
W WARSZAWIE
Przewodnik, Warsaw, 1957

WATERHOUSE, D. B.
"Fire-Arms in Japanese History: with notes on a Japanese Wall Gun"
The British Museum Quarterly, *Vol. XXVII, No. III, IV, p. 94.... London, Winter 1963-1964*

WATROUS, GEORGE
Winchester Rifles and Shotguns
(second edition).... New Haven, Conn., 1950

WEGELI, RUDOLF
"Inventar der Waffensammlung des Bernischen Historischen Museums in Bern"
Historical Museum
Volume I.... Bern, 1920-1921

K. J. Wyss Erben, Bern, 1927
Volume II.... 1929
Katalog der Waffensammlung im Zeughaus
zu Solothurn, *Solothurn, Switzerland, 1905*

WEIGEL, CHRISTOPH
Illustrated Abraham à Sancta Clara's Centifolium
Stultorum (Der Narrenspiegel)

WETTENDORFER, EDWARD
"Ein Salve-Rohr"
Z.H.W.K., *p. 57.... 1944*
"Zur Technologie der Steinbüchsen"
Z.H.W.K., *Vol. VI (new), p. 147.... 1938*

WHELAN, MAJOR TOWNSEND
The American Rifle
The Century Co., New York, 1918

WHITEHORNE, PETER
The Arte of Warre, Certain Waies of Orderyng
Souldiers in Battelray
(Translation of Machiavelli)
Kingston, London, 1562
Williamson, London, 1575

WHITELAW, C. E. and JACKSON
A Treatise on Scottish Hand Firearms
Holland Press, London, 1959

WIEN—Codex 10824—Hofbibliothek zu Wien

WILKINSON, FREDERICK
Arms and Armour
A. & C. Black, London, 1963
Small Arms
Hawthorne Books, New York, 1966

WILLEMIN, NICHOLAS XAVIER

Monuments Français
(Sculpture including firearms)....Paris, 1839

WILLIAMS, SIR ROGER
Discourse of Warre
London, circa 1590

WILLIAMSON, HAROLD F.
Winchester, the Gun that Won the West
Combat Forces Press, Washington, D.C., 1952

WILSON, A. W.
The Story of the Gun
Woolwich, 1944

WILSON, R. L.
The Arms Collection of Colonel Colt
Herb Glass, Bullville, N. Y., 1964
L. D. Nimschke, Firearms Engraver
John J. Malloy, Teaneck, N. J., 1965
Samuel Colt Presents
Wadsworth Atheneum, Hartford, Conn., 1961

WINANT, LEWIS
Early Percussion Firearms
London, 1961
Firearms Curiosa
St. Martin's Press, New York, 1955
Pepperbox Firearms
New York, 1952

WINGATE, COL.
"Colonel Wingate's Letters"
Army and Navy Journal (U.S.)....1869-1870

WOLF, PAUL J.
"English All-Metal Flintlock Pistols"
J.A.A.S., Vol. IV, No. XII, p. 241
December, 1964
"Some Segalas Variations"

J.A.A.S., Vol. III, No. I, p. 207
London, March, 1959

WOLFF, ELDON B.
Air Guns
Milwaukee Public Museum, Milwaukee, 1958

WORCESTER, EDWARD SOMERSET, EARL OF
A Century of Inventions
(Multi-firing weapons)....London, 1660

WORSHIPFUL COMPANY OF GUNMAKERS
See: ANONYMOUS

WROTTESLEY, GEORGE
Crecy and Calais, from the Public Records
Harrison & Sons, London, 1898

ZANCHI, GIOVANNI BATTISTA
Del Modo di Fortificar le Citta
Plinio Pietrasanta, Venice, 1554

ZEITSCHRIFT FUR HISTORISCHE WAFFENKUNDE
(Edited initially by Wendelin Boeheim)
Variously published in Berlin, Dresden, Leipzig,
Munich, 1897-1944

ZEITSCHRIFT FUR HISTORISCHE WAFFEN-UND
KOSTUMKUNDE
(Edited by Alexander Freiherr von Reitzenstein)
Munich, 1959 to date

ZUBLER, LEONHARD
Nova Geometrica Pyrobulia
Jonas Gessner, Zurich, 1608

INDEX

References in bold type refer to the captions to the illustrations.

INDEX

INDEX

INDEX

INDEX

INDEX

INDEX